Master Cookbook

Collard Valley Cooks

A Celebration of Southern Tradition and Togetherness

Thank you for making this cookbook a part of your culinary journey. I am thrilled to be a part of your family through food. Since childhood, the kitchen has always been my favorite part of our home. As young girls, mama would send my sister and I to the grocery store with a list. The Casey family owned a local grocery store. They lived in Collard Valley, too, and Daddy enjoyed "shooting the bull" with the men, as Mama called it, while we strolled through the store placing items in the buggy.

When we got home, I would organize the groceries under the counter. I took pride in everything I did and enjoyed being a help to Mama. She worked hard in the kitchen, preparing our meals. We rarely ate out, and when we did, it was usually a fast-food burger while we were out for a doctor's appointment. That did not happen often; Mama cooked every meal for us. She was an extraordinary cook. We learned from the best, and by the time I was a pre-teen, I was cooking whole meals. I could not cook as well as Mama, but it was a start.

It took years of practice to reach the level I am at now, a place where I feel confident and privileged to share my knowledge and experience with you. I would have loved to have had this cookbook when I was just starting out. Back then, I relied solely on the package instructions. I recommend watching tutorials if you are an inexperienced cook. There should be a video tutorial for every recipe covered in this book on my YouTube channel. Cooking is more than just following a recipe; it is also about learning by observing. You must observe how a cook navigates the kitchen and times a meal so that everything finishes cooking simultaneously. This way, everything is served fresh and hot.

With my recipe tutorials and this cookbook, you will become an outstanding Southern cook—one your family will remember for years to come. Thank you for allowing me to guide you.

Collard Valley Cooks Master Cookbook

Collard Valley Cooks LLC

1870 Belle Island Rd.

Richmond Hill, Georgia 31324

Collard Valley Cooks Master Cookbook

Author: Tammy Nichols

ISBN: 9798318819025

CVC CONTACT INFORMATION:

WEBSITE: www.collardvalleycooks.com

EMAIL: collardvalleycook@gmail.com

Amazon Affiliate Influencer Program:

Publishing Company
Palmetto Publishing
1501 Belle Isle Ave
Mt Pleasant, SC 29464

Book Citations:
Microsoft Copilot used in Microsoft Word for Book edits.

Microsoft Copilot, **1. Wikipedia Article:**
Cabbage. (2024, June 16). In *Wikipedia*.
https://en.wikipedia.org/wiki/Cabbage
(Note: Update the retrieval date if you accessed the article on a different day.) [en.wikipedia.org]
2. Herbs in History Article:
Touwaide, A., & Appetiti, E. (2024, June). Herbs in history: Cabbage. *American Herbal Products Association*.
https://www.ahpa.org/content.asp?contentid=375 [ahpa.org]

Table of Contents

Master Cookbook.. A

Information Page ....B

About the Author...D

A Cookbook to Treasure ....E

Tammy's Kitchen Helps........................... F

Air Fryer Recipes............................... 1

Appetizer Recipes 9

Beef Recipes.................................. 19

Beverage Recipes 38

Breads & Pastry Recipes..................... 42

Biscuits... 43

Cornmeal Recipes 48

Pastry & Sweet Bread Recipes 54

Muffin Recipes.................................. 60

Bread Recipes...................................62

Breakfast Recipes 67

Cakes from Scratch Recipes..................... 77

Cake Mix Creations 104

Casseroles & Skillets 114

Cookie & Bar Recipes 127

Dessert Recipes............................ 137

Fish & Seafood Recipes 147

Frostings, Fillings & Toppings Recipes 152

Pie & Cobbler Recipes........................159

Pork Recipes................................180

Poultry Recipes............................189

Salad Recipes 205

Sandwich Recipes...........................216

Sauces, Gravy & Spice Recipes..................221

Soup & Stew Recipes..........................227

Southern Sides Recipes 237

Beans & Peas 238

Corn Recipes... 244

Leafy Greens 246

Rice Side Recipes 247

Root Vegetables 248

Vegetables 252

Tammy's Cooking Tips 258

Where is Collard Valley?............................259

The Family of Collard Valley Cooks..............260

Tammy Over the Years 263

Tammy's Holiday Recipes 264

Index...267-277

> My two favorite bible verses are:
>
> **John 1:1**
> "In the beginning was the Word, and the Word was with God, and the Word was God."
>
> **Psalm 116:8**
> "For thou hast delivered my soul from death, mine eyes from tears, and my feet from falling."

"Jesus is the Word, Jesus was in the beginning, Jesus was with God, and Jesus is God. Jesus is the whole meaning of the Bible. It is all about Him and all points to Him. He is the Way, the Truth, the Life and no one comes to the Father but by Him. I Praise the Lord in heaven for His precious gift of salvation. Jesus is the only one worthy of being in the presence of God. We must go through Him. I pray you trust in Jesus Christ and that I will see you in heaven some sweet day! I love you." -Tammy

Who is Tammy Nichols?

I grew up in the beautiful hills of Northwest Georgia, in an area called Collard Valley. I learned the art of comfort cooking from my mama and granny. Growing up in the country with access to land allowed us to have our own pork, beef, fresh vegetables, fruit, and even pecans and walnuts. Why, Granny even had a chestnut tree when I was little, and I remember Daddy eating them at Christmas. So, you can imagine, there was good food and lots of love in the kitchens of our family, and not just ours; it was like that for our whole community.

I was born a middle child and was always a busybody. I also loved pleasing people from an early age. I wanted everyone to be proud of me. I was taught to work hard and to be honest by my parents and grandparents.

I married at the age of 15, and instead of ruining my life, it made me grow up quickly. I had to get up and work on a dairy farm before getting ready for the school bus every day. I was divorced by the age of 16 because he wanted me to quit school, and that was never going to happen.

I wanted to make up for my mistakes by going to college. I wanted to be remembered for something good. I graduated from college in 1992 with a bachelor's degree in Architectural Engineering.

I married Chris Nichols in 2000, and we had two girls quickly. I worked as a project manager for an Architectural Firm for many years, until I was laid off during the 2009 recession. Six months later, I was diagnosed with triple-negative breast cancer and also had it in 12 of my lymph nodes. The statistics were alarming, but despite them, I am still here today.

This cookbook is a great accomplishment for me. A dream of mine, really, and the thought of helping you make delicious food for your family makes my heart happy. I know that somewhere, a little kid is going to wake up and smell the aroma of scratch cooking because their mama or daddy is taking pride in feeding their family. I want the traditions to continue and the smiles and laughter in the kitchen to be a large part of your family. Thank you for letting me come into your world of food and family.

I accepted Jesus Christ into my life as a young child. He has always been my counselor and friend. I pray that you, too, come to know Him and trust Him as your personal Savior. Our salvation is more important than anything else, for we shall live eternally through Christ.

A Cookbook to Treasure!

"I love this picture of us on the couch! It captures the style from that time, and our dirty socks—I'm even wearing two different colors! My older brother and cousin playing chess with overalls on! Just look at Daddy and Barry's Easter suits! Daddy went to church on Holidays only! And lastly Mama was trying her best to get a picture of us when Eddie was a baby."

Precious Memories

Tammy's Kitchen Help

Over the years as a content creator, I have received a variety of kitchen tools. Some of these have become my favorites, and throughout this book, I will share images illustrating their usefulness in various recipes. You will notice a small icon next to the recipes indicating when these tools are particularly beneficial. Additionally, other icons will represent helpful appliances like a conventional oven or a Crockpot. This design aims to facilitate your navigation through recipes tailored to the specific cooking methods you seek.

Blending Fork

Food Hook

Gravy Whisk

French Whisk

Jar Opener

Magnetic Measuring Spoons

Measuring Scoops

Garlic Press

Hamburger Separator

Can Punch for Evaporated milk

Can Opener

Biscuit Cutters

Crank Sifter

Microplane

Batter Bowl

Infrared Thermometer

Pull Chopper

Bench Scraper

Mini Spatulas

Cut Resistant Gloves

Olive Oil Dispenser

13 QT mixing bowl

3"Deep 10.5" cast iron skillet

Casserole Dish

standard pie plate

Instant Pot

Stand Mixer

Wok

Funnel & Jars

Shop Kitchen:

nonstick pot

7 x 11 Baking Pan

Hand Mixer

Braiser

Micro -wave

Crock Pot

COLLARDVALLEYCOOKS.COM
AMAZON AFFILIATE LINKS

https://www.collardvalleycooks.com/

F

Recipe #1

Air Fryer Recipes

Enjoy crispy textures with less oil and more flavor!

If you are seeking a way to create healthier versions of your favorite fried foods without compromising on taste or texture, look no further than the air fryer. This ingenious countertop appliance uses rapid air circulation to achieve the satisfying crunch and golden color of deep-frying, all while using a fraction of the oil. Perfect for busy home cooks, the air fryer offers versatility, speed, and easy cleanup—making it a must-have tool for everyday meals or special occasions alike. From crisp veggies to perfectly browned proteins, air fryer cooking is all about maximizing flavor with minimal effort. Oh, and the fact that it turns itself off is a great safety feature for the kids and us old folks.

Discover the ultimate convenience with this dependable and user-friendly air fryer! Featuring pre-set buttons for popular foods like bread and steak, cooking has never been easier. Plus, a QR code links directly to Collard Valley Cooks' website's Shop Kitchen/Appliances tab, making it simple to purchase through Amazon!

Visit Tammy's Recommend Appliances!

Use your phone's camera to scan! When the link appears on your screen, click it to access the site! https://www.collardvalleycooks.com/

1

1) Brussels Sprouts, Roasted

→ 16 oz. package fresh brussels sprouts
→ olive oil
→ dried shallots (or chopped green onion)
→ salt & pepper
→ chopped roasted almonds
→ parmesan cheese
→ toasted sesame seeds, optional
→ fresh lemon

Wash and trim the brussels sprouts, slicing them in half or thirds if large.

In a bowl, toss the Brussels sprouts with olive oil. Add dried shallots or green onion, roasted almonds, and toasted sesame seeds, and toss again. Spray the air fryer basket with cooking oil. Place the Brussels sprouts in the basket and season with salt and pepper to taste.

Cook at 370°F for 6 minutes, then shake and increase the temperature to 400°F and cook for an additional 2 minutes.

 Notes & Tips: Add fresh lemon juice and Parmesan to hot Brussels sprouts before serving.

Conventional Oven: Bake at 400°F on a sprayed cookie sheet for 10-15 minutes, until crispy.

Tips for Cutting a Blooming Onion:

To create a blooming onion, start with a large, sweet onion. Cut off the top inch and peel off the outer skin, leaving the root end intact. Place the onion cut-side down and make vertical cuts, about 1/2 inch apart, down to the root end, but not through it. Turn the onion and repeat the cuts, creating a crosshatch pattern. Gently separate the petals. It's ready for battering and frying.

2) Blooming Onion

→ 1 large, sweet onion
→ 1/2 cup all-purpose flour
→ 1 Tbsp buttermilk
→ 2 eggs
→ 1/2 cup panko breadcrumbs
→ 1 Tbsp paprika
→ 1-1/2 tsp seafood seasoning

Read 'Tips for Cutting a Blooming Onion,' then coat the onion in flour and shake off the excess. Beat the eggs and buttermilk together, then thoroughly coat the onion—season with salt, pepper, and seafood seasoning. In a separate bowl, combine panko, the remaining flour, and paprika. Evenly coat the onion pieces in this mixture. Spray the air fryer basket with cooking oil. Place the onion cut side up. Cook at 390°F for 10 minutes. Spray the onion with cooking spray, then lower the temperature to 350°F and cook for an additional 5 minutes. Serve with Recipe #3, Horsey Dipping Sauce.

3) Horsey Dipping Sauce

→ 1/2 cup light mayonnaise
→ 2 Tbsp horseradish
→ 1 Tbsp ketchup
→ 1/4 tsp paprika
→ 1/8 tsp cayenne
→ pepper to taste
→ 1/8 tsp dried oregano

In a small bowl, combine the mayonnaise, horseradish, ketchup, paprika, cayenne pepper, oregano, and pepper. Stir until everything is well combined.

Psalm 116:8
"For thou hast delivered my soul from death, mine eyes from tears, and my feet from falling." KJV

4) Bacon, Air Fryer

Place 4 or 5 slices of <u>thick-sliced</u> bacon side by side in the bottom of the air fryer. Set the air fryer to 400°F and cook for 6 minutes. Flip the bacon slices, then reduce the temperature to 350°F. Cook for an additional 4 minutes.

 Tips: This cooking time and temperature will result in bacon that is golden brown. If the temperature is set too high, the bacon may burn and become dry.

5) Bread Pudding Singles

- → 2 Tbsp salted butter
- → a dinnersized roll, cubed
- → 1 large egg
- → 1/3 cup evaporated milk
- → 2 Tbsp sugar
- → 1/4 tsp vanilla extract
- → 1/4 tsp ground cinnamon
- → 1/4 tsp ground nutmeg

Place one tablespoon of butter in a ramekin. Add the bread cubes to the ramekin. In a bowl, whisk together the egg, evaporated milk, one tablespoon of sugar, vanilla extract, cinnamon, and nutmeg. Pour this mixture over the bread in the ramekin and let it sit for 20 minutes. Sprinkle with sugar and add one tablespoon of butter on top before baking. Bake two at a time in an air fryer at 300°F for 20 minutes. Check for doneness by inserting a fork; if there is runny milk or egg, cook for an additional 4 minutes at 280°F. Once cooked, dust with cinnamon sugar.

 Conventional Oven: Place the ramekins on a baking sheet and bake at 350°F for 30 minutes.

 Baked Potato Tip: After baking carefully butter the outside and sprinkle with kosher salt before placing in aluminum foil to rest.

6) Buttermilk Biscuits

- → 2 cups self-rising flour
- → 1/4 tsp baking soda
- → 2/3 to 3/4 cup full-fat buttermilk
- → 5 Tbsp salted butter, room temperature (or 1/4 cup vegetable shortening, Crisco)

Add soda to the flour and whisk. Cut butter into flour with a blending fork or pastry blender until the mixture resembles coarse crumbs, about the size of peas. Gradually add buttermilk, mixing until the flour is combined into the dough. Place the dough on a floured surface, fold it 4-7 times, then roll it out to about one-half inch thick. Cut the biscuits, place them in a greased air fryer basket, and pat the tops with buttermilk. Bake at 320°F for 8-10 minutes. Biscuits may need to be flipped over and baked longer if the bottom is not toasted.

7) Baked Potato

Wash two medium sweet potatoes or regular baking potatoes. Place in an air fryer and bake at 380°F for 25 minutes. Then, flip and bake for an additional 25 minutes. Larger potatoes may require an additional 5 minutes of cooking time. To test doneness, squeeze gently with a dishcloth until it sinks or pierce with a fork — if it slides in easily, it is ready. Wrap in foil and rest for 5-10 minutes for a tasty crust.

8) Chicken Fries

→ large chicken breast
→ 2 Tbsp olive oil
→ 2 Tbsp Hidden Valley Ranch dry seasoning
→ salt and pepper to taste
→ 1 cup self-rising flour
→ 1 cup panko crumbs
→ cooking spray

Cut chicken into half-inch strips. Season with Ranch, salt, and pepper, then coat with olive oil. Lightly dust with flour, then coat with panko crumbs, pressing them gently into the mixture. Arrange in the air fryer and spray with cooking spray. Bake at 400°F for 10 minutes, then flip and bake for 5-8 more minutes, or until done. Serve with Recipe 603: Honey Mustard Sauce. Enjoy!

9) Chicken Tenders

→ about 1/2" thick chicken tenders
→ Recipe #597 Chris's Special Seasoning
→ salt and pepper
→ salted butter, melted
→ self-rising flour
→ 1-1/2 cups panko crumbs
→ cooking spray

Sprinkle the chicken tenders with a mixture of seasoning, salt, and pepper. Dip each tender in melted butter to coat thoroughly. Lightly dredge each in flour, then press panko onto the chicken so it sticks to the flour. Place the coated tenders in the air fryer basket and spray them generously with cooking oil or spray. Cook at 400°F for 10 minutes. Carefully turn each tender and cook for an additional 10 minutes. Serve with Recipe #603 Honey Mustard Sauce or Recipe #599 Dippen Chicken Sauce.

"These tenders are delicious! They are tender and juicy on the inside with an incredible crunch!"
- Tammy

10) Chicken Wings

→ 10 or 12 raw chicken wings
→ 1/2 cup olive oil or melted salted butter
→ salt and pepper to taste
→ Recipe #597 Chris's Special Seasoning
→ all-purpose or self-rising flour

Pat the wings dry. Sprinkle with salt, pepper, and Chris's special seasoning. Toss them in the oil or melted butter. Lightly dredge in flour. Place the wings in the Air Fryer basket. Cook at 380°F for 20 minutes. Flip the wings and cook for an additional 20 minutes. Once crispy to your liking, remove from the Air Fryer. Toss in your favorite sauce and serve.

 Wings will stay crunchy if you serve the sauce on the side.

11) Cinnamon Toast

→ 2 slices thick-sliced sandwich bread
→ 2 Tbsp salted butter, room temperature
→ 1 Tbsp sugar
→ 1 tsp ground cinnamon

Spread the butter evenly over one side of each bread slice, ensuring the edges are coated. Sprinkle with cinnamon and sugar. Place the bread in the air fryer and set the temperature to 380°F. Cook for 6 to 7 minutes, checking periodically to avoid burning.

 Notes & Tips: Serve cinnamon toast with scrambled eggs for a delicious meal. For perfect cinnamon toast, cover the entire bread surface with butter, scrape off the excess for even browning, and sprinkle enough cinnamon sugar to create a crisp crust when toasted.

It may take a few tries to master the ideal ratio of butter, sugar, and cinnamon.

12) Coconut Custard

→ 1 Tbsp salted butter, melted.
→ 1 Tbsp sugar
→ 1 medium or large egg
→ 1/8 cup buttermilk
→ 1/4 tsp vanilla extract
→ 1/8 cup sweetened flaked coconut

Spray the ramekin with cooking spray. In a small bowl, whisk the first five ingredients together well. Put coconut in the bottom of a ramekin and pour custard over it.

Place two ramekins in the air fryer and cook for 16 minutes at 310°F. Check for doneness by inserting a fork; if there's runny milk or egg, cook for an additional 4 minutes at 280°F.

 Conventional Oven: Place the ramekins on a baking sheet. Bake at 350 degrees for 30 minutes.

"Creating a classic old-fashioned dessert in the air fryer is incredible. You can prepare individual portions in just a few minutes. Each bite will make you feel as if your mom is right there in your kitchen! It will truly be a blessing." -Tammy

13) Corn On the Cob

→ fresh ears corn (shucked and silk removed)
→ cooking spray
→ salted butter.
→ salt and pepper

Wash the corn thoroughly. Spray the corn with cooking spray or rub it with butter. Place the corn in the air fryer basket. Cook at 380°F for about 7 minutes. Use tongs to remove the corn and transfer it to a plate. Let it cool for 5 to 8 minutes, then season with salt, pepper, and butter.

 Notes & Tips: Prepare an herb butter by finely mincing fresh herbs and thoroughly incorporating them into softened butter at room temperature.

14) Croutons

→ leftover bread, cut into small cubes.
→ olive oil
→ herb blend (your preference)
→ shredded parmesan cheese

Place bread pieces in a bowl and drizzle with olive oil. Toss bread to coat evenly.

Sprinkle with herb blend and Parmesan cheese; toss again. Arrange bread in the air fryer basket. Cook at 350°F for about 4 minutes or until crisp. Let cool before serving or storing.

 Notes & Tips: For extra crunch, check the croutons after 4 minutes and cook an additional minute if needed.

Store cooled croutons in an airtight container for up to two weeks.

Try adding garlic powder or smoked paprika to vary the flavor profile. For an even coating, use cooking spray Instead of tossing in olive oil.

15) Nachos

→ tortilla chips
→ queso dip, mild or spicy
→ non-stick spray
→ your choice of toppings

Spray an 8" cake pan with non-stick spray. Place tortilla chips in the pan. Add queso dip and desired toppings over chips. Air fry at 350°F for 3-4 minutes.

Top with additional toppings if desired and serve immediately.

 Notes & Tips: Try pairing with Recipe #38 Guacamole Dip or Recipe #546 Avocado Salad.

If using other cheeses, purchase block cheese and shred it for creamier melting.

"I love air fryer nachos! It only takes about 4 minutes at 350 degrees to make your nachos hot and crispy. Pair them with my Guacamole or Avocado Salad." - Tammy

16) Home Fries

→ 3 medium potatoes
→ 3 Tbsp olive or vegetable oil
→ kosher salt
→ black pepper
→ onion powder, salt-free
→ roasted garlic powder, salt-free
→ 1/4 cup all-purpose flour

Wash potatoes thoroughly and leave the skin on. Cut potatoes into fries about half an inch thick. Spread fries out and season with kosher salt, black pepper, onion powder, and roasted garlic powder. Toss fries in oil to coat evenly. Sprinkle flour over the fries and toss again to ensure an even coating. Place fries in the air fryer basket. Cook at 380°F for 25 minutes, then shake the basket and lightly spray the fries with oil halfway through. Serve hot with your favorite dipping sauce.

If you own a Cosori 5.8 qt. air fryer, an 8" cake pan may fit. Use tongs for easy removal.

Scan with your phone camera!

collardvalleycooks.com

SHOP Tammy's Kitchen Bakeware Items

USA BRAND
Round Cake Pans
All Sizes Available

Buy the 8" size for the air fryer!

17) Panko Crusted Fish

→ 3-4 fish fillets (1/2" thick or less)
→ olive oil or yellow mustard
→ self-rising flour
→ 1-1/2 cups panko crumbs

→ salt
→ black pepper
→ seasoning of your choice
→ olive oil cooking spray

Pat fish fillets dry and season with salt, pepper, and your chosen seasonings. Coat each fillet with olive oil - dust both sides of each fillet with flour. Press panko crumbs onto both sides of the fillets to adhere. Place fillets in the air fryer basket and spray with olive oil cooking spray. Air fry at 350°F for 8 minutes. Flip, spray again, and air-fry at 400°F for 5-8 more minutes, or until golden.

Tips: Use yellow mustard instead of olive oil for a unique flavor twist.

Before you begin ensure fish fillets are patted dry so the coating sticks better.

18) Hot dogs

→ 4 beef hot dogs (such as Ball Park)
→ 4 hot dog buns
→ ketchup, to serve
→ mustard, to serve
→ Recipe #555 Cole Slaw

Slice hot dogs across the top. Place them in the air fryer basket and cook at 400°F for 6 minutes. Shake the basket and cook for an additional 3 minutes to achieve a charred finish. Warm the hot dog buns if desired and assemble the hot dogs with ketchup, mustard, and coleslaw.

Tips: Add cole slaw to hot dogs for extra flavor and crunch

Make Recipe #602 Hot Dog Chili Sauce for the ultimate dog!

I love my hot dogs cooked in an air fryer. They get a perfect char on the outside, like they have been on a charcoal grill. There is no need to waste lighter fluid, y'all!" - Tammy

"As an Amazon Associate, I earn from qualifying purchases."

19) Potato Chips

→ 1 russet potato
→ cooking oil (corn oil)
→ salt
→ pepper
→ french fry seasoning (optional)

Wash and scrub the potato, then dry. Slice the potato thinly using a sharp knife, mandolin, or grater. Season with salt, pepper, and French fry seasoning if desired. Place slices in a bowl and coat with cooking oil. For the air fryer: Cook at 350°F for 10 minutes, then shake the basket and continue cooking for an additional 10 minutes.

 For a conventional oven: Spread the slices on a parchment- or foil-lined baking sheet and bake at 400°F for 25 minutes, or until golden brown.

 Tips: For extra crunch, soak potato slices in cold water for 20 minutes, then dry before adding seasoning and oil.

Slice potatoes as evenly as possible for uniform cooking. Adjust seasoning to taste after cooking, if needed.

20) Peach Cobbler Singles

→ 1 Tbsp. salted butter
→ 1/8 cup granulated sugar
→ 1/8 cup milk
→ 1/8 cup self-rising flour
→ chopped pecans, optional
→ cinnamon and nutmeg, optional
→ white sugar crystals, optional
→ 14.5 oz. can slice peaches in syrup.

Spray a ramekin with cooking spray and add butter to the bottom. Whisk together granulated sugar, milk, seasonings, and flour. Pour flour batter into a ramekin until it is half full. Add Peaches and a little syrup to each ramekin, filling it to 3/4 full.

Place the ramekin in the air fryer and bake at 320°F for 8 minutes. Sprinkle the tops with white sugar crystals and bake for an additional 8 minutes. A total 16 minutes of cooking time.

 For oven baking, set ramekins on a baking sheet and bake at 375°F for 30 minutes.

 Tips: For added crunch, use chopped pecans and sprinkle extra sugar on top before baking.

Use canned pie fillings or other fruits packed in syrup.

Make sure not to overfill ramekins to avoid bubbling over.

21) Potato Skins

→ 3 russet potatoes
→ 3 Tbsp melted salted butter (or olive oil)
→ cheddar cheese slices
→ 1/2 cup sour cream
→ 3 green onions, diced
→ salt
→ pepper

Microwave potatoes until tender. Cut one-halfinch slices from each side and reserve the insides for another use. Brush potato skins with melted butter. Season with salt and pepper. Air fry skins, skin side down, at 350°F for 10 minutes. Add cheddar cheese to each skin; air fry 2 minutes more. Dip these in Recipe #43 Sour Cream and Onion Dip.

 For the oven option, bake the skins at 425°F for 14 minutes, then add the cheese and continue baking for an additional 4 minutes.

 Tips: For extra crispiness, broil skins for 12 minutes after adding cheese.

When using cheese in an air fryer, use slices instead of grated cheese, as it can blow off the food.

Use the reserved potato insides for mashed potatoes or Recipe # 675 Potato Cakes.

22) Sausage, Pepperoni Bread

→ pizza dough, fresh or refrigerated
→ marinara sauce, for dipping
→ 1 cup breakfast sausage, browned
→ sliced pepperoni
→ sliced mozzarella cheese
→ shredded mozzarella cheese
→ Italian seasonings
→ 1 large egg
→ 2 Tbsp water

Roll the dough into a rectangle and stretch it out. Top half of the rectangle with sliced mozzarella, sausage, pepperoni, Italian seasonings, and shredded mozzarella. Beat egg with water for an egg wash. Brush the egg wash along the edges of the dough using a pastry brush or use your fingers. Fold the empty side of the dough over the ingredient side. Seal the edges with the tongs of a fork. Brush the top of the dough with egg wash. Spray the bottom of air fryer with cooking spray. If the rectangle is too large to fit in the air fryer basket, slice it in half and cook the sections separately. Cook on 380°F for 8 minutes. Slice and serve with marinara sauce.

 For oven: bake on parchment or a greased sheet pan at 425°F for 15 minutes.

 Notes & Tips: Let the bread cool slightly before slicing for a less messy experience.

Tip: For a golden crust, brush with egg wash again halfway through baking.

Tip: Try adding bell peppers or onions for an extra burst of flavor.

It took almost 3 years to gain 100k subscribers! We began CVC in May of 2017 and received this plaque in January of 2020.

23) Southern Fried Chicken

→ 1 young fryer chicken (not a hen)
→ 2 tsp Recipe #597 Chris's Special Seasoning
→ 1 cup self-rising flour
→ 2 large eggs
→ 1/2 cup milk
→ cooking spray
→ water

Cut the chicken into pieces and slice the breasts in half. Beat eggs with water in a shallow dish. Mix flour with seasoning in another shallow dish. Dip each chicken piece in the egg mixture, then coat it in the flour mixture, pressing to adhere. Let the coated chicken rest for 10 minutes. Spray chicken pieces with cooking spray. Place it in the air fryer at 380°F for 20 minutes. Turn and spray again, then cook for an additional 15 minutes or until the internal temperature reaches 180°F. Rest the chicken for 10 minutes before serving.

 Notes & Tips: Spray both sides of the chicken with cooking spray thoroughly to ensure even browning.

Allowing chicken to rest after coating helps the crust adhere better.

We were so excited when we got our YouTube plaque for 100k Subscribers!

Recipe 28

Recipe 32

Crowd Pleasing Appetizers!

Pull up a chair and welcome to the appetizer table! Here in this section, you will find the spirit of Southern hospitality in every bite. These recipes are not just about food, they are about connecting, sharing stories, and building memories with family and friends. Whether you are craving the signature tang of Granny's 14 Day Sweet Pickles or the irresistible crunch of potato chips dipped in Tammy's homemade chip dip, there is something for everyone. You will learn how simple ingredients—like cucumbers, sugar, and vinegar—transform into pickles that are sweet and tart, perfect alongside classic southern sides. So, roll up your sleeves, gather the folks, and dive into these beloved starters. You are sure to discover why these dishes turn every get-together into a celebration of good company and great taste.

Recipe 34

Recipe 38

24) 14 Day Sweet Pickles

→ 1 peck sliced cucumbers
→ 1-gallon boiling water
→ 1 pint pickling (canning) salt
→ 1-1/2 gallons of clean water
→ 2 tsp powdered alum
→ 2.5 quarts of vinegar
→ 12 cups of sugar
→ 1 Tbsp celery seed

Place cucumbers in a large glass jar or churn. Pour salt over cucumbers, then add boiling water. Let them stand for 7 days, skimming any residue daily and keeping cucumbers submerged.

On day 8, drain and cover cucumbers with clean water. Let them stand for 24 hours.

On day 9, drain water. Boil clean water and powdered alum, then pour the mixture over cucumbers and soak for 24 hours.

On day 10, drain the alum water. Boil vinegar, sugar, and celery seeds together, then pour the mixture over cucumbers and soak for 24 hours.

From days 11 to 14, drain and reheat the vinegar-sugar mixture daily, pour it back over cucumbers, and let them soak for another 24 hours each day.

Sterilize jars and lids. Pack pickles into jars. Boil the brine, then pour it over the pickles, leaving a 1/4-inch space at the top. Seal the jars and cool. Store sealed jars in a cool, dry place, and refrigerate any unsealed ones.

This is my large canning jar. I use it for pickles. This 2.5-gallon jar is available on our website.

Notes & Tips: Use only pickling or pure kosher salt—avoid table salt to prevent cloudy brine or discoloration.

Process jars in a pressure canner for long-term storage, following the guidelines of the NCHFP.

Lids should "ping" when sealed. Refrigerate any unsealed jars and use them first.

"When I was a kid, I always got excited when Granny opened a jar of sweet pickles or pickled beets. I so vividly remember sitting at her little round kitchen table and enjoying them with the lunch she prepared for us in the summer." -Tammy

The NCHFP: The USDA's primary canning guidelines website is the National Center for Home Food Preservation (NCHFP), which is supported by the USDA's National Institute of Food and Agriculture. It offers the USDA Complete Guide to Home Canning, along with recipes and information on safe preservation methods.

https://nchfp.uga.edu/how/can

Visit the NCHFP Website "HOW TO CAN" By following the link in this QR CODE.

Scan with your phone camera! When link pops up on screen click it and it will take you there!

25) Dill Pickles, Tammy's

- → whole small pickling cucumbers
- → 1-gallon boiling water
- → 1 1/2 pints pink Himalayan salt
- → onion, sliced thin (1/2-inch pieces)
- → garlic, two cloves per jar
- → fresh dill or dill weed
- → 1 1/2 cups water (per quart jar)
- → 1/2 cup vinegar (per quart jar)

Wash the cucumbers, remove the ends, and slice them. Layer the cucumbers and salt in a large glass jar or churn. Pour salt over the layered cucumbers, then add boiling water. Let them stand at room temperature for 14 days.

Start tasting after 10 days; pickles are ready when the brine is cloudy, and they are crunchy. Drain the pickles and place them in a large bowl (do not rinse them).

Sterilize jars and rings. Prepare flat seals.

Pack jars with pickles, onion slices, dill, and garlic. Bring vinegar and water to a boil. Pour over the pickles in jars, leaving a 1/4-inch space at the top. Seal jars with rings until they are just tight. Cool completely.

Check for proper seals. Refrigerate any unsealed jars and consume first. Process jars in a pressure canner for long-term storage if desired.

 Notes & Tips: Choose small, firm cucumbers for the crunchiest pickles.

The water and vinegar amounts are per jar. Once you pack pickles into jars, you will know how much you need to prepare by multiplying the amount by the number of quart jars.

Large glass jars make it easier to monitor the clarity of the brine.

The "ping" sound indicates a successful seal.

Always use pickling or kosher salt—never table salt—for best results

John 1:1
"In the beginning was the Word, and the Word was with God, and the Word was God." KJV

26) Artichoke & Spinach Dip

- → 1 cup sour cream
- → 4 oz. cream cheese, room temperature
- → 1 tsp ranch dressing mix
- → 1 tsp onion powder
- → 1/4 cup olive oil
- → 2 cloves garlic, pressed
- → 14 oz. Marinated artichoke hearts drained and chopped
- → 1/2 cup frozen spinach, drained and chopped (use 32 oz. cooked, drained spinach for more flavor; squeeze excess moisture out with a towel)
- → 8 oz. mozzarella, shredded
- → 4 oz. Romano cheese, grated
- → 8 oz. Parmesan cheese, grated (divided)

Preheat oven to 375°F.

Blend sour cream, cream cheese, ranch dressing mix, onion powder, and olive oil until smooth. Add pressed garlic and mix well. Fold in artichoke hearts, spinach, mozzarella, Romano, and half of the Parmesan; mix thoroughly. Transfer mixture to a greased baking dish and sprinkle with remaining Parmesan. Bake for 20 minutes, or until hot and bubbly.

 Notes & Tips: Serve warm with crackers, bread, or chips.

Tip: Squeeze out as much liquid as possible from the spinach for a thicker dip.

Tip: Try broiling for 2-3 minutes at the end for an extra golden top.

"Skip the baking; microwave to warm when ready to serve. No baking needed." - Tammy

27) Cheese Straws

→ 2 cups shredded cheddar cheese, room temperature
→ 1/2 cup salted butter, room temperature
→ 1-1/2 cups all-purpose flour
→ 1/4 tsp cayenne pepper (or 2 tsp dry Hidden Valley Ranch)

Mix butter and cheese until smooth and creamy using a food processor or stand mixer. Add flour and seasoning - blending until the dough forms. Roll the dough out on a floured surface and cut into cracker shapes, or pipe it with a pastry bag. Arrange on a parchment-lined baking sheet. Bake at 375°F until golden, for about 12 minutes. Cool on a rack and transfer to an airtight container.

 Notes & Tips: Freeze baked cheese straws for extended storage.

For an extra flavor boost, use both cayenne and ranch seasoning.

Ensure butter and cheese are at room temperature for more effortless blending.

"I remember mama making cheese stick dough and piping them onto baking sheets. She would carefully transport them to wedding reception halls and serve them alongside other delicious appetizers." - *Tammy*

28) Chex Mix

→ 3 cups corn Chex™ cereal
→ 3 cups rice Chex™ cereal
→ 3 cups wheat Chex™ cereal
→ 1 cup mixed nuts
→ 1 cup bite-sized pretzels
→ 1 cup garlic-flavor bite-size bagel chips
→ 1/2 cup of salted butter
→ 2 Tbsp Worcestershire sauce
→ 1 1/2 tsp seasoned salt
→ 3/4 tsp garlic powder
→ 1/2 tsp onion powder

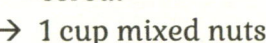

Combine cereals, mixed nuts, pretzels, and bagel chips in a large bowl.

Melt butter; stir in Worcestershire sauce, seasoned salt, garlic powder, and onion powder. Pour the butter mixture over the cereal mixture and toss to coat evenly. Spread the mix on two baking sheets. Bake at 250°F for 1 hour, stirring every 15 minutes, using two oven racks if possible.

Cool to room temperature before storing in an airtight container for up to 2 weeks.

 Tip: Stirring every 15 minutes ensures even baking and maximum crunch.
Tip: For an extra flavor boost, sprinkle a pinch of your favorite seasoning blend over the top before baking.

29) Cucumber Salad Sandwiches

→ 1 seedless cucumber, diced
→ 2 Tbsp grated onion
→ 1/2 tsp salt
→ 1/2 tsp black pepper
→ 8 oz. cream cheese, room temperature
→ 2 tsp vinegar
→ white or dark bread
→ pimento, for garnish, optional
→ parsley, for garnish, optional

Combine cucumber, onion, salt, pepper, cream cheese, and vinegar in a bowl and mix until smooth and well combined. Spread the mixture on the bread.

For open-faced sandwiches, cut rounds from bread with a biscuit or cookie cutter, top with cucumber spread, and garnish with pimento or parsley if desired as shown in picture below.

 Tips: Chill the spread for 30 minutes before serving for an enhanced flavor.

Pat the diced cucumber dry with a paper towel to avoid extra moisture.

Use thinly sliced bread for a more delicate presentation.

"Go outside, look at the sky, the plants, the birds and see God's glory! It is so evident in nature. Feel His presence, He is everywhere!" - *Tammy*

30) Chocolate Strawberries

→ 1 lb. fresh strawberries
→ 3/4 cup milk chocolate chips
→ 3/4 cup semi-sweet chocolate chips
→ 1/2 cup white chocolate chips
→ 1 Tbsp shortening
→ parchment paper

Wash the strawberries and leaves gently, then let them dry completely. Combine milk chocolate chips, semi-sweet chocolate chips, and shortening in a microwave-safe bowl. Heat in 30-second intervals, stirring until smooth. Dip strawberries into the melted chocolate, shake off excess, and place on parchment paper. Melt the white chocolate chips, then drizzle them over the dipped strawberries using a spoon. Let strawberries sit until dry, then store them in an airtight container in the refrigerator.

Notes & Tips: Use a tall slender container for melting chocolate for easy dipping.

Do not substitute shortening; butter may cause chocolate to seize.

Ensure strawberries are completely dehydrated before dipping for optimal results.

31) Cocktail Meatballs, Mama's

→ 2 lb. ground sirloin
→ 2 large eggs
→ 2 Tbsp dried onion flakes
→ 1/4 tsp black pepper
→ 1/3 cup ketchup
→ 1 cup crushed cornflakes (or saltine crackers)
→ 1/3 cup parsley flakes
→ 2 Tbsp soy sauce
→ 1/2 tsp salt
→ 16 oz. can jellied cranberry sauce (or grape jelly)
→ 2 Tbsp Lemon juice
→ 12 oz. jar chili sauce
→ 2 Tbsp firmly packed brown sugar

Combine ground sirloin, eggs, dried onion flakes, black pepper, ketchup, crushed cornflakes, parsley flakes, soy sauce, and salt in a bowl and mix well. Roll the mixture into walnut-sized ballsand place on a lined baking sheet. Bake at 400°F for 25 minutes.

Meanwhile, add jellied cranberry sauce, lemon juice, chili sauce, and brown sugar to a saucepan, and stir over medium heat until smooth. Add baked meatballs to the sauce and heat through. Keep meatballs warm until serving.

Tips: Use parchment or foil to line the baking sheet for easy cleanup.

To save time, substitute frozen meatballs and simmer directly in the sauce.

Serve from a slow cooker set to low to keep meatballs warm during gatherings.

"When I was growing up, my mama was a member of Collard Valley Homemakers Club. The ladies in the community would gather in homes once a month. They raised money for the club and charities. They quilted, canned food, designed booths every year for the county fair, and so much more.

Those ladies were friends. I never heard my mama gossiping about or with other ladies. I am so thankful she raised me like that. We were taught to love everyone. These ladies were not high-faulting' ladies like you see in Southern Bell movies; they were ordinary homemakers who cared about family and the community they lived in.

I recall how I enjoyed tagging along with mama. Granny was always there, too. You may wonder why I am discussing this in the appetizer section. Well, if I had to be honest, this is how I was introduced to appetizers. Seeing what all the ladies brought was a joy, and now I know it was also a privilege. I thank God for my upbringing." - Tammy

32) Cream Cheese Ball, Pineapple

→ 28-oz cream cheese, softened
→ 8 oz. can crushed pineapple, drained
→ 1/4 cup finely chopped green bell pepper
→ 2 Tbsp finely chopped onions
→ 1 1/2 tsp seasoned salt
→ 1 cup finely chopped pecans

Combine cream cheese, crushed pineapple, green bell pepper, onions, seasoned salt, and pecans in a mixing bowl. Mix until thoroughly blended. Shape into a ball, wrap in plastic, and refrigerate until firm. For extra appeal, roll the cheese ball in additional chopped pecans before serving. Serve with crackers.

 Tips: Ensure the pineapple is well-drained to prevent a runny mixture.

Chill the cheese ball for at least 2 hours to allow flavors to meld.

For a festive look, roll in chopped parsley or paprika along with pecans.

33) Cream Cheese Rangoons

→ 8 oz. cream cheese, room temperature
→ 1/4 cup sugar
→ 1 green onion, diced
→ 1 large egg
→ 1 package egg roll wrappers
→ 1/4 cup of sweet crab meat, optional

Mix cream cheese and sugar until smooth. Fold in diced green onion and crab meat (if using). Cut egg roll wrappers into squares. Beat the egg to make an egg wash and brush it onto the wrapper edges. Add the filling to the center, fold the wrappers into triangles, and seal the edges. Fry until golden brown; drain on a rack. Serve with your favorite dipping sauce.

 Notes & Tips: For extra crispiness, avoid overfilling wrappers.

Chill the filling for easier wrapping.

If using crab meat, reduce or omit sugar for a savory flavor.

Pair with sweet chili sauce for a delicious dip.

34) Deviled Eggs

→ 6 large eggs
→ 2 Tbsp mayonnaise
→ 1/4 tsp sugar
→ 1/2 tsp yellow mustard
→ 1/4 tsp black pepper
→ 2 tsp sweet pickle juice
→ 1 Tbsp sweet pickle relish, optional paprika

Bring water to a boil in a saucepan, then gently lower eggs into water with a spoon and boil for 12 minutes. Rinse under cold water. Add 2 cups of ice to the water. After 2 minutes, peel the eggs; the eggshells should come off easily. Slice eggs in half and remove yolks. Using a fork, mash yolks with mayonnaise, sugar, mustard, black pepper, pickle juice, and relish (if using). Spoon or pipe yolk mixture into egg whites. Sprinkle with paprika before serving.

 Notes & Tips: If you are using fresh eggs, they are harder to peel. You can prick the large end with a needle or a sharp, thin object before boiling. This will work great every time. There is no need to do this step if you have store-bought eggs.

Piping the filling makes for a neater presentation.

Lay the eggs sideways in the refrigerator 24 hours before boiling to center the yolk in the egg.

Enhanced Flavors:

For extra tang, increase mustard..

Use dill pickle juice and relish instead of sweet pickles.

Use crumbled bacon and 1/2 tsp Hidden Valley Ranch seasoning while omitting pickle relish and juice

Use chopped olives and olive juice in place of pickles.

35) Fried Green Tomatoes

→ 2–3 yellow or green tomatoes
→ wash, dry, and slice the tomatoes.
→ 1 cup whole buttermilk
→ corn oil for frying

Flour batter:

→ 2/3 cup self-rising flour
→ 3/4 tsp pepper
→ 1 1/2 tsp salt

Cornmeal batter:

→ 1/8 cup self-rising flour
→ 1/2 cup self-rising cornmeal mix
→ 3/4 tsp pepper
→ 1 1/2 tsp salt

Soak tomato slices in buttermilk for 10 minutes. Mix self-rising flour, pepper, and salt to create a flour batter, or combine self-rising flour, cornmeal mix, pepper, and salt to create a cornmeal batter. Shake off excess buttermilk from each tomato slice, then coat both sides with one of the batter recipes above.

Preheat the skillet and add oil. Test oil with a bit of batter; when it sizzles, add tomatoes. Fry tomatoes, flipping once, until golden on both sides. Drain on paper towels. Serve with Recipe

#599 Dippen Chicken Sauce, or Recipe #3 Horsey Dipping Sauce.

 Tips: Soak tomatoes thoroughly in buttermilk for the best flavor.

For extra crunch, use self-rising flour on all of your vegetables when frying.

Fry on medium heat for even browning.

Drain on a wire rack, not paper towels, to keep tomatoes crisp.

36) Fried Mozzarella Sticks

→ 8 oz. mozzarella cheese, cut into 8 sticks
→ 1/3 cup all-purpose flour
→ 1 tsp seasoned salt (or Badia Complete)
→ 1 Tbsp Italian seasoning
→ 1 large egg
→ 1 1/4 cups dry Italian breadcrumbs
→ 16 oz. bottle vegetable oil pizza sauce, for dipping

Cut mozzarella cheese into sticks and freeze. Mix flour, seasoned salt, and Italian seasoning in a bag. Shake cheese sticks in flour mixture to coat. Beat egg in a bowl and place breadcrumbs in another bowl. Dip each stick in egg, then coat with breadcrumbs. Repeat this step for a double coating, if desired. Chill the breaded sticks on a sheet pan for 1 hour. Heat the vegetable oil to 370°F. Test oil with a bit of batter; when it sizzles, fry 3-4 sticks at a time until golden. Drain on paper towels and serve hot, accompanied by pizza sauce.

 Tips: Freeze cheese before breading. Chill before frying to prevent cheese from melting too quickly in the oil. Double-coat with egg and breadcrumbs for extra crunch. Serve immediately for best taste.

"There are so many kitchen gadgets that have been mailed to me by viewers over the years! One of my very favorites is the pig tail food hook. I absolutely love this thing. It is super sharp and will pick up meats without knocking off the crispy batter. Scan the code below with your phone's camera for a link to this product. If you cook, it will be one of the best tools you have ever been introduced to! - Tammy

SHOP TAMMY'S KITCHEN TOP SELLERS

Scan with your phone camera!
collardvalleycooks.com   GET A Food Hook TODAY!

15

37) Fruit Dip – Mama's

→ 7 oz. marshmallow cream
→ 12 oz. sour cream
→ 14 oz. can sweetened condensed milk.
→ 2 lemons (for zest and juice)
→ 1/3 cup lemon juice

Zest the lemons before juicing. Combine marshmallow cream, sour cream, sweetened condensed milk, and lemon juice in a medium bowl. Blend until smooth using a hand mixer. Fold in most of the lemon zest, saving a small portion for garnish.

 Refrigerate in an airtight container overnight.

Before serving, sprinkle with reserved zest.

Refrigerating overnight allows the flavors to meld.

Serve cold for optimal texture and flavor.

"Mama always served this when she catered weddings. She would make a beautiful fruit bowl out of a watermelon and serve this dip alongside it." - *Tammy*

38) Guacamole Dip

→ 3 ripe avocados
→ 1/2 freshly squeezed lemon or lime
→ 2 Tbsp fresh cilantro, chopped
→ 3 Tbsp minced onion
→ 1 small tomato, chopped
→ 1/2 tsp salt
→ 1/4 tsp pepper

Peel and pit the avocados, mash them with a fork. Add lemon juice, cilantro, onion, tomato, salt, and pepper. Stir gently to combine.

 Tips: Place an avocado pit in the dip to help maintain freshness.

Store with plastic wrap pressed directly on the surface to help prevent browning.

Cilantro should be roughly chopped, not minced, to obtain authentic flavor.

How to Choose the Right Avocado

 Check the color: Look for avocados with an even green-black color. Bright green usually indicates underripe fruit, while a dark, almost black color can signal ripeness. Just beware of any overly dark,

shriveled skin, which might mean it's overripe.

Give it a gentle squeeze: Hold the avocado in your palm and press lightly—if it yields slightly but doesn't feel mushy, it's just right. If it's firm, it needs more time; if it's too soft, it's likely overripe.

Peek under the stem: Flick off the small stem at the top. If the flesh underneath is bright green, the avocado is perfectly ripe. If it's brown or mushy, that's a sign it's past its prime.

"I enjoy Recipe #546 Avocado Salad and often snack on sliced avocado with salt and pepper. Avocados are rich in healthy fats and contain protein. So, the next time you're at the grocery store, consider picking one up," - *Tammy*

39) Ham Spread

→ 2 cups diced ham
→ 8 oz. cream cheese, room temperature
→ 8 oz. can crushed pineapple, drained
→ 1/2 cup chopped pecans
→ 1 tsp Worcestershire sauce

Add the above ingredients to a mixing bowl. Mix well with a hand mixer until the mixture is smooth. Serve chilled with crackers.

 Notes & Tips: Let the cream cheese soften at room temperature before mixing for a smoother, more spreadable consistency.

Drain pineapple thoroughly to prevent excess moisture.

For a festive touch, garnish with extra chopped pecans or fresh herbs.

Store leftovers in an airtight container in the refrigerator.

"The only good in me is the goodness of God. I need His love to have a joyful life." - *Tammy*

40) Onion Rings, Best Ever!

→ 1 large, sweet onion
→ 3/4 cup milk
→ heaping 1/8 cup cornstarch
→ 3/4 cup self-rising flour
→ 1 tsp onion powder
→ 1 tsp roasted garlic powder, Bidia
→ 1/2 tsp cayenne pepper
→ corn oil for frying

Peel and slice the onion into rings. Whisk milk, cornstarch, self-rising flour, onion powder, roasted garlic powder, and cayenne pepper in a bowl until smooth. Heat the oil over medium to medium-low heat. Dip the onion rings into the batter, coating well. Fry the onion rings a few minutes on each side, until they are golden brown and the onion is tender inside. Remove with a slotted spoon or tongs, then drain off excess oil.

 Tips: Keep oil at the right temperature for the best texture. Too hot will over-brown, too cool will make the rings greasy.

Separate onion slices carefully for even coating.

Drain on a wire rack for a crispy crust.

Serve immediately for crispness.

41) Pimento Cheese, Eddie's

→ 8 oz. cream cheese, room temperature
→ 1/2 cup mayonnaise
→ 1/4 tsp garlic powder
→ 1/4 tsp onion powder
→ 1/4 tsp cayenne pepper
→ 2 oz. jar pimentos
→ 8 oz. sharp cheddar cheese, shredded
→ 8 oz. white American cheese, shredded
→ 1 jalapeño, grilled, seeded, diced, optional

Place cream cheese in a mixing bowl and blend until smooth. Add mayonnaise, garlic powder, onion powder, and cayenne pepper, mix until well combined. Stir in pimentos. Fold in sharp cheddar cheese and white American cheese until evenly combined. Add jalapeño if desired and mix thoroughly. Refrigerate until ready to serve. Enjoy with crackers or as a sandwich spread.

 Tips: For a milder spread, omit the jalapeño or use less cayenne.

Shred your own cheese for the best texture and flavor.

Serve cold for optimal consistency and flavor.

 "My onion ring recipe pairs perfectly with a grilled burger topped with my brother Eddie's pimento cheese—a great combo for any celebration." – *Tammy*

My Brother Eddie

Eddie was always a gentle soul. A kid who was loving and kind. He played fair and had a humble nature. I was not surprised when he surrendered to God and became a Preacher. He is now the Pastor of our community's church, Collard Valley Baptist Church in Cedartown, Georgia. The people there are loving and caring. They can all cook, and their cooking styles are very similar to what you will find in this book. If you ever have the chance to eat there at Homecoming, I highly recommend it. It is a true Collard Valley Cooks feast! You can also watch the church services on Facebook and YouTube. I hope you give Eddie's pimento cheese a try, but I know he would rather you try "Jesus." -*Tammy*

42) Sausage Balls from Scratch

→ 2 cups self-rising flour
→ 2 large eggs
→ 1 lb. breakfast sausage (half hot, half mild)
→ 1/2 cup salted butter, melted
→ 1 Tbsp nosalt salad blend
→ 1 Tbsp Onion powder (or granulated onion or 3 Tbsp minced green onion and parsley) use NO SALT Seasonings
→ 16 oz. sharp cheddar cheese, grated

Melt butter in a microwavable bowl. Add the butter, sausage, spices, and flour to a large bowl. Mix the mixture well by hand until it is evenly blended. Pour the cheese out on counter and knead in grated cheese a little at a time until thoroughly incorporated. Pinch off the dough and roll it into balls about one inch in diameter. Place the balls on a parchment-lined baking sheet. Bake at 350°F for 25 minutes. Refrigerate leftovers.

 Notes & Tips: Use a stand mixer to mix sausage balls.

"Swaggerty's Farm breakfast sausage instantly won me over. Growing up with homemade sausage from our pigs, it brought back the memories of what sausage should taste like. The spices are perfect, and it is worth every penny you spend. Put some in your skillet—I know you'll enjoy it!"-Tammy

 Use a mix of hot and mild Swaggerty's Farm breakfast sausage for optimal flavor!

Shred cheese from a block for optimal texture and flavor.

If parchment is not available, spray baking sheet with oil or cooking spray.

Store sausage balls in an airtight container in the refrigerator.

This contains meat, so please don't leave it out on the table for over three hours. Keep refrigerated.

"Our Favorite Sausage is Swaggerty's Farm! They are from Tennessee and have an excellent family business. Give their sausage a try today, you will be so glad you did!" -Tammy

43) Sour Cream & Onion Dip

→ 1 sweet onion (Vidalia if available)
→ 3 tsp garlic powder
→ 1 tsp salt
→ 24 oz sour cream
→ 1/8 cup chopped chives or green onions

Thinly slice and dice the onion. Mix onion, garlic powder, and salt in a bowl. Add sour cream and chopped chives/onion. Stir until evenly combined. Store dip in an airtight container and refrigerate until serving.

 Notes & Tips: Serve with potato chips or raw vegetables.

Store leftovers in the sour cream container for convenience.

You can use garlic salt in place of salt and omit garlic powder.

"I make this dip for parties and gatherings, and everyone loves it." - Tammy

Recipe #54, Recipe #674
Recipe #642, Recipe # 613, Recipe # 103

Beef Recipes

Welcome to Tammy's Hearty Beef Recipes
A Taste of Home in Mama's Kitchen

If there is one aroma that fills the kitchen and brings everyone running to the table, it is the scent of Mama's beef cooking on the stove, Our beef recipe collection is full of simple ingredient cooking that you will love.

Inside this section, you will discover delicious classics like Mama's Chuck Roast, made with tender chuck roast, fresh carrots, and potatoes. It has just the right blend of spices to make it taste like the Sunday pot roast you remember. And do not miss Recipe #64 Meatloaf Topping, a perfect zesty companion that reminds me of that little extra care Mama always added to make every dish special.

So, whether you are looking to recreate those cozy weeknight dinners or whip up a feast for your own family gatherings, these recipes will transport you back to Mama's kitchen—where every bite tastes like home.

44) Beef Burrito Supreme

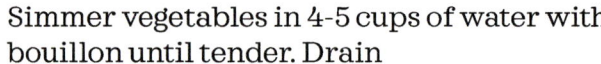

- → 1-1/2 lb. ground beef or ground chuck
- → 1 cup salsa
- → 1 tsp chili powder
- → 1/4 tsp cumin
- → 1 tsp salt
- → 1/4 tsp pepper
- → Recipe #593 Cheese Sauce
- → 1 onion, sliced
- → 1 bell pepper, sliced
- → 3 Tbsp olive oil
- → 2-15.5 oz. cans red kidney beans
- → 2 tsp onion powder
- → 1 tsp garlic powder
- → burrito flour tortillas
- → cooking spray or oil
- → toppings: lettuce, tomato, sour cream

Start by browning and draining the ground beef, then mix it with salsa, chili powder, cumin, salt, and pepper. Prepare Recipe #593 Cheese Sauce.

Sauté the sliced onion and bell pepper in olive oil until it is soft. In a small saucepan or microwave-safe bowl, heat the beans and then mash them. Stir in the onion and garlic powders.

Spray a 13x9x2-inch baking dish with cooking spray or lightly oil it. Lay out the tortillas and fill them with cooked beef, beans, and sautéed vegetables. Roll up each tortilla and place them seam-side down in the dish. Pour the cheese sauce over the rolled tortillas, then sprinkle with extra salsa and shredded cheese.

Bake at 350°F until bubbly, for about 40 minutes. Serve with shredded lettuce, diced tomato, and sour cream. Kidney beans can be substituted with pintos.

45) Beef Pot Pie

- → 3 carrots, peeled and cubed
- → 4 potatoes, peeled and cubed
- → 1/2 onion, cubed
- → 2 tsp beef bouillon granules
- → 3 cups hot water

Simmer vegetables in 4-5 cups of water with bouillon until tender. Drain

- → 1 lb. ground chuck
- → 1/2 onion, chopped
- → 1/2 bell pepper, chopped

Add the beef, onion, and pepper to a skillet and cook over medium-high heat until browned. Drain excess oil from the meat and return it to the skillet.

- → milk
- → 3/4 cup brown gravy mix, McCormick

Place gravy mix in milk and stir well. Pour liquid over meat in the skillet and simmer until it has thickened. Add drained vegetables and stir.

- → 2 ready-made 9-inch pie crusts (find in refrigerated section near biscuits)

Place the pie crust at the bottom of a round baking dish or a cast-iron skillet. See below for the size of the cast iron. Fill with the beef mixture. Top with the remaining crust. Cut 6 slits into the top crust and bake at 375°F for 1 hour. The bottom crust should be golden brown!

Option: Use canned mixed veggies in place of fresh vegetables but drain them first.

Use a 10.25-inch cast iron skillet that is 3" high (chicken frying skillet) or a 12-inch regular cast iron skillet. It will be too much filling for a regular 10.25-inch skillet.

46) Beef Enchiladas

- → 1-1/2 lbs. ground chuck
- → 1 tsp salt
- → 1/4 tsp black pepper
- → Recipe #47 Enchilada Sauce
- → Recipe #593 Cheese Sauce
- → corn tortillas (or *flour tortillas*)
- → cooking oil
- → toppings: lettuce, tomato, sour cream, additional beef, and onion

Brown the ground chuck in a skillet, breaking it apart with a hamburger separator. Drain excess fat—season with salt and pepper. Prepare the enchilada and cheese sauces as instructed+. Lightly coat a 13x9-inch baking pan with cooking oil. Fill the corn tortillas with the beef mixture, fold the sides over the filling, and arrange them in the pan. Top the filled tortillas evenly with enchilada sauce and cheese sauce, then sprinkle with additional shredded cheese. Bake at 350°F until bubbly, for about 40 minutes. Serve with shredded lettuce, sliced tomato, and sour cream.

Tips for Folding Corn Tortillas
How to Fill and Fold Corn Tortillas Without Cracking

*Warm Them Up: Corn tortillas are naturally less flexible than flour tortillas and are prone to cracking when cold. Before folding, wrap a stack in a damp paper towel and microwave for 30–45 seconds, or heat them individually in a dry skillet for 15–20 seconds per side. This softens them and makes them much easier to work with.

*Don't Overfill: Add just enough filling to create a plump tortilla that can still be easily folded. Overfilling will cause the tortillas to split or spill open.

*Filling Placement: Spoon your beef, cheese, or other filling slightly off-center, then fold one side over the filling, tuck it gently, and roll it up snugly but not too tightly to prevent tearing.

*Work quickly: Corn tortillas stiffen as they cool, so fold them soon after heating for the best results. If making a large batch, keep them wrapped in a warm kitchen towel as you work.

*Steam for Extra Flexibility: Place tortillas in a steamer basket over simmering water for 1–2 minutes, or use a tortilla warmer lined with a damp cloth. The steam will make them pliable and less likely to crack.

*Brush with Oil: Lightly brushing both sides of each tortilla with oil before heating can help them become softer and prevent sticking or splitting during folding.

*Store Properly: Always keep corn tortillas sealed in their original package or in a zip-top bag to prevent drying out, which makes them more brittle and prone to cracking when folded.

47) Enchilada Sauce

- → 1/4 cup cooking oil
- → 2 Tbsp flour
- → 1/4 cup chili powder
- → large garlic clove, diced or pressed
- → 1 Tbsp diced onion
- → 8 oz. can tomato sauce
- → 1 1/2 cups water
- → 1/2 tsp ground cumin
- → 1 tsp salt
- → 1/2 cup ketchup

Add oil to a hot skillet. Add flour and whisk well. Then, add chili powder, garlic, onion, tomato sauce, and whisk again. Add water, cumin, salt, and ketchup, and whisk until thoroughly combined. Reduce the heat and let it simmer for 10 minutes. Allow to cool, then pour into a jar for refrigerator storage. It will stay for up to 3-4 weeks.

 This is a great use of a funnel and mason jar!

48) Beef Shanks

→ 2 or 3 large, meaty beef shanks
→ olive (or vegetable oil)
→ kosher salt and black pepper
→ 2 sprigs fresh rosemary (or 1 tsp dried)
→ 2 sprigs fresh sage (or 1/2 tsp dried)
→ 1 red bell pepper, sliced
→ 1 large onion, quartered
→ 2 large carrots peeled and chopped
→ 1 stalk celery, chopped

Remove the shanks from the refrigerator about 90 minutes before cooking—season with kosher salt and pepper. Preheat a large stockpot over high heat, then add oil and brown the shanks on both sides. Add the vegetables and spices, then cover with water and simmer for at least 2 hours.

Remove the shanks and strain the broth, setting aside large vegetable chunks. Place the shank in a non-stick pan or stockpot, ensuring it is not overcrowded. Pour half of the broth over the shanks, cover, and simmer until the liquid has evaporated and turned into a sticky gravy. Flip the meat, then add the remaining broth and vegetables. Continue cooking until all the stock has cooked off and a rich gravy has formed.

49) Beef Tips & Gravy

→ 1 medium onion, chopped
→ 2 green onions, diced

→ 2 Tbsp chopped red bell pepper
→ olive oil
→ 1 1/2 lbs. beef tips (or stew meat)
→ 1 pack Lipton onion soup mix
→ 1 Tbsp buttermilk
→ 1/2 cup all-purpose (or self-rising flour)
→ 3/4 tsp Worcestershire sauce
→ 2 Tbsp cornstarch
→ 1/2 cup milk

Sauté onion and pepper in 3 tablespoons of olive oil until tender, then set aside. Toss beef stew meat in buttermilk, onion soup mix, and flour. Sear in a pressure cooker with oil until browned. Add hot water, sautéed vegetables, and Worcestershire sauce. Cook on medium pressure for 30 minutes. Whisk cornstarch into the cold milk and pour it over the meat. Cook until gravy thickens. Serve over rice or potatoes.

Saucepan: Cook in a saucepan over medium/low heat until beef is fork-tender.

Thicken as directed above.

50) Chip Beef & Gravy

→ 1 jar chipped beef, sliced thin option: rinse to reduce salt
→ 1/2 cup salted butter
→ 1/2 cup flour
→ 1/2 tsp black pepper
→ 2 1/2 cups beef broth
→ 1/2 cup evaporated milk
→ 1 tsp dried parsley (or fresh)

Melt butter in a large skillet. Sift the flour into the hot, melted butter and whisk until smooth. Add pepper and cook on high heat, stirring constantly until the flour turns brown. Add chipped beef, broth, and milk. Use a gravy whisk and cook, stirring continuously, until the mixture is thick and bubbly. Pour into a serving dish. Serve gravy over toasted bread topped with Recipe#674 Creamed Potatoes.

51) Cabbage Roll Skillet

- → 1/2 lb. ground chuck (or breakfast sausage)
- → onion, sliced thinly.
- → small bell pepper, sliced thin, optional
- → grated carrot
- → large tomato, chopped
- → 1/2 head cabbage, sliced thin
- → 1 Tbsp fennel seed (crushed or chopped to enhance flavor)
- → 5 oz. can tomato sauce
- → 1 Tbsp apple cider vinegar
- → large garlic clove, minced or pressed
- → 15 oz. can navy beans, drained
- → 3/4 tsp salt
- → 1/2 tsp black pepper

Brown ground chuck with onion and pepper. Grate and prepare the vegetables while the beef browns. Drain excess grease from the meat. Add the remaining ingredients and simmer on medium heat for 10 minutes. Serve and enjoy! This dish tastes even better the next day once the flavors have had a chance to meld.

Notes & Tips: Use a spice blend, such as 1/2 teaspoon of Goya salad vegetable spice. If the spice blend contains salt, reduce the salt in the recipe accordingly.

Beans can be substituted for other types that you have on hand.

I recommend Swaggerty's Farm breakfast sausage.

"If you like cabbage rolls, try my cabbage roll skillet recipe; it is a shortcut version of traditional cabbage rolls."- *Tammy*

Eph 1:3
"Blessed be the God and Father of our Lord Jesus Christ, who hath blessed us with all spiritual blessings in heavenly places in Christ:" KJV

A Brief History of Cabbage
From Ancient Fields to Modern Kitchens

Cabbage has been around forever — it is one of those vegetables that just never goes out of style. It originated in the Mediterranean, where the ancient Greeks and Romans grew early varieties for food and medicine. Over the centuries, people kept tweaking and cultivating it until we got the round, leafy heads we recognize today.

In medieval Europe, cabbage gained popularity due to its durability, ease of cultivation, and ability to stay fresh for an extended period. People used it in everything—stews, soups, and especially sauerkraut once fermentation gained popularity. As people began to move around the world, cabbage accompanied them and found its way into many different dishes.

These days, cabbage remains a staple in many kitchens. It is crunchy, tasty, ultra-healthy, and versatile in many recipes. Whether you eat it raw, cooked, or pickled, cabbage has a way of bringing people together and making meals feel a little warmer, no matter where you are.

When I grew up, we planted plenty of cabbage in the garden. Granny loved sauerkraut, and she canned it every year. Mama did not feed us kraut very often, but now and then, Daddy would get a hankering for it. - *Tammy*

52) Corned Beef and Cabbage

→ corned beef with seasoning packet
→ 3 cups water
→ 1 Tbsp beef bouillon granules
→ black pepper
→ 6-8 small new potatoes onion, peeled and cubed
→ 5 carrots, peeled and sliced
→ half a head of cabbage

Mix the bouillon with 3 cups of warm water. Wash the cabbage and slice it into 1-inch-wide strips. Note: Salting is not necessary because bouillon is salty. Add the meat, bouillon, water, seasoning packet, onion, and enough additional water to cover the beef completely.

Crockpot: Cook on low for 7 hours. Then add potatoes and carrots, sprinkle with black pepper, and cook on high for 2 hours. Add the cabbage, sprinkle with black pepper, and cook until both the cabbage and vegetables are tender.

Saucepan: Follow the exact instructions as above. Cooking time may vary depending on when the meat becomes tender enough to be fork-tender. Cook the meat on low heat; avoid boiling, as this can cause it to become tough. Once meat is tender add vegetables and cook until fork tender.

Braiser: This method has the fastest cooking time! The braiser should have a heavy lid without a vent to keep all the moisture inside. Follow the exact instructions as above. The beef and vegetables will become tender quicker with this method of cooking.

 For extra flavor, add a couple of bay leaves and a few peppercorns to the cooking liquid.

Slice the corned beef against the grain to ensure each bite is tender and easy to chew.

53) Cottage Pie

For Potatoes:

→ 5 lbs. Russet potatoes
→ 2 tsp salt
→ 1/4 cup sour cream
→ 3/4 tsp black pepper
→ 1/4 cup salted butter
→ 3/4 cup milk

Peel and cut potatoes, then simmer in a stockpot over medium heat for 25 minutes. Drain, add salt, sour cream, black pepper, milk, and butter. Beat with a stand mixer or hand mixer until the mixture is light and fluffy.

Beef filling:

→ small onion, diced
→ 1-1/2 lb. ground chuck (or ground beef)
→ 1 tsp steak seasoning, Weber Steak & Chop
→ 1/2 cup brown gravy mix, McCormick
→ 1 tsp Worcestershire sauce
→ 2- 15 oz. cans mixed vegetables

Cook and brown the beef with diced onion, then drain if necessary. Mix in steak seasoning, gravy, Worcestershire sauce, and the liquid from the vegetables. Cook until the liquid evaporates. Spray a baking dish, layer half the potatoes, drained vegetables, and beef, then the remaining potatoes. Bake at 400°F until golden and bubbly.

 The recipe works well in a 3-quart, 3-inchdeep, 10.25-inch cast-iron skillet.

"Cottage pie and shepherd's pie are comforting classics—both topped with mashed potatoes and baked. The main difference? Cottage pie uses beef; shepherd's pie uses lamb. Otherwise, they are the same comfort food!" - *Tammy*

54) Cubed Steak, Fried

→ cubed steak
→ 1 1/2 cups self-rising flour
→ 1 large egg
→ 1/4 cup buttermilk
→ steak seasoning, Weber Steak n Chop
→ black pepper
→ salt

Remove meat from the package 30 minutes before cooking. Place flour on a shallow pie plate. Beat eggs and buttermilk in another. Season steak with seasoning, pepper, and salt. Dip in egg mixture then in flour, pressing into the meat. Coat both sides, sit for 5 minutes. Fry in 1/2-inch hot oil: 3 minutes on first side, then flip and cook 2 more minutes, adjust heat to prevent burning. Remove oil, use drippings for Recipe #613 White Milk Gravy. Serve gravy over steak.

55) Nana's Steak Fries

→ cubed steaks
→ salt
→ black pepper
→ roasted garlic powder, Badia
→ 1 cup self-rising flour
→ 1 large egg
→ 1/4 cup buttermilk

Cut steak into 1/2-inch strips, season with salt, pepper, and garlic powder. Beat egg and buttermilk, pour into a dish. Place flour in another dish. Dip steak in egg, coat with flour, pressing to stick. Let them sit 5 minutes. Preheat skillet with 3/4-inch oil. Fry 2 minutes per side, total 4 minutes, over high or medium-high heat. Serve with a dipping sauce!

"This recipe was Chris's mamas! She still cooks these for the family. They are great served with Heinz 57 Sauce! I hope you enjoy them as much as we do." -*Tammy*

56) Crescent Roll Taco Pie

→ 1 1/4 lb. lean ground beef
→ 1 packet taco seasoning mix (2 Tbsp)
→ 1/2 cup of water
→ 1/2 cup salsa, Herdez brand if available
→ 8 oz. can crescent roll sheet dough
→ 1 1/2 cups crushed corn chips, divided
→ 8 oz. carton sour cream
→ 6 slices American cheese
→ shredded lettuce
→ sliced black olives, optional
→ diced tomatoes

Option: substitute sliced cheese with 8 oz. Shredded Mexican blend. You can also substitute corn chips for tortilla chips, but the flavor may be less pronounced.

Cook the ground meat in a skillet, then drain it. Add taco seasoning, water, and salsa, and simmer for 5 minutes. Add half of the meat to the casserole dish. Top with 1 cup of corn chips, the remaining meat mixture, sour cream, olives, cheese, and the remaining chips. Roll out the crescent dough, press the edges, and fit it on top of your casserole. Bake at 350°F for 40 minutes until the crust is golden brown. Serve with lettuce, tomatoes, and sour cream.

57) Hamburger Steak

- → 1 lb. 80/20 ground beef
- → 1 small onion, sliced
- → 1 small bell pepper, sliced
- → 3 Tbsp salted butter
- → 1 tsp onion powder
- → 1/2 tsp each salt & black pepper
- → 1/2 tsp steak seasoning

Make ground beef patties that are 3/4 inch thick. Preheat the skillet over medium-high heat. Add the patties without oil—season with salt, pepper, and steak spices. Cook for 4 minutes on each side until browned. Add peppers and onions, then lower the heat to medium or low, cover, and simmer until tender. Ensure the patties are fully cooked to prevent the risk of consuming raw beef.

58) Hamburger Steak Deluxe

- → Make Recipe #57
- → Make Recipe # 59

Serve Hamburger Steaks with the Easy Mushroom Gravy.

59) Mushroom Gravy - Easy

- → 1/2 cup McCormick brown gravy mix
- → 2 cups milk
- → 1/2 cup sliced mushrooms
- → 1/4 cup chopped onions
- → 3 Tbsp salted butter

Use the same skillet that the steaks were cooked in making sure that the drippings are not burnt. Pour off excess grease from skillet. Melt butter in the skillet used for cooking the steaks. Add onion and mushrooms and cook until tender. Mix the gravy powder with milk and pour it into the skillet. Cook until it thickens and becomes bubbly. Serve over the hamburger steaks.

 Be careful not to burn the drippings. If they turn too brown, do not use them for gravy

WHEN SEARING BEEF IN A PREHEATED CAST-IRON SKILLET, THE MEAT WILL ADHERE TO THE SURFACE. FOR THE INITIAL TURN, USE A STAINLESS-STEEL SPATULA; SLIDE IT BENEATH STEAKS, SCRAPING IT ALONG THE BOTTOM OF THE PAN. THIS TECHNIQUE WILL EFFECTIVELY RELEASE THE SEARED BEEF FROM THE SKILLET.

Combine the marinade ingredients and marinate the steak in a gallon zip-top bag in the fridge for 24 hours. Let the steak sit at room temperature for an hour before grilling. Use an oven-safe skillet, such as a cast-iron grill pan. Preheat the skillet in the oven to 400°F. Insert a thermometer into the steaks and grill the steak on a hot stovetop grill pan for 2 minutes per side. Transfer to the preheated skillet and broil for 5 minutes per side in the oven. Grill to medium or cook for a longer time to achieve your preferred doneness. Rest for 5 minutes, then carve against the grain.

60) Hamburger Steak, Battered

→ 1 lb. 80/20 ground beef
→ 1/2 tsp salt
→ 1/2 tsp black pepper
→ steak seasoning
→ Dry Hidden Valley Ranch seasoning
→ 1 egg, beaten and placed in a shallow dish
→ self-rising flour
→ 1 small onion, sliced into rings
→ 1 bell pepper, sliced into strips
→ cooking oil (or corn oil)

Preheat the skillet over medium heat. Make four beef patties and season them with salt, pepper, steak seasoning, and ranch seasoning. Dip each patty in egg wash, then coat with self-rising flour. Increase the heat to medium-high, add 1/2 inch of oil, and cook the patties for 4 minutes per side until they are seared. Add peppers and onions, then turn the heat to medium-low, cover, and cook until all pink has disappeared. Never eat raw ground beef. Enjoy with sides!

"I got this idea from a viewer. It turned out good, so I added it to my cookbook!" - *Tammy*

61) London Broil Marinade

→ London Broil
→ 1/8 cup Worcestershire sauce
→ 1/2 cup soy sauce
→ 1/8 cup red wine vinegar
→ 1/8 cup balsamic glaze, optional
→ 1/8 cup brown sugar
→ 1 tsp dry mustard
→ 1 tsp black pepper
→ 1 tsp meat tenderizer
→ juice one lemon
→ 2 garlic cloves, pressed
→ 1/8 cup fresh chopped rosemary or use 2 tsp dried rosemary, or 1 tsp ground rosemary

Option: Sauté fresh mushrooms in a bit of olive oil with onions, then add 1/2 cup of leftover marinade and serve with steak.

62) Mississippi Crockpot Roast

→ crockpot liner, optional
→ 1 large chuck roast
→ 1 packet Lipton onion soup mix
→ 2 Tbsp or one packet Hidden Valley Ranch Dressing Mix
→ 4 small, sweet peppers or one bell pepper
→ pint of fresh sliced mushrooms, optional
→ 1/4 cup salted butter
→ 1 onion, cubed

This recipe is intended for a chuck roast. The recipe requires a roast that has an ample amount of fat. Do not substitute it with a different type of roast.

Place a crockpot liner in a crockpot. Add the roast and other ingredients to the slow cooker. Cook on low for 8-10 hours or until the roast is very tender. Serve as a main meat dish!

"I always say cook a roast until it is falling apart done! The London Broil, Prime Rib, and the Roasted Rump are the only ones you will slice to serve. My other recipes are cooked until they are fork tender." - *Tammy*

63) Meatloaf, Mama's

Mama

→ 1.5 lbs. ground beef
→ two eggs
→ half sleeve saltine crackers
→ 5-6 dashes Worcestershire sauce
→ 1/2 tsp salt
→ 1/2 tsp black pepper
→ 1 package Lipton Onion Soup Mix, 2 Tbsp
→ 1/2 tsp Badia roasted garlic powder, (or garlic powder but not garlic salt)

Mix all ingredients thoroughly, then place in a loaf pan and bake at 375°F for 40 minutes. Remove and drain any excess grease. Add the topping (recipe below) and bake for another 15 minutes.

64) Meatloaf Topping

→ 3/4 cup ketchup
→ 3 Tbsp brown sugar
→ 1/2 tsp onion powder

Whisk all ingredients well and spread over the meatloaf during the final 15 minutes of baking.

"Both of the meatloaf recipes on this page are delicious. The Tomato Sauce meatloaf is Chris's mama's meatloaf, which I spruced up with gravy mix and stuffing. Chris's mama's name is Virginia Nichols, and she is from Ft. Payne, Alabama! -Tammy

65) Meatloaf, Tomato Sauce

Virginia - Nana

→ 2 lbs. ground beef
→ 1 medium onion, diced
→ 1/2 bell pepper, diced
→ 8 oz. can tomato sauce
→ 5 shakes Worcestershire sauce
→ 2 raw eggs
→ 1/4 cup brown gravy mix, McCormick
→ 6 oz. Chicken or traditional dry stuffing mix
→ ketchup for topping

Mix all ingredients in a large bowl. It is best to use your hands. Spray a 3-quart oblong or rectangular baking dish with cooking spray. Place the meatloaf in the dish and bake at 375 degrees for 60 minutes. Remove the meatloaf from the oven and drain any excess grease. Then spread ketchup on top. Continue baking for another 20 minutes.

66) Marvelous Meatballs & Gravy

- → 1-1/2 lbs. ground chuck
- → 1 tsp steak seasoning, Weber Steak n Chop
- → 1/4 cup brown gravy mix, McCormick
- → 2 cups milk
- → 5-6 shakes Worcestershire sauce
- → 1/4 tsp black pepper
- → 10.25-inch cast iron skillet

Preheat a cast-iron skillet. Shape beef into walnut-sized meatballs and cook over medium-high heat, adding oil if needed. Season with steak seasoning and black pepper, then brown on all sides for 10-15 minutes; drain excess grease if necessary. Whisk together milk, Worcestershire sauce, and gravy mix, then add it to the skillet with drippings and cook until thickened. Cover and keep warm.

Notes & Tips: A simple way to drain ground beef is to use paper towels to absorb the grease with a set of tongs. Carefully discard the paper in the trash.

When searing beef in a hot cast-iron skillet, it sticks. Use a stainless steel spatula to flip, sliding it under the meatballs and scraping along the pan's bottom. This releases the beef effectively.

"This was one of my kids' favorite meals growing up. If you have a large family, you will have to double it." - *Tammy*

67) Pepper Steak

- → 2 lbs. sirloin steak (sliced very thin) *freeze steak 1 hour before slicing*

Spice bowl: In a small bowl, combine:
- → 1 garlic clove, pressed
- → 1 tsp ground ginger
- → 1/2 tsp black pepper
- → a dash salt

Liquid Gold: Combine in a liquid measuring cup:

- → 2 tsp beef bouillon granules
- → 1/4 cup soy sauce
- → 1/2 tsp sugar
- → 1 cup hot water
- → 1 Tbsp corn starch

Additional Ingredients:
- → 1 onion, cut into thin strips
- → 1 bell pepper, cut into thin strips
- → 1/8 cup olive oil

Have all ingredients above ready before you begin!

Heat a wok or large skillet over medium-high heat. Add 2 tablespoons of oil, the spice bowl, and the meat to the wok. Stir constantly for 2 minutes, then transfer it to a platter. Now add the peppers and onions, along with 1/4 cup of the liquid gold. Simmer on medium-low for 5 minutes. After the peppers are soft, add the remaining liquid gold and heat on high until thickened. Add the steak and remove from the heat. Serve immediately over white rice or as a main course.

68) Butter Basted Ribeye or Fillet

- → 10.25-inch cast-iron skillet
- → 1 1/2 inches thick, well-marbled ribeye or filet mignon
- → kosher salt
- → black pepper
- → fresh rosemary
- → 3-4 cloves fresh garlic, pressed
- → extra virgin olive oil
- → 1/2 cup salted butter

Tammy's tip: Salt ideally 24 hours before cooking; if not, add it right before. Timing is crucial.

Preheat an oven-safe skillet at 400°F for 20 minutes, then place it on high heat. Baste the steak with olive oil. Add 3 Tbsp olive oil to the skillet, then sear the steak for 3 minutes on each side. Add butter, garlic, and rosemary to the skillet. Carefully tilt the skillet using a spoon to baste the steak in hot butter for 1 minute per side, creating a brown, crunchy sear. The garlic and herbs flavor the butter.

For a medium, medium-well, or well-done steak, use a steak thermometer while cooking. Then, transfer skillet to the oven and finish cooking until it reaches your desired temperature.

Simmer roasts at low heat for tenderness; high temperatures toughen beef.

McCormick Unseasoned Meat Tenderizer uses bromelain from pineapple to soften tough meat. It's salt-free, kosher, and MSG-free, allowing natural flavors to shine. To use, moisten meat and sprinkle about 1 teaspoon per pound before cooking.

69) Roast & Vegetables, Crockpot

→ roast
→ steak Seasoning, Weber Steak n Chop
→ garlic salt
→ 1/4 cup all-purpose flour
→ 1/8 cup olive or vegetable oil
→ 5 large carrots, washed and peeled
→ 5 medium potatoes, washed and peeled
→ 1 large onion, peeled
→ 1/2 cup brown gravy mix
→ 5 dashes Worcestershire sauce
→ salt and pepper

Option: add 1/2 stick salted butter (if eye of round, bottom round, shoulder, sirloin, or leaner roast is being used)A meat tenderizer can be used, but I prefer the non-flavored type. Watch the salt content if using. It may be salty.

Use a crockpot liner or spray the pot with cooking spray for easy cleanup. If the roast is large, cut it in half. Season the roast with meat tenderizer, steak seasoning, and garlic salt. Lightly coat with flour. Preheat a large skillet or stockpot over medium heat. Brown the meat in olive oil, then transfer it to a crockpot. Slice the carrots, potatoes, and onions into pieces. Sprinkle the gravy mix and Worcestershire sauce over the roast. Add the vegetables to the crockpot, then season with salt and pepper. For lean meat, add 1/2 cup butter. Pour water around the edges to cover. Cook on low 8-10 hours.

→ 1/2 cup cold milk
→ 3 heaping Tbsp corn starch (or 6 heaping Tbsp flour)

To thicken broth with gravy, whisk together milk and cornstarch until smooth. Whisk very well until all the starch is combined. Pour into the roast. Cook at a higher temperature until the sauce thickens.

70) Prime Rib Roast, Eddie's

→ prime rib roast, wash, trim, and pat dry
→ 1 cup salted butter
→ fresh chopped herbs: rosemary, thyme, basil, and garlic
→ 2 1/2 cups beef broth
→ 1 large onion, sliced
→ salt and black pepper
→ steak seasoning

Mix butter with chopped herbs. Rub the roast with this butter, saving a portion for basting. In a pan with a roasting rack, add more rosemary, onion, and broth. Place the roast on the rack and season it with salt, pepper, and steak seasoning. Roast at 400°F for 20 minutes, then lower the temperature to 300°F. Insert a thermometer; once the center hits 120°F, remove and rest for 10-15 minutes. Strain the drippings to serve as au jus with each slice.

If you prefer to cook the loin longer, remember the ends will be more welldone, for those who want a fully cooked steak.

"We enjoy my brother Eddie's Prime Rib at our Christmas gathering and feast!" - Tammy

71) Roast, Chuck - Braised

- → 1 large chuck roast
- → coarse ground pepper and kosher salt
- → olive or corn oil flour for dredging
- → roasted garlic powder, Badia brand
- → 2 tsp dried parsley
- → 2 tsp dried basil
- → 1 tsp fresh rosemary, diced or ground rosemary
- → 1 onion, cut into large pieces
- → 1 garlic clove
- → 1 stalk celery, cut into large pieces
- → 1 large carrot, peeled and chopped
- → 5 shakes Worcestershire sauce
- → 1/4 cup all-purpose flour
- → 1/4 cup salted butter
- → 3 cups strained stock

Set the roast out at room temperature for 1 hour, then season with salt and pepper on both sides. Dredge with flour and brown on all sides in a preheated skillet with oil. Add garlic powder, parsley, basil, rosemary, onion, garlic, celery, carrots, stock, Worcestershire, and butter. Cover with water and simmer on low for 5-6 hours, until the meat is tender enough to be separated with a fork. Remove the meat and strain the broth.

Put 1/4 cup of flour in a pan with 1/4 cup of butter and cook until the mixture is browned. Finally, add 3 cups of stock and cook until the mixture thickens into a gravy. Serve with roast.

 Tammy's Tip: Heat the spices in a braiser before you start the recipe and set them aside. This will enhance the flavors of the spice.

72) Roast, Chuck – Pressure Cook

- → chuck roast
- → 1/4 cup brown gravy mix
- → 2 tsp steak seasoning, Weber Steak-n-Chop
- → salt & pepper
- → 1/4 cup all-purpose flour
- → 1/8 cup olive or cooking oil
- → 4-5 shakes Worcestershire sauce
- → if using a lean cut of meat, add 1/4 stick of butter
- → water

Remove the roast from the fridge for 30 minutes to an hour before cooking. If it is larger than your pressure cooker, cut it in half before seasoning and browning—season with brown gravy mix, steak seasoning, salt, and pepper. Lightly coat with flour. Heat oil in the cooker, then brown the meat on all sides over medium-high heat. Add Worcestershire sauce and then add enough water so that it is about an inch below the top of the contents. Bring the contents to medium pressure and cook for 40 minutes. Check if it is tender; if not, cook for another 20 minutes. Thicken juices with cornstarch and milk as instructed.

- → 1/2 cup cold milk
- → 3 heaping Tbsp cornstarch or 6 heaping Tbsp flour

To thicken broth with gravy, whisk together milk and cornstarch. Whisk very well until all the starch is combined. Pour into the roast. Cook at a higher temperature until the sauce thickens.

Instant Pot:

 This recipe can be prepared in an Instant Pot using the same cooking time and pressure settings.

Instant pots are great to use; however, they take longer to reach pressure, so the total cook time is longer than that of an old-fashioned pressure cooker.

"When I worked, I always used my pressure cooker to make roasts because it was much faster, and I could have dinner on the table in minutes." - *Tammy*

73) Roast, Rump – Dutch Oven

→ roast rump (must be labeled rump, not bottom round)
→ 2 Tbsp all-purpose flour
→ 1 tsp salt
→ 1/2 tsp black pepper

Preheat a Dutch oven. Mix flour, salt, and pepper, then rub mixture evenly all over roast. Add 1/4 cup of shortening or cooking oil to Dutch oven. Brown all sides thoroughly.

→ 1/4 tsp hot sauce, used sriracha chili sauce
→ one 14.5 oz. can petite diced tomatoes
→ 1/2 tsp steak seasoning, Weber Steak-n-Chop
→ 1 onion, sliced thin
→ 2 tsp thyme
→ 1/2 cup water
→ remaining flour, rub

Add hot sauce, tomatoes, seasoning, onion, thyme, water, and the remaining flour rub. Stovetop instructions: Simmer on low for 1.5 hours with the lid on. Turn the roast and continue simmering for another 2 hours. Slice the roast across the grain. The ingredients form a sauce at the bottom of the pot, which can be served over the meat.

Oven directions: Use a meat thermometer and cook at 325°F until the internal temperature reaches the desired level. Remove from the oven. Slice across grain.

"The trick to cooking a great, tender roast is not to boil the meat. Cook all roasts at a low temperature," - *Tammy*

74) Roast, Chuck – Mama's

→ 1 large chuck roast
→ steak seasoning, Weber Steak-n-Chop
→ 1 cup self-rising flour
→ 1/2 tsp pepper
→ 1 tsp salt
→ 1/8 cup of olive oil
→ water
→ 1 onion, peeled and quartered
→ 1 stalk of celery, cut into three pieces
→ 1 bay leaf
→ 2 tsp beef bouillon granules
→ 1 Tbsp Dales Steak Seasoning
→ 5 medium potatoes, washed and peeled
→ 6 fresh carrots, washed and peeled

Season the roast with salt, pepper, and dry steak seasoning. Rub flour all over it. Brown in preheated oil, then brown all the edges. Cover the meat in water, then add onion, bay leaf, celery, bouillon, and Dales. Simmer on low heat for 4 to 6 hours until it is fork-tender. Cut potatoes and carrots into quarters and add them to the roast. Cook on medium heat for 40 minutes or until the carrots are tender enough to be pierced with a fork.

→ 1/2 cup cold milk
→ 3 heaping Tbsp cornstarch or 6 heaping Tbsp flour

To thicken broth with gravy, whisk milk and cornstarch until thoroughly combined. Pour into the roast. Cook at a higher temperature until the sauce thickens. Then lower the heat. Enjoy!

"When I was a kid, Mama's roast was always my favorite. To this day, it remains one of my favorites, and it never grows old. With beef prices so high, consider buying a less expensive cut of roast and using a meat tenderizer, as shown in Recipe #69's idea call out image."- *Tammy*

75) Roast, Rump - Roasted

→ 3 lb. roast rump, must be labeled rump, not bottom round
→ 2 tsp steak seasoning, Weber Steak N Chop
→ 2 tsp Weber Chicago Steak Seasoning, or another seasoning of your choice
→ 3 cloves garlic
→ 1/8 cup olive or vegetable oil

Remove the roast from the refrigerator for 30 minutes to 1 hour before cooking. Place seasonings on a plate. Peel and smash garlic cloves to release their juices. Make 3-4 slits in the roast with a sharp knife and insert garlic. Rub the meat with olive oil and seasonings. Place on a rack, fat side up, or use a cooling rack on a foil-lined or sprayed sheet pan. Insert a digital meat thermometer into the center of the roast. Sear in oven at 450°F for 25 minutes, until browned, then reduce the temperature to 350°F and cook until the desired internal temperature is reached. Medium – Cook until the internal temperature reaches 150°F, then remove and let rest for 15 minutes before carving. Medium well – Cook until it reaches 155°F, then remove and let rest for 20 minutes before cutting against the grain.

 *If you get a chance to by a rump roast on sale, remember it is one of the BEST cuts of roast you can buy! It is delicious roasted and doesn't need to be submerged in water like other cuts of meat.*

76) Round Steak, Fried

→ round steaks
→ 1 1/2 cups self-rising flour
→ salt (omit if using a salty meat tenderizer)
→ roasted garlic powder
→ ground rosemary, optional
→ black or white pepper
→ 2 eggs, room temperature
→ McCormick unseasoned meat tenderizer

Remove the meat from the fridge an hour before tenderizing to warm the fibers. Lightly season with tenderizer and generously with spices. Pound the steaks on both sides with a mallet, preferably a day ahead, and refrigerate in a Ziplock bag overnight. Before battering and frying, take the meat out an hour earlier. Place flour in a shallow pie plate; beat eggs in another. Dip the steaks in eggs, then coat them in flour, pressing the flour into the meat to ensure a thorough coating on both sides. Fry in 1/3-inchdeep hot oil for 3 minutes on one side, then flip and fry for 2 minutes, lowering the heat slightly. Remove steaks and place on a paper towel-lined plate. Pour out excess oil. Use the drippings to make Recipe #613 White Milk Gravy.

77) Stuffed Bell Peppers

→ 6 large bell peppers
→ 1 lb. ground beef
→ 1/2 cup chopped onion
→ 1 tsp onion powder
→ 1 cup cooked rice
→ 1 tsp salt
→ 15 oz. can tomato sauce
→ 1/2 cup ketchup
→ 1 Tbsp mustard
→ 1/2 tsp chili powder
→ 1 cup shredded cheese of your choice

Cut the tops off peppers and remove the centers. Drop the peppers into boiling water for 5 minutes. Use tongs to take them out and place them in a baking pan. Next, cook the beef and onion until browned, then drain. Add the remaining ingredients, except for half of the tomato sauce. With the peppers standing upright, fill their centers with the beef mixture. Pour the remaining tomato sauce over the peppers, then add 1 cup of water directly into the bottom of the baking dish. Cover with foil and bake at 350°F for 45 minutes. Finally, remove the foil and bake for another 15 minutes. Enjoy!

78) Salisbury Steak

→ 1-1/2 lb. ground chuck
→ 1/2 tsp black pepper
→ 1 pack Lipton beefy onion soup mix
→ 1 large egg
→ 2 tsp yellow mustard
→ 2 Tbsp ketchup
→ half a sleeve Saltine cracker, crushed
→ 2 or 3 fresh green onions, diced
→ 1 Tbsp Worcestershire sauce

Place the ground beef in a large bowl. Add black pepper, soup mix, egg, mustard, ketchup, crushed Saltine crackers, Worcestershire sauce, and diced green onions. Mix well using a stand mixer with the paddle attachment or mix by hand. Divide the mixture into five equal patties, about 3/4 inch thick. Place the patties on a parchment-lined baking sheet. Bake at 350°F for 30 minutes, or until the meat is fully cooked and no pink remains.

Tip: Serve Salisbury Steak topped with Recipe #79 Mushroom Gravy.

Note: Ensure the ground beef is cooked thoroughly for safety.

79) Mushroom Gravy

→ 1/4 cup salted butter
→ 1/2-pint white mushrooms, chopped
→ 1 small onion, sliced into strips
→ 4 cups of beef broth (preferably unsalted or low sodium)
→ 5 Tbsp cornstarch
→ 1 Tbsp Worcestershire sauce
→ 1/2 tsp black pepper
→ 1 garlic clove, pressed, to be added at the end of cooking

Melt butter in a large skillet or saucepan. Add mushrooms and onions, and sauté until the onions have softened, and the juice from the mushrooms has evaporated. In a measuring cup, whisk the beef stock and cornstarch together until smooth. Add Worcestershire sauce to the stock mixture. Once the mushrooms and onions are ready, add 1/2 tsp of black pepper, then pour in the stock mixture. Bring to a simmer and cook until the gravy thickens and turns a rich brown color. Finally, add the pressed garlic clove and stir until well combined. Serve over Salisbury Steak.

"This dish impresses guests, is easy to make, and requires no attention in the oven, freeing you to prepare other dishes. It looks beautiful and tastes perfect." - *Tammy*

80) Italian Meatballs:

→ 1/2 lb. ground chuck
→ 1/2 lb. Italian sausage, used Swaggerty's Farm brand
→ 1 raw egg
→ 1 cup crushed croutons
→ 1/2 tsp Dale seasoning
→ 1/2 medium onion, finely chopped
→ 1 tsp fresh Italian parsley, chopped, optional
→ 1 tsp fresh basil, chopped, optional
→ 1 Tbsp Italian seasoning

Mix all the ingredients and form them into small meatballs, approximately 1 inch in diameter. Brown all sides in a preheated skillet. Remove and drain excess grease. Cover and cook on low 15 minutes.

Air Fryer: Use an air fryer to cook meatballs. Cook at 350°F for 20 minutes.

Tammy's Tip: Use one lb. of ground beef and omit the Italian sausage if desired. If it is omitted, add 1 tsp of Italian sausage seasoning.

81) Basic Italian Pasta Sauce:

→ 2-8 oz. can crushed tomatoes
→ 1 tsp sugar
→ 1/2 tsp salt and black pepper
→ 3 Roma tomatoes, chopped
→ 1/2 medium onion, chopped
→ 2 cloves garlic, pressed

Combine the ingredients above in a saucepan (excluding garlic) and simmer for 10-15 minutes. Stir occasionally. Add pressed garlic and meatballs. Serve over pasta topped with shredded mozzarella cheese. Enjoy.

82) Swiss Steak

- → three 1/2-inch-thick round steaks
- → salt and black pepper
- → self-rising flour
- → corn oil
- → 1 bell pepper, chopped into medium chunks
- → 1 large onion, chopped into medium chunks
- → 3 garlic cloves, sliced
- → 14.5 oz can diced tomatoes
- → Worcestershire sauce
- → onion powder
- → roasted garlic powder, used Bidia brand
- → paprika
- → steak seasoning, Weber Steak 'n Chop
- → 2 1/2 cups beef stock (or use beef bouillon to make stock)
- → meat tenderizer, unseasoned

Set out the beef for 1 hour before tenderizing. Trim off the perimeter fat so the meat can flatten evenly around the edges. To tenderize, sprinkle meat tenderizer and black pepper on both sides and lightly dredge in flour. Beat very well on each side until the beef begins to break down and become tender and flat. Once the steaks are tenderized, cut each in half. Dip in self-rising flour and fry until golden brown on both sides in a preheated skillet with oil. Remove the meat and add chopped onion and pepper; cook for about 3-4 minutes. Return the beef to the skillet, sprinkle with all spices and sauces. Add the canned tomatoes and stock. Cover and simmer on low for two hours.

"What a wonderful beef dish. It is so delicious served with mashed potatoes and peas or your favorite vegetable side dish." - *Tammy*

83) Taco Skillet

- → 1 lb. ground beef
- → medium onion, chopped
- → 16 oz. can refried beans
- → 4 oz. can chopped green chiles
- → 1/2 tsp garlic powder
- → 3/4 cup sour cream
- → 1/2 tsp ground cumin
- → 1/2 tsp chili powder
- → medium tomato, seeded and chopped
- → 4 oz. can sliced black olives
- → small green pepper, chopped
- → 6 or 8 oz. pack Mexican blend shredded cheese
- → tortilla chips (or taco shells)

In a large skillet, cook ground beef with onion and green pepper until browned. Drain excess fat, then add spices. Mix in beans and chiles and cook until heated through. Spread sour cream over the mixture in the skillet. Top with tomato and olives, then sprinkle with cheese. Cover with a lid just long enough for the cheese to melt. Serve with chips or taco shells.

"This is a recipe the whole family will love! It is also great to have when you are serving a crowd for the kids or as an appetizer."-*Tammy*

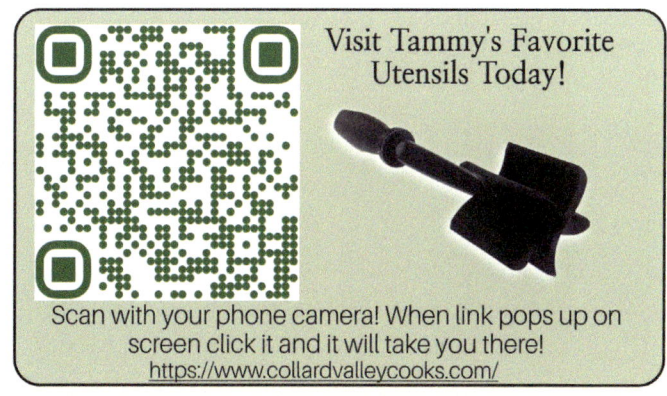

Visit Tammy's Favorite Utensils Today!

Scan with your phone camera! When link pops up on screen click it and it will take you there!
https://www.collardvalleycooks.com/

84) Texas Hash with Beans

→ 1 onion, chopped
→ 3 Tbsp bell pepper, chopped
→ 3 Tbsp olive oil
→ 1-1/2 lb. ground chuck
→ 1-1/2 cups hot boiling water
→ 2 tsp beef bouillon granules
→ 1 Tbsp chili powder
→ 14.5 oz can diced tomatoes
→ 14.5 oz can kidney beans, drained
→ 2 tsp salt
→ 1 tsp black pepper
→ 1 cup uncooked rice
→ 8 oz package grated cheese (Mexican blend)

In a large skillet, sauté the onion and pepper in olive oil for 4-5 minutes. Add the ground beef and cook until it is broken apart and browned. Drain the excess grease from the meat. Microwave the water in a liquid measuring cup until it boils, about 1 minute. Add the bouillon; stir well. In a separate large bowl, combine the water, bouillon, chili powder, diced tomatoes, kidney beans, salt, pepper, and rice, then mix thoroughly. Add half of the meat mixture to this bowl and stir again. Spray a 4- to 5-quart baking dish with cooking spray. Pour the mixture from the bowl, including beans, rice, and tomatoes, into the baking dish. Sprinkle the entire top with shredded cheese and add the remaining meat on top. Bake at 350°F for 45 minutes.

85) Taco Cabbage Skillet

→ 1 lb. ground beef, brown & drain
→ 1 or 2 Tbsp. taco seasoning
→ 1 cup of salsa (Herdez brand used)
→ 3 cups cabbage, shredded
→ 1 cup shredded cheddar cheese

Brown ground beef and drain. Add salsa and taco seasoning. Stir well. Add cabbage, mix well and cover with a lid. Cook on lowest setting for 20 minutes. Remove the lid and stir in cheese. Serve immediately with Cornbread or Tortilla Chips.

86) Beef (or Turkey) Stroganoff

→ 1 medium onion, chopped.
→ 1/8 cup chopped red bell pepper, optional
→ olive oil
→ 1 1/2 lbs. ground beef or turkey, browned and drained
→ 1 clove garlic, minced
→ 1 packet beefy onion soup mix
→ 4 dashes Worcestershire sauce
→ 1/2 tsp black pepper
→ 1 tsp salt
→ 2 cups milk
→ 3 heaping Tbsp cornstarch
→ 1 cup sour cream
→ cooked egg noodles or rice

Sauté onion and pepper in a bit of olive oil, then set aside. Brown your beef or turkey and drain the grease. Next, add the sautéed onion and peppers, garlic, soup mix, Worcestershire sauce, black pepper, and salt to the meat and stir over medium-high heat. Mix cornstarch and milk with a whisk, then add. Finally, stir in sour cream and combine well. Simmer on low for 5 minutes. Serve over egg noodles or rice.

💡 For a lower-fat version: Use ground turkey and low-fat sour cream.

Cream of Soup Option:

Omit: onion soup mix, 2 cups of milk, and cornstarch and add:

→ two 10.5-oz cans cream of mushroom soup 1 cup of milk

87) Secret Spaghetti Sauce

→ 1 bell pepper, chopped
→ onion, chopped
→ 2 cloves garlic, pressed
→ 1 Tbsp Italian seasoning
→ 1 Tbsp Salad blend seasoning, no salt type
→ 2-8 oz. can diced tomatoes
→ 1 tsp salt
→ 1 Tbsp granulated sugar
→ 1/2 tsp pepper
→ 8 oz. marinated Italian mushrooms chopped
→ 1 Tbsp the marinated mushroom juice
→ 1-1/2 pounds ground beef, browned and drained

In a 2-cup measuring cup whisk together:

→ 6 oz can of tomato paste
→ 1 Tbsp beef bouillon granules & 1 cup of hot water

In a large skillet sauté onion, peppers, garlic, Italian seasoning, & salad blend seasoning. Remove from skillet. Add tablespoon of olive oil and brown ground chuck until no pink shows. Drain beef but do not rinse with water. Add vegetables back to skillet with beef. Add diced tomatoes. Add tomato bouillon mixture to skillet. Add salt, pepper, chopped mushrooms, mushroom juice and sugar. Cover pan and simmer on low for 1 hour. Serve with spaghetti noodles of your choice. Note: better the next day after sitting in refrigerator overnight.

"I took this to a bible study one night. Our pastor said, "I don't eat spaghetti." He said his wife made something for him to eat. Before we left, he had ate a big bowl of this spaghetti. I thought it was so funny. So, this is not your regular spaghetti, it is even better!" - *Tammy*

88) Chris's Goulash

→ 2 Tbsp olive oil
→ 2 medium yellow onions (chopped)
→ 2 large cloves garlic (minced)
→ 1 lb. ground beef
→ 1/4 tsp salt
→ 1/4 tsp ground black pepper
→ 3 Tbsp tomato paste
→ 1-1/4 cups low-sodium beef broth
→ 15-oz can tomato sauce
→ 15-oz. can diced tomatoes
→ 1-1/2 tsp Italian seasoning
→ 1-1/2 tsp paprika
→ 1-1/2 cups elbow macaroni (uncooked)
→ 1-1/2 cups shredded cheddar

In a large skillet over medium heat, heat oil. Add onion and cook until soft, about 5 minutes. Add garlic and cook until fragrant, about 1 minute more. Add ground beef and cook until it is no longer pink. Drain fat and season with salt and pepper. Add tomato paste broth, tomato sauce, diced tomatoes, Italian seasoning, and paprika. Stir in macaroni. Bring to a simmer and cook, stirring occasionally, until pasta is tender, about 15 minutes. Stir in cheese and remove from heat.

89) Ukrainian Goulash

→ 1-1/2 to 2 lb. boneless beef chuck cubed (or ground beef)
→ 1 onion chopped
→ 2 Tbsp. butter or olive oil
→ 8 oz. can tomato sauce
→ 3/4 cup water
→ 1 tsp sugar
→ 1 tsp paprika
→ 1 tsp salt
→ 1 tsp caraway seed
→ 1/2 tsp dill weed
→ 1 Tbsp knorr beef bouillon granules
→ 1 tsp Worcestershire sauce
→ 1/4 tsp garlic powder
→ 1/4 tsp black pepper
→ 1/8 tsp dry mustard
→ 1/8 tsp basil
→ 1/2 cup sour cream
→ hot butter noodles, cooked per package directions.

Put all ingredients in a crock pot (minus the noodles) and cook on high 4-6 hours or until beef is fork tender. Serve over buttered noodles.

Beverage Recipes

The Heart and Soul of Southern Sips

There is a cherished ritual in Southern kitchens that begins with the whistle of a kettle and ends with a pitcher glistening in the sunlight: the making of Sweet Tea. In Georgia, every glass is a declaration of hospitality, and every sip is a memory of family gatherings and porch swings.

Sweet tea is not just a beverage, it is a tradition, passed down by our mamas, who knew that the secret to the perfect glass started with patience. Tea bags would be steeped in simmering water until the color deepened, and the aroma filled the house, then, while the tea was still warm and strong, generous scoops of sugar were stirred in, melting to create a golden sweetness that set Georgia tea apart.

Once the sweetened brew was cooled, it was poured over ice—never skimping on the cubes in the blazing summer heat—and sometimes topped with a wedge of lemon. Simple, yet sublime, Georgia Sweet Tea is more than refreshment; it is Southern comfort in a glass, made with the care and devotion only a mama could summon.

This beverage section celebrates that same spirit, inviting you to savor the timeless flavors that have defined Southern tables for generations.

90) Coffee Frappe

→ 1 cup ice cubes from the freezer
→ 3/4 cup almond milk, non-flavored
→ 1 Taster's Choice Instant Colombian Singles
→ 1 cup vanilla ice cream

Add ice to a blender, then pour in milk and the coffee packet, followed by ice cream. Blend using crushed ice or the smoothie setting. Blend thoroughly. Top with whipped cream and drizzle with Hershey's chocolate syrup. Have a wide straw ready and enjoy!

For Java Chip: Use the instructions and ingredients above, and add 2 Tbsp of mini semi-sweet chocolate chips to the blender after adding your coffee.

"My kids wanted to drive by the specialty coffee shop for this frappe, so I decided I would learn to make it. This is the closest I came to it. I would make the kids one before they went to high school in the mornings. It was a money saver, and they loved it." -Tammy

91) Coffee Punch

→ 1 gallon of your favorite coffee, brewed
→ 1 cup sugar
→ 16 oz. powdered creamer
→ 2 quarts whole milk
→ 3 tsp vanilla extract
→ 3 quarts ice cream, vanilla, or chocolate

Make 1 gallon of coffee, then add sugar to the hot coffee. Mix in creamer and chill thoroughly. After chilling, add whole milk and vanilla. When it is time to serve, combine the coffee mixture and ice cream in a punch bowl.

92) Egg Nog, Old Fashioned

→ 6 large eggs, separated
→ 1/2 cup sugar
→ 1 cup heavy whipping cream
→ 2 cups whole milk
→ 1 tsp vanilla extract
→ 1/2 tsp cream of tartar
→ 1/2 tsp ground nutmeg
→ 1/8 tsp salt

Beat the egg yolks and sugar together thoroughly with a hand mixer and set aside. In a saucepan, combine the cream, milk, nutmeg, and salt. Heat the mixture over medium heat until it starts to bubble, then remove it from the heat. Gradually whisk the warm milk and egg mixture together, stirring constantly to ensure thorough blending. The mixture should be smooth and free of lumps. If you notice any lumps, pass the mixture through a mesh strainer to remove them. Next, beat the egg whites with cream of tartar until stiff peaks form. Return the milk mixture to the saucepan and bring it to a gentle simmer, heating it to about 160°F to 170°F. Once it reaches this temperature, remove it from the heat and gently fold in the whipped egg whites. Mix until the mixture is smooth and creamy. Finally, store the mixture in an airtight container in the refrigerator.

Notes & Tips: Go by the date on your whole milk to know when it will expire. Make with the freshest milk available.

Make Recipe #225 Egg Nog Pound Cake with this homemade egg nog.

93) Fruit-Flavored Sweet Tea

→ 2 family-sized black tea bags
→ 2 flavored tea bags
→ 1 cup sugar

Bring 4 cups of water to boil. Once boiling, add tea bags and simmer for one minute. Turn off the heat and let the tea bags steep for 15 minutes. Remove the tea bags, then add 1 cup of sugar and stir until dissolved. Pour into a 1-gallon pitcher and fill with water. Chill overnight before serving. Add extra sugar if desired.

94) Georgia Sweet Tea

→ 3 family-size Tetley tea bags
→ water
→ 1 cup granulated sugar, adjust amount per taste but not until it is fully chilled
→ plain, clean milk jug

In a medium saucepan, fill it halfway with water. Add tea bags and place pan on the stovetop. Bring to boil over medium-high heat. Boil the tea for one minute. Turn off the heat and remove the pan from the stove. Let it sit for 15 minutes. My favorite way to make tea is using a gallon jug, like a milk jug. Take a clean jug and place it in the sink. Use a funnel to add sugar to the jug. DO NOT add boiling water to a plastic jug! Make sure the water has cooled for at least 15 minutes, but it should still be warm. Pour the warm tea through a funnel into the jug over the sugar. Put the lid on the jug. Turn the jug upside down and shake it very well until all the sugar dissolves. Add water to fill it up, leaving an inch from the top. Shake well again. Do not serve it the same day you make it.

Important Tea Tips:

Tips: Tea tastes much sweeter after it has cooled in the refrigerator overnight. If you make it the same day you plan to drink it, you'll need to add more sugar to achieve the desired sweetness. To enjoy the best flavor, always prepare tea at least a day in advance. Letting it sit overnight is especially helpful for those who are mindful of their weight or sugar intake.

If you need to drink the tea the same day and have a deep freezer, you can place it in the freezer until it is very cold before serving.

When my kids were young, I used to add 1 and 1/3 cups of granulated sugar. Now they prefer it with just 3/4 cup of sugar per gallon. Feel free to adjust the amount according to your taste.

If you're looking to reduce the sugar in your tea, start by cutting it down by 1/4 cup at a time to make the change gradual.

"I personally prefer to boil my tea. I find that the Tetley brand does not taste bitter after boiling, unlike other brands. The strength of the tea is a matter of personal preference. My mother did not boil her tea; she simply added hot tap water and let it sit all day in a jug on the kitchen counter. I, however, like to boil it in my kettle." -Tammy

95) Hot Chocolate Mix

→ 1 cup sugar
→ 1 cup powdered creamer
→ 1 cup powdered milk
→ 1/2 cup Hershey's cocoa
→ 1/4 cup instant coffee, optional

Combine all ingredients and store mixture in a jar with a sealed lid. Use 1/8 Cup of mix with 8 oz. hot water. Adjust amount of mix to your taste.

96) Lemonade

- → 3/4 cup lemon juice
- → 1 cup granulated sugar
- → 2 cups hot water
- → Pulp and zest from one lemon

Using a grater or zester, zest one lemon before starting. Place the zest in the bottom of a large pitcher or bowl. Juice the lemons until you have 3/4 cup of lemon juice. Pour the juice into the pitcher with the zest through a strainer, discarding the seeds. Add sugar and 2 cups of hot water, then whisk well. Cut a few lemon slices very thin and place them in your serving pitcher or container. Finish filling with water and mix well. Refrigerate! Makes 64 oz. which is 8 cups.

97) Mama's Orange Punch

- → 2 packages of orange Kool-Aid
- → 2 packages of lemon Kool-Aid
- → 4 cups sugar
- → 4 cups water
- → 2-4 6 oz. cans pineapple orange juice
- → 2 quarts ginger ale
- → 1/2-gallon orange sherbet

Mix everything except the sherbet and store in a sealed container in the refrigerator, preferably in an empty gallon jug. When guests arrive, pour the mixture into a punch bowl and add the sherbet just before serving. This makes about 2 gallons of punch. This makes 32 cups of punch.

"Oh, how I remember mama making this in large gallon jugs for weddings."- *Tammy*

98) Peach Milkshakes

- → 1 cup fresh or frozen peaches, diced
- → 1/4 cup honey, or 1/4 cup sugar
- → 1 tsp vanilla extract
- → 1 1/2 cups milk
- → 1-pint vanilla ice cream

Blend peaches and honey in a blender, then add the remaining ingredients. Blend until smooth. Serve in a tall glass topped with whipped cream. Makes 3 shakes.

Our daughter, May, enjoying lemons at Long John Silvers

"Our oldest daughter, May, has a love for lemons. We first noticed this when, as a baby in a restaurant, we gave her one to entertain her, and she ate it! So, Tammy always ordered tea with lemons, and May was preoccupied while we enjoyed our meal." - *Chris*

Master A Southern Classic: The Biscuit!

"Every time I smelled bacon cooking, my feet hit the floor! It did not matter if the house was freezing cold and my windows were glazed over with ice I wanted to be near my mama in the kitchen. Mama got up at 5am to cook daddy's breakfast. She would make enough grits, bacon, toast, and sausage for the whole family. But she would go back to the kitchen and cook more eggs for us when it was time for us to get up for school. Mama was an amazing cook, and her love was on every plate she sat on the table.

Down here in the South, our mama's mostly made cornbread and biscuits. On special occasions they would make homemade dinner rolls and cinnamon rolls. Most of the time, a quick bread was used in our kitchens. When mama took the time out and made fresh bread, the smell of yeast would encompass the whole house. We would anxiously stand watching and waiting for the dough to rise. These days were special, and we looked forward to them. Even my cousins and aunts would ask for a fresh cinnamon roll from mama's kitchen!

In this section you will find Biscuits, Cornmeal Recipes, Pastry & Sweet Breads, and Muffins. My biscuit recipes tell you to add milk a little at a time, as it is hard to give a definite measurement for milk. This is due to the difference in flours and thicknesses of buttermilk.

This section is overflowing with love from my kitchen. From granny's cut out biscuits, mama's cornbread dressing, and my biscuit cinnamon rolls you will find so many recipe treasures here.

Come check out my cooking tutorials on YouTube—you will pick up all kinds of handy tips for Southern dishes. Sure, recipes are helpful, but they do not always show you the tricks you really need to cook like mama did. I made these videos to help you feel right at home in the kitchen and you will get comfortable cooking real Southern style foods."- *Tammy*

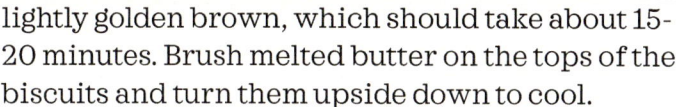

99) 2-Ingredient Biscuits

→ 2 cups self-rising flour
→ 2/3 to 3/4 cup heavy whipping cream

Note: Amount of cream will vary

Put flour in a bowl and gradually add whipped cream to make a thick dough. Dust a surface with self-rising flour, place the dough on it, sprinkle more flour on top, and gently fold 6–7 times. Pat dough 3/4 to 1 inch thick, cut out biscuits, and arrange them on a greased pan. Bake at 450°F for 15-20 minutes until golden brown. Flip biscuits upside down after baking to prevent sweating.

100) Angel Biscuits

Yeast Mixture: In a separate small bowl, combine:

→ 1-1/2 tsp fast-rise yeast
→ 2 Tbsp warm water (baby bottle warm)
→ 1-1/2 tsp granulated sugar

For the dough:

→ 2 1/2 cups self-rising flour
→ 1/4 cup granulated sugar
→ 1/3 cup shortening
→ 1 cup warm whole buttermilk

Combine the flour and 1/4 cup of sugar using a whisk. Use a fork to cut in the shortening until the mixture becomes crumbly with pea-sized pieces. Add the buttermilk and yeast mixture, stirring until the ingredients are well blended. Sift flour onto the dough's surface and knead it 4 to 5 times, adding more flour as necessary for ease of rolling. Form biscuits by either cutting them out or rolling small pieces of dough, approximately 1/4 cup each, in your hands. Arrange the biscuits in a greased aluminum sheetpan. Bake at 500 °F until

lightly golden brown, which should take about 15-20 minutes. Brush melted butter on the tops of the biscuits and turn them upside down to cool.

101) Blueberry Biscuits

→ 1 cup self-rising flour
→ 1/4 cup salted butter, room temperature
→ 1/2 cup sugar
→ 1/2 cup whole buttermilk, amount may vary
→ 1/2 cup fresh blueberries
→ Recipe #102 Sweet Biscuit Glaze

Combine flour, butter, and sugar with a blending fork or pastry blender until it is crumbly. Gradually add milk until the mixture is thick and no dry flour remains. Turn dough onto a floured surface, sift more flour on top, and fold by hand 4-5 times. Pat dough 1/2-inch high and add blueberries on top. Gently fold the dough over them, turning the dough 2-3 more times. Do not push down hard and crush berries. Pat dough to 3/4-inch tall, cut out biscuits, place close together on a greased aluminum pan, and bake at 450°F for 20-25 minutes until golden brown.

 Option: Use a a different type of berry for another flavor profile. If using frozen berries, do not thaw before folding into the dough. Enjoy y'all!!

102) Sweet Biscuit Glaze:

→ 3 Tbsp salted butter, melted
→ 1 cup powdered sugar
→ 1 tsp vanilla
→ 2 Tbsp cream

Mix the glaze ingredients until creamy. Spread glaze over the top of warm biscuits. Enjoy y'all!!

103) Buttermilk Biscuits

→ 2 cups self-rising flour
→ 1 pinch baking soda
→ 3/4 to 1 cup whole buttermilk, amount varies
→ 1/4 cup vegetable shortening, Crisco

Blend shortening and flour until shortening is pea-sized. Mix in a little soda, then gradually add milk until no dry flour remains and the dough is thick.

 Note: The Amount of buttermilk will vary depending on the type you buy. Some are thin while others are thick.

Sift flour onto the counter, add dough, and sift more flour on top. Knead 4-7 times, then pat to 3/4 to 1 inch thick. Cut biscuits, place in a greased pan, pat tops with buttermilk, and bake at 500°F for 15-20 minutes. Flip biscuits upside down after baking to keep bottoms crisp.

"Granny Benefield made 1 1/2 dia. biscuits in an 11x7 pan. She had a small side oven she always made her bread in." - *Tammy*

Tammy's Tip: Mama baked biscuits at 450°F, while Granny used 500°F for smaller ones. Try both temperatures to see which you prefer—500°F browns biscuits faster and yields a softer crumb.

104) Cheddar & Garlic Biscuits

→ 2 cups self-rising flour
→ 1/4 cup salted butter, room temperature
→ 1-1/2 cups grated cheddar cheese
→ 1 tsp garlic powder, optional
→ 1 Tbsp salad spice blend (unsalted)
→ 1 tsp onion powder
→ close to 1 cup whipping cream (or whole buttermilk)

Place the flour into a mixing bowl. Incorporate the butter using a fork until combined. Add the cheese, herbs, and onion powder, stirring thoroughly. Gradually pour in the whipped cream, mixing until the batter becomes sticky and all the flour is fully incorporated. Portion out heaping spoonfuls onto a greased baking pan. Bake at 500°F for 15 to 20 minutes.

105) Spoon Biscuits

→ 2 cups self-rising flour
→ 1 pinch baking soda
→ 3/4 to 1 cup whole buttermilk
→ 1/4 cup vegetable shortening, Crisco

Combine shortening and flour using a pastry blender or fork until the shortening is in pea-sized pieces. Add baking soda and mix thoroughly. Gradually pour in milk, stirring until all flour is fully moistened and the dough achieves a thick consistency. Portion heaping tablespoons of dough onto a greased pan or a parchment-lined baking sheet. Bake at 500°F for 15-20 minutes. After baking, invert the biscuits to minimize moisture retention. Serve as desired.

 When making spoon biscuits, the dough should be slightly thinner and wetter than typical biscuit dough.

For an easier batter, use Southern Biscuit Mix Formula L.

106) Hand-Rolled Biscuits

→ 5 lb. bag self-rising flour
→ 1/4 tsp baking soda
→ 5 Tbsp salted butter, room temperature or: 1/4 cup shortening (Crisco)
→ 2/3 to 3/4 cup buttermilk; for lighter biscuits, use whole milk (sweet milk).

Press all the flour against the sides and bottom of a large bowl using the outside of your fist. After the flour is compacted, add the shortening and milk. Mix the shortening and milk thoroughly by hand with a squeezing motion. Rotate the mixture in the bowl to loosen the flour and incorporate it. Continue squeezing the dough through your fingers until the consistency is appropriate. Since this step can be difficult to describe precisely, viewing a YouTube tutorial and practicing may be helpful. Refer to the video for instructions on shaping the biscuits by hand before placing them in a greased iron skillet or bread pan. Bake at 500°F for 15 to 25 minutes, or until golden brown. After removing the biscuits from the oven, invert them to prevent moisture accumulation on the bottom.

 Biscuits may take longer to brown in a cast iron skillet.

Biscuits placed close together may take longer to bake.

Biscuits on an aluminium sheet pan will take less time to bake.

Once you figure out the best time for making biscuits in your oven, mark the time on this recipe here. The temperature that is best for biscuits in my oven is _____.

"This is the biscuit my mama made every day when I was growing up. She made them with whole milk. We called it sweet milk." - *Tammy*

107) Hoecake Biscuit

Family Favorite:

"If you find making biscuits intimidating, this is the recipe for you!" -*Tammy*

→ 2 cups self-rising flour
→ 1 pinch baking soda
→ 1/4 cup shortening or butter at room temperature
→ 1 1/2 cups whole buttermilk, amount varies

Combine flour and baking soda in a bowl. Use a blending fork to mix in shortening or butter until the mixture resembles pea-sized crumbs. Add enough buttermilk to create a wet mixture. Pour the mixture into a well-greased 10-inch cast-iron skillet, greasing the skillet with shortening. Bake at 450°F for 25 to 30 minutes, or until golden brown. After baking, flip the bread and cut it into triangles as typically done for cornbread.

 If you prefer, melt the shortening or butter and mix it in rather than cutting it into the flour.

This dough should be wetter than traditional biscuit dough. It should be about the consistency of cornbread batter.

"I love a hoecake biscuit the best for making biscuits and gravy! We loved it when mama made breakfast for supper. It was such a treat to sit down and enjoy a plate of biscuits and gravy with slices of cantaloupe from the garden. As I remember our dining room, it had sliding doors when we were young. Daddy removed them and installed a brick chimney and installed a wood burning heater that had a flat top for cooking. In the winter, we heated the entire house with that stove. If the power went out mama would cook on it. Bringing in the wood was a real chore!" - *Tammy*

108) Lard-Fried Biscuits or Puffs

→ 2 cups self-rising flour
→ 1 pinch baking soda
→ 3/4 to 1 cup whole buttermilk
→ 1/4 cup lard

Blend lard and flour with a pastry blender or fork until you get pea-sized pieces. Stir in a bit of soda, then mix until combined. Add milk gradually until no flour remains at the bowl's bottom; the mixture should be thick.

 Note: This recipe is intended to be made after frying chicken in lard. You are to use the chicken grease after you fry your chicken.

Sift flour onto the counter, add dough, sift more flour on top, and knead 4-7 times. Flatten dough about 1/3-inch thick and cut out biscuits.

Use lard in a cast iron skillet. It should be melted to a depth of at least 1-inch and heated to medium. Evaluate readiness with a small piece of dough-it should float and fry. Fry biscuits in batches without crowding, flipping when golden; cook 4-5 minutes per side. Keep oil at a moderate temperature so biscuits cook through without browning too fast.

109) Mayonnaise Biscuits

→ 2 cups self-rising flour
→ 1 Tbsp sugar
→ 1/3 cup mayonnaise
→ 1 cup milk
→ 1 Tbsp salted butter, melted

Mix the ingredients in a medium bowl. Place dough on a surface dusted with flour. Dust the top of the dough with flour and knead 4 to 7 times, adding more flour as needed. Pat dough about 3/4 to 1-inch high and cut with a biscuit cutter. You can also hand form into 2-inch rolls and place on a greased baking sheet or cast-iron skillet. Bake at 500°F for 15 minutes. Remove, brush with butter, and bake for an additional 5 minutes. The biscuits will be golden brown. Flip the biscuits upside down after removing them from the oven to keep the bottoms crispy.

110) Sour Cream Biscuits

→ 2 cups self-rising flour
→ 16 oz. sour cream
→ 1/2 cup salted butter, room temperature

Mix the flour and butter with a blending fork or pastry cutter until the butter is the size of peas. Add sour cream and stir until all the flour is incorporated into the dough. Lightly dust the counter with flour and place the dough on it. Dust the top of the dough with flour and knead 4 to 7 times, adding more flour as needed. Pat the dough to about one inch thick and cut with a biscuit cutter. Arrange the biscuits close together in a greased baking pan coated with shortening. Bake at 500°F for 15 to 20 minutes, or until golden brown.

"These are my new favorite biscuit. I am sure it has to do with the fact they have 1/2 cup of butter. They are so moist and delicious!"

 Note: These biscuits are very soft and delicious. They taste similar to buttermilk biscuits but don't require buttermilk. This is great if you live in an area where buttermilk isn't available.

111) Stovetop Biscuits

→ 2 cups all-purpose flour
→ 3 tsp baking powder
→ 1-1/2 cups whole buttermilk
→ 1 tsp salt
→ 1/3 cup shortening (or room temperature salted butter)
→ Non-stick skillet with lid

If the flour is lumpy, sift it with salt and baking powder; if smooth, whisk together in a bowl. Cut in shortening or butter until the mixture looks like pea-sized crumbs. Stir in milk gradually until dough forms. Lightly flour a counter, knead the dough 4-7 times, then flatten to 3/4 inch thick. Cut biscuits, arrange them in a non-stick skillet, cover, and cook on medium-low heat until browned on the bottom and risen. Flip, cover, and finish cooking until they are done.

 Note: Buttermilk varies in thickness. Add it gradually when making biscuits, mixing after each addition. Stop once all flour is combined; avoid adding excess milk.

112) Biscuit Mix

→ 2 cups self-rising flour
→ 1/4 tsp baking soda, optional
→ 1/8 cup butter-flavored shortening (or butter at room temperature)
→ 1/8 cup vegetable shortening, Crisco

In a mixer with a paddle attachment, add flour, baking soda, shortening, and mix on low until shortening is about pea sized. Pour into a container and repeat until you have 8 cups of biscuit mix. Store in an airtight container for up to 4 months. Note: If you substitute butter for shortening, it must be refrigerated.

113) Biscuit Mix Pancakes

→ 2 cups biscuit mix
→ 1 tsp vanilla extract
→ 1 large egg
→ 1 cup milk
→ 2 Tbsp sugar

Mix all the ingredients above to make pancake batter. In a non-stick skillet on medium heat add 1/3 or 1/4 cup of batter for each pancake. Cook until bubbles uniformly appear on top of dough. Flip and finish cooking. Serve with butter and pancake syrup.

114) Biscuit Mix Dumplings

→ 1 cup biscuit mix
→ whole milk

Add milk gradually until all the flour is incorporated and the mixture is thick. Knead on a floured surface until the sheet of dough can be lifted without cracking. Cut into dumplings using a fork or a non-scratch pizza cutter. Add to boiling broth, cover, and simmer for 10 minutes.

115) Biscuit Mix Biscuits

→ 2 cups biscuit mix
→ 3/4 to 1 cup buttermilk

Add milk gradually until no flour remains at the bottom of the bowl. The mixture should be thick. Knead dough on a floured surface for 4-7 turns. Cut out with a biscuit cutter. Bake at 500°F for 15-20 minutes, or until golden brown. Also use rolled dough for cobbler toppings.

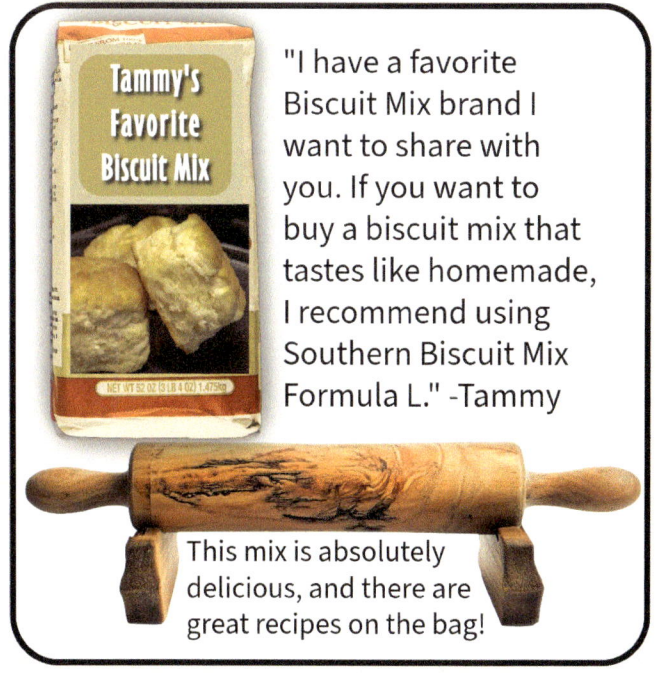

"I have a favorite Biscuit Mix brand I want to share with you. If you want to buy a biscuit mix that tastes like homemade, I recommend using Southern Biscuit Mix Formula L." -Tammy

This mix is absolutely delicious, and there are great recipes on the bag!

116) How to Boil a Chicken

- → boil a young fryer chicken
- → 1-1/2 tsp salt
- → 1/2 tsp black pepper
- → 1 Tbsp chicken bouillon granules
- → 2 celery stalks, cut into thirds
- → onion, quartered
- → water

Place the chicken breast side down in a large stock pot, add water to 3/4 high. Add the remaining ingredients to the pot. Turn heat to medium/low and cook for 1 hour. Remove chicken with two large spoons and place on a pie plate. Once cooled to touch, remove chicken from bones. Discard bones, fat, onions, and celery. Straining broth is optional. I do not strain it myself for dressing. Reserve broth.

 Boiling a chicken like this makes Chicken Broth. In order to make Chicken Stock, you have to boil the bones at least 1-1/2 to 2 hours.

 Use two one quart jars to store the broth. Pour the broth through a wide-mouth funnel with a mesh strainer into the jars. This process should give you roughly 1 1/2 to 2 quarts.

117) Cornbread for Dressing

- → 3 cups self-rising buttermilk cornmeal mix
- → 6 Tbsp salted butter, melted
- → 2 1/2 cups whole buttermilk
- → 1/4 cup corn oil
- → 1 large raw egg

Mix the ingredients above and bake in a 13"x9"x2" aluminum pan at 350 degrees for 35 minutes. (Should be light in color)

118) Mama's Chicken and Dressing

- → Recipe #117 Cornbread for Dressing
- → 10.5 oz. can cream chicken soup
- → 4-5 slices loaf bread, cut into cubes
- → 3 boiled eggs, chopped - optional
- → 1 cup chopped onion
- → 1 cup chopped celery
- → 1/2 to 3/4 tsp poultry seasoning
- → 5 1/2 cups chicken broth from recipe #116
- → 1 Tbsp chicken bouillon granules
- → 1/2 tsp salt
- → 1/2 tsp black pepper
- → 2 cups milk
- → 3 raw large eggs
- → chicken from Recipe #116
- → lasagna-sized baking dish

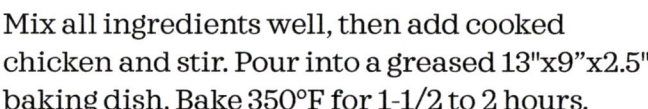

Mix all ingredients well, then add cooked chicken and stir. Pour into a greased 13"x9"x2.5" baking dish. Bake 350°F for 1-1/2 to 2 hours.

Make sure it is fully cooked! The dressing should rise and crack in the middle as well as on the sides when done. Allow at least 2 hours of baking before serving.

 Making dressing in advance enhances the flavor as it marinates. You can also freeze it in disposable baking dishes for travel. Refrigerate to thaw, it will take at least 48 hours to thaw in the refrigerator.

Day of the meal: mix it well. Pour it into sprayed baking pans. Let the dressing sit at room temperature for 2 hours before baking. Serve with Mama's Giblet Gravy.

"It took time and patience to figure out just the right amount of ingredients to make this dressing taste just like mamas! Mama never wrote down amounts, but I have just for you! Y'all are going to love my dressing! Make sure it is runny after you mix it up, and remember, it will not look as runny when cold. This dressing stays fluffy even after it cools, unlike other cornbread dressings that get dense." - Tammy.

119) Broccoli Cornbread

- → 2-8.5 oz. boxes Jiffy cornbread mix
- → 4 eggs, lightly beaten
- → 1/2 cup salted butter, melted
- → 1 cup sour cream
- → 1-1/2 cups broccoli cooked and finely chopped; frozen broccoli can be used
- → small onion, chopped

Begin by melting butter in a skillet, then add the broccoli and onion. Sauté until both are tender. In a separate bowl, combine the cornbread mix, eggs, and sour cream thoroughly. Carefully fold the cooked broccoli and onion into the mixture, ensuring that all the butter is evenly incorporated.

For square cornbread: Transfer the batter to a greased 9x13-inch pan and bake at 375°F until the surface is uniformly browned.

For muffins: Fill each muffin cup to threequarters full and bake at 350°F for approximately 40 minutes, or until golden brown.

"When I started Collard Valley Cooks, I did not know that mama had used a cornmeal mix all my life. When viewers started asking about the flour amounts in my cornbread, I had no idea what they meant. In the south, when mama says, "get me some cornmeal," it means a 5lb. bag of self-rising cornmeal mix. " -Tammy

Note: Cornbread is delicious reheated in the air fryer. Store leftovers in the refrigerator in a sealed container or bag.

120) Cornbread for Two

- → 1 cup self-rising cornmeal mix
- → 1 large egg
- → 2 Tbsp salted butter, melted
- → 1/8 cup vegetable or canola oil
- → 1/2 cup whole buttermilk
- → shortening for greasing the skillet

Combine cornmeal mix, egg, butter, oil, and buttermilk in a bowl. Grease an 8-inch cast-iron skillet with shortening and dust with cornmeal. Pour batter in and bake at 425°F for 25 minutes until browned. Remove and flip upside down onto a plate, bottom side up.

"Enjoy it with a meal or crumble it into a bowl, add milk, and savor! I like to cut tomato into chunks and sprinkle salt and pepper on my cornbread and milk. Daddy always enjoyed his with a green onion" - Tammy

121) Cornbread Fritters

- → 2 cups self-rising cornmeal mix
- → 6 Tbsp salted butter, melted
- → 1 Tbsp granulated sugar, optional
- → 1-1/2 cups buttermilk
- → 1 large egg

Mix the ingredients above in a bowl. Place onehalf inch of oil and 1/4 cup of butter in a preheated ten-inch cast-iron skillet. Drop by tablespoons and fry the patties on a medium/high heat.

"I prefer to use buttermilk cornmeal mix. I will use any brand of buttermilk cornmeal mix. To me they are all good! We typically buy White Lily, or Aunt Jemima which is now Pearl Milling." - Tammy

122) Cornbread Dressing, Granny's

→ 1/2 cup salted butter, melted
→ 1 cup diced celery
→ 1 large onion, chopped
→ 2 large eggs
→ one 2-cup cornbread recipe, baked and crumbled
→ 4 or 5 leftover homemade biscuits, crumbled and toasted
→ 1 tsp rubbed sage
→ 4 cups chicken stock (preferably homemade)
→ 1/2 tsp salt
→ 1/2 tsp black pepper

Mix the above ingredients in a large bowl. Spray a 13x9-inch cake pan. Bake at 350°F until set, which takes at least 1.5 hours. This recipe serves 12 and do not forget to serve it with Granny's Giblet Gravy.

"This is my Granny Benefield's recipe. This one is old-fashioned with day old biscuits and no soups!"- *Tammy*

123) Tammy's Shortcut Dressing

→ 2 cups self-rising cornmeal mix
→ 10.5 oz. can cream of chicken soup
→ 3 pieces loaf bread, cut into cubes
→ 1 onion, chopped
→ 3 stalks celery, chopped

→ 1/4 tsp salt
→ 1/4 tsp black pepper
→ 1/2 tsp poultry seasoning, used McCormick
→ 2 cups chicken stock
→ 1 Tbsp chicken bouillon granules
→ 1-1/2 cups whole buttermilk
→ 3 raw eggs
→ 1/4 cup vegetable oil
→ 4 Tbsp melted salted butter

Mix all ingredients together (excluding loaf bread) until well blended. The mixture will be runny. Spray a 13x9x2.5-inch baking dish with cooking spray. Note: If you use a regular aluminum pan, grease it well with shortening. Put loaf bread cubes in the bottom of the pan, then add the dressing mix. Cook at 350°F until golden brown and firm, about 1.5 hours. Dressing should crack in the middle and on the sides when it is fully done. Enjoy!

"I always wanted to make dressing without cooking cornbread first. Well, I tried it, and it is good. I would not make it for Thanksgiving day, but it is fine for a weeknight meal. So, mix this up quickly and enjoy!" - *Tammy*

124) Cornbread Dressing Cakes

→ 2 or 3 green onions, chopped
→ 2 Tbsp bell pepper, chopped
→ 2 Tbsp olive oil
→ 1 stalk celery, chopped
→ 1/2 tsp pepper
→ 1/4 cup sour cream
→ 3 large eggs
→ 2 tsp poultry seasoning, used McCormick or 1 tsp rubbed sage
→ 1/2 pone of Recipe #128: Crunchy Cornbread, leftover and crumbled
→ 2 oz. jar chopped pimentos, optional

Sauté onion and bell pepper in olive oil for 2 minutes until soft. Mix with all other ingredients in a bowl. Heat an iron skillet, add 1/4 inch of oil, and spoon the mixture in. Cook on medium until browned on both sides. Drain on paper towels and serve.

In the mood for dressing and do not want to make a whole pan? Just mix up these delicious dressing cakes and enjoy them with dinner! -*Tammy*

125) Crackling Cornbread

→ 2 cups cracklings
→ 2 cups self-rising cornmeal mix
→ 2 cups buttermilk or milk
→ 1/2 tsp black pepper
→ 1/2 tsp salt
→ 1/4 cup cooking oil
→ shortening as needed
→ 10.25-inch cast iron skillet

Preheat oven to 425°F. Crush cracklings in a freezer bag with a meat mallet. Grease an iron skillet with shortening and dust with cornmeal mix. In a bowl, combine cornmeal mix, buttermilk, pepper, salt, oil, and the crushed cracklings. Pour into the skillet and bake until browned, about 20-30 minutes. Serve with greens and beans!

"Before making Recipe #125, know that some people like it cracklings soaked to soften them, while others do not. Try both ways and mark which way you like it in this book, so you remember."-*Tammy*

126) Crackling Corn Pones

→ 2 cups cracklings
→ 1 2/3 cups self-rising cornmeal mix
→ 1 cup water
→ 1 cup milk
→ 1/2 tsp black pepper
→ 1/2 tsp salt
→ 1/4 cup salted butter
→ cooking oil and 3 Tbsp salted butter

In a skillet, add the cracklings and heat until hot. Then, add water and milk and simmer for 3-5 minutes. Season with salt and pepper, then stir in the cornmeal. Mix well. Form into 1/2-inch-thick patties and fry in hot oil with a little butter until very brown. Remove and place on a plate lined with paper towels. Enjoy!

127) Hot Water Cornbread

→ 1 cup cornmeal mix
→ 1/2 tsp black pepper
→ 1 cup boiling hot water
→ 3/4 cup corn oil
→ 1/4 cup salted butter

Combine the cornmeal, pepper, and water, allowing the mixture to rest for five minutes as you heat butter and oil in a cast iron skillet. Once the butter has melted, fry the cornbread in thin portions until both sides are golden brown. Maintain medium heat to ensure thorough cooking. The batter may be dropped into the pan by spoonful's or rolled into balls and then flattened upon reaching the pan. These are best served at room temperature rather than immediately from the skillet.

128) Crunchy Cornbread

→ 2 cups self-rising cornmeal mix
→ 6 Tbsp salted butter, melted
→ 1 Tbsp granulated sugar, optional
→ 1-1/2 cups whole buttermilk
→ 1/4 cup corn oil
→ 1 raw egg

Grease a 10.25-inch cast iron skillet with shortening and sprinkle 1/4 cup cornmeal mix on the sides and bottom. In a large bowl, mix all ingredients well and pour into the skillet. Bake at 425°F for 25-30 minutes until browned. Immediately remove, flip onto a plate, and use a thick potholder as the pan will be hot.

"Granny made a pone of regular cornbread every single day along with a pan of biscuits in the morning." -*Tammy*

129) Hushpuppies

- → 2-3 Tbsp chopped onion
- → 2 Tbsp diced jalapenos, optional
- → 1 large egg
- → 1/4 tsp black pepper
- → 1 cup self-rising cornmeal mix
- → 1/2 to 3/4 cup buttermilk (to moisten)

In a glass bowl, mix onion, jalapeños, egg, pepper, and cornmeal. Gradually add milk until the mixture is moist, then let it stand for 10-15 minutes. Pour 1/2 inch of oil into a skillet and heat until a small piece of mix sizzles. Drop by spoonful's into the hot oil and fry until golden on both sides. For deep-frying, use 350°F oil and cook for 8 minutes, lowering heat if they brown too fast. Drain on paper towels for 3-4 minutes, then keep warm in the oven until serving. Serve as a side or appetizer.

 Tip: Make smaller hushpuppies to ensure they cook through.

130) Cornbread And Milk

Crumble the cornbread while still slightly warm into a cereal bowl and cover it with milk. Add salt and pepper and eat with a spoon!

Option: Chopped summer tomatoes are great in it. Be sure to season it with salt and pepper! Some people enjoy it with buttermilk.

131) Mexican Cornbread, Nana's

- → 1-1/2 cups self-rising cornmeal mix
- → 3/4 cup vegetable oil
- → 1/4 cup chopped onion
- → 1/8 cup chopped bell pepper
- → 6 or 8 oz. can cream corn
- → 2 large eggs
- → 1 chopped jalapeño pepper (or 2 Tbsp diced jalapeños from a jar)
- → 2 oz. pimentos
- → 1 cup sour cream
- → 8 oz. bag shredded Mexican cheese blend (or medium cheddar)

Use a 13x9x2-inch aluminum pan or a 10-inch cast iron skillet. Preheat the skillet and grease it with shortening. Coat the sides and bottom with 1/4 cup of cornmeal. In a medium bowl, mix the ingredients, then pour the mixture into the skillet. Bake at 400°F until it turns dark brown, about 50 to 60 minutes. Once done, remove it from the oven and carefully flip it upside down onto a regular-sized plate.

 Caution: The cast iron skillet will be very hot. Use a thick potholder to handle it when removing it from the oven and flipping!

"Nana uses a 13x9x2-inch aluminum cake pan when she makes her Mexican Cornbread. It makes it crunchy and delicious. She takes it to all the family gatherings at every holiday meal." -Tammy

132) Mighty Good Cornbread

- → 10.25" cast iron skillet
- → 1-1/2 cups self-rising cornmeal mix
- → 1/2 cup of corn or vegetable oil
- → 1 cup cream-style canned corn
- → 1 cup sour cream
- → 2 large eggs

Grease a cast-iron skillet thoroughly. Sprinkle the inside with cornmeal mix. Combine the above ingredients and pour the mixture into the skillet. Bake at 425°F for 30 minutes or until golden brown. Carefully remove from the oven and immediately flip the skillet upside down to release the cornbread.

133) Oven-Fried Cornbread

→ 2 cups self-rising cornmeal mix
→ 1 large egg
→ 1/4 cup salted butter, melted
→ 1-1/2 cups whole buttermilk

Grease a 10-inch cast iron skillet with shortening, add 1/4 cup oil, and preheat in a 450°F oven. Mix the cornbread batter in a large bowl. When the skillet is hot, move it to the stove, pour in the batter (it should sizzle), and bake at 425°F for 25–30 minutes. Flip upside down onto a plate, cut into triangles, and serve with butter.

"Many people prefer this method of making cornbread; however, my personal favorite is greasing the skillet and sprinkling it with cornmeal mix, just like my mama did." -*Chris*

"In 2020 we moved from Paulding County, Georgia to Saint Mary's, Georgia with the girls. It was a fun time and there we shared great memories of food. We were confined to the house during the Covid lockdown and of course we all gained weight that year! There was not much to do but eat. These three pictures are in our Saint Mary's kitchen. Kaysha also came to live with us that summer. She is our god daughter. She is missing from the picture below because she was out of town with her family for Thanksgiving. The four of us and one of Amy's friends from college had lots of food to eat! Everyone had small gatherings that year." -*Tammy*

"Chris is getting ready to make a meatloaf sandwich after getting home from fishing. He loves meatloaf so very much!" -*Tammy*

134) Apple Nut Bread

→ 2 cups apples, Golden Delicious
→ 1 lemon
→ 1/3 cup all-purpose flour
→ 1/2 cup raisins
→ 1 cup chopped pecans
→ 3 eggs
→ 1/2 cup salted butter or vegetable oil
→ 1 cup brown sugar
→ 1 tsp vanilla extract
→ 1/2 cup sour cream
→ 1 tsp cinnamon
→ 2 cups self-rising flour

Peel and chop the apples, then add a little lemon juice to prevent discoloration and set aside.

In a separate bowl, combine 1/3 cup of flour with raisins and pecans, tossing to coat.

In a third bowl, thoroughly mix eggs, vegetable oil, and brown sugar. Stir in vanilla, sour cream, and cinnamon. Gradually add the flour mixture and blend well. Gently fold in the apples, nuts, and raisins.

Pour the batter into a well-greased 9x5x3 inch pan, Bundt pan, or two small loaf pans. Bake at 400°F for 20 minutes. Then, lower the oven temperature to 350°F and continue baking for 35-40 minutes.

Shop Now

Bundt Pan

135) Apple Fritters

Glaze:

→ 1 cup powdered sugar
→ 1 tsp vanilla extract
→ 3 Tbsp milk

Mix the above ingredients well. Set aside.

Apples:

→ 2 medium apples (cored, peeled, and chopped)
→ 3 Tbsp salted butter
→ 1/2 tsp ground cinnamon
→ 1/3 cup sugar

Combine apples, butter, cinnamon, and sugar. Cook on the stove or in the microwave until soft before adding to the dough batter.

Dough:

→ 1 cup all-purpose flour
→ 1-1/2 tsp baking powder
→ 1/2 tsp salt
→ 1 tsp ground cinnamon, optional
→ 1 large egg
→ 1/3 cup milk

Mix the dough ingredients. Stir in cooked apples. Preheat a saucepan with oil for frying. Add 1/4 cup of butter to the oil before dropping in the batter. Use a spoon to carefully drop the batter into the hot oil. Brown on both sides, then remove and place on a cooling rack with parchment paper or paper towels underneath. Dip the warm fritters into the glaze and let them dry on a cooling rack.

"As an Amazon Associate, I earn from qualifying purchases."

136) Banana Bread, Tammy's

- → 1/2 cup salted butter, melted
- → 2 large eggs
- → 1 tsp vanilla extract
- → 3 very ripe bananas
- → 1 cup sugar
- → 2 cups self-rising flour
- → 1/4 cup buttermilk
- → 1 tsp baking soda
- → 1/2 tsp salt
- → 1/2 tsp ground cinnamon
- → 1/4 tsp nutmeg
- → 8-oz. can crushed pineapple, drained
- → 2/3 cup chopped pecans

Combine butter, eggs, bananas, and vanilla in a bowl. Add sugar, then mix in flour gradually (1/2 cup at a time). Stir in buttermilk, baking soda, salt, cinnamon, nutmeg, pineapple, and pecans until well blended. Pour into a greased and floured cake or loaf pan. Bake at 325°F for 1 hour. Cool for 10 minutes before removing it from the pan.

137) Bear Claws

- → Pepperidge Farm puff pastry sheets (Each sheet makes 3 bear claws)
- → almond filling or almond paste
- → slivered almonds
- → 1 egg white
- → large sugar crystals, optional

Preheat the oven to 350°F. Thaw and unfold the pastry, then cut along the folds to make three rectangles. Spoon 2-3 tablespoons of filling on one side. Dampen edges with egg white, fold over, and crimp all edges with a fork. Cut 1-inch slits every 3/4 inch along the crimped edge. Place pastries on a parchment-lined sheet, pull edges apart slightly, brush with egg white, and top with almonds and sugar crystals. Bake for 25-30

minutes until golden brown and risen. If using almond filling, refrigeration is not necessary.

 Note: pastry sheets are usually found in the freezer near pie crusts and Cool Whip. Almond filling is located near other pie fillings in the supermarket.

138) Berry Scones

- → 2 cups self-rising flour
- → 1/4 cup salted butter, room temperature
- → 1/2 cup sugar
- → 1 large egg
- → 3/4 to 1 cup whipping cream, amount varies
- → Cinnamon
- → Nutmeg, optional
- → Sugar crystals
- → Fresh berries

Cut butter into flour until pea-sized. Mix in sugar, then eggs. Mix in whipping cream a little at a time until dough comes together. Knead lightly on a floured surface, roll into a circle 1/4-inch tall. Place berries in the center, sprinkle with cinnamon, fold edges over to form a 1/2-inch high circle. Cut into 8 triangles. Brush with butter and sprinkle nutmeg (optional) and sugar. Transfer folded side down to a parchment-lined sheet and bake at 375°F for 30 minutes.

See Recipe #422 Vanilla Cream Sauce

139) Biscuit Bread Pudding, Granny's

→ 5-6 leftover homemade buttermilk biscuits
→ 9x9 or 7x11-inch pan
→ 4 large eggs
→ 1/2 cup brown sugar, packed
→ 1/2 cup granulated sugar
→ 12 oz. can evaporated milk
→ 1/2 cup water

Optional: 2 cups of whole milk can be substituted for evaporated milk and water

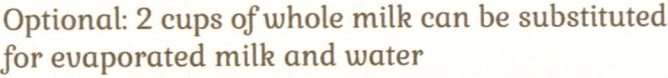

→ 1/2 cup salted butter, melted
→ 1/2 tsp ground cinnamon, optional
→ 1/4 tsp ground nutmeg

Whisk eggs, sugars, milk, water, butter, and spices in a bowl. Crumble biscuits into a greased pan and pour the mixture over them. Soak for 20 minutes, then bake at 350°F for 40 minutes (or 300°F if using a toaster oven) until set. Serve warm or cold.

"This is my granny's recipe, and oh, how my little brother loved her bread pudding."- *Tammy*

140) Banana Bread Pudding

→ 2.5-quart casserole dish
→ 5 seedless hamburger buns
→ 1/2 cup salted butter, room temperature
→ 3 ripe bananas, mashed
→ 1/2 cup granulated sugar
→ 6 large eggs
→ 3 cups milk
→ 1 tsp vanilla extract
→ 1/4 tsp almond extract, optional
→ 3/4 cup chopped pecans

Spray the casserole dish with cooking spray for easy cleanup. Butter each piece of bread

andarrange it in two layers in your dish. Remove the top layer and set it aside. Place bananas in a mixing bowl with sugar and mix until creamy. Add eggs and mix well. Add milk and extracts, blending thoroughly. Pour half of the mixture over the single layer of bread in your baking dish. Place the top layer of buns in the dish and pour the remaining liquid over them. Do not overfill; fill up to about 3/4 inch from the top of the casserole. Top with pecans and let it sit at room temperature for 1 hour to allow the mixture to soak into the bread. After soaking, bake at 350 degrees for 1 hour. Serve while warm.

141) Bread Pudding

→ 4 eggs
→ 1/2 cup brown sugar, packed
→ 1/2 cup granulated sugar
→ 1 cup evaporated milk and 1 cup water (or 2 cups whole milk)
→ 1/2 cup salted butter, melted
→ 1/2 tsp ground cinnamon, optional
→ 1/4 tsp ground nutmeg, optional
→ 7 large slices old loaf bread in cubes
→ 9"x9" or 7"x11" brownie pan

Whisk eggs in a bowl, then mix in sugar, evaporated milk, water (or whole milk), butter, and spices. Layer bread cubes in a baking dish and pour the mixture over them. Soak for 20 minutes, then bake at 350°F for 40 minutes until set. If using a small toaster or convection oven, bake at 300°F for 40 minutes, or until set. Enjoy warm or cold!

Chocolate Bread Pudding:

→ 5 Tbsp cocoa powder, Hershey's
→ dash of salt
→ omit cinnamon and nutmeg in the above recipe

Follow the same instructions as above, excluding cinnamon and nutmeg. Whisk the cocoa thoroughly into the sugars. This step helps incorporate the cocoa into the dry ingredients before proceeding with the pudding.

Psalm 86:5

"For thou, Lord, art good, and ready to forgive; and plenteous in mercy unto all them that call upon thee." KJV

142) Biscuit Cinnamon Rolls

Dough:
- → 2 cups self-rising flour
- → 3/4 to 1 cup whole buttermilk
- → 1/4 cup Crisco shortening or 1/4 cup salted butter, room temperature

Filling:
- → 1/2 cup salted butter, room temperature
- → 4 Tbsp ground cinnamon
- → 1/3 cup granulated sugar

Icing:
- → 3 Tbsp salted butter, room temperature
- → 1-1/2 cup powdered sugar
- → 1/4 cup milk

For Dough: Mix shortening, and flour together with a fork until the shortening is pea sized. Gradually add buttermilk until all the flour is moist and the mixture is just combined. Sift flour onto the counter and turn out the dough. Lightly sift more flour on top, then knead the dough 7-10 times. Roll out into a large rectangle about 1/2 inch thick.

For Filling: Mix the sugar, butter, and cinnamon together with a hand mixer in a medium size bowl. Spread the filling evenly across the sheet of dough.

Roll up the dough starting with the short side. Lightly sprinkle with flour if needed while rolling. Using a bread knife, cut the roll into 1 1/2-inch-wide slices and place them close together in a greased pan with shortening. Bake at 425°F for 25 minutes.

For the Icing: Prepare a glaze with room-temperature butter, powdered sugar, and milk. Spread the glaze over the rolls while they are hot. Enjoy!

143) Cinnamon Rolls

- → 1/4 cup warm water
- → 1/4 oz. pack yeast (2 1/4 tsp)

Combine water and yeast. Let it sit 5 minutes.

- → 1 cup warm milk (microwave 60 seconds if refrigerated)

Add milk and yeast water to a stand mixer (bowl) with a whisk attachment. Whisk at medium speed for 5 minutes. Put on a dough hook attachment and add:

- → 3 cups bread flour

Blend for 5-7 minutes at the lowest speed.

Grease bowl with oil. Place the dough inside, set in a warm place to double in size.

Punch down the Dough and put it back in the stand mixer with the dough hook & add:

- → 1/3 cup granulated sugar
- → 2 eggs at room temperature
- → 1 tsp salt
- → 1 tsp cinnamon
- → 1-1/2 cup bread flour, add 1/4 cup at a time

slowly beating after each addition of flour. Mix for 5 minutes. In a bowl combine:

- → 3/4 cup salted butter, room temperature
- → 5 Tbsp cinnamon
- → 2/3 cup sugar
- → 1/2 tsp vanilla extract

Mix well with a hand mixer. Roll the dough on a floured surface into a rectangle, spread with cinnamon filling, roll from the short side, and cut into 1 1/2-inch slices. Place 1/2-inch apart in a greased 13x9-inch dish, spray the tops, and cover with plastic wrap. Once it is nearly doubled in size, remove the wrap and bake at 350°F until golden.

For the Icing: Prepare a glaze by mixing

- → 3 Tbsp salted butter, room temperature
- → 1-1/2 cups powdered sugar
- → 1/4 Tbsp milk

Spread the glaze over the rolls while they are hot. Enjoy!

> ### Luk 11:4
> "And forgive us our sins; for we also forgive every one that is indebted to us. And lead us not into temptation; but deliver us from evil." KJV

144) Cream Puffs

- → 1/2 cup salted butter
- → 1 tsp granulated sugar
- → 1/4 tsp salt
- → 1 cup all-purpose flour
- → 1/2 cup water
- → 1/2 cup milk
- → 4 large eggs

Preheat the oven to 375°F and line two baking sheets with parchment paper. Melt butter in a medium saucepan over medium-high heat, then add sugar, salt, and water. Bring to a boil, quickly sift in the flour, and stir until a film forms on the bottom of the pan. Remove from heat and let cool for 6 minutes. Mix the mixture with a hand mixer or by hand. Add eggs one at a time, stirring vigorously to incorporate each. Using a hand mixer makes this process easier.

Prepare an egg wash by whisking the following together:

- → 1 egg
- → 1 Tbsp water

Use a large tablespoon and spoon out puffs about 1-1/2 inches apart on a lined baking sheet. Brush with egg wash and bake until golden, about 30 minutes. Cool on racks. Fill with Recipe #145 Pastry Cream. Dip in melted chocolate if desired. These freeze well so freeze the leftovers.

145) Pastry Cream, Easy

- → 1-3.4 oz. instant vanilla pudding
- → 1 cup milk
- → 2 cups whipping cream

Add milk to the pudding mix and stir. Whisk in 2 cups of whipping cream until stiff peaks form.

 If you are not serving with chocolate topping, Add 1/4 tsp of cinnamon if desired.

146) Doughnuts, Buttermilk

- → 2 Tbsp shortening
- → 3/4 cup sugar
- → 2 large eggs
- → 4 cups all-purpose flour, sifted
- → 2 tsp baking powder
- → 1/2 tsp cinnamon
- → 1/2 tsp nutmeg, optional
- → 1/2 tsp salt
- → 1/2 tsp baking soda
- → 1 cup buttermilk, can use whole milk
- → oil for frying, used corn oil

In a mixing bowl, cream together the shortening and sugar until smooth. Add the eggs and mix thoroughly. In a separate bowl, sift together the flour, baking powder, cinnamon, nutmeg, salt, and baking soda, then stir well to combine. Gradually add the buttermilk and the egg-sugar mixture to the dry ingredients, mixing until the dough comes together and no dry flour remains. Cover the bowl with a damp cloth and refrigerate the dough for at least an hour. Once chilled, roll out the dough to a 1/2-inch thickness on a lightly floured surface. Cut out doughnuts and, if desired, the doughnut holes. Heat oil in a deep fryer or heavy-bottom pot to 370°F using a thermometer. Fry the doughnuts, turning them to brown both sides evenly, then remove and drain on a cooling rack. This recipe makes approximately 2 1/2 dozen doughnuts.

Vanilla Glaze

- → 2 cups sifted powdered sugar
- → 1/3 cup milk
- → 1 tsp vanilla extract

Whisk the above ingredients together until smooth and creamy. Then, glaze the doughnuts by dipping the tops into glaze and resting them on a cooling rack. Doughnuts can also be dipped into powdered sugar instead of glazing.

147) Orange Date Nut Bread

→ 1 large egg
→ 3 Tbsp salted butter, room temperature
→ 3/4 cup sugar
→ 1 tsp vanilla extract
→ 1 cup chopped dates
→ 1/2 cup boiling water
→ 1 orange, peeled and sliced
→ 1 cup chopped pecans
→ 2 cups all-purpose flour
→ 1 tsp baking powder
→ 1/2 tsp baking soda
→ 1/4 tsp salt

Boil 1/2 cup water in the microwave, add dates, and set aside. Mix egg, butter, sugar, and vanilla. Blend dates with water and oranges using an immersion blender or regular blender. Stir into the mixture. Add combined soda, baking powder, salt, and flour; mix well. Fold in nuts. Pour into a greased loaf pan, filling up to threequarters. Bake at 350°F for 1 hour. Test doneness with a skewer or toothpick—remove if clean.

 This is bread and not sweet like cake. If you want it to be sweeter, use 1 1/2 cups of sugar instead of 3/4 cup. And bake at 325°F. It is delicious y'all!

148) Pumpkin Bread or Layer Cake

→ 1 cups white sugar
→ 1 cup packed brown sugar
→ 1/4 tsp salt
→ 16 oz. can pumpkin
→ 1/2 cup vegetable oil
→ 1/2 cup salted butter, melted
→ 1 tsp vanilla extract
→ 3 large eggs
→ 2 cups self-rising flour
→ 1/2 tsp cinnamon
→ 1/2 tsp nutmeg
→ 1/4 tsp cloves or pumpkin pie spice
→ 1 cup chopped pecans

Combine sugar, salt, pumpkin, oil, butter, vanilla, and eggs; mix well. Add cinnamon, nutmeg, and cloves; mix well. Gradually add flour in 1/2 cup increments, then mix for another minute. Stir in chopped pecans. Pour into a wellsprayed Bundt pan and bake at 350°F for 45 minutes. Check with a toothpick. Cool before removing it from pan. Enjoy!

 Tip: Can bake in cupcake pan with paper liners and ice with Recipe #208 Cream Cheese Frosting if taking to an event!

"This is my 'go-to' recipe every year! It is like cake, not bread! So good with coffee."-*Tammy*

149) Vanilla Scones

→ 2 cups self-rising flour
→ 1/4 cup salted butter, room temperature
→ 1/2 cup sugar
→ 1 large egg
→ 3/4 to 1 cup whipping cream
→ 1 1/2 tsp vanilla extract
→ A dusting spice (cinnamon or nutmeg), optional
→ large sugar crystals, optional

 Tip: You may not need all the whipping cream.

Cut butter into flour with a fork until pea-sized. Stir in sugar, then mix in eggs. Gradually add whipped cream until dough forms and leaves the bowl sides. Knead lightly on a floured surface, roll into a circle and pat 1/4 inch high. Cut into 8 wedges. Brush with butter, sprinkle with spices and sugar. Place scones on parchment-lined sheet and bake at 375°F for 30 minutes.

The picture shows the scones being served with Recipe #419, Lemon Curd.

Muffin Recipes

150) Cheesy Sausage Muffins

- → 1 cup self-rising flour
- → 1/4 cup salted butter, room temperature
- → 1/4 cup mild cheddar cheese, shredded
- → 1/2 cup sharp cheddar cheese, shredded
- → 3 oz. cream cheese, cubed
- → 2 large eggs
- → 1/3 lb. sausage, used Swaggerty's Farm
- → 1/8 cup chopped onion or green onion
- → 2/3 cup buttermilk

Brown sausage in a skillet, add onion if desired. In a bowl, blend butter with flour, cheese, beaten eggs, and milk. Stir in the sausage and fold in cream cheese cubes. Fill greased muffin tins—24 mini or 12 regulars. Bake at 375°F for 25 minutes for mini size muffins and 30 min for regular.

151) Streusel Topping, Muffins

- → 4 Tbsp salted butter, room temperature
- → 2/3 cup flour
- → 1/2 cup brown sugar, packed
- → 1/4 cup chopped pecans, optional
- → 1/2 tsp ground cinnamon, optional
- → 1 cup quick oats, optional

Using a blending fork, combine butter, flour & sugar until mixture is crumbly. Add remaining ingredients and mix. Sprinkle over muffins.

152) Banana Muffins, Brown Sugar

- → 3-4 Tbsp salted butter, room temperature
- → 1 cup self-rising flour
- → Pinch baking soda
- → 1/2 cup packed brown sugar
- → 1 large egg
- → 1 tsp vanilla extract
- → 1 ripe banana, mashed with a fork
- → 1/2 cup buttermilk

Combine butter and flour with a blending fork until the mixture is crumbly. Add baking soda and stir. Incorporate sugar, egg, vanilla, banana, and buttermilk, mix with a spoon until combined. Fold in nuts. If the batter appears dry, add a small amount of milk. The batter may remain lumpy. Fill greased muffin tins to threequarters full and sprinkle with Recipe #151 Streusel. Bake at 375°F until the muffins are golden brown and set, check in 30 minutes.

153) Banana Nut Muffins

- → 2 cups self-rising flour
- → 1/3 cup cooking oil
- → 1 large egg
- → 1 cup mashed ripe bananas
- → 1/2 cup milk
- → 1 tsp vanilla extract
- → 1/2 cup chopped nuts (pecans or walnuts)
- → 1/2 cup sugar, optional

In a mixing bowl combine above ingredients and mix until blended. Place it in well-greased muffin pan. Makes 12 large muffins. Distribute batter evenly in all 12 cups.

Top with Recipe #151: Streusel and Bake at 350°F for 25-30 minutes.

 To make a low sugar option banana muffin, omit sugar and streusel topping.

154) Pineapple Muffins

→ 1/3 cup salted butter, melted.
→ 1 large egg
→ 8 oz. sour cream
→ 1 tsp vanilla extract
→ 8 oz. can crushed pineapple
→ 2 cups self-rising flour (or if using all-purpose flour, add:
  ▪ 1/2 tsp baking soda
  ▪ 1/2 tsp salt
  ▪ 2 tsp baking powder)
→ 1/2 cup brown sugar, packed
→ 1/4 cup pecans, optional

Mix butter, egg, sour cream, and vanilla. Fold in pineapple with its juice. In a separate bowl, combine flour, sugar, and pecans. Make a well in dry ingredients, pour in wet mixture, and stir. Spray muffin pan. Fill muffin cups 3/4 full. Sprinkle with cinnamon sugar or Recipe #151 Streusel if desired. Bake at 350°F for 35-40 minutes. Serve hot with butter!

"This recipe is quick, easy, and a treat without the calories of cake or store-bought pastry. A must-try." -Tammy

155) Blueberry Muffins

→ 3 Tbsp salted butter
→ 1/2 cup granulated sugar
→ 2 raw eggs
→ 3/4 cup buttermilk
→ 1 tsp vanilla extract
→ 2 cups self-rising flour
→ 6 oz. or 3/4 cup fresh blueberries

Melt butter in a glass dish. Whisk in sugar and eggs, then add milk and vanilla, whisking again. Stir in flour (batter may be lumpy). Fold in blueberries. Fill greased muffin tins 3/4 full, top with Recipe #151 Streusel, and bake at 375°F until golden and raised in the middle. (check after 25 minutes).

Tammy's Tip: Remove from muffin pans with a fork quickly to prevent bottoms from sweating. Cool on a cooling rack. Top with Recipe #151 Streusel Topping prior to baking with cinnamon added.

Amy ♥ May
Little
Helpers

156) 1927 Spoon Bread

- → iron skillet 10.25"
- → 3 egg yolks
- → 3 egg whites
- → 2 cups whole milk, scalded
- → 1/2 cup cornmeal (plain, not self-rising)
- → 1 tsp salt
- → 1/2 tsp baking powder
- → 2 Tbsp melted fat (salted butter)
- → 2 Tbsp shortening for skillet

Place a cast iron skillet in the oven and preheat to 375°F. While it heats, separate the eggs, beat the yolks with a fork, and set them aside. In a double boiler or non-stick pan, heat the milk until it is hot but not boiling. Beat egg whites until stiff peaks form. Slowly stir cornmeal into hot milk, cook until mushy. Remove from heat, add salt, baking powder, and butter. Mix in yolks. Fold in the egg whites. Remove the skillet from the oven and melt two Tbsp of shortening around the edges. Then, pour the batter into the skillet. Bake for 30 minutes and serve warm directly from the skillet.

1Jo 1:9

"If we confess our sins, he is faithful and just to forgive us our sins, and to cleanse us from all unrighteousness." KJV

157) Easy Butter Rolls

- → 1 package quick-rise yeast, or 2 1/4 tsp
- → 3/4 cup evaporated milk mixed with 1/2 cup warm water
- → 1 tsp granulated sugar
- → 5 Tbsp salted butter, melted
- → 1 1/2 tsp salt
- → 1 large egg yolk
- → 3-4 cups bread flour, sifted

Combine yeast, milk, water, and sugar in a stand mixer with wire whisk attachment. Mix on low for 5 minutes. Yeast should be activated and become bubbly. Add melted butter, salt, and egg yolk; mix on low. Add 2 cups of bread flour and mix until well combined. Then, switch to the dough hook. Add the remaining flour 1/4 cup at a time, waiting 1-2 minutes between additions. When the dough pulls away from the bowl and is sticky but manageable, knead briefly, then let it rest for 10 minutes.

Reattach the dough hook, beat on low for 8 minutes. Divide the dough into 16 pieces, roll each into a ball, and tuck the folds underneath.

Grease a 13x9 dish (or two 9-inch pans). Place the rolls one inch apart, leaving the sides ungreased for rising. Cover loosely and let the dough rise until it has doubled in size. Drizzle melted butter over the rolls. Do not brush butter because they may fall.

Bake at 400°F for 20 minutes. Pour more butter over hot rolls and listen to it sizzle. Enjoy!

Rising Tip: Use a warming pad on low and place the rolls on top to allow them to rise. It is the perfect temperature. I learned this from Phyllis Stokes, a former YouTuber!

Another great place to rise them is in the sunlight coming through a window.

"This is a quick dinner roll that takes only one rise. They turn out fluffy and delicious! I used my temptations baking dish to make these, and it did a better job than my aluminum pan did. If you have a ceramic baking dish, use it! These are worth the trouble y'all."-Tammy

158) Crazy Crust Pizza

→ 1 cup all-purpose flour
→ 1/2 tsp salt
→ 2 large eggs
→ 1 tsp pizza seasoning
→ 2/3 cup milk
→ pizza toppings
→ mozzarella cheese

Beat the ingredients thoroughly with a fork or whisk, then pour into a greased 10 or 12-inch cast iron skillet. Top with browned Italian sausage and pepperoni. Bake at 425°F for 20 minutes until the crust pulls from the sides. Add your preferred pizza toppings and bake for another 10 minutes. For convection ovens, bake at 380°F.

 Sauce Application Note: Applying sauce directly on the crust after removing it from the oven will make the top soggy. To keep the crust crispy, add the sauce last or serve it as a dipping sauce.

Crust Thickness Note: Do not skip the precook stage for the crust! The smaller the cast-iron skillet, the thicker the crust!

John 3:16
"For God so loved the world, that he gave his only begotten Son, that whosoever believeth in him should not perish, but have everlasting life." KJV

159) Corn Fritters, Fresh Corn

→ 2 large eggs, separated
→ 1 cup fresh sweet corn (cut off cobb or cream corn) Important: Do not use canned cream corn
→ 1 tsp baking powder
→ dash salt
→ 1/2 tsp black pepper
→ 1/2 cup self-rising flour

Beat the two egg whites until stiff. In a separate bowl, combine the remaining ingredients and mix well. Fold the beaten egg whites into the mixture. Fry in a preheated skillet with butter. Flip when the cake rises and turns brown. Cook the other side until browned. Remove and enjoy!

 Tammy's Tip: Beating only two egg whites is best done in a tall, skinny bowl, such as a 4-cup glass measuring cup, or tilt the bowl you are using so they beat up faster.

Option: beating the egg whites is optional. If you choose to do this step, you will be making the traditional version of a corn cake. If you want to skip this step, just use the whole eggs when mixing the batter.

160) Fritters, Cheese

→ 1 tsp Worcestershire sauce
→ 1 egg, beaten
→ 1/2 cup milk
→ 1 green onion, diced
→ dash hot sauce, optional
→ 2 cups biscuit mix, Recipe #112
→ 1 1/2 cups American cheese, cut into small cubes. Cheese should be very cold prior to frying.

Mix the first five ingredients. Add the flour and stir well. Fold in the cheese. Drop by teaspoons into hot oil. Cook at 365 degrees F until golden brown. Remove and place on paper towels. Enjoy!

If you do not have biscuit mix, use 2 cups of self-rising flour combined with 1/4 cup of butter or shortening. Cut the shortening into the flour until it reaches pea-sized crumbs, then use this mixture instead of biscuit mix in the recipe.

Romans 5:8
"But God commendeth his love toward us, in that, while we were yet sinners, Christ died for us." KJV

161) Drop Dumplings

→ 2 cups self-rising flour
→ 1/4 cup shortening or use a biscuit mix, Recipe #112
→ broth from a cooked roast

Cut the shortening into the flour using a blending fork or pastry blender until the pieces are pea sized. Add enough roast broth to create a thick, sticky dough. The dough should be thick enough to drop from a spoon, like spoon biscuit dough.

 Tammy's tip: thicken the pot roasts broth before adding dumplings, as you can't stir the pot afterward.

Push the roast and vegetables to the side of the pot, then drop each dumpling by heaping tablespoon into the broth with the roast. Cover with a lid and cook the dumplings (lid on) for at least 15 minutes. Spoon broth over the dumplings to coat them well before serving.

My Best Dumpling Tip!

Hold sheet of dough up, if it tears, you need to incorporate more flour and get it sturdy enough to hold it's shape when lifted

162) Dumplings

→ 2 cups self-rising flour
→ 1/8 cup vegetable shortening
→ 2/3 cups milk

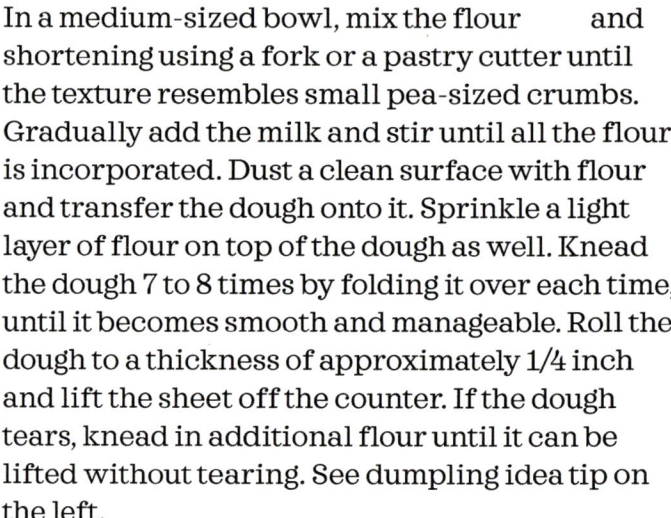

In a medium-sized bowl, mix the flour and shortening using a fork or a pastry cutter until the texture resembles small pea-sized crumbs. Gradually add the milk and stir until all the flour is incorporated. Dust a clean surface with flour and transfer the dough onto it. Sprinkle a light layer of flour on top of the dough as well. Knead the dough 7 to 8 times by folding it over each time, until it becomes smooth and manageable. Roll the dough to a thickness of approximately 1/4 inch and lift the sheet off the counter. If the dough tears, knead in additional flour until it can be lifted without tearing. See dumpling idea tip on the left.

Cut the dough into strips about 1 inch by 2 inches using a pizza cutter or a fork. Lightly dust the pieces with flour to prevent sticking.

To cook the dumplings, add them to boiling chicken broth or a chosen cobbler filling. Reduce the heat to the lowest setting after adding them, cover the pot, and cook for 10 to 15 minutes. Stir the bottom of pot periodically while cooking to prevent broth from sticking.

"These are perfect for sweet potato and blackberry cobblers. I typically use two recipes for chicken and dumplings." -Tammy

163) Pizza Popovers

- → cooking spray (olive oil)
- → frozen Italian-style meatballs
- → mozzarella cheese or Italian cheese blend
- → pizza seasoning
- → pizza sauce or marinara
- → 1/4 cup melted salted butter
- → 2 garlic cloves, pressed
- → 2 refrigerated Pillsbury pizza doughs

Melt butter in a small measuring cup, then mix with pressed garlic and set aside. Spray a 12-cup muffin pan with olive oil. Unroll one package of pizza dough, place it over the pan, and press into each cup, poking holes for shaping. Add 1 tablespoon of marinara sauce to each cup, followed by 2 meatballs, cheese, and pizza seasoning. If using fresh vegetables such as onions or peppers, sauté them beforehand. Cover with the second sheet of dough, cut between cups with a pizza cutter, and fold the dough over the popovers. Brush with garlic butter and, if desired, top with pepperoni. Bake at 350°F for 20-30 minutes, or until golden

164) Hot Cross Buns

- → 2 envelopes active dry yeast (2 1/2 tsp)
- → 1/2 cup very warm water
- → 1/2 cup salted butter
- → 2/3 cup evaporated milk
- → 1/2 cup granulated sugar
- → 1 tsp salt
- → 2 large eggs
- → 1 cup dried fruit (raisins, currants, dates)
- → 4 1/2 cups sifted bread flour
- → 1/4 tsp ground cinnamon
- → 1/4 tsp ground nutmeg

Add yeast to warm water in a large stand mixer bowl; the water should be comfortably warm to the touch. Stir 5 minutes until dissolved. Melt butter and remove from heat. Add sugar, stir to combine, then mix in milk and salt, stirring until the sugar dissolves. Combine this mixture with the yeast. Beat eggs in a small bowl, reserving 2 tablespoons and covering them to prevent drying out. Add the remaining eggs to the yeast mixture. Sift 2 cups of flour and whisk in spices. Attach a dough hook to the mixer and gradually add flour to the yeast mixture, mixing on low speed until a soft, sticky dough forms. Add an additional 2 cups of flour, continue to mix until the dough is sticky but manageable. Transfer to a floured surface and knead in dried fruits until the dough is smooth and elastic, about 5 minutes. Place the dough in a greased bowl, turn to coat, cover with a towel, and let sit in a warm, draftfree location for 1 hour or until doubled in size. Punch down the dough and place it on a floured surface. Divide into two halves, then split each half into 16 balls. Arrange 16 balls in a 9x9x2 inch pan, spray with oil, cover, and allow to rise until doubled. Brush with reserved egg and bake at 350°F for 20-30 minutes, or until golden. Allow to cool and decorate with lemon vanilla glaze in a cross pattern.

Glaze:

- → 1 cup powdered sugar
- → 4 tsp milk
- → 1/4 tsp lemon extract
- → 1/4 tsp vanilla extract

Mix glaze ingredients until smooth and creamy. Put in a piping bag or Ziplock bag and clip off the end to create a circular tip. Pipe icing in a cross pattern on rolls.

"Hot cross buns are traditionally served on Easter. Make it a tradition at your house this year!" -Tammy

165) Irish Soda Bread

- → 2 cups self-rising flour
- → (or if using all-purpose flour add:
    - ▪ 1/2 tsp of salt
    - ▪ 3 tsp baking powder)
- → 1 tsp soda
- → 1/4 cup shortening
- → 1 large egg, beaten
- → 1 cup whole buttermilk or sour cream
- → 1/2 tsp rosemary or carraway seed
- → 1/2 tsp dill

 If using butter instead of shortening, use the same amount, melt the butter, and add it to the beaten egg mixture.

In a bowl, combine flour and baking soda. Add shortening and blend with a fork until crumbly. Mix in egg, milk or sour cream, and spices. Stir to combine. Flour your surface, turn out the dough, knead briefly, and shape into a circle seam-side down. Place in a greased 10-inch cast-iron skillet, cut an X about 1/2 inch deep on top. Bake at 375°F for 30 minutes or increase to 425°F if needed until golden brown. Remove, butter the top, and serve hot.

This is picture of my older Brother Barry, me, and my sister Malissa on Christmas of 1969.

166) Holiday Bread Dressing

- → 1 lb. breakfast sausage, Swaggerty's Farm
- → 2 stalks celery, chopped
- → 1 small onion chopped
- → 1/4 cup salted butter
- → 1/2 cup chopped green onion
- → 4 cups hot water
- → 2 Tbsp chicken bouillon granules
- → 2 large apples, Honeycrisp or Golden Delicious
- → 12 cups stuffing (half cornbread & half herb), used Pepperidge Farm Brand
- → 1 cup fresh cranberries, finely chopped, optional

Preheat the oven to 350°F. In a skillet, cook the sausage, breaking it into small pieces as it browns. Once the sausage is thoroughly browned, add the onion, celery, and butter; sauté for 2-3 minutes. In a separate bowl, whisk together the water and bouillon. Peel, core, and chop the apples. In a large mixing bowl, combine the stuffing mix, chopped apples, and the cooked sausage mixture. If desired, incorporate cranberries at this stage. Mix all ingredients until well combined. Evenly pour the prepared broth over the stuffing and stir to ensure uniform moisture distribution. Transfer the mixture to a well-greased, large baking dish comparable in size to a lasagna pan. Bake for 40 minutes.

"This is delicious. I love the tart cranberries, while Chris would prefer it without them. Give it a try." – *Tammy*

Oh Breakfast, my favorite meal of the day!

I was given so many tools to use in the kitchen from viewers like you! Like some of you, I had never had the pleasure of using these gadgets. They are all very useful for making breakfast! I wanted to show and tell you about them here.

Shop our Best Sellers!

#2 The Jaccard Food Flipper!
I got this amazing gift, and I can't believe I lived without it! It's perfect for flipping bacon, searing meats, and even lifting a whole roast with ease. Seriously, it's a total game changer for browning and handling battered foods. Just a heads up though—don't fall for cheaper alternatives! They might promise a sharp hook, but nothing beats the Jaccard with its ultra-fine point. It's one of the best investments you can make!

Use your phone's camera to scan! When the link appears on your screen, click it to access the site!

#1 The blending fork
I discovered this tool in my first year of cooking on YouTube in 2017, and it's been my top kitchen sidekick ever since! It's a game-changer for blending shortening and butter with flour for delicious treats, and many of you love it for flipping meats and stirring pasta. It is the ultimate blending tool!

https://www.collardvalleycooks.com/

167) 2 Egg Omelet

→ 1 small non-stick fry pan
→ 2 eggs
→ 3 Tbsp milk
→ Salt & black pepper
→ Toppings:
→ ham, diced or cubed
→ shredded cheese, your choice
→ green peppers, diced
→ onions, diced
→ mushrooms, chopped
→ If you use fresh vegetables, sauté them in butter until soft
→ Browned breakfast sausage pieces

Whisk eggs and milk in a small bowl. Preheat a skillet on low, add 1 tablespoon of butter. When melted, pour in eggs. Cook on low, tilt, and gently push edges to let the runny parts flow into the pan.

Recommendation: Place a lid on the skillet and maintain a very low temperature to allow for gentle, slow cooking. This technique ensures the eggs cook evenly without browning on the bottom. Achieving a non-browned finish is recommended, as browning can negatively affect the flavor.

Once the runny parts of the eggs are cooked, add your toppings. Slide the omelet onto a plate, letting the second half fold over into a half-moon shape. Serve topped with shredded cheese and condiments like ketchup, salsa, or your favorite sauce.

> **1Jo 5:3**
> "For this is the love of God, that we keep his commandments: and his commandments are not grievous." KJV

168) Biscuits & Gravy

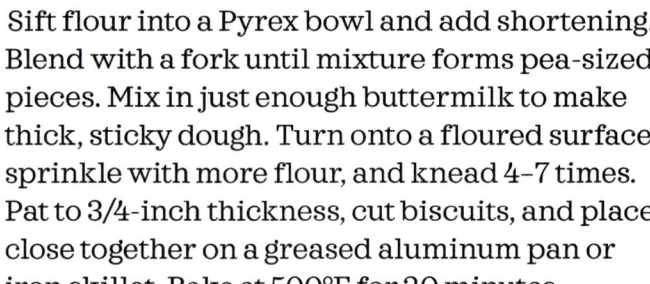

→ 2 cups self-rising flour
→ 1/4 cup shortening, Crisco
→ A pinch baking soda
→ 3/4 to 1 cup whole buttermilk
→ Extra flour for your sifter

Sift flour into a Pyrex bowl and add shortening. Blend with a fork until mixture forms pea-sized pieces. Mix in just enough buttermilk to make thick, sticky dough. Turn onto a floured surface, sprinkle with more flour, and knead 4–7 times. Pat to 3/4-inch thickness, cut biscuits, and place close together on a greased aluminum pan or iron skillet. Bake at 500°F for 20 minutes.

169) Milk & Butter Gravy

→ 1/2 cup self-rising flour
→ 1/2 cup salted butter
→ 1 tsp salt
→ 1/2 tsp black pepper
→ 3 cups whole milk or 2% milk

Melt butter in a large skillet over medium heat, then raise to medium-high. Sift in flour and whisk until smooth; add salt and pepper. Brown the mixture slightly, then pour in milk, stirring constantly to avoid lumps. Once thickened, transfer to a serving dish. If it is too thick, whisk in more milk until desired consistency is reached.

"Mama made biscuits and gravy with cantaloupe for supper during the summer. We loved this combo then, and it remains a favorite of ours to this day. If you have not tried this pairing, I recommend it. The sweetness of cantaloupe complements the savory gravy."
-Tammy

170) Broccoli Cheese Quiche

→ 1 pie shell
→ 1/2 lb. broccoli, chopped small
→ 1/2 cup diced cooked ham, optional
→ 1/4 cup onion, diced, optional
→ 1-1/2 cups shredded cheese
→ 4 large eggs, beaten
→ 1 cup half-and-half
→ 1/2 tsp onion powder
→ 1/2 cup mayonnaise (or 1/2 cup salted butter, melted)
→ 1/2 tsp black pepper
→ 1/4 cup self-rising flour

Pre-bake the pie shell at 400°F for 20 minutes, then reduce the oven temperature to 350°F. Fill shell with broccoli, optional ingredients, and 1 cup of cheese. Mix eggs, half and half, onion powder, mayonnaise (or butter), pepper, and flour; beat well. Pour the mixture over the broccoli and top with 1/2 cup cheese. Bake at 350°F for 40 minutes.

The Smell of Breakfast

My feet hit the floor as soon as mama's did when I was little. I could smell the bacon and sausage, and it always woke me up. I was the only kid who got up earlier than I had to. I couldn't wait to sit by the bottom of the refrigerator and feel the warmth coming from the motor. It was my favorite place to be in the morning, sitting there watching my beautiful mama cook breakfast. It's comforting now just thinking about it. Where were your favorite places to be when you were a child? Even if you have bad memories, hopefully you can focus on a few good times.

The Lord tells us to think on good things. Let your mind go to these places instead of drifting to the negative thoughts throughout the day. God is good and worthy to be Praised!

171) Breakfast Pizza

→ 1 cup all-purpose flour
→ 1/2 tsp salt
→ 2 large eggs
→ 2/3 cup milk
→ Bacon or breakfast sausage
→ 10.25-inch cast iron skillet

Mix the ingredients thoroughly by beating them with a fork or whisk. Pour into a well-greased 10- to 12-inch cast iron skillet (greased with shortening or meat drippings). Add browned sausage and bacon on top of the runny crust. Bake for 20 minutes at 425°F. The crust will pull away from the sides of the pan.

Make Recipe # 172 One Cup Gravy Recipe

Once the crust has baked, remove it from the oven and top with gravy.

→ 5 large eggs
→ 1-1/2 cups cheese, shredded
→ toppings of your choice

Crack eggs on top of the pizza. Season the eggs with salt and pepper. Place in a 450-degree oven and bake for 10 minutes. Open, add the cheese on top, and cook for an additional 5-10 minutes.

Option: add additional toppings and seasonings if desired.

172) One Cup Gravy Recipe

→ 1/8 cup meat drippings
→ 1/8 cup all-purpose or self-rising flour
→ 1 cup milk
→ dash of salt and black pepper

Add flour to the bottom of the skillet where you fried your meat. Stir with a whisk. Add milk, salt, and pepper. When the gravy boils, turn off the heat.

Grease a 9" x 13" pan. In a skillet, brown half of the hashbrowns with half of the butter until golden on both sides, then place them in the baking dish. Repeat with the remaining hashbrowns and butter. Season with salt and pepper, then add to the dish. Cook the sausage until browned, break it into small pieces, then add the onion and cook until browned. Spread evenly over the potatoes. Beat the eggs with milk, pour over the casserole, then top with shredded cheese. Bake at 350°F for 60 minutes.

 Option: You do not have to brown the hashbrowns. Just add the butter to the casserole and then the potatoes.

173) Casserole, Chris's Breakfast

→ 7 frozen hashbrowns
→ 8 large eggs
→ 3/4 cup milk
→ 1 medium onion, diced
→ 1/2 cup bell pepper, diced
→ 3/4 lb. (or 7 sausage patties), used Swaggerty's Farm brand
→ 1-1/2 cups grated cheese

In the egg mixture:

→ 1/2 tsp salt
→ 1/4 tsp black pepper

Brown the hashbrowns as directed on the package. Fry and separate the sausage. Mix eggs with milk, salt, pepper, onion, and bell pepper. Spray a large casserole dish with spray. Layer the hashbrowns, then half of the cheese. Pour the egg mixture over, add the sausage, and top with the remaining hashbrowns and cheese. Bake at 350°F for 1 hour until set.

 Note: Pierce the casserole with a large spoon and pull it back to see if all the liquid from the eggs is set. Do not serve with raw eggs. It could take longer to cook in your oven.

174) Breakfast Hashbrowns Casserole

→ 30 oz. frozen hashbrowns, thawed
→ 1/2 cup salted butter
→ 1/2 tsp black pepper
→ 1/2 tsp salt
→ 1 lb. pork breakfast sausage, used Swaggerty's Farm brand
→ 1/2 cup onion, diced
→ 9 large or 12 medium eggs
→ 1 cup heavy cream or half and half
→ 8 oz. cheddar cheese, shredded
→ 4 oz. pepper jack cheese, shredded

175) Fireman's Breakfast Casserole

→ 12 large eggs
→ 1 cup heavy cream or half and half
→ 16 oz. Cheddar cheese, shredded or other cheese can be used
→ 1 lb. pork breakfast sausage, used Swaggerty's Farm brand
→ 1 small can mushrooms, optional
→ 1/2 large onion, chopped
→ 1 green pepper, chopped
→ salt and black pepper
→ 2 Tbsp salted butter

Grease a 9-inch by 13-inch pan. Crack the eggs into the pan and poke each yolk or lightly scramble. Pour the cream over the eggs. Add half of the grated cheese. Brown the sausage and drain. Add onions, peppers, and mushrooms to the sausage and cook with butter. Spread the sausage mixture evenly over the eggs and top with the remaining cheese. Bake at 350°F for 1 hour until set.

176) Cinnamon Rolls, Shortcut

→ 1 tube refrigerated pizza dough
→ 1/3 cup sugar
→ 2 Tbsp ground cinnamon
→ 6 Tbsp salted butter, room temperature

Preheat your oven to 375°F. Combine cinnamon, butter, and sugar until smooth. Roll out the dough and spread the cinnamon filling evenly over it. Roll the dough from the shorter side to create more layers. Slice into 1-inch pieces and place on a parchment-lined baking sheet. Bake for 30 minutes. Meanwhile, prepare the butter glaze. Once baked, remove the cinnamon rolls from the oven and coat them with Recipe # 177 Butter Glaze. Enjoy!

177) Butter glaze for Sweet Breads

→ 1-1/2 cups powdered sugar
→ 1/2 tsp vanilla extract
→ 3 Tbsp melted salted butter
→ 1/3 cup milk or heavy cream
→ 1/4 tsp salt

Mix until creamy. Spread on warm rolls.

178) Egg in a Hole

→ 1 large egg
→ 1 slice of bread
→ salted butter
→ shredded cheese
→ 2" cookie or biscuit cutter
→ salt & black pepper

Butter both sides of a bread slice. Use a 2-inch round cookie or biscuit cutter to cut out the center of the bread. Brown one side in a moderately hot non-stick skillet. Then flip it over and crack an egg into the hole. Sprinkle the egg with salt and black pepper. Cook until the whites are set. Cover the skillet to help the egg whites cook completely done.

Tip: For a perfectly cooked egg, crack it directly onto the bread as soon as you place it in the skillet. This allows the egg to cook while both sides of the bread are browning. Feel free to brown the circles as well.

One method is to sprinkle shredded cheese on top and allow it to melt as the last side browns. Various cutters can be used for different occasions, such as a heart shape for Valentine's Day.

179) Coffee Cake, Banana

→ 1/2 cup salted butter
→ 1 cup granulated sugar
→ 2 large eggs
→ 3 ripe bananas, mashed
→ 1 tsp vanilla extract
→ 1/2 cup sour cream
→ 1/2 tsp cinnamon
→ 2 cups self-rising flour

Preheat the oven to 350°F. Cream the butter, then gradually mix in the sugar. Beat in the eggs one at a time. Add mashed bananas, vanilla, cinnamon, and sour cream, then mix thoroughly. Gradually add the flour until fully combined. Pour the batter into a well-greased 13x9x2 aluminum cake pan. Top with Recipe # 180 Streusel Topping, then bake for 45 minutes or until a cake tester inserted in the center comes out clean. Let the cake cool on a rack for 10 minutes. Since it has a topping, serve it directly from the pan. Enjoy!

180) Streusel Topping for Cakes

→ 1 cup chopped nuts
→ 1/2 cup light brown sugar
→ 1 tsp cinnamon

Combine and set aside; this streusel is ideal for sheet cakes. Simply sprinkle it over the batter and bake as directed for a sweet, crunchy topping—no frosting needed. See the Sour Cream Banana Pound Cake picture below.

Over-easy — Over denotes the flipping of the egg. Easy denotes the doneness of the yolk.

"Chris tends to get upset when he orders this and is served an egg that is not cooked. The white should be cooked, and the yolk should stay runny." -*Tammy*

181) Coffeecake, Cherry

- → 1/4 cup salted butter, room temperature
- → 1 pkg. white cake mix
- → 1/4 oz. Packet dry yeast, 2 1/4 tsp.
- → 1 cup all-purpose flour
- → 2 large eggs
- → 21 oz. can cherry pie filling
- → 2 Tbsp granulated sugar
- → 8 oz. cream cheese, cubed, optional

Preheat the oven to 375°F; if using convection, set it to 350°F. Reserve 1/2 cup of dry cake mix in a bowl. In a large bowl, combine the remaining cake mix, yeast, flour, eggs, and 2/3 cup warm water, then mix until well blended. Spread the dough in a greased 13x9-inch pan. In another bowl, mix the reserved cake mix with butter and sugar to make the streusel; it will be crumbly. Set aside. Spoon pie filling in three rows; add cubed cream cheese on top if desired. Sprinkle streusel in four rows. Bake at 375°F for 30 minutes.

Glaze Topping: mix up and pour onto cake.

- → 1 cup confectioner's sugar (sift if lumpy)
- → 1 Tbsp corn syrup
- → 2 Tbsp water

182) Eggs Over Easy

- → 2 large eggs
- → 2 Tbsp salted butter
- → salt & black pepper

Use a small skillet that fits two fried eggs with minimal space left. Preheat the skillet on low to medium heat while melting butter. Crack your egg into the skillet with the butter. Salt and pepper the egg. Cook on medium to low heat until the whites are just set. Carefully slide your spatula underneath the yellow part of the egg and flip. Cook just until the whites are no longer clear and the yolk is still runny. Carefully remove the egg from the skillet and place it on a plate.

183) Coffeecake, Strawberry

- → 1/2 cup granulated sugar
- → 2 large eggs
- → 3 Tbsp salted butter, melted
- → 1 tsp vanilla extract
- → 3/4 cup buttermilk or milk
- → 1-1/2 cups self-rising flour

In a mixing bowl, combine the ingredients listed above in the order they are given, mixing after each addition. Set aside and prepare your pan: pan size should be 7x11 or 9x9, sprayed with cooking or baking spray.

- → 16 oz. strawberries, frozen or fresh
- → 1/2 cup chopped pecans
- → 4 Tbsp salted butter, melted
- → 1/3 cup granulated sugar

Place slices of strawberries, pecans, and butter in the bottom of the pan. Sprinkle sugar over the fruit and nuts, mixing with a spatula to distribute evenly. Pour the cake batter into the pan. Bake at 350°F until golden brown, about 25-30 minutes. When it is done, remove the cake from the oven and let it cool for 5 minutes. Then, flip it out (upside down) like you would with an upside-down cake. Use a spatula to help and adjust any fruit as needed. If it sticks, scoop it onto the cake. Do not worry if it is not perfect because it is so good! Enjoy your breakfast cake!

"Feel free to substitute different fruit like blueberries for the coffee cake." - *Tammy*

184) Egg Sandwich

→ 2 slices of bread
→ salted butter, room temperature
→ 1 large egg
→ salt & black pepper
→ 1 slice of cheese
→ mayonnaise or preserves, optional

Spread butter on one side of the bread and broil on low until golden brown. While monitoring the bread, melt butter in a non-stick skillet, add an egg, season to taste, break the yolk, and cook until set on both sides. Place a slice of cheese on the untoasted side of the toasted bread, add the cooked egg, assemble the sandwich, and cut before serving.

"I have been told this is the best egg sandwich they have ever had! I think you should try it." -Tammy

185) Grits, Creamy

→ 3/4 cup quick grits
→ 1-1/2 cup milk
→ 2 cups water
→ 3-4 Tbsp salted butter
→ 1/4 tsp black pepper
→ 1/2 tsp salt
→ 3 Tbsp granulated sugar, optional

Place the grits, milk, and water in a batter bowl. If you do not have a batter bowl, use a tall, microwave-safe container to prevent the grits from boiling over and making a mess in the microwave!

Place the grits in the microwave and cook on high for 3 minutes. Remove and stir well. Return to the microwave and cook for another 3 minutes. Continue cooking for 2-minute intervals until they are creamy. Take out, then add butter, pepper, salt, and sugar. Mix well. The grits should have a pourable consistency when served. If they thicken before serving, add enough water to make them creamy again. Enjoy!

"Using the Microwave for grits is fantastic! The grits come out nice and creamy, making every bite a delight. If you have not already, consider getting a batter bowl—it is a game changer for making grits, puddings, and so much more. You are going to love it." - Tammy

186) Hard Boiled Eggs

→ water
→ large eggs

In a small saucepan, add water until it is about 2 inches high. Cover and bring to boil. Use a slotted spoon to add each egg. Set a timer for 12 minutes for large eggs and 10 minutes for medium ones. When the timer goes off, remove the pot from heat and rinse the eggs thoroughly with cold water. Cover eggs with cold water and add 2 cups of ice and stir. These should peel very easily! The trick is to add eggs to boiling water. It works with room temperature or cold, refrigerated eggs.

 If you are using these for deviled eggs, lay them on their sides in the refrigerator 24 hours before boiling. This helps center the yolk in the eggs.

"If your eggs crack when you add them to boiling water, it is usually because the shells are quite thin. To help prevent this, consider choosing a higher-quality egg when you are preparing for a special occasion. Options like Egg land's Best or cage-free eggs often have sturdier shells, making your cooking experience smoother. -Tammy

73

187) Cinnamon Roll French Toast

→ 1-1/2 cups milk
→ 3 large eggs (whisk before adding)
→ 1 tsp ground cinnamon

Whisk the ingredients together and put them in a shallow dish large enough to dip bread into. I prefer to use a pie plate.

→ 1" large gourmet cinnamon rolls (slice rolls in half)
→ salted butter
→ cinnamon sugar

 Note: iced sides of cinnamon rolls and cinnamon sugar-coated sides will brown faster because of the sugar, so be careful and adjust the temperature if needed.

The most popular ratio for cinnamon sugar is 4:1. Mix 1 tablespoon of cinnamon with 4 Tbsp sugar.

Use a large non-stick skillet - two slices of rolls should fit comfortably. Preheat the skillet over medium heat. When you slice the rolls, icing will be visible on top. Scrape off most of the icing before dipping the egg.

Dip the roll into the egg mixture and flip. Repeat to coat both sides twice. If desired, sprinkle cinnamon sugar on the sides of the roll. Place 1 tablespoon of butter in a skillet for each bread slice, then add the rolls to the preheated, buttered skillet. Cook until the egg is set and the roll is light brown, then flip and cook the other side. Remove from the skillet and place it on your plate. Drizzle or spread with

Cream Cheese Spread.

→ 4 oz. cream cheese, room temperature
→ 3 Tbsp salted butter, room temperature
→ 1 cup powdered sugar

Mix the ingredients above thoroughly until smooth and creamy.

188) French Toast

→ 1-1/2 cups milk or orange juice
→ 3 large eggs
→ 1 tsp vanilla extract
→ 1 tsp cinnamon
→ 1/4 tsp nutmeg, optional
→ 2 Tbsp granulated sugar

In a medium bowl, whisk the ingredients together and place in a shallow dish large enough for dipping bread. I like to use a pie plate.

→ Loaf of bread, works great with thick slices
→ 1 Tbsp salted butter per piece of toast
→ Powdered sugar
→ Pancake syrup

Use a skillet large enough to hold at least two pieces of bread. Preheat the skillet on medium heat. Put butter in the bottom of the skillet. Dip each slice of bread into the milk mixture and flip quickly; repeat for both sides, dipping twice. Place the toast in the preheated, buttered skillet. Cook until the egg is cooked and the bread is light brown. Flip and cook the other side. Remove it from the skillet and place it on a serving plate. Sprinkle with a dusting of powdered sugar. Serve with bacon, sausage, pancake syrup, and fresh fruit!

"This breakfast is quick and easy! It is so delicious, especially when served with bacon or sausage— Swaggerty's Farm is my favorite! I personally adore French toast and usually do not use syrup; instead, I like to sprinkle it with cinnamon sugar or powdered sugar and enjoy it with some fresh fruit pieces. The Cinnamon Roll Frech Toast is something I got while on vacation! Oh, my goodness, I fell in love and had to put it in my cookbook!" - *Tammy*

189) Hashbrowns

- → 2 Tbsp cooking oil
- → 2 Tbsp salted butter
- → 1 medium potato
- → 1/8 cup chopped onion, optional
- → 1/4 cup shredded cheddar cheese
- → Salt and black pepper
- → 8-inch non-stick skillet

 Note: water on the potatoes will cause the oil to pop excessively. Dry them well. Each medium potato makes 1 serving.

Wash and scrub the potato, leaving skins on if you like. If not, peel the potato. Dry it with a towel or paper towel. Using a hand grater, grate the potato. It is best to wear safety gloves while using the grater. Soak the grated potatoes in ice water for 10-15 minutes. Drain the potatoes and dry them with paper towels. Add oil and butter to a skillet. Carefully add the potatoes to the preheated skillet. Season with salt and pepper. Cook on medium heat until golden brown, then flip with a large spatula. Cook both sides until done. Serve with breakfast or a sandwich. Sprinkle with cheese if desired.

190) Oatmeal, Microwave

- → 1 cup quick oats (1-minute)
- → 2 cups milk
- → 1/4 cup salted butter
- → 2 tablespoons sugar, granulated or brown
- → 1/2 teaspoon salt

Warning: Oats will rise while cooking, so use a TALL bowl - I like to use a glass batter bowl. Put oats and milk in a large microwave-safe bowl. Place the bowl in the microwave and cook for 3 minutes. Take it out and stir well. Oatmeal should be very moist and almost runny. (Add enough water to achieve this if necessary). Then, cook for another 2 minutes on high. Take it out, add sugar, butter, and stir. Add salt and serve warm.

"I will always remember the moment when my daddy started paying attention to his cholesterol levels. He was not much of a cook before, but suddenly, he began making his own oatmeal every morning. I was in my twenties at the time. He would add raisins and nuts, and he would do it with such pride, telling me about what he put in it. I felt a warm sense of pride for him, too."- *Tammy*

191) Pancakes & Sausage

- → 1/4 cup melted salted butter
- → 2 cups whole buttermilk (or 1 3/4 cup low-fat buttermilk)
- → 2 Tbsp sugar
- → 1 large egg
- → 2 cups self-rising flour
- → 1 tsp vanilla extract

Use a glass or microwave-safe bowl. Microwave butter the bottom of the bowl. Add sugar and mix well. Add egg, vanilla, and buttermilk, then whisk thoroughly. Add flour and whisk again. Preheat a non-stick skillet over medium heat. The skillet should have a flat surface. If it is a good one, I prefer not to grease it. If you are using an older skillet, spray it with cooking spray before making pancakes.

Add a 1/2 cup scoop of batter to the skillet and gently spread into a circle. Wait for the pancake to become bubbly across the entire surface before flipping with a flat spatula. Brown both sides.

Adjust the temperature as needed for your desired level of browning. I use medium on a gas stove. Serve with butter and pancake syrup.

 Option: Use regular milk instead of buttermilk. Pancakes will be thinner. Use a 1/3 cup scoop of mix for each pancake instead of 1/2 cup.

"Chris is the pancake King in our family! He loves pancakes more than French toast and always makes them every Sunday morning while all the girls are getting ready for church. It is a special family tradition for us, and you cannot eat pancakes without some Swaggerty's Farm breakfast sausage!" – '*Tammy*

192) Sausage & Egg Pie

→ 1 pie shell
→ 1/2 lb. breakfast sausage, used Swaggerty's Farm
→ 1 small onion diced, optional
→ 1-1/2 cups cheddar cheese, shredded
→ 4 large eggs, beaten
→ 1 cup half and half
→ 1/2 tsp onion powder
→ 1/4 cup salted butter, melted
→ 1/2 tsp black pepper
→ 1/4 cup self-rising flour

Pre-bake the pie shell at 400°F for 20 minutes, then reduce the temperature to 350°F. Cook sausage with onion, drain. Mix eggs, half-andhalf, onion powder, butter, and pepper. Then, add flour and whisk until smooth. Stir in sausage, onion, and 1 cup cheese. Pour into shell. Bake at 350°F for 40 min, top with remaining cheese, and bake 20 min. The pie must rise in the middle as high as it is on the sides to be done. It could take longer.

Important: if using all-purpose flour, add 1/2 tsp baking powder.

193) Sausage Milk Gravy

→ 1/2 cup self-rising flour
→ 1/4 cup shortening

→ 1/4 cup salted butter
→ 1 tsp salt
→ 1/2 tsp black pepper
→ 3 cups milk
→ 1/2 lb. Swaggerty's Farm breakfast sausage, browned

Begin with a large, 10" cast iron that is 3" deep or 12" skillet. Brown and crumble the sausage, then set aside. Melt shortening over medium heat, raise to high, and add butter. Quickly sift flour into the pan, whisking until combined. Add salt and pepper; let it brown slightly. Pour in milk, stirring constantly. Return sausage to the pan and whisk to avoid lumps. Pour gravy as it thickens— it will continue to thicken. If needed, add more milk and whisk to adjust consistency.

Gravy will bubble and rise, so make sure your skillet it large enough or you will have a mess.

194) Waffles, Mama's

→ 1/4 cup salted butter, melted
→ 3 large eggs, separated
→ 2 cups sifted self-rising flour
→ 1 tsp vanilla extract
→ 2 cups buttermilk
→ 2 Tbsp granulated sugar

Melt butter in a batter bowl. Add buttermilk, egg yolks, and vanilla, then whisk until well combined. In a separate bowl, beat egg whites until stiff peaks form. Turn on the waffle iron to preheat. Sift flour into the batter and mix thoroughly. Pour the batter into a larger bowl, then gently fold in the egg whites. Add 1/2 cup of batter to the waffle iron and cook until it reaches your preferred color. (I prefer mine dark!) You can also prepare a batch ahead, transfer them to a wire rack to prevent sogginess, and reheat in the waffle iron or air fryer for extra crispy waffles. These freeze well!

Tammy's
Fruit Cake
Recipe 216

Cakes from Scratch Recipes

Welcome to Tammy's Homemade Cake Recipe

Share the Love of Sugar With the People You Love Most!

"Mama began making cakes when I was young, and by the time I left elementary school, she was decorating wedding cakes. She was very talented, and we were used to her baking cake layers and making large batches of icing every weekend. Once I reached middle school, I started helping her cater weddings and rehearsal dinners. She took great pride in her work and was always preparing delicious food at home.

I found her white cake layer recipe written on the inside cover of one of her favorite cookbooks, and I've included it in this cookbook. I spent many hours researching cakes and different recipes before developing my own cake layer recipes. Many in this section are my original creations, including the carrot, German chocolate, spice, chocolate coffee, red velvet, hummingbird, buttery fruitcake, apple stack cake, and several others.

Homemade cake has a different texture than cake mix. If you're looking for that spongy, moist texture, add a 3.4 oz. package of vanilla instant pudding to your homemade layer cake. For a moister pound cake, like those bought in stores, incorporate one 14 oz. can of sweetened condensed milk into the batter. If you decide to use the pudding or condensed milk, you do not have to alter the recipe.

Don't forget, you can mix things up with the liquids too! Whether you prefer coffee, milk, water, or even fruit juice, feel free to swap them around. The same goes for the fats—you can use cooking oil, shortening, butter, or a mix of them! Baking a cake is easier than you might think, so have fun with it, y'all! Happy baking!" -*Tammy*

195) 5 Flavor Pound Cake, Mark's

→ 1 cup salted butter
→ 1/2 cup butter-flavored shortening
→ 3 cups sugar
→ 5 eggs, well beaten
→ 3 cups all-purpose flour
→ 1/2 tsp baking powder
→ 1 tsp salt
→ 1/2 cup buttermilk
→ 1/2 cup evaporated milk or half and half
→ 1 tsp each extract: rum, butter, lemon, vanilla, and coconut

Cream butter, shortening, and sugar until fluffy. Beat eggs until pale yellow and add. Mix flour with baking powder and salt, then add to the creamed mixture alternately with milk. Stir in flavorings. Pour into a greased 10-inch tube pan and bake at 325°F for 1-1/2 hours, or until done. Cool 10 minutes before removing it from the pan. Top with recipe #196 Five Flavor Glaze if desired.

196) Five Flavor Glaze

→ 1/2 cup granulated sugar
→ 1/4 cup water
→ 1/2 tsp each extract: rum, butter, lemon, vanilla, and coconut.

Mix ingredients and heat to boiling; boil for 2 minutes. Pour over the hot cake.

197) Mama's Angel Food Cake

→ 1-1/2 cups confectioner's sugar
→ 1 cup all-purpose flour
→ 1-1/2 cups egg whites, room temperature
→ 1-1/2 tsp cream of tartar
→ 1 tsp almond extract
→ 1 tsp vanilla extract
→ 1/4 tsp salt
→ 1 cup granulated sugar

Sift confectioners' sugar and flour into separate bowls. In a stand mixer, beat egg whites, cream of tartar, extracts, and salt, gradually adding granulated sugar until stiff peaks form. Fold onethird of the egg whites with one-third of the dry ingredients in a large bowl; repeat until everything is combined. Pour into an ungreased tube pan and bake at 375°F for 40 minutes, or until the cake springs back. Invert the pan to cool completely, then loosen the cake with a flat knife.

 Great served with Recipe #421 Strawberry Topping and Whipping Cream or Cool Whip!

This cake requires a tube pan that has two parts. Do not use an Angel food pan for a pound cake or regular cake mix. It can only be used for Sponge & Angel Food Cakes. When using a regular batter it will ooze out of the cracks and make a mess in the oven.

"This 5 Flavor Pound Cake recipe comes from my friend Mark Fuller, a Marietta, Georgia resident, and skilled pianist who sells cakes.

Discover Mark's Gospel Music page on Facebook by scanning the qr code!

A trip to the North Georgia Apple Orchards!

As a child, visiting the apple orchards in North Georgia was a cherished family ritual. Often, Mama's homemakers club would head out together, and joining them felt like a delightful privilege. It was a day filled with adventure, returning home with bushels brimming with tasty apples!

Keep Precious Memories Alive!

North Georgia boasts more than 10 delightful apple orchards. If you grew up in the neighboring states, it's likely your family also took trips to pick apples. Unlike my grandmother, who had her own apple tree, it was crucial for my mom to stock up on apples for the freezer! Nothing ushers in the fall quite like the aroma of apple pies, apple cakes, fried apple pies, and just simple fried apples on a plate. While many enjoyed them fresh during the season, a lot of folks peeled them and laid them out to dry in the sun. After drying, they would freeze the apples, using them throughout the year, and often, by the time it was time for another trip, their stock would be completely gone!

Apple varieties for baking cakes

Use your phone's camera to scan! When the link appears on your screen, click it to access the site!

https://www.collardvalleycooks.com/

198) Applesauce Cake

→ 1 cup shortening
→ 1-1/2 cups granulated sugar
→ 2 large eggs, room temperature
→ 1-1/2 cups sweetened applesauce
→ 1 tsp cinnamon
→ 1/4 tsp nutmeg
→ 1/2 tsp salt
→ 1 tsp baking soda
→ 1 tsp baking powder
→ 2 cups all-purpose flour (or use self-rising flour and omit salt, baking soda, and baking powder)
→ 1/2 cup golden raisins
→ 1/2 cup chopped walnuts

Cream shortening and sugar. Add eggs, applesauce, cinnamon, nutmeg, salt, baking soda, baking powder. Mix well. Gradually add flour, half a cup at a time. Dust raisins and walnuts in flour. Fold in raisins and walnuts. Divide batter between two greased and floured 8- or 9-inch pans. Bake at 325°F for 30-40 minutes, or until golden and set (a toothpick inserted in the center comes out clean). Frost with Recipe #208 Cream Cheese Frosting!

199) Apple Dapple Cake

→ 1-1/2 cup salad oil
→ 2 cups granulated sugar
→ 3 large eggs
→ 3 cups all-purpose flour
→ 1 tsp. baking soda
→ 1 tsp salt
→ tsp vanilla extract
→ 3 cups apples, peeled & chopped
→ 1 cup sweetened flaked coconut
→ 1 cup pecans, chopped

Preheat oven to 325°F. Mix the oil, sugar, and eggs until blended. Add flour, soda, salt, and vanilla. Blend for 2 minutes with mixer. Stir in the apples, coconut, and nuts. Bake in a well-greased tube pan for 90 minutes. Remove it from oven and let it cool completely before flipping out of the pan.

Topping:

→ 1 cup of light brown sugar, packed
→ 1/2 cup salted butter
→ 1/2 cup milk

Heat until boiling. Stir 2 minutes. Pour over cake and enjoy!

 Any apple can be used, however, it is recommended that you use an apple that is both sweet and tart. Not a granny smith. I would recommend Golden Delicious, Honeycrisp, & Rome Beauty

"This recipe was given to me by my Aunt Shirley Benefield. This was my uncle Noah's favorite cake. I felt it fitting to include in my Master Cookbook!" -*Tammy*

200) Apple Skillet Cake

→ 4 Tbsp salted butter
→ 2/3 cup packed light brown sugar
→ 3 large, firm Golden Delicious apples, sliced thin
→ 1/2 tsp cinnamon with 1/4 cup sugar

Melt butter in cast iron skillet, add brown sugar & sliced apples. Sprinkle with Cinnamon Sugar if desired.

→ 1/2 cup shortening
→ 1/2 cup light brown sugar, packed
→ 1 cup granulated sugar
→ 2 large eggs, room temperature
→ 1-1/2 cups self-rising flour
→ 3/4 cup buttermilk
→ 1 tsp vanilla extract

Cream the shortening and sugars, then add eggs one at a time. Mix remaining ingredients for 2 minutes. Spray skillet well. Pour batter over apples. Bake 35-45 minutes at 350°F. Using oven mitts, flip onto a plate immediately. Use spatula to position apples. Enjoy! Apples tend to darken over time, so it is best to serve them on the day you make them if you are bringing them to an event. Use a 12" cast iron skillet, or 3" deep 10" cast iron skillet. Batter will run over in a regular 10-inch skillet.

201) Apple Stack Cake, Tammy's

For the Layers:
- → 1-1/4 cup shortening
- → 3 1/2 cups granulated sugar
- → 2 large eggs, room temperature
- → 1/2 cup sorghum molasses
- → 1/2 cup buttermilk
- → 1 tsp each cinnamon & ground ginger
- → 1/2 tsp nutmeg
- → 1 tsp vanilla extract
- → 5 cups self-rising flour
- → 1/2 tsp each baking soda & salt

Cream the shortening and sugar until fluffy, then add eggs and mix. Add the remaining ingredients in the order listed above. Add flour one cup at a time, mixing well after each addition. Place one cup of batter in well-greased 8-inch round cake pans, or 1 1/4 cups if using 9-inch pans. Bake at 350°F for 15 to 20 minutes. Makes 5-7 layers depending on pan size.

Option: If using all-purpose, add 2 Tbsp baking powder and 1 1/2 tsp salt

For the Apples:
- → 5 cups dried apples
- → 3/4 tsp cinnamon
- → 3/4 tsp nutmeg
- → 1/2 tsp allspice
- → 3/4 cup salted butter
- → 3/4 cup light brown sugar, packed
- → 3 cups water & 1/2 tsp salt

Combine the ingredients in a large pot and simmer on low until the apples are semitransparent and soft. Place the filling between each cake layer and on top of the cake. Let it sit in a cool dry place (not refrigerator) for at least 24-48 hours to absorb the juice of apples. Refrigerate afterward, wrapping it airtight. Important: Cake is best served at room temperature.

202) Banana Pound Cake, Malissa's

- → 3 tsp plus 3 cups sugar, divided
- → 1 cup salted butter, softened
- → 6 large eggs, room temperature
- → 1 cup mashed ripe bananas (about 2 medium)
- → 1-1/2 tsp vanilla extract
- → 1/2 tsp lemon extract
- → 3 cups all-purpose flour
- → 1 tsp salt
- → 1/4 tsp baking soda
- → 1 cup sour cream

Glaze:
- → 1-1/2 cups confectioner's sugar
- → 1/2 tsp vanilla extract
- → 3 to 4 tsp milk

Grease a 10-inch fluted tube pan with lots of shortening and sprinkle with 3 teaspoons sugar; set aside. In a large bowl, cream butter and 3 cups sugar until fluffy, about 5-7 minutes. Add eggs one at a time, beating well after each addition, then stir in the bananas and extracts. Mix flour, salt, and baking soda; add to the creamed mixture alternately with sour cream, just until combined. Pour it into the pan. Bake at 325°F until a toothpick inserted near the center comes out clean, about 75-85 minutes. Cool for 10 minutes, then remove from pan onto a wire rack. Whisk glaze ingredients and drizzle over the cake. Store refrigerated; freeze up to a month.

 This cake tends to stick use lots of shortening in place of cooking spray.

"This banana cake recipe came from my sister, Malissa Benefield. She got it from an old Taste of Home magazine. It is the best banana pound cake I have ever tasted! I hope you try it." - *Tammy*

203) Banana Custard Cake, Tammy's

- → 1/2 cup shortening
- → 1-1/2 cups granulated sugar
- → 3 large eggs, divided
- → 3 ripe bananas
- → 1/2 cup buttermilk
- → 2 cups self-rising flour
- → 1 tsp vanilla extract
- → 32 oz. heavy cream, non-sweetened

Preheat the oven to 350°F. In a bowl with an electric mixer, blend shortening and sugar until light and fluffy. Add egg yolks, bananas, and buttermilk; mix thoroughly. Gradually incorporate the flour, stirring for 2 minutes. Transfer the batter to a large bowl. Wash and dry the original bowl, then beat the egg whites until stiff peaks form. Gently fold the egg whites into the batter. Pour the mixture into three greased and floured round cake pans. Bake until a toothpick inserted in the center comes out clean, for about 25 minutes. Allow to cool, then invert onto parchment paper and wire racks. Fill layers with Recipe #204 Banana Custard and ice sides with whipped cream. Additionally, top the cake with custard as in picture above.

204) Banana Custard

- → 1 cup evaporated milk
- → 1 cup water
- → 1/3 cup self-rising flour
- → 1/2 cup granulated sugar
- → 3 large egg yolks
- → 1 cup mashed ripe bananas

Combine the flour and sugar in a glass batter bowl and whisk until smooth. Add milk, water, and egg yolks, whisk after each addition. Mix in mashed bananas. Microwave on high for 3 minutes, then stir well, scraping the bottom and sides of the bowl. Return to the microwave and cook for 1-minute intervals until the mixture is thick and creamy. Cool in a shallow dish.

Use as a filling in between cake layers or in a banana cream pie. (Cool filling before adding sliced bananas if applicable)

205) Brown Beauty Cake

- → 1/2 cup semi-sweet chocolate chips
- → 1/2 cup butterscotch chips
- → 1/4 cup boiling water
- → 1/2 cup shortening
- → 1-1/2 cups granulated sugar
- → 3 large eggs
- → 2 1/4 cups self-rising flour
- → 1/2 cup buttermilk

Preheat the oven to 350°F. Grease the round cake pans well and lightly dust them with flour. In a separate bowl, stir the chocolate and butterscotch with hot water until the chocolate is melted. In another bowl, add the shortening and sugar and beat with an electric mixer. Add the eggs and chocolate and continue beating for another minute at medium speed. Add 1 cup of flour, mix, then incorporate the buttermilk. Next, add the remaining flour and mix on medium speed for 2 minutes. Bake in round layers for 3035 minutes until a toothpick inserted in the center comes out clean. Frost with Recipe #206.

206) Brown Beauty Frosting

Tip: If you are frosting a 13x9x2 sheet cake, you can reduce this recipe to half.

- → 2 cups semi-sweet chocolate chips
- → 2 cups butterscotch chips
- → 1 cup strong coffee
- → 2 lb. powdered sugar
- → 1/4 tsp salt

Combine the chocolate pieces and coffee in a saucepan. Stir over low heat until the chocolate is just melted. Remove from heat; stir in confectioners' sugar and salt. Beat until smooth, glossy, and easy to spread. If it is not shiny, stir in a few drops of hot water.

207) Carrot Cake, Tammy's

→ 2 1/2 cups granulated sugar
→ 4 large eggs, room temperature
→ 2 tsp vanilla extract
→ 1 cup cooking oil *see note below (or 1 cup salted butter, melted)
→ 2 tsp cinnamon
→ 1/2 tsp ground ginger
→ 1/2 tsp nutmeg, optional
→ 2 1/4 cups self-rising flour
→ 1/2 tsp. salt
→ 1 cup chopped pecans
→ 3 cups peeled carrots, grated.
→ 8 oz. can crushed pineapple with juice
→ 1/2 cup golden raisins (tossed in flour)

Combine sugar, eggs, and vanilla in a bowl; mix well. Add oil, spices, then flour and salt, blend. Fold in pecans, carrots, pineapple, and raisins. Mix for 1 minute at medium speed. Pour into two greased 9-inch pans and bake at 325°F for about 1 hour, until golden. Cool on wire racks for 15 minutes, then flip onto parchment. Frost with Recipe #208 Cream Cheese Frosting.

 For cakes and baked goods, always use fresh, neutral oils like canola, vegetable, sunflower, corn, or safflower. This is crucial for oily recipes such as carrot cake

and check that your oil isn't expired and has no strong smell before using.

208) Cream Cheese Frosting

→ 1/2 cup salted butter, room temperature
→ 12 oz. cream cheese, room temperature
→ 2 lb. powdered sugar
→ 1 tsp vanilla extract
→ 1 Tbsp evaporated milk, omit if piping
→ 1/4 tsp. salt

In a bowl, beat butter and cream cheese until smooth. Gradually mix in powdered sugar, 1/2 cup at a time. After 2 cups, add milk and vanilla, then finish adding the rest of the sugar. Whip on high for 1 minute to fluff the frosting.

Red Velvet Frosting:

Add 1 cup of toasted chopped pecans to icing.

Banana Bread & Carrot Cake Frosting:

This icing is perfect for icing carrot cake.

Italian Cream Frosting:

Add 1/2 cup of toasted coconut and 1/2 cup of chopped toasted pecans to the icing.

209) Mini Cheesecakes

→ 2-8 oz. cream cheese, room temperature
→ 2 large eggs
→ 1/2 cup sugar
→ 1 tsp vanilla extract
→ vanilla wafers Nabisco Brand
→ pie filling, your choice
→ mini foil bake cups

Combine eggs, cream cheese, sugar, and vanilla on high speed until the mixture is smooth. Arrange vanilla wafers in baking cups and divide the filling evenly among 12 muffin cups. Bake at 350 degrees Fahrenheit for 20 minutes. Allow to cool, then add pie filling as a topping.

Option: Use Oreo Thin Cookies on bottom and garnish with a mini-Oreo cookie.

SHOP Tammy's Kitchen Bakeware Items

USA BRAND
Round Cake Pans
All Sizes Available

Scan with your phone camera!

collardvalleycooks.com

Buy the 8" size for the air fryer!

210) Cheesecake-plain or Oreo

For Crust:

- → 60 vanilla wafers, crushed
- → 1/3 cup salted butter, melted
- → 1/4 cup granulated sugar

Mix the ingredients above and press into a 9-inch springform pan. Bake at 350°F for 15 minutes. Remove and cool completely.

For Cake:

- → 3-8 oz. cream cheese, room temperature
- → 3/4 cup granulated sugar
- → 1/2 tsp salt
- → 3 large eggs
- → 2 tsp vanilla extract
- → 1 cup heavy whipping cream
- → 1/2 cup sour cream

Preheat oven to 350°F. Set a water-filled cake pan on the bottom rack. Freeze whipped cream for 10 minutes. Beat cream cheese and sugar until fluffy; add eggs one by one. Scrape bowl, then mix in cold cream, sour cream, and vanilla. Pour into springform pan and fill to the top. Bake for 30 minutes at 350°F, then reduce to 325°F and bake another 30 minutes. Turn off oven and let rest in oven for 1 hour. Remove from pan, chill, and serve with fruit or pie filling if you like.

Oreo Version: Omit wafer crust and bake Recipe # 346 Brownies, cool- press into the bottom of a springform pan. Fold 20 crushed Oreos into cheesecake batter before baking.

211) Chocolate Pound Cake

- → 1 cup salted butter, room temperature
- → 1/2 cup butter-flavored shortening
- → 2 cups light brown sugar, packed
- → 1 cup granulated sugar
- → 5 large eggs, room temperature
- → 2 tsp vanilla extract
- → 2 1/2 cups all-purpose flour
- → 1 tsp. baking powder
- → 3/4 tsp salt
- → 1/2 cup cocoa powder, used Hershey's
- → 1/2 cup strong coffee
- → 1/2 cup heavy cream or evaporated milk
- → 1/2 cup buttermilk
- → 1/2 cup chopped pecans, optional
- → confectioner's sugar, optional

Cream butter shortening and sugars, then beat in eggs one at a time. Add vanilla. Stir in baking powder, salt, cocoa, coffee, and cream. Gradually add flour and buttermilk. Mix 2 minutes after the flour is in. Fold in nuts if you like. Bake at 325°F for 1-1/2 hours until a tester comes out clean. Cool briefly, then transfer to rack. Dust with powdered sugar if desired or ice with Recipe #417 Favorite Fudge Frosting.

212) Coconut Hack Cake, Mama's

- → 2-6 oz. bags fresh frozen coconut (thaw in refrigerator)
- → 1/2 cup can cream of coconut (or coconut milk)
- → 1 Pepperidge Farm frozen three-layer cake (lemon or coconut)
- → 2 Tbsp Sugar add if using coconut milk

Do not thaw coconut in microwave. Mix coconut with cream of coconut or coconut milk and sugar. Take top layer of cake off with a spatula and spread a layer of coconut mixture inside. Place top layer back on and pile remaining coconut on top and sides of cake. The cake must be refrigerated and wrapped with plastic wrap.

"When mama got older making a fresh coconut cake was hard to do so she used this trick, and it was so much easier to make and still tastes homemade." - Tammy

213) Favorite Choc. Cake, Tammy's

→ 2 1/2 cups self-rising flour
→ 1/2 tsp soda
→ 1 tsp baking powder
→ 1/2 tsp salt
→ 3/4 cup cocoa
→ 2 1/4 cups granulated sugar

→ 1 stick salted butter, room temperature
→ 3/4 cup cooking oil
→ 3 large eggs room temperature
→ 1/2 cup sour cream
→ 1 cup milk
→ 1 cup hot dark espresso or strong coffee
→ 1 tsp. vanilla extract

Preheat oven to 350°F. Whisk flour, baking soda, baking powder, salt, and cocoa in a large bowl; set aside. Beat sugar, butter, oil, and eggs with a mixer, then add sour cream and milk. Gradually mix in dry ingredients, adding 1-1/2 cups first, then pour in hot coffee, followed by the rest of the flour. Stir in vanilla. Batter will be thin. Pour into three greased and floured 8-inch or 9" round cakepans. Do not fill pans beyond 3/4 full. Bake until the center rises and sides pull away: check after 25 minutes, Frost with Recipe #417 for layer cakes.

 Bake at 325°F if using a 13x9x2. And frost with Recipe#214

214) Sheet Cake Chocolate Frosting

→ 1 lb. powdered sugar (4 cups)
→ 6 Tbsp cocoa

Whisk sugar and cocoa together in a large mixing bowl.

→ 3/4 cup salted butter
→ 6 Tbsp evaporated milk
→ 1/4 tsp salt
→ 1 tsp vanilla extract
→ 1/2 cup pecans, chopped, optional

Combine wet ingredients, add dry ingredients, mix well, and add pecans if desired.

This icing is for pouring over cakes that are left in a 13x9 pan. It is great on Recipe #262 Mexican Meets Cola sheet cake!

"This frosting is so simple to make and even easier to spread over the cake (just leave it in the pan). If you are looking for a delicious and hassle-free cake, this icing is a perfect choice. Plus, you do not need a mixer—it is thin and easy to mix!"
- Tammy

215) Blackberry Cake

→ 1 cup fresh blackberries
→ 2 cups all-purpose flour, divided
→ 1/2 cup butter, softened
→ 2 cups granulated sugar
→ 2 large eggs, room temperature
→ 1 tsp baking soda
→ 1 tsp ea. ground cinnamon & nutmeg
→ 1/2 tsp salt
→ 1/4 teaspoon ground cloves, optional
→ 1/4 teaspoon ground allspice, optional
→ 3/4 cup buttermilk
→ Optional: Whipped cream and confectioners' sugar

Preheat oven to 325°F. Toss blackberries with 1/4 cup flour and set aside. Cream butter and sugar until fluffy, then beat in eggs. Mix baking soda, spices, salt, and remaining flour; add to cream mixture alternately with buttermilk. Fold in blackberries. Pour into a greased, floured bundt pan and bake for 45–50 minutes, or until a toothpick comes out clean. Cool before serving; top with whipped cream, confectioner's sugar, and extra blackberries if desired.

"You're either a fan of blackberries or you can't stand them, and this girl truly loves them! I recall gathering them from the bushes in the cow fields and enduring the scrubbing and itchy chiggers afterward, but the joy of tasting that blackberry made it all worthwhile!"
-Tammy

216) Tammy's Buttery Fruitcake

For the Cake:

- → 2 cups salted butter
- → 2 cups packed light brown sugar
- → 6 large eggs
- → 2 tsp Apple pie spice, used Penzey's
- → 3 Tbsp vanilla extract
- → 1/2 cup grape juice
- → 2 2/3 cups self-rising flour
- → 3 1/2 cups candied fruit
- → 10 oz. chopped dates
- → 4 cups chopped pecans

Read the recipe first. Do not preheat the oven. Cream butter and sugar, then add eggs one at a time, followed by apple pie spice and vanilla. Mix in grape juice, then flour; beat for 2 minutes. In another bowl, coat fruit with 1/3 cup flour, add pecans and dates, and combine well. Stir fruit mixture into batter, mix thoroughly. Put in a well-greased 12 cup tube pan. Fill almost full, it until there is about 1" left empty. If there is extra batter, use a loaf pan. Put cakes in a cold oven, set to 350°F for 30 minutes, then reduce to 250°F for 3 to 4 hours. Wait until center rises before adding fruit topping; otherwise, topping will sink. After topping, bake for 30 minutes at 350°F to toast pecans.

For pecan and fruit topping:

- → 8 oz. jelly or marmalade, used orange marmalade
- → 2 cups large mixed colored candied fruits (your choice). I like red and green cherries with light pineapple
- → 4 cups whole pecans

Heat jelly (your choice of apple or orange marmalade) in a small non-stick pot or skillet. Pour over the fruit and stir until the fruit and nuts are well coated.

My choice of fruits for cake batter:

- → 8 oz. fruit and peel old English mix or extra fancy (these are chopped small)
- → 8 oz. tropical mix
- → 8 oz. mixed pineapple and cherries, cut fruit in half for cake batter
- → 10 oz. chopped dates

 Tips: When you buy fruit and nuts, get plenty for the top of cakes too! Do not put topping on the cake before the middle is set, or it will sink into the cake.

Do not use old English fruit unless you taste it and make sure you like the citron and fruits; replace with other mixed fruits if you don't.

217) Coconut Condensed Milk Pound Cake

- → 2 cups salted butter, softened
- → 2 cups granulated sugar
- → 1 tsp salt
- → 8 large eggs, separated
- → 3 1/2 cups all-purpose flour
- → 14 oz. can sweeten condensed milk
- → 12 cup bundt pan
- → 1 tsp vanilla extract
- → 2 tsp coconut extract, optional
- → 2 bags of 6 oz. frozen fresh coconut or 12 oz. flaked sweet coconut.

Preheat oven to 325°F and spray a tube pan with non-stick spray. Beat butter and sugar until fluffy, then add egg yolks, extracts, condensed milk, salt, and gradually the flour. Stir in coconut. Whip egg whites to stiff peaks and fold into batter. Pour batter into a well-greased and floured 12-cup Bundt pan, filling only threequarters full; use extra batter in another pan as needed. Bake for 1 hour 30 minutes or until a toothpick comes out clean. Cool for 20 minutes in the pan before unmolding.

 Note: This cake gets its height from air beaten into the egg whites and needs no baking powder or soda. Do not use self-rising flour.

218) Fresh Coconut Cake, Mama's

Prepare Recipe #219 White Cake Recipe in 4 round cake pans. Ice with Recipes #220 & 221. Instructions in Filling Recipe!

219) White Cake Layers

→ 1/2 cup salted butter, room temperature
→ 1/2 cup shortening
→ 1 3/4 cups granulated sugar
→ 6 large egg whites, room temperature
→ 3/4 tsp salt
→ 2 tsp baking powder
→ 1/2 tsp baking soda
→ 2-1/2 cups all-purpose flour
→ 1-1/2 cups buttermilk
→ 2 tsp clear vanilla extract

Preheat oven to 325°F. Cream butter and shortening, then add sugar and egg whites. Mix in salt, baking powder, and baking soda. Add flour (1/2 cup at a time) with milk, then mix in vanilla. Beat on low for 2 minutes. Pour batter into greased pans—use three if round; if only two, set aside 1 cup of batter. Bake for 30-35 minutes, checking with a toothpick for doneness.

 Bake at 325°F if using a 13x9x2. Check after it cooks 40 minutes.

"This white cake layer is good to use for fresh coconut cake. If you use it for the coconut and want to make Recipe #419 lemon curd, you can use the 6 egg yolks in the curd." -*Tammy*

220) Coconut Buttercream Frosting

Note: The buttercream will be thin, which is ideal for this cake.

→ 3/4 cup salted butter, room temperature
→ 4 1/2 cups powdered sugar
→ 2 tsp vanilla extract

→ 1/4 tsp salt
→ 1 1/2 Tbsp cream, used evaporated milk
→ 1/2 cup cream of coconut * see note

 Note: Cream of coconut will have a hard layer of grease on top. Mix well before adding butter cream, then use what is left in your filling.

In a stand mixer's mixing bowl, add butter and beat with the whisk attachment on high speed until it is white and fluffy. Gradually add 2 cups of powdered sugar. Then add cream, cream of coconut, and vanilla. Continue adding the powdered sugar. Finish by adding a dash of salt.

221) Coconut Filling and Topping:

→ 6-8 oz. packs fresh frozen coconut
→ 3/4 cup lukewarm water
→ 1/2 cup cream of coconut

 Note: When preparing the layered cake with frosting and coconut filling, use a deep sided plate like a pie plate. The cake is soggy and will ooze with goodness. It will make a mess if you put it on a flat cake server.

Put the frozen coconut in the fridge for 2 days to thaw before mixing the filling. Combine the coconut, water, and cream of coconut in a large bowl and mix until well blended. It will be a little soggy. You should have at least 4 layers. If you have fewer, split them in half before adding the icing and filling. Place a thin layer of coconut buttercream, then a generous layer of coconut filling between each cake layer. Frost the outside of the cake with a thin layer of buttercream. Cover the entire cake with the remaining coconut filling. This cake tastes better after sitting in the refrigerator for 2-3 days.

 Caution: Fresh coconut goes sour easy. Do not thaw in microwave. Make sure to store filling and finished cake in the refrigerator until ready to serve.

Note: Fresh frozen coconut is in the freezer section of grocery near frozen fruit. In addition a thin layer of Recipe #419 Lemon Curd can be spread in between each layer.

"This cake was a family tradition. Mama made it for both sides of the family every year. I can remember her cracking fresh coconuts. You will not find a better fresh coconut cake recipe, I guarantee it!" -*Tammy*

222) Flaked Coconut Cake, Tammy's

Moist Yellow Cake Recipe #266

Coconut Buttercream Recipe #220

→ 14 oz. Bag baker's sweetened flaked coconut

Bake a yellow cake in 3 or 4 round cake pans. Prepare Coconut Buttercream Icing. The buttercream will be thin, which is best for this cake. Place a layer of icing and a generous amount of flaked coconut between each layer. Ice the outside of the cake and cover it with the remaining coconut.

223) Coconut Cake, Magdalene's

→ 1-1/2 cup granulated sugar
→ 1/2 cup salted butter
→ 1/2 cup shortening
→ 4 eggs
→ 2 cups self-rising flour
→ 1 tsp pure vanilla extract
→ 1 tsp pure coconut extract
→ 1 cup canned coconut milk (not cream of coconut)

Preheat the oven to 325°F. Sift the flour and set aside. In a mixing bowl, cream together the butter, shortening, and sugar until fluffy. Add the eggs one at a time, mixing after each addition, until well combined. Add half a cup

of flour, then a quarter cup of coconut milk, and mix, alternating between the two until all the flour and coconut milk are incorporated, finishing with the flour. Bake for about 28 to 35 minutes in three greased and floured 9- or 10-inch round cake pans. (Line the bottoms with parchment to prevent sticking.) Let the cakes cool before icing with Recipe #224 Magdalene's Coconut Icing.

224) Magdalene's Coconut Icing

→ 4 cups granulated sugar
→ 1/4 tsp salt
→ 6 6-oz. bags of fresh frozen coconut
→ 3 Tbsp cornstarch, heaping
→ 13.5 oz can of coconut milk

Combine all the icing ingredients in a saucepan and bring to a low simmer, stirring frequently to avoid burning. The icing will start to boil. Let it boil or simmer for about 6 minutes or more until thick. Set aside and cool until warm. The icing is much easier to spread onto and between the cake layers when it is still warm.

Tammy's tips: Use a non-stick pot to cook the icing. Cook the icing long enough that the cornstarch turns clear—about 15 minutes, stirring frequently to prevent sticking. Sticking won't be an issue if you use a good non-stick saucepan.

This coconut cake is a favorite among many. The Gaither Vocal Band would rush to the arena door to grab one of these cakes baked for them by my mom. Bill Gaither once told her, "You should be put in jail for making something that good." – Mark Fuller

Mark Fuller, the son of the late Magdelene Fuller

Mark resides in Marietta, Georgia and is a busy man during the holidays making his mother's cakes for others! He is carrying on her traditions!

225) Egg Nog Pound Cake, Tammy's

→ XL 12-cup bundt or tube pan
→ 1 cup shortening
→ 3/4 cup salted butter, room temperature
→ 3 cups granulated sugar
→ 9 large eggs, room temperature
→ 1 cup eggnog, Recipe #92
→ 2 tsp baking powder
→ 1 tsp of salt

→ 3 cups of all-purpose flour or cake flour
→ 2 tsp vanilla extract
→ 1 tsp almond extract

Preheat the oven to 350°F. Using an electric mixer and mixing bowl, combine the shortening and butter for 3 minutes. Next, add the sugar and beat until fluffy. Incorporate the eggs one at a time, mixing well after each addition. Then, add the baking powder, salt, 1 cup of flour, and flavorings.

Stir in the eggnog, then add the remaining flour. Mix at a medium-low speed for 2 minutes.

Pour the batter into a well-greased and floured fluted Bundt pan. Bake at 350°F for 40 minutes, then reduce the oven to 325°F and bake for an additional 30 minutes.

 Important Tip: Fill the baking pan 3/4 full and avoid overfilling. If you have extra batter, bake it in a separate pan.

OPTIONAL: When greasing the tube pan, grease the bottom well and sprinkle it with slivered almonds. When inverted, this will create a pretty cake.

See Recipe #92 Old Fashioned Egg Nog to make homemade egg nog.

226) Hot Fudge Pudding Cake

→ 1 cup all-purpose flour
→ 3/4 cup sugar
→ 2 tsp baking powder
→ 1/4 tsp salt
→ 1/2 cup milk
→ 2 Tbsp melted salted butter
→ 1 sq. (1 oz.) semi-sweet chocolate, melted
→ 1/2 cup chopped nuts, optional
→ 1 tsp vanilla extract
→ 1 cup packed light brown sugar
→ 1/4 cup cocoa
→ 1 3/4 cup boiling water

Preheat the oven to 350°F. Combine flour, sugar, baking powder, and salt. Mix milk, butter, and melted chocolate; add to the dry ingredients. Stir in nuts and vanilla. Pour the batter into a greased 9 x 9 or 7 x 11-inch pan. Use your fingers to mix brown sugar and cocoa, then sprinkle over the batter. Pour boiling water evenly over the top (do not stir). Bake for 45 minutes. Cut into squares, then scoop out the sauce from the bottom of the pan and pour it over each serving. Serve with ice cream or whipped cream, if desired.

This is a picture of me with Mama's Fresh Coconut Cake in 2023.

227) German Choc. Cake, Tammy's

- → 2 1/2 cups all-purpose flour
- → 1/2 cup cocoa
- → 2 tsp baking powder
- → 1/2 tsp baking soda
- → 3/4 tsp salt
- → 1/2 cup salted butter
- → 1/2 cup shortening
- → 2 1/4 cups granulated sugar
- → 3 large eggs, room temperature
- → 1 cup evaporated milk
- → 1/2 cup water
- → 1 tsp vanilla extract

Preheat oven to 350°F. In a bowl, whisk together flour, cocoa, baking powder, baking soda, and salt. In another bowl, beat butter, shortening, and sugar until fluffy. Add eggs one at a time, then mix in milk and water. Gradually add dry ingredients, mixing well, and finish with vanilla. Beat for 2 minutes. Pour batter into three greased and floured round pans (no more than 3/4 full). Bake without opening the oven for 25 minutes. Remove cakes when a toothpick comes out clean.

 Bake at 325° for sheet cake and don't open oven until 40 minutes has passed.

If you take the time to make my homemade German chocolate cake layers, please make my homemade German chocolate icing too!

"Very moist cake layers. Ice with Recipe #228. This is my husband Chris's favorite cake. He likes it with round layers because he gets more icing. It is also my brother Barry's favorite too!" - *Tammy*

228) German Chocolate Icing

- → 4 large eggs
- → 2-2/3 cups evaporated milk
- → 2-2/3 cups granulated sugar
- → 1 cup salted butter
- → 1/4 tsp salt
- → 2 tsp vanilla extract
- → 14 oz. Baker's sweetened flaked coconut
- → 1-1/2 cups pecans, chopped

Crack eggs into a large microwave-safe bowl. Add evaporated milk and sugar, then whisk well. Add melted butter and salt and whisk again. Microwave on high for 3 minutes, then stir well. Return to microwave and cook for another 3 minutes. Take out and stir thoroughly; it should start to thicken. This icing does not truly thicken but becomes creamy. Continue cooking in 1–2-minute intervals until it reaches a creamy consistency. Overcooking may cause butter to separate, making it look curdled. About 8-10 minutes should suffice! Mix in coconut and pecans, then fold into the filling. Pour into shallow pans to cool. This makes enough icing to frost a large three-layer cake.

NOTE: If you think the filling has started to curdle, it's okay to stop cooking and go ahead and add the coconut and pecans. There is no need to start over. Once it cools, it will still be tasty.

229) Hershey's Syrup Cake

- → 1-1/2 cups sugar
- → 3/4 cup salted butter
- → 6 large eggs, room temperature
- → 24 oz. Hershey's chocolate syrup
- → 1-1/2 cups self-rising flour
- → 1 tsp vanilla extract

Cream together sugar and butter, then add eggs one at a time. Stir in chocolate syrup, then add flour gradually, half a cup at a time. Add vanilla and mix for 2 minutes on medium speed. Pour batter into a greased and floured 13x9 inch cake pan and bake at 350°F for 30 minutes. After 30 minutes, lower the oven temp. to 325°F and continue baking until a toothpick inserted in the center comes out clean. (Mine takes about 40-45 minutes total). Frost with Recipe #214

230) Hummingbird Cake

→ 2 1/2 cups granulated sugar
→ 3 large eggs, room temperature
→ 3/4 cup vegetable oil
→ 2 cups mashed bananas
→ 1 tsp baking soda
→ 1 tsp salt
→ 1 tsp ground cinnamon
→ 20 oz. can crushed pineapple, divided
→ 3 cups all-purpose flour
→ 1 tsp vanilla extract
→ 1 cup chopped pecans plus 1/2 cup for top
→ Option: Make the cake moister: add a small box of vanilla instant pudding mix to the batter.

Combine sugar, eggs, oil, bananas, 8 oz. crushed pineapple (with juice), and vanilla. Stir in baking soda, salt, and cinnamon, then mix in flour for 1-1/2 minutes on medium speed. Fold in 1 cup chopped pecans, taking care not to overmix (total mixing after flour should be 2 minutes). Grease and flour three 8-inch or two 9-inch round pans; sprinkle pecans on the bottom of one pan. Bake all cakes at 325°F for about 35 minutes, until a toothpick comes out clean and edges pull away. Place the pecan-topped cake layer on top. Frost between layers and sides with Recipe #208 but leave top unfrosted.

Pineapple Topping: Combine remaining pineapple and its juice with 1/2 cup brown sugar in a non-stick pot or skillet and cook about 5 minutes until it thickens a little. Put on top of cake like picture. Enjoy!

"Picture above shows the cake with the extra pineapple cooked with brown sugar. This puts my Hummingbird Cake above others because it is so moist! If you love Hummingbird Cake, I hope you try my recipe." - *Tammy*

"This was on granny's dessert table every year for Christmas. Her dessert table was the floor freezer that she had in the dining room. I can still remember running to that freezer and having to tip toe to see what was there. I was always excited about dessert!" - *Tammy*

231) Ice Box Fruitcake

→ 2 cups graham crackers (or 16 oz. vanilla wafers, crushed)
→ 4 cups toasted pecans, chopped
→ 15 oz. box golden raisins
→ 10 oz. package miniature marshmallows
→ 1 cup salted butter
→ 12 oz. jar maraschino cherries

Drain and chop cherries, reserving the juice. Crush crackers, then place them in a mixing bowl with the reserved juice. In a saucepan, melt butter, then add marshmallows and cook on medium heat, stirring constantly until the marshmallows and butter have melted together. Pour the mixture into the mixing bowl with the crackers and cherry juice. Add pecans, raisins, and chopped cherries, and mix well. Use two large pieces of parchment paper to roll the mixture into two logs, then place them in the refrigerator for 4 hours to chill. Remove the bars, unwrap, and slice into serving pieces. Bars can be wrapped in foil and stored in the refrigerator for up to one month. Enjoy!

 Many had this with vanilla wafers and some of you remember it with graham crackers. You can use either as I have stated above.

When you accept Jesus Christ as your personal Savior, the Holy Spirit dwells within you. You can then love other's with God's love. This love is called agape love. It is a love without boundaries, an endless and unconditional love. - *Tammy*

232) Japanese Fruit Cake

For the Icing:

- → medium lemon, juice, and zest
- → medium naval orange
- → 2 cups granulated sugar
- → 4 Tbsp corn starch
- → 1/2 cup water
- → 1/2 cup cherry juice
- → 1/4 tsp salt
- → 20 oz. can crushed pineapple, drained
- → 1 cup flaked or fresh coconut
- → 1/2 cup maraschino cherries halved
- → 1 cup chopped pecans

Zest lemon on paper towel, and then juice it, and set aside. Zest orange onto same paper towel as lemon zest, then peel and cut into small pieces. Combine lemon juice, orange pieces, and zests in a small bowl. In a medium saucepan whisk sugar and cornstarch together. Add water, cherry juice, salt, zests, and juices from small bowl. Bring to a slow boil on medium heat. Once boiling well turn up to high heat and Boil 2 minutes. Add drained pineapple, coconut, halved cherries, and pecans. Cook for another minute. Pour icing into shallow dish to cool.

For the Cake:

Prepare Recipe #255 Spice Cake and Recipe #266 Yellow Cake, then split one layer of each to make 4 layers. Stack them alternately with filling between each layer. You can ice the sides with 7-minute icing or cover the whole cake with filling. Poke holes while stacking and use hot filling to let it soak in but be cautious. Avoid getting pulp in the zest to prevent bitterness. This classic cake is delicious.

 Option: Ice the sides with Recipe #399 Seven Minute Icing.

233) Maple Pecan Pound Cake

- → an extra-large 12-cup bundt pan required
- → 1-1/2 cups salted butter, room temperature
- → 3 cups granulated sugar
- → 9 large eggs, separated
- → 1 cup sour cream
- → 3 cups all-purpose flour
- → 1/2 tsp baking soda
- → 1 tsp salt
- → 2 Tbsp maple extract
- → 1 cup chopped pecans

Preheat the oven to 300°F. Using a stand mixer, cream the butter and sugar until light and fluffy. Add the egg yolks individually, ensuring each is well incorporated before adding the next. Blend in the baking soda, salt, chosen flavoring or extract, and sour cream until the mixture is smooth. Gradually add the flour, approximately half a cup at a time, mixing on medium-low speed for two minutes once all the flour has been added. Gently fold in the pecans. In a separate bowl, beat the egg whites until stiff peaks form, then carefully fold them into the batter. Transfer the batter to a thoroughly greased fluted bundt pan and bake at 300°F for 90 minutes.

 This cake will get lots of compliments. Slice your cakes and freeze them in freezer bags, or if frosted in plastic containers. Pull them out and have them later. The freezer makes the crumb of the cake more moist and they are just absolutely delicious!

234) Mississippi Mud Cake

→ 1 cup salted butter, room temperature
→ 2 cups granulated sugar
→ 4 large eggs
→ 1/3 cup cocoa, heaping
→ 1 tsp vanilla extract
→ 1-1/2 cups self-rising flour
→ 1 cup chopped pecans
→ 1 cup flaked coconut, optional
→ 10 oz. miniature marshmallows or 8 oz. marshmallow cream
→ chocolate icing (recipe below)

Preheat oven to 350°F. Beat butter and sugar with an electric mixer until blended, then mix in eggs one at a time. Add cocoa and vanilla; mix well. Incorporate flour for 2 minutes at a medium speed. Stir in nuts and coconut. Pour batter into a greased, floured 13" x 9" x 2" pan. Bake for 40 minutes, watching near the end and removing when a toothpick comes out clean. Top with miniature marshmallows or spread marshmallow cream immediately after baking. Prepare Recipe #235 Easy Chocolate Frosting below.

235) Easy Chocolate Frosting

→ 1/3 cup of cocoa & 1/4 tsp salt
→ 1 lb. powdered sugar
→ 1/4 cup of melted salted butter
→ 1/3 cup of evaporated milk
→ 1 cup chopped pecans, add last

Mix well, then add 1 cup chopped pecans. Spread on top of the cake over the marshmallows!

Psalm 111:10
"The fear of the LORD is the beginning of wisdom: a good understanding have all they that do his commandments: his praise endureth forever." KJV

236) 1 Egg Spice Cake

→ 1/4 cup salted butter, room temperature (or shortening)
→ 1 cup light brown sugar, packed
→ 1 egg, beaten
→ 2 cups all-purpose flour
→ 1-1/2 tsp baking powder
→ 1/2 tsp baking soda
→ 1/2 tsp cinnamon, ground
→ 1/2 tsp allspice, ground
→ 1/2 tsp nutmeg, ground
→ 1/2 tsp cloves, ground
→ 1/2 tsp salt
→ 1 cup buttermilk or sour cream

In a bowl, beat together sugar, butter or shortening, and egg until smooth. Sift flour, baking soda, baking powder, and salt in another bowl, add spices, and whisk to combine. Gradually mix dry ingredients with milk into the wet mixture; beat on medium for 2 minutes. Pour batter into a greased, floured tube pan and bake at 350°F for 30–40 minutes, until the center springs back or a toothpick comes out clean. Cool for 10 minutes, invert it onto a plate, dust with powdered sugar, and serve.

 This cake is low in sugar, has only one egg, and has no oil. Chris loved this for breakfast warmed with a little butter spread on it. He also liked it just as a snack at room temperature.

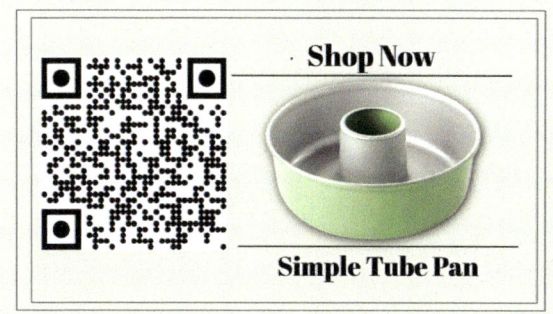

Shop Now

Simple Tube Pan

then uncover and stir for two more minutes. Add vanilla, pecans, and coconut. Ice the cake immediately. Broil in oven on low until the icing is bubbly and golden. Serve.

 Tammy's Tip: Toast whole pecans before chopping to prevent scorching. If chopped pecans are only available, toast them on low heat in a non-stick skillet, stirring frequently.

237) Oatmeal Cake, Lazy Daisy

→ 1 cup 1-minute oatmeal
→ 1-1/4 cup boiling water
→ 1 cup granulated sugar
→ 1 cup light brown sugar, packed
→ 1 cup salted butter, room temperature
→ 2 large eggs, room temperature
→ 1 tsp vanilla extract
→ 3/4 tsp cinnamon
→ 1/4 tsp nutmeg, optional
→ 1/2 tsp salt
→ 1 tsp baking soda
→ 1-1/2 tsp baking powder
→ 2 cups all-purpose flour
→ (or use self-rising flour and omit salt, soda, and baking powder)

Boil water and add oatmeal; let stand. Cream butter with sugars, then mix in eggs and vanilla. Add cinnamon, nutmeg, salt, baking soda, and baking powder; mix thoroughly. Stir in soaked oatmeal. Gradually add flour. Pour batter into a greased 9x13 pan. Bake at 325°F for 40-50 minutes, until golden and a toothpick comes out clean. Top with Recipe #238.

"This has got to be one of the most delicious cakes I have ever tasted." - *Tammy*

238) Broiled Coconut Icing

→ 3/4 cup salted butter
→ 3/4 cup brown sugar, packed
→ 1/3 cup half & half (or evaporated milk)
→ 1-1/2 tsp vanilla extract
→ 1/2 cup flaked coconut
→ 1/2 cup toasted pecans, chopped

Melt butter in a saucepan over low heat. Stir in both sugars and cream, then bring to a gentle boil over medium-low, letting the sugar dissolve completely before raising the heat. Boil vigorously; cover for one minute to keep sugar off the sides,

239) Tammy's Favorite Pound Cake

→ Extra-large 12-cup bundt or tube pan
→ 1 cup shortening
→ 3/4 cup salted butter, room temperature
→ 3 cups granulated sugar
→ 9 large eggs
→ 2 tsp baking powder
→ 1 tsp salt
→ 3 cups all-purpose flour or cake flour
→ 2 tsp vanilla extract
→ 1 tsp almond extract

Preheat the oven to 350°F. Using an electric mixer, cream together the shortening and butter for three minutes in a mixing bowl. Incorporate the sugar and continue beating until the mixture is light and fluffy. Add the eggs individually, ensuring each one is thoroughly mixed before proceeding. Blend in the baking powder and salt. Gradually add the flour in half-cup increments, followed by the desired flavorings. Mix on medium-low speed for two minutes. Transfer the batter to a fluted Bundt pan that has been prepared with both grease and flour. Fill pan 3/4 full. Bake at 350°F for 40 minutes, then reduce the temperature to 325°F and bake for an additional 30 minutes.

240) Orange Juice Cake

→ 2 1/2 cups self-rising flour
→ 1/2 cup salted butter
→ 1-1/4 cups granulated sugar
→ 3/4 cup light brown sugar, packed
→ 3 large eggs, room temperature
→ 1/2 cup sour cream
→ 3/4 cup cooking oil
→ 1 tsp vanilla extract
→ 1 tsp orange extract
→ 1 cup orange juice

Sift flour and set aside. Using a stand mixer, beat butter and sugars on medium until fluffy (about 1-1/2 minutes). Add eggs one at a time, mixing after each. Mix in sour cream, oil, and flavorings. Gradually add flour, pouring in orange juice halfway through. Finish adding flour and beat for 2 minutes on medium/low (do not exceed 2 minutes after adding flour). Grease and flour four 8" or three 9" cake pans. Bake at 350°F for 30 minutes, or until a toothpick comes out clean and the cake pulls from the pan sides.

 Important: If you are baking this in a sheet cake pan or in thicker layers, Bake at 325°F . Check the cake for doneness after 40 minutes. Bake until the center has risen and bounces back when touched.

241) Orange Juice Cake Frosting

→ 6 cups powdered sugar
→ 1/2 cup frozen orange juice concentrate
→ 3/4 cup salted butter
→ 1/4 tsp salt
→ 1 tsp vanilla extract
→ 1 tsp orange extract
→ fresh orange, for zesting

Add powdered sugar and a pinch of salt to the bowl. Combine orange juice concentrate and butter in a measuring cup, microwave until hot.

Pour into the mixer and blend on medium, then mix in extracts. (Icing thickens as it cools.) Finish by zesting orange over the iced cake.

242) Frozen Fruit Topping & Filling

→ 16 oz. bag of frozen fruit
→ 1 cup granulated sugar

Combine fruit and sugar. Microwave for 8 minutes. Remove and transfer to a shallow dish to cool. Cut the fruit into smaller pieces if desired. Serve over cake with whipped topping. You can also use this for a pie filling, but if you use it for fried pies, you must cook it until it is thick like preserves being careful not to burn.

Great served on Recipe #239, Tammy's Favorite Pound Cake.

243) Peach Skillet Cake

→ 4 Tbsp salted butter
→ 2/3 cup light brown sugar, packed
→ 2 cups sliced ripe peaches
→ cinnamon sugar, optional

Melt butter in 10.25" cast iron skillet, add brown sugar and sliced peaches. Sprinkle with cinnamon sugar if desired.

Cake Batter:

→ Cooking Spray
→ 1/2 cup shortening
→ 1/2 cup light brown sugar, packed
→ 1 cup granulated sugar
→ 2 large eggs
→ 1-1/2 cups self-rising flour
→ 3/4 cup buttermilk
→ 1 tsp vanilla extract

Use an electric mixer to mix shortening and sugars until fluffy, then add eggs one at a time. Mix in remaining ingredients for 2 minutes. Grease the skillet, pour batter over peaches, and bake at 350°F for 35-45 minutes. Invert it onto a plate and arrange fruit with a spatula. Serve.

 Tip: fruit will turn dark, so serve day that you make it if you are taking it to a function.

James 3:17 KJV

"But the wisdom that is from above is first pure, then peaceable, gentle, and easy to be intreated, full of mercy and good fruits, without partiality, and without hypocrisy."

244) Peanut Butter Cake

- → 1/4 cup shortening
- → 1/2 cup salted butter, room temperature
- → 1-1/2 cups granulated sugar
- → 3 large eggs, room temperature
- → 1 cup peanut butter, used 1/2 crunchy and 1/2 creamy
- → 2 cups self-rising flour
- → 1-1/2 cups whole buttermilk
- → 1/2 cup water

Blend butter and shortening with an electric mixer, then add sugar and beat until fluffy. Scrape the bowl, add eggs one at a time, mixing after each, then add peanut butter. Mix in 1 cup flour, alternate with buttermilk and water, then add remaining flour and mix for 2 minutes. Grease or spray a 13"x9"x2" pan, pour in batter, and bake at 325°F for 40-50 minutes or until a toothpick comes out clean.

Bake round layers at 350°F, and check after 35 minutes.

245) Peanut Butter Buttercream

- → 1/2 cup salted butter, room temperature
- → 1/2 cup shortening or salted butter
- → 1/4 cup creamy peanut butter
- → 1 tsp vanilla extract
- → 5 cups powdered sugar & 1/4 tsp salt
- → 6-8 Tbsp evaporated milk or heavy cream

Use an electric mixer to blend butter and shortening until smooth. Add peanut butter, vanilla, salt, and 1 1/2 cups of powdered sugar. Mix until creamy. Then add milk and the remaining powdered sugar. Add more milk if needed. The mixture should be light, fluffy, and spreadable.

246) Peanut Butter & Jelly Cake

- → 1 large jar grape jam, not jelly

Make Recipe #244, Peanut Butter Cake. Bake it in a 13x9x2 inch baking pan. Leave cake in pan. Frost with Recipe #245, Peanut Butter Buttercream. Spread jam over the top of icing and swirl or decorate as pictured above.

247) Peter Paul Mounds Cake

Bake Recipe # 213, my Chocolate Cake layer, in a 13x9 pan. Leave the cake in the pan and top with filling, then pour frosting over the top of cake.

Mound Cake's Coconut Filling:

- → 1 cup sugar & 1/4 tsp salt
- → 1 cup milk
- → 12 oz. sweetened flaked coconut, used Baker's brand
- → 12 large marshmallows or 120 miniatures
- → 1 tsp vanilla extract
- → 1/2 cup finely chopped pecans

Bring sugar and milk to a boil. Add coconut and marshmallows, then return to a boil. Cook for 5 minutes, stirring often. Stir in vanilla, salt, and pecans, then spread hot filling over the cake.

Mound Cake's Frosting:

- → 2 cups granulated sugar
- → 2 Tbsp cocoa, Hershey's
- → 1/2 cup salted butter
- → 12 oz. can evaporated milk
- → 1 tsp vanilla extract

Mix sugar and cocoa with a wire whisk, then add the mixture and all other ingredients except vanilla to a saucepan. Cook over medium heat, stirring constantly until it reaches the softball stage. Transfer to a mixing bowl and add vanilla. Beat until it is pourable (slightly thickened), then pour all over the top of the cake.

248) Pineapple Pound Cake

→ Extra-large 12 cup tube pan required
→ 1 cup shortening
→ 3/4 cup salted butter, room temperature
→ 3 cups granulated sugar
→ 9 large eggs
→ 2 tsp baking powder
→ 1 tsp salt
→ 3 cups all-purpose flour
→ 2 tsp vanilla extract
→ 20 oz. can crushed pineapple
→ 1/2 cup light brown sugar, packed

Preheat oven to 350°F. Drain half of can of pineapple in a separate bowl and set aside. Cream shortening and butter with a mixer; add granulated sugar-mix until fluffy. Add eggs one at a time, then baking powder and salt. Gradually mix in flour, then flavorings. Mix for 2 minutes, then fold in the remaining pineapple.

Spread 1/4 cup of soft butter on the bottom of a solid tube pan and coat with cooking spray, including the flute. Sprinkle brown sugar on the bottom. Add drained pineapple, pressing flat. Fill pan 3/4 full of batter. Bake for 30 minutes at 350°F, then reduce heat to 325°F and bake another 35–40 minutes.

249) Prune Cake

→ 1 cup vegetable oil
→ 1-1/2 cups sugar
→ 3 large eggs, room temperature
→ 1 tsp cinnamon
→ 1/2 tsp nutmeg
→ 1/2 tsp allspice
→ 1 tsp vanilla extract
→ 2 cups self-rising flour
→ 1 cup buttermilk
→ 2 cups ready-to-eat prunes, chopped
→ 1 cup chopped pecans

Combine oil, sugar, and eggs. Add spices and vanilla, then 1 cup flour and buttermilk. Mix, add remaining flour, and beat for 2 minutes. Stir in prunes and nuts. Pour into a greased 13x9x2-inch pan and bake at 325°F for 40 minutes. Cool, then dust with confectioner's sugar or frost as desired.

"This cake is packed with fruit and raisins. It is best to make it in a sheet pan and not as a layer cake. This is an old-timer favorite!"
- *Tammy*

250) Pineapple Skillet Cake

→ 2/3 cup light brown sugar, packed
→ 4 Tbsp salted butter
→ fresh cut pineapple
→ small jar maraschino cherries
→ 3" Deep 10-inch or 12-inch cast iron skillet

Melt butter and sugar in cast iron skillet. Simmer on low for 4-5 minutes. Place fresh pineapple rings in skillet with cherries.

For Cake Batter:

→ 1/2 cup shortening
→ 1/2 cup light brown sugar, packed
→ 1 cup granulated sugar
→ 2 large eggs, room temperature
→ 1-1/2 cups self-rising flour
→ 1 tsp vanilla extract
→ 1/2 cup milk (whole or 2%)

Mix shortening, brown sugar, sugar, and eggs until creamy. Add flour and milk alternately and then mix in the vanilla. Mix 2 minutes. Spray edges iron skillet with cooking spray. Pour batter over pineapple and cherry topping. Bake at 350°F for 25-35 minutes, until golden and a toothpick comes out clean. Cool for 15 minutes, invert it onto a plate, and serve.

251) Pound Cake for Round Layers

→ 8" or 9" round cake pans
→ 8 large eggs, separated
→ 1-1/2 cups salted butter, room temperature
→ 3 cups granulated sugar
→ 3 cups self-rising flour
→ 2 tsp vanilla extract
→ 1 cup milk or canned milk

Preheat the oven to 325°F. Whip the egg whites until stiff peaks are achieved; set aside. Cream the butter and sugar using a mixer until light and fluffy. Incorporate the egg yolks individually, blending thoroughly after each addition. Mix in the vanilla extract. Add flour in 1/2-cup increments, alternating with milk, and mix for two minutes. Gently fold the whipped egg whites into the batter until just combined. Transfer the batter into round cake pans that have been thoroughly greased and floured. Bake at 325°F until a toothpick inserted in the center emerges clean.

For thin cake layers, use 1-1/2 cups of batter per pan. This method produces layers that are ideal for icing.

 Option: Bake in 3 cake layers and split layers in half before icing. (This will give you 6 layers.)

"Ice with Recipe #417 Favorite Fudge Frosting or Recipe #416 Stovetop Fudge Icing!"
- Tammy

Add a 3.4 oz. box of Vanilla Instant Pudding to a homemade cake recipe to give it a softer crumb (make it moister).

252) Sweet Potato Pound Cake

→ 12 cup bundt pan (required)
→ 1 cup shortening
→ 1 cup salted butter, room temperature
→ 3 1/2 cups granulated sugar
→ 2 tsp baking powder
→ 1 tsp salt
→ 9 large eggs, room temperature
→ 2 cups sweet potatoes, cook & whip
→ 3 cups all-purpose flour
→ 2 tsp vanilla extract
→ 1 tsp cinnamon or pie spice, optional

Options for sweet potatoes:

Bruce's Candied Yams: Put drained potatoes in a microwaveable bowl and heat on high for 4 minutes. Blend well with an electric mixer until smooth.

Fresh Sweet Potatoes: will have more flavor. Bake them, cool, peel and blend them until smooth.

Preheat oven to 350°F. Cream shortening and butter with an electric mixer, then add sugar until fluffy. Mix in baking powder and salt. Add eggs one at a time. Blend in potatoes, then gradually add flour (1/2 cup at a time). Stir in flavoring and spices. Mix on medium-low for 2 minutes. Pour batter into a greased 12-cup Bundt pan (fill 3/4 full). Bake for 40 minutes, then reduce heat to 325°F and bake another 50 minutes.

253) Red Velvet Cake

- → 2 1/2 cups all-purpose flour
- → 3 Tbsp cocoa, Hershey's
- → 3 tsp baking powder
- → 1/2 tsp soda
- → 3/4 tsp salt
- → 3/4 cup salted butter, room temperature
- → 2 1/2 cups granulated sugar
- → 3 large eggs, room temperature
- → 1 Tbsp white vinegar
- → 3/4 cup vegetable oil
- → 1 fluid oz. red food coloring
- → 1-1/2 cups buttermilk
- → or 1/2 cup water & 1 cup evaporated milk
- → 2 tsp vanilla extract

Preheat oven to 350°F. Whisk flour, cocoa, baking powder, baking soda, and salt. Beat butter and sugar until fluffy, then add eggs, vinegar, oil, food coloring, buttermilk, and vanilla. Mix in dry ingredients for 2 minutes on medium-low. Pour into greased pans, filling no more than 3/4 full. Bake 25-30 minutes until set; test with a toothpick. Cool and frost with Recipe #208 Cream Cheese Frosting.

 For a sheet cake bake at 325°F sheet cake will take at least 20 more mintues to bake. Avoid checking for at least 40 minutes.

254) How to Toast Pecans:

Toast whole pecans at 325°F for 5-8 minutes, stirring once during the process. Toast until they are dry and their flavor is enhanced but not darkened. If chopped pecans are needed, chop them after toasting.

Toast chopped pecans in a non-stick skillet over low heat, stirring until fragrant.

255) Snikerdoodle Cake, Spice Layers

- → 3/4 cup salted butter, room temperature
- → 2 cup granulated sugar
- → 3 large eggs, room temperature
- → 2 tsp baking powder
- → 3/4 tsp salt
- → 1/2 tsp ground ginger
- → 1 tsp ground cinnamon
- → 1/2 tsp ground nutmeg.
- → 1-1/2 cups milk
- → 2 tsp vanilla extract
- → 2 1/2 cups all-purpose flour

Preheat oven to 350°F. Beat butter and sugar until fluffy, for about 2 minutes. Add eggs one at a time. Mix in baking powder, salt, ginger, cinnamon, nutmeg, milk, and vanilla. Gradually add flour 1/2 cup at a time, then mix for 2 minutes on medium speed. Pour batter into 3 greased and floured pans Avoid filling more than 3/4 full. Bake 25-30 minutes, until the middle rises and edges pull away. Remove when a toothpick comes out clean.

 For a sheet cake bake at 325°F. Cake will take at least 20 more mintues to bake. Avoid checking for at least 40 minutes.

Frost with Recipe #208 Cream Cheese Frosting, but add:

- → 1 tsp. ground cinnamon to icing!

"Very mild spice flavor and is good iced with caramel or cream cheese frosting. If frosting with cream cheese or buttercream frosting, add 1 tsp of cinnamon to frosting."
- Tammy

256) Spanish Bar Cake

- → 2 cups all-purpose flour
- → 1-1/2 cups sugar
- → 1-1/2 tsp baking soda
- → 1 Tbsp cocoa powder, used Hershey's
- → 1 tsp ground cinnamon
- → 3/4 tsp salt
- → 1 tsp ground nutmeg
- → 1 tsp allspice, ground
- → 1/2 cup vegetable oil
- → 2 cups apple butter
- → 2 large eggs, slightly beaten
- → 1 cup raisins... Plump them in orange juice overnight, drain, and use. (Add these last, after everything else is mixed.)

Preheat the oven to 325°F. Assemble all spices and remaining ingredients before beginning. In a large mixing bowl, combine flour, sugar, and baking soda. Incorporate cocoa powder, cinnamon, salt, nutmeg, and allspice, blending thoroughly. Add vegetable oil, applesauce, and beaten eggs to the dry mixture, mixing until smooth. Gently fold in the prepared raisins. Transfer the batter to a greased and floured 9x13-inch cake pan. Bake at 325°F for 45 to 60 minutes, or until a toothpick inserted into the center comes out clean.

For The Frosting:

- → 8 oz. cream cheese, softened
- → 4 Tbsp salted butter, softened
- → 2 tsp vanilla extract
- → 2 cups confectioner's sugar
- → 1/3 cup milk
- → 1 Tbsp lemon juice, fresh
- → 1/2 cup walnuts, chopped - optional

Mix the cream cheese, butter, vanilla, confectioner's sugar, milk, and lemon juice together. Spread over the cake.

> **Rom 1:16**
>
> "For I am not ashamed of the gospel of Christ: for it is the power of God unto salvation to everyone that believeth; to the Jew first, and also to the Greek." KJV

257) Southern Praline Cake, Tammy's

- → 1 cup salted butter, room temperature
- → 2 1/2 cups granulated sugar
- → 4 large eggs, room temperature
- → 2 tsp vanilla extract
- → 1 tsp butter extract
- → 3 tsp baking powder
- → 1 tsp salt
- → 1-1/4 cup milk
- → 3 cups all-purpose flour

Preheat oven to 350°F. Beat butter in a stand mixer for 2 minutes, then add sugar and mix until fluffy. Mix in eggs one at a time, then add baking powder and salt. Alternate adding flour and milk, mixing for 2 minutes. Pour batter into 3 greased, floured cake pans (no more than 3/4 full) and bake until a toothpick comes out clean. Cool layers and ice with Recipe #258 Browned Butter Icing.

258) Browned Butter Icing

- → 5 cups confectioner's sugar, sift if lumpy
- → 1/4 tsp salt
- → 1 cup salted butter, browned
- → 1/2 cup half and half (half milk, half cream)

Add butter to a saucepan or skillet and cook on medium heat until brown. Take off heat, cool 20 minutes. Add butter to a stand mixer with salt, powdered sugar, and milk- beat until creamy. Add more milk to make it more spreadable if desired.

Topping:

- → 1 Jar Caramel Topping

Remove lid from the jar and microwave for 30 seconds, or until spreadable. Pour it over the center of the cake. Use a spatula to spread the icing across the top, letting it drizzle down the sides. Garnish sides with toasted chopped pecans.

259) Sponge Cake, Mama's Blue-Ribbon

→ 3/4 cup sugar
→ 1-1/2 cups self-rising flour

Sift the above ingredients together in an x-large bowl

→ 6 large eggs, room temperature
→ 1/4 cup water
→ 1 tsp vanilla extract
→ 1/4 cup granulated sugar
→ 1 tsp cream of tartar

Begin by separating the eggs, placing the whites into a mixing bowl, and reserving the yolks in another container. Add the egg whites to a mixer set at low speed, then gradually incorporate 1/4 cup of sugar and cream of tartar. Increase the mixer speed to high and continue beating until stiff peaks form and the mixture appears glossy; set the egg whites aside once finished. In a separate bowl, whisk together the yolks, water, and vanilla until the mixture becomes very foamy and frothy. Carefully add the dry ingredients to the yolk mixture, beating on high speed until a creamy consistency is achieved. Transfer the beaten whites to an extra-large bowl, pour the yolk mixture over them, and gently fold with a spatula—ensuring not to stir— until fully combined. Pour the batter into a dry, ungreased tube pan. Bake at 350°F for 45 minutes. Once baked, invert the cake to cool completely. Use a spatula to loosen the cake from the sides of the pan, then remove both the bottom and flute in the same manner.

"Mama got a blue ribbon at our county fair for this cake. She was so proud." -Tammy

260) Sweet Potato or Pumpkin Cheesecake

→ 2-8 oz. cream cheese, room temperature
→ 1 cup granulated sugar (1 3/4 cups if using pumpkin)
→ 2 cups cooked sweet potatoes, whipped or 16 oz. can pumpkin
→ 2 tsp vanilla extract
→ 2 Tbsp flour
→ 1/2 tsp salt
→ 1 cup sour cream
→ 1/2 cup whipping cream
→ 6 large egg whites
→ 1/4 cup granulated sugar

Preheat oven to 350°F. Set a water-filled cake pan on the bottom rack. Beat cream cheese and sugar until smooth. Mix in sweet potatoes or pumpkin, vanilla, flour, salt, then sour cream. In a clean bowl, beat egg whites on high until frothy; gradually add 1/4 cup sugar until soft peaks form. Fold into cheesecake mixture. Pour into a 9- or 10-inch springform pan with a Recipe #261, graham cracker crust. Bake for 30 minutes at 350°F, then reduce to 325°F and bake another 30 minutes. Turn off oven and let rest in oven for 1 hour. Remove from pan, chill, and serve with fruit or pie filling if you like.

261) Graham Cracker Crust:

→ 12 whole graham crackers, crushed
→ 1/3 cup salted butter, melted
→ 1/4 cup granulated sugar

Mix the ingredients above and press into a 9-inch spring-form pan. Bake at 350°F for 15 minutes. Remove and cool completely.

262) Mexican meets Cola Cake, Tammy's

→ 2 1/2 cups self-rising flour
→ 2 1/4 cups granulated sugar
→ 3/4 cup cocoa, Hershey's
→ 1/4 tsp salt
→ 1/2 tsp ground cinnamon
→ 1/2 tsp baking soda
→ 3 large eggs, room temperature
→ 1/2 cup sour cream
→ 1 cup Coca Cola
→ 1 cup milk
→ 1/2 cup salted butter, melted
→ 1 tsp vanilla extract
→ 3/4 cup cooking oil

Combine dry ingredients in a bowl and whisk until cocoa is blended. In a mixing bowl, mix eggs, sour cream, cola, milk, butter, vanilla, and oil. Add dry ingredients 1/2 cup at a time, then mix at medium-low for 2 minutes. Pour into a greased and floured 13 x 9 x 2-inch pan. Bake at 325°F for 40-45 minutes until a toothpick inserted in the center comes out clean.

For the Frosting:

→ 1/2 cup butter
→ 6 tablespoons Coca cola
→ 2 tablespoons unsweetened cocoa powder
→ 4 cups confectioners' sugar
→ 1 cup chopped pecans

Combine butter, cola, and cocoa in a saucepan; bring to a boil. Pour over confectioners' sugar in a large bowl; mix well. Stir in chopped nuts.

Rom 3:10
"As it is written, There is none righteous, no, not one:"

Mexican Meets Cola

3 Popular Cakes in One!

"I created this recipe from 3 different popular cakes! Mexican Chocolate Cake, Texas Sheet Cake and Coca Cola Cake. It has everything that makes those 3 chocolate cakes stand out above all others! My Aunt Susan made a cake very similar to this each Christmas, and we loved it and looked forward to it as kids...Tammy"

263) Toffee Pecan Crunch Cake

Topping: combine and set aside

→ 1/2 cup brown sugar
→ 1 cup Heath English toffee bits
→ 1 cup chopped pecans
→ 1 Tbsp cinnamon
→ 1 cup sweetened flaked coconut, optional

Cake Batter:

→ 1 cup water
→ 3/4 cup oil
→ 1 tsp vanilla extract
→ 4 large eggs, room temperature
→ 3.4 oz. pkg. Instant vanilla pudding
→ 3.4 oz. pkg. Instant butterscotch pudding
→ 1 cup granulated sugar
→ 2 cups self-rising flour

 Option: if you use all-purpose flour in cake batter, add 2 tsp baking powder and 1 tsp salt.

Preheat the oven to 350°F. Grease and flour a 13"x9"x2" sheet cake pan. In a bowl, mix water, oil, vanilla, and eggs. Add puddings and blend on low speed, then mix in sugar and gradually add flour. Beat at a medium speed for 2 minutes. Pour half the batter into a pan, layer with half the topping, add the rest of the batter, and top with remaining topping. Bake at 350°F for 45 minutes.

264) Whoopie Pies:

→ 1-1/2 cups granulated sugar
→ 1/2 cup Hershey's cocoa
→ 2 cups self-rising flour
→ 1 large egg
→ 1/2 cup shortening
→ 1/2 cup water
→ 1/3 cup oil

Place ingredients in a large bowl and mix thoroughly. Drop onto a cookie sheet lined with parchment with 2 Tbsp cookie scoop or by tablespoons. Bake at 350°F for 10 minutes.

265) Whoopie Pie Fluff:

→ 1/2 cup shortening
→ 3 Tbsp Salted butter
→ 1/2 cup confectioner's sugar
→ 7 oz. marshmallow fluff
→ 1 tsp vanilla extract
→ 1/4 tsp salt

Mix the ingredients for the filling until creamy and smooth. Pipe it between two cooled cookies. Cakes are very delicate, so piping the filling is the best option. If you spread it, you must do so very carefully. Filling can be doubled if desired. Makes one dozen whoopie pies

266) Yellow Cake Layers, Tammy's

→ 2 1/2 cups self-rising flour
→ 2 cups granulated sugar
→ 1/2 cup salted butter, room temperature
→ 3/4 cup cooking oil
→ 3 large eggs room temperature
→ 1 egg yolk
→ 1/2 cup sour cream
→ 1/2 cup milk
→ 1/2 cup water
→ 1 tsp vanilla extract

Preheat oven to 350°F. Mix sugar, butter, oil, eggs, sour cream, and milk. Gradually add 1/2 cup flour at a time, then water after 1 1/2 cups of flour has been added. Continue with the remaining flour, add vanilla. Batter will be thin. Pour into three greased and floured round pans. Do not fill more than 3/4 full. Bake until the middle rises and edges pull away. Do not open oven for 25 minutes for layers

 If you are baking a sheet cake use a 13x9x2-inch well greased and floured aluminum pan. Bake at 325°F and don't check on it for at least 40 minutes. Cake should rise in the middle as tall as sides. Check with a toothpick or cake tester in the center for doneness. Remove and cool on a wire rack for 15 minutes prior to removing from the pan.

"This is a great birthday cake layer! It is very moist and delicious. The cake in the picture is frosted with Recipe #407, Sour Cream Chocolate Frosting. This is my personal favorite chocolate frosting!" -Tammy

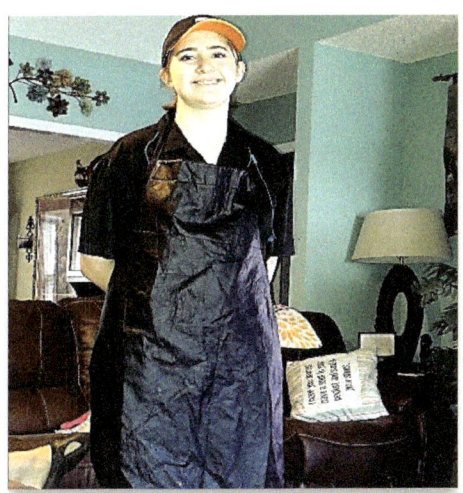

May gets her first job in high school at a pizza place! She was so excited.

70'S GELATIN! STRAWBERRY CAKE

Recipe 295

Cake Mix Creations

Easy, Delicious Cakes Anyone Can Master

Welcome to Cake Mix Creations—a section devoted to making baking approachable, fun, and fool-proof for everyone. If you have ever felt intimidated by homemade cakes, you are about to become a confident baker! With just a box of cake mix and a few simple add-ins, you can whip up desserts that look and taste like they came from a bakery. From ultra-moist birthday layers to crowd-pleasers like Earthquake Cake, these recipes are designed for both seasoned bakers and total beginners. You will find step-by-step instructions, handy baking tips, and plenty of encouragement along the way.

Do not worry about fussy techniques or complicated ingredients—these cakes are all about getting fantastic results with minimal effort. So, grab your favorite cake mix, gather your mixing bowls, and let your kitchen fill with the wonderful aroma of something delicious baking in the oven. Dive in, experiment, and enjoy the sweet satisfaction that comes from creating homemade treats the easy way. You've got this—and your friends and family are in for a treat! - *Tammy*

Peter Paul Mounds Cake, Recipe#247 Use a cake mix layer to make this amazing sheet cake! It is so moist and delicious!

104

267) Banana Nut Pound Cake

- → 4 bananas
- → 4 large eggs, room temperature
- → 1/3 cup vegetable oil
- → 1 box yellow cake mix
- → 1/2 tsp ground cinnamon
- → 1/2 tsp ground nutmeg
- → 1 cup chopped pecans

Mash bananas in a bowl. Mix in eggs and oil, then add cake mix and beat for 1 minute. Stir in cinnamon, nutmeg, and 1 cup chopped pecans; mix for another minute. Spray a bundt pan with baking spray, pour in the batter, and sprinkle with more pecans. Optionally, dust with fresh nutmeg. Bake at 350°F for 1 hour.

268) Black Forest Cake, Easy

- → 1 Devil's Food cake mix
- → eggs, water, oil (per directions)
- → 20 oz. can cherry pie filling

Prepare cake batter per package directions. Bake in two round cake pans. Cool the cake before icing. Trim the top mound off both cake layers. Leave this extra cake out until dry enough to crumble. Crumble cake through handheld mesh strainer or cooling rack grid. Continue with Recipe #269.

269) Whipping Cream Frosting:

- → 3 cups heavy whipping cream
- → 1-1/2 cups powdered sugar
- → 3/4 tsp vanilla extract

Chill the mixing bowl and whipping cream in the freezer for 10 minutes. Sift powdered sugar. Beat the chilled cream in the cold bowl until slightly thick, then add powdered sugar and vanilla and beat until thick (do not overbeat). Place one cake layer on a plate, pipe whipped cream around the edge and fill middle with half the cherry filling. Add the top cake layer. Cover the sides with whipped cream, smoothing it out, and pipe a border on top. Add the remaining pie filling to the center, sprinkle chocolate crumbs on borders, and pipe circles topped with drained maraschino cherries. Keep refrigerated and serve cold.

270) Eggnog Pound Cake, Easy

- → 2 Tbsp salted butter
- → 1/2 cup slivered almonds
- → 1 yellow or white cake mix
- → 3.4 oz. Instant vanilla pudding
- → 4 large eggs, room temperature
- → 2 Tbsp rum or rum extract
- → 1/8 tsp ground nutmeg
- → 1 cup commercial eggnog, or Recipe#92
- → 1/4 cup salted butter, melted

Preheat oven to 350°F. Butter the Bundt pan base, spray the sides and center, then add almonds. Mix all other ingredients until smooth, pour into pan, and bake for 45 minutes or until a skewer or cake tester comes out clean. Cool on a wire rack before removing it from pan.

 Tammy's tip: for a tall cake double the recipe. But do not use two pudding mixes if you double it.

Rom 3:11,12

"There is none that understandeth, there is none that seeketh after God."

"They are all gone out of the way, they are together become unprofitable; there is none that doeth good, no, not one." KJV

271) Chocolate Chip Pound Cake

→ 1 box yellow Butter cake mix
→ eggs, water, oil (per directions)
→ 2 large eggs
→ 8 oz. sour cream
→ 3.4 oz. box chocolate or vanilla instant pudding mix
→ 12 oz. pkg. chocolate chips
→ 1/2 cup chopped pecans, optional

Prepare cake batter per package directions then add sour cream, pudding and 2 extra eggs, and mix 1 minute. Fold in the chips and nuts. and pour into a greased and floured tube pan. Bake at 325°F for about 1 hour. Let it set in the pan for 30 minutes.

Topping:

→ 2 Tbsp salted butter
→ 1/2 cup evaporated milk
→ 1/4 cup powdered sugar
→ 12 oz. chocolate chips
→ 1 tsp vanilla extract

Combine the first four ingredients in a double boiler over hot water. Stir well. Pour the mixture over the cake. (can microwave low and slow, and mix well)

272) Daddy Dump Cake

→ 20 oz. can crushed pineapple
→ 20 oz. can cherry filling
→ 1 box yellow cake mix
→ 1 cup pecans, chopped
→ 1 cup salted butter

Grease a 9 x 13-inch pan. Spread pineapple with juice on bottom of pan. Dump in pie filling (we place it over pineapple by the spoonful until all is added evenly). Do not mix up. Pour cake mix over evenly. Sprinkle nuts over the top evenly. Drop butter in slices across the entire top. Bake at 350°F for 1 hour. This is like a buttery cobbler!

 Option: use different types of cake mixes and or fruit filling. Enjoy it is so good y'all.

273) Earthquake Cake

→ 1 German chocolate cake mix, prepare batter as per box directions
→ 1/2 cup salted butter, room temperature
→ 8 oz. cream cheese, room temperature
→ 2 cups powdered sugar
→ 1-1/2 cups flaked coconut
→ 1 cup chopped pecans

Preheat oven to 350°F. Prepare cake mix and set batter aside.

Combine butter, cream cheese, and sugar. Blend with an electric mixer until creamy. Spray a 13x9x2" cake pan well with baking spray (or grease and flour).

Sprinkle coconut evenly across bottom of pan. Next, sprinkle nuts evenly over coconut. Pour cake batter over coconut and pecans. Drop cream cheese mixture over top of batter, using a Tbsp, in dollops evenly across top. Take your spatula and carefully run it through top of cake to marble cream cheese in a little. (NOT TOO MUCH or it will not make craters while baking)

Bake at 350°F for 1 hour. Take out and enjoy hot or cool!

274) Easy Fruit Bar Cakes

- → 1 box white cake mix (NOT yellow)
- → 20 oz. can pie filling (your choice of fruit) fresh fruit for garnish
- → 8 oz. container of Cool Whip topping
- → 8 oz. cream cheese, room temperature

Bake cake per package directions in a 13"x9"x2" sheet cake pan. Remove, cool 5-10 min. Then, flip out on parchment paper.

Cake:

Cool Cake completely. Cut sheet cake into 3 wide sections crosswise or 2 long sections lengthwise. Split each bar of cake into two layers. Stack pieces and trim off brown edges.

Filling:

Use canned pie filling or mix half a can of pie filling with 8 oz. room temp. cream cheese for a richer bar cake. Wash, dry, and slice fresh fruit if using. Place the bottom layer of the bar on a serving plate. Spread the filling over the bottom layer and top with pieces of fruit. Then place the top cake layer on the bar. Add a generous layer of Cool Whip (or whipping cream). Swirl the top and garnished with pieces of fresh fruit or canned drained fruit.

 Option: Lemon, use lemon filling blended with 8 oz. cream cheese. Garnish with lemon zest.

275) Gooey Butter Cake

1st Layer:

- → 2 large eggs
- → 1/2 cup salted butter, room temperature
- → 1 box of poundcake mix (not regular cake mixes)

Mix the ingredients above (batter will be sticky and thick). Spray a 7x11 or 9x9 brownie pan with baking spray. Using a spatula, spread batter evenly across the bottom of the pan.

2nd Layer:

- → 2 large eggs
- → 8 oz. cream cheese, room temperature
- → 1 tsp vanilla extract
- → 1 lb. powdered sugar (reserve 1/8 cup for garnish)

Cream together two eggs, vanilla, and cream cheese until well blended. Add powdered sugar, reserving a little for the cake topping. Mix until smooth, then pour over the bottom layer in the pan. The pan will look full, but that is okay! Bake for 25 minutes at 325°F. Sprinkle powdered sugar on top of the cake and return to the oven to bake for an additional 35 minutes at 300°F! (The total baking time is 1 hour.) Remove and enjoy it warm or cold!

"Prepare to be amazed!"-Tammy

276) Lemon Gooey Butter Cake

Make Recipe #275 but use a

- → Lemon Pound Cake mix

in place of the regular pound cake mix for the 1st layer. Then add:

- → 1/2 tsp. lemon extract

to the 2nd layer. Finish making per Recipe #275's instructions.

 This cake is popular, and many use a regular cake mix. I think the pound cake mix is a better choice because it creates great crunchy edges and it is more like bars.

Red velvet cake is a great choice for Christmas, and specialty mixes like Lemon Supreme will work well too.

Use the small brownie size pan for all types of mixes as it makes a tall bar with a thicker cream cheese layer.

277) Tammy's Tropical Dream Cake

→ 3 large eggs, room temperature
→ 1/2 cup water
→ 3/4 cup vegetable oil
→ 8 oz. can crushed pineapple with juice
→ 2 medium, ripe bananas, mashed
→ 1 tsp vanilla extract
→ 1 tsp lemon extract
→ 1 strawberry cake mix
→ 3 oz box strawberry flavored gelatin
→ 3.4 oz. vanilla instant pudding mix
→ 1/2 cup self-rising flour
→ 14 oz. bag sweetened flaked coconut
→ 1/2 cup chopped pecans
→ 16 oz. container whipped topping

Combine eggs, water, and oil in a mixing bowl on low speed. Stir in pineapple, bananas, and extracts. Mix in cake mix, sweetened gelatin, pudding mix, and flour thoroughly. Fold in 1/2 cup coconut and pecans. Pour batter into three greased, floured pans. Bake at 325°F for 40 minutes; test with a toothpick—bake longer if needed, as fruit cakes require extra time. Avoid opening the oven for 30 minutes.

Ice cake with whipped topping or fresh whipping cream. Cover cake with remaining coconut if desired.

For richer cake, ice with Recipe #296 Strawberry icing.

 This cake must be refrigerated because it has so much moisture.

"I hope you enjoy this Tammy original!"
- Tammy

278) Tammy's Italian Cream Cake

→ 1 cup chopped pecans
→ 12 oz. flaked coconut (reserve 1/2 cup unbaked for cake batter)
→ 4 oz. cream cheese, room temperature
→ 1/4 cup salted butter, room temperature
→ 3 large eggs
→ 1 box white cake mix
→ 1 cup buttermilk
→ 1/2 cup warm water

Preheat oven to 350°F. Toast pecans with coconut (except reserved coconut) until golden, stirring occasionally. Set aside for batter and icing. Blend cream cheese and butter until smooth, then add eggs, cake mix, buttermilk, and water; beat for 2 minutes. Stir in 1/2 cup toasted coconut with pecans and 1/2 cup unbaked coconut. Mix well and divide into three greased, floured round pans. Bake until the centers rise and cakes pull from pan sides; do not open oven for at least 25 minutes to check on cake.

The remaining toasted coconut/pecans will be used in icing and to decorate outside of cake. Make Recipe # 208 and Italian cream option. Ice cooled layers and top with remaining toasted coconut and pecans. This cake must be refrigerated.

"Each time I make this cake, people RAVE about how delicious it is. This is an AMAZING cake, and you will not find a better recipe, I promise."-Tammy

Rom 3:17
"And the way of peace have they not known: There is no fear of God before their eyes." KJV
Rom 3:20
"Therefore by the deeds of the law there shall no flesh be justified in his sight: for by the law is the knowledge of sin." KJV

279) Better Than Sex Cake

→ 1 box yellow cake mix
→ 1/3 cup self-rising flour
→ 3.4 oz. instant vanilla pudding mix
→ 1/2 cup water
→ 1/2 cup vegetable oil
→ 3 large eggs, room temperature
→ 1 cup sour cream
→ 4 oz. German's sweet chocolate melted
→ 6 oz. semi-sweet chocolate chips
→ 1 cup pecans, toasted
→ 1 cup flaked coconut, toasted

Preheat oven to 350°F and grease a tube pan. Mix cake mix, flour, pudding, water, and oil with an electric mixer. Add eggs one at a time, beating well, then blend in sour cream and melted chocolate. Stir in chocolate chips, nuts, and coconut. Pour into pan and bake for 50-60 minutes, until a tester comes out clean. Cool for 15 minutes, loosen the edges, and turn onto a rack. Serve cake with whipping cream.

 Toast pecans whole, then chop. If they are already chopped, toast them in a non-stick skillet on the stovetop until they become fragrant.

280) Honeybun Cake

→ 1 cup salted butter, room temperature
→ 1 box of butter cake mix (reserve 1/2 cup of dry mix for cinnamon layer)
→ 4 large eggs, room temperature
→ 8 oz. sour cream

Beat butter until it is fluffy and light in color. Add the remaining ingredients (minus the reserved dry cake mix) and mix on medium speed for 2 minutes. Pour half of the batter into a well-greased 13"x9"x2" cake pan.

Cinnamon Layer:

→ 1/2 cup reserved cake mix
→ 1/2 cup light brown sugar, packed
→ 2 tsp ground cinnamon
→ 1/2 cup chopped pecans

Mix the cinnamon layer ingredients above and spread evenly over the batter in the pan. Top with the remaining cake batter and bake at 325°F for 45 minutes.

Glaze:

→ 1 cup powdered sugar
→ 1 tsp vanilla extract
→ 2 Tbsp milk

"Spread over the cake while still hot. "Best Cake Ever" -*Tammy*

281) Lemonade Cake

→ 1 box of white cake mix
→ 3 oz. box lemon flavored gelatin (Jell-O)
→ 3.4 oz. Box vanilla instant pudding
→ 3/4 cup vegetable oil
→ 1 cup lemonade
→ 4 large eggs, room temperature
→ 1 cup sour cream
→ 1 tsp lemon extract

Mix all ingredients and pour into a well-greased 13x9x2 sheet cake pan, or two round cake pans. Bake at 350°F for 30-35 minutes or until a toothpick comes out clean and the cake has begun to pull away from the edges of the pan. Leave in the pan and cool on a cooling rack. If making round layers, let them cool for 5-10 minutes, then flip them out onto parchment paper and cool on a cooling rack.

 Frost with Recipe #208 Cream Cheese Frosting

282) Nutmeg Cake

- → 4 large eggs
- → 3/4 cup oil
- → 3/4 cup sherry or fruit juice
- → 1 tsp vanilla extract
- → 1 tsp nutmeg
- → 1 yellow cake mix (or white cake mix)

Note: Omit the box of pudding if your cake mix already contains pudding in the mix.

- → 3.4 oz. instant vanilla pudding

Mix oil, sherry (or juice), and eggs, then add cake mix. Stir in pudding and nutmeg. Pour into a well-greased Bundt pan. Bake at 325°F for 50 minutes. Dust the cake with powdered sugar before serving.

"This recipe was given to me by a viewer. It is so good if you are a fan of nutmeg. It is easy to make, and it does not have to be frosted."
- *Tammy*

283) Pie Filling Cake

- → 1 box white cake mix
- → 1 can of pie filling (your choice)
- → 1/2 cup vegetable oil
- → 2 large eggs

Mix the white cake mix with oil and eggs. Gently fold in the pie filling with a spatula to avoid crushing the fruit. Make sure all the batter is well incorporated. Bake the cake at 325°F for 40 minutes in a well-greased and floured tube pan.

Frost with Recipe #284, Pudding Frosting

284) Pudding Frosting

- → 3.4 oz. pkg. instant pudding (your choice of flavor)
- → 1 cup milk
- → 8 oz. container of cool whip

Stir the milk into the pudding mix, wait 2 minutes, then use a mixer to blend in Cool Whip. Spread the mixture over the cake. Serve it the same day it is iced. Keep any leftover cake covered and refrigerated.

"Have fun mixing your favorite flavors together for this cake! I think peach filling would be delicious with vanilla pudding.!"
- *Tammy*

285) Pig Pick' in Cake

- → 1 white cake mix
- → 1 cup milk or 3/4 cup orange juice
- → 3 oz. box orange flavored gelatin (Jell-O)
- → 3 large eggs, room temperature
- → 1/2 cup salted butter, room temperature
- → 15 oz. can mandarin oranges, drained

Mix the ingredients above together (excluding drained oranges). Mix the batter for 2 minutes. Do not use an electric mixer to mix the oranges. Fold in the oranges with a large spoon. Divide the batter evenly into two well-greased and floured 8" or 9" round cake pans and bake at 350°F for about 35-40 minutes. (It may take longer, so check with a toothpick and continue baking until done.) Flip onto parchment paper and cool on a wire rack before icing the cake. Frost with Recipe #286 Pineapple Pudding Frosting.

286) Pineapple Pudding Frosting

- → 8 oz. cool whip topping
- → 20 oz. can crushed pineapple with juice
- → 5 oz. box instant vanilla pudding

Mix a can of pineapple with pudding. Add Cool Whip and mix until well blended. Ice orange cake layers, wrap, and refrigerate the cake.

"This picture was taken during my cancer treatments. I had a tea party for the kids. I am wearing my favorite wig a Gabor wig." -*Tammy*

287) Tunnel of Fudge Cake

- → 1 devil's food cake mix eggs, oil, water per package directions.
- → 1 cup sour cream

Go by ingredients on cake mix box. Put eggs, oil, and water in mixing bowl, then dry cake mix. Add sour cream and mix well. Grease and flour (or spray well) a 10 cup Bundt pan. Put all batter in Bundt pan.

Pudding Filling:

- → Recipe #288 Dark Chocolate Pudding

Put pudding in a plastic quart freezer bag. Starting 1" from corner cut bag at a 45° angle. Squeeze pudding around the center of cake one time. Bake at 325°F for 1 hour and 15 minutes. Let cool fully on a wire rack before turning out. Finish with Recipe #415 Vanilla Glaze.

288) Dark Chocolate Pudding

- → 1/4 cup cocoa, used Hershey's or 1/8 cup for milk chocolate pudding
- → 1 1/2 cups granulated sugar
- → 1 cup of boiling water, use microwave to boil in a 2-cup glass liquid measuring cup
- → 3 Tbsp corn starch
- → 1 large egg
- → 1 tsp vanilla extract
- → 2 Tbsp. salted butter
- → 1/4 tsp salt

In a batter bowl, whisk cocoa, sugar, and cornstarch. Add boiling water and mix well, then add the egg and whisk thoroughly. Microwave for 3 minutes. Microwave for a longer time if needed. Add vanilla and butter and salt-mix.

 Tip: Replace homemade pudding using an instant pudding, Mix a 5 oz. chocolate or vanilla pudding in 1.5 cups of milk.

289) Peaches & Cream Cake

Peaches

- → use 15 oz. can sliced peaches in syrup
- → or use 1-1/2 to 2 cups of fresh peaches (or frozen) sliced thin
- → 1/2 cup sugar

Microwave sugar and peaches for 2 minutes, then mash and chill.

Drain the peaches and set the syrup aside for the cake batter. Put the peaches in a chopper and chop them. Use 1/3 cup of chopped peaches in the batter. Strain the remaining peaches WELL for icing.

For the Cake:

- → 1 box white cake mix
- → 3 oz. peach flavored gelatin
- → 3/4 cup oil
- → 1/2 cup reserved peach syrup/juice
- → 4 large eggs, room temperature
- → 1/3 cup chopped peaches

Combine all ingredients thoroughly and transfer the mixture to a well-greased 1/4 sheet cake pan. Bake at 325°F for 40 to 45 minutes, or until a toothpick inserted into the center comes out clean. Allow the cake to cool in the pan on a wire rack. Frost with Recipe #290 Peach Frosting.

290) Peach Frosting

- → 1/2 stick salted butter, room temperature
- → 4 oz. cream cheese, room temperature
- → 3 1/2 cups powdered sugar
- → Well strained peaches

Mix the ingredients well. Make sure the peaches are not too syrupy, or the icing will be runny. Chill the cake in the pan.

291) Pina Colada Pound Cake

- → 16 oz. can cream of coconut
- → 1 white or yellow cake mix
- → 3.4 oz. instant vanilla pudding mix
- → 1/3 cup cooking oil
- → 4 large eggs, room temperature
- → 8 oz. can crushed pineapple

Combine cream of coconut in a bowl, whisk until smooth, and set aside 1/4 cup for glaze. Mix cake mix, pudding, oil, eggs, pineapple, and the remaining cream of coconut. Pour into a greased Bundt pan and bake at 325°F for 60 minutes. Cool and glaze with Recipe #292 Coconut Glaze.

 Option: can omit pudding if cake mix has pudding in mix.

292) Coconut Glaze:

- → 1 1/2 cups powdered sugar
- → 1 tsp vanilla extract
- → reserved 1/4 cup cream of coconut

Mix powdered sugar, vanilla, and the reserved cream of coconut to make a glaze. Pour it over the cake. Enjoy!

293) Easy Hummingbird Cake

- → 3/4 cup oil
- → 1/4 cup water
- → 3 large eggs, room temperature
- → 1 coconut supreme cake mix
- → 1 tsp vanilla extract
- → 2 medium ripe bananas, mashed.
- → 1/2 cup flaked coconut, Baker's brand
- → 8 oz can crushed pineapple with juice
- → 1/2 cup chopped pecans

Combine oil, water, eggs, and cake mix in a mixer; beat for 2 minutes on medium. Add vanilla, bananas, coconut, pineapple, and pecans, mixing for one more minute. Pour into a greased Bundt pan and bake at 325°F for 45

minutes. Test with a cake tester before removing. Cool before serving. Glaze if desired. Recipes #402 Buttermilk glaze is pictured above with cake.

294) Pecan Upside-Down Bundt Cake

Spray your Bundt pan with baking spray.

- → 1/2 cup melted butter
- → 1/3 cup light brown sugar
- → 1/2 cup pecans

Pour butter in the bottom of your prepared bundt pan. Add brown sugar and pecans and set aside.

- → 1 Butter Golden cake mix
- → 3.4 oz vanilla instant pudding mix
- → 3 large eggs
- → 1 cup water
- → 1/2 cup vegetable oil

Combine cake mix, pudding mix, eggs, water, and oil; beat for 2 minutes. Pour over pecans in a bundt pan and bake at 350°F for 40–45 minutes. Cool for 10 minutes, tap the pan, and invert it onto a plate.

"I got this recipe and photo from my sister, Malissa! She ensured me it was delicious, so I added it to the cookbook. Nothing says Southern like delicious pecans!" -Tammy

295) Strawberry 70's Cake

→ Strawberry Topping Recipe #421 (or 16 oz. container of frozen sweetened sliced strawberries.)
→ 1 box of white cake mix (must be white)
→ 3 oz. strawberry flavored gelatin
→ 3/4 cup vegetable oil
→ 1/2 cup water
→ 4 large eggs, room temperature
→ 1/2 heaping cup of Strawberry Topping

Mix all ingredients and pour into a well-greased 13x9x2 sheet cake pan. Bake at 350°F for 35-40 minutes or until a toothpick inserted in the center comes out clean and the cake has started to pull away from the edges of the pan. Leave it in the pan to cool on a cooling rack.

296) Strawberry Buttercream Frosting

→ 1/2 cup salted butter
→ 3 1/2 cups powdered sugar
→ 1/2 cup Recipe #421 Strawberry Topping strained very well, or icing will be runny

Mix the ingredients thoroughly. Ensure the strawberries are not too syrupy or the icing

In the picture I made the strawberry cake in round layers and topped the cake with strawberry preserves!

"This is the best strawberry cake! Everyone loves it, so please try it." -Tammy

297) Watergate Cake

→ 1 box white cake mix
→ 3.4-oz. box Instant pistachio pudding mix
→ 1 cup vegetable oil
→ 3 large egg whites
→ 1 cup Sprite or Club soda

Note: Buy a cake mix that doesn't already contain pudding.

Mix the cake mix and pudding together. Add eggs, oil, and soda. Mix all ingredients for 4 minutes at medium speed. Stir in the nuts. Bake for 40-45 minutes at the temp. specified on the box. Allow it to cool. Frost with Recipe #298!

298) Pistachio Pudding Frosting

→ 1.3 oz. pkg. dream whip (1 envelope)
→ 1-1/4 cup cold milk
→ 3.4 oz. box instant pistachio pudding mix

Blend Dream Whip and milk. Beat at high speed to peaks. Gradually add pudding. Beat until light and fluffy.

Options: Decorate the top of the cake with flaked coconut, chopped pecans, and maraschino cherries. You can also add 1/2 cup chopped pecans to the cake layer before baking if desired.

299) Whole Shebang Cake

→ 1 yellow or white cake mix
→ 15 oz. can fruit cocktail, drained
→ 2 ripe bananas, mashed
→ 1/2 cup flaked coconut, Baker's
→ 1/2 cup chopped pecans
→ 1/2 cup applesauce
→ 3 large eggs, room temperature

Place eggs in a mixing bowl and beat well. Add the remaining ingredients and mix on medium/low speed for 2 minutes. Pour into a well-greased (or sprayed) Bundt pan and bake at 325°F for 1 hour and 20 minutes. Enjoy! These can also be made into cupcakes.

Baker's coconut is so moist and delicious. Please use it if it's available. It is worth the extra dollar in the grocery store!

Casseroles & Skillets

Welcome to the Casseroles & Skillets section! Here you will find many of my family recipes like my old-fashioned mac n cheese, squash casserole, and green bean casserole. Above you can see my Mama's sweet potato souffle. This recipe is a true treasure. I used to make it for several families every holiday. This is the BEST one I have ever tasted!

Please give it a try! Each recipe is designed to bring warmth and tradition to your table, making this section an essential part of the cookbook for hearty, home-cooked meals.

300) Baked Spaghetti Casserole

→ 1/2 lb. Italian sausage (Swaggerty's farm)
→ 1 lb. ground chuck
→ olive oil
→ onionchopped
→ 1 bell pepperchopped
→ 2 cloves garlic, pressed
→ 1 Tbsp. Italian seasoning
→ 1 Tbsp. beef bouillon granules
→ 2-8 oz. can crushed tomatoes
→ 2-8 oz. can diced tomatoes
→ 1 lb. spaghetti or angel hair pasta
→ 8 oz. cheese, grated (your choice)
→ 8 oz. mozzarella cheese, grated
→ salt
→ parmesan cheese, grated

Cook pasta according to package directions. Drain and rinse with water. In a skillet, brown the sausage and beef, drain and set aside. In the same skillet, sauté pepper and onion until soft. Add the cooked beef and sausage, garlic, Italian seasoning, bouillon granules, crushed and diced tomatoes, and stir well. Put the cooked pasta and sauce into a large pot used to boil the pasta. Mix thoroughly. Add two cups of shredded cheese and stir again. Pour the mixture into a well-greased deep lasagna baking dish. Top with grated mozzarella cheese and sprinkle with fresh or dried parsley. Bake in a 350°F oven for 60 minutes or until hot bubbly. Serve with grated Parmesan and garlic bread. If baking a cold casserole, it will take it longer to cook.

301) Baked Chicken Salad

Mix:

→ 3 cups cooked chopped chicken
→ 1 cup diced celery
→ 2 hard-boiled eggs, chopped
→ 1/2 cup mayonnaise
→ 10.5 oz. can cream of chicken soup
→ 2 Tbsp. chopped green onion, or onion
→ 1 tsp of Worcestershire
→ 1/2 tbsp. lemon juice, optional
→ 8 oz can water chestnuts, drain- chop

After mixing put in a 9"x9" or 9" round baking dish.

Topping:

→ 1/2 sleeve of saltine crackers, crushed
→ 1/2 cup slivered almonds
→ 1/2 stick melted butter poured over crackers and almonds

Bake at 350°F for 30 minutes. Enjoy as a dip or on a sandwich.

302) Pepper Jack Mac

→ 8 oz. creamy Havarti cheese (used Amish country cheese)
→ 12 oz. pepper jack cheese
→ 1-1/2 cups milk
→ 1 egg, beaten
→ 1/2 tsp pepper
→ 1/2 tsp salt
→ 3 cups macaroni, cooked and drained
→ 1/3 cup salted butter, melted (omit for cheesier mac)

Melt butter in your casserole dish or coat with cooking spray. Add cooked macaroni. Beat egg into milk, then combine with salt, pepper, and most of the cheese. Mix with macaroni, top with remaining cheese, and bake at 375°F for 35-40 minutes.

Some pepper jack cheeses have habanero pepper, which is too hot for me. Pick a cheese that has the right amount of heat.

Carefully remove water, add bouillon, and soup mix, whisk well. Drain brown beef. In a large crockpot, add onion, beef, mixed vegetables, cream of mushroom soup, sliced mushrooms with juice, water with bouillon, black pepper, and macaroni noodles. Mix well. Cook on low for 8 hours or high for 4 hours.

Casserole: Transfer the mixture into a thoroughly greased lasagna-sized casserole dish and bake at 350°F for 1-1/2 hours.

 If you cook this on the stovetop it has a tendancy to scorch and burn due to the gravy. It is best to cook in a crockpot.

303) Buffalo Mac N Cheese

→ 6 cups milk
→ 8 oz cream cheese, room temperature
→ 2 1/2 cups shredded cheddar cheese (8 oz. pack)
→ 4 oz. feta cheese
→ 1 tsp. salt
→ 1 tsp. black pepper
→ 3 cloves garlic, minced or pressed
→ 1/2 cup buffalo wing sauce
→ 16 oz. box macaroni noodles-uncooked
→ cooked chicken (rotisserie, grilled, roasted, your choice)

Heat milk in microwave in a batter bowl or glass microwavable bowl until "hot," about 9 minutes on high. Cut cream cheese into 1" cubes and add to a large bowl with the other cheeses. Add salt, pepper, minced garlic, buffalo wing sauce. Pour hot milk over it and stir until cheese melts. Add pasta (uncooked) and stir. Place it in a large well-greased casserole dish and bake at 350°F for 1 hour. Serve at once with chopped chicken. I use a rotisserie chicken from the grocery store.

304) Beefy Mushroom Macaroni

→ 1/8 cup vegetable oil
→ 1 medium onion
→ 2 lbs. Ground chuck
→ 3 cups boiling water
→ 1 Tbsp beef bouillon granules
→ Paket of Lipton Onion Soup Mix
→ 2- 14.5 oz. cans mixed vegetables (drained)
→ 2- 10.5 oz. cans cream of mushroom
→ 3 cups elbow macaroni noodles, uncooked
→ 1/2 tsp black pepper and Salt to taste
→ 4 oz. can sliced mushrooms

Add vegetable oil to a preheated skillet, wok, or stockpot. Add onion and cook until tender. Remove onion and set aside. Brown beef on medium high heat. While beef is browning, microwave 3 cups of water until boiling.

305) Chicken & Rice Casserole

→ 4 to 6 oz. box long-grain wild rice
→ packet of rice seasoning from box
→ 1 cup milk
→ 1 cup hot water
→ 10 oz. can cream of chicken
→ 10 oz. can cream of mushroom
→ 1 cup frozen green peas, optional
→ 1 medium onion chopped
→ 4 oz. can sliced mushrooms, drained
→ 3 1/2 cups cooked chicken chopped
→ 6 oz. French's crispy fried onions

Mix the seasoning pack (from the rice box), milk, and water together in a large bowl. Add the cream of chicken & cream of mushroom soup, then mix it all up and add rice and peas. Finally, add onion, mushrooms, and chicken. Spray a 9x13 pan with cooking spray. Pour chicken mixture into baking pan. Add crispy fried onions on top and bake for 1 hour at 350°F.

Take it out of oven and let it sit 20 minutes prior to serving. Enjoy! This is a delicious casserole.

306) Broccoli Cheese Casserole

→ 3 cups fresh steamed broccoli florets
→ 3 cups chicken broth
→ 1 cup milk
→ 8 Tbsp salted butter, divided
→ 1/2 cup large onion, chopped
→ 3 Tbsp bell pepper, chopped
→ 1 cup rice, uncooked long grain white
→ 1 cup pepperidge farm herb stuffing (traditional)
→ 1/2 cup mayonnaise
→ 1/2 cup sour cream
→ 2 cups shredded mild cheddar cheese, divided
→ 1/4 cup all-purpose flour
→ 1/2 tsp each salt & black pepper
→ pinch cayenne pepper

Steam broccoli for 8 minutes. Combine broth with milk. Sauté onion and pepper in 4 tbsp butter until soft. In a large bowl, mix rice, herb stuffing, mayo, sour cream, black pepper, and 1 cup cheese. Add sautéed onion and pepper. Melt remaining 4 tbsp butter; whisk in flour, salt, and cayenne until lightly browned. Stir in broth and milk, bring to a boil. Pour over rice mixture, mix, and transfer to a well-greased 13x9 baking dish. Sprinkle 1 cup shredded cheese on top. Bake at 325°F for 1 hour.

These are my 3 siblings: Barry, Malissa & Eddie

307) Reuben Casserole

→ 1 can (16 oz.) sauerkraut, rinsed
→ 16 oz. corned beef (used boar's head from deli)
→ 12 oz. Swiss cheese, shredded
→ 1 cup mayonnaise
→ 1/2 cup thousand island dressing
→ 2 fresh sliced tomatoes, optional
→ 4 Tbsp salted butter, room temperature
→ loaf of pumpernickel rye, pepperidge farm

Spray a 13x9x2 or large oblong baking dish with cooking spray. Place a layer of bread on the bottom. Put sauerkraut on top of bread. Mix the mayonnaise and dressing together. Spread half of the dressing on top of the beef. Add cheese (reserve a little for the top). Spread the rest of the dressing on top of the cheese. Place sliced tomatoes on top. Cut 3 slices of bread into small 1/2-inch cubes. Put them in a mixing bowl. Spread butter on your hands and toss the bread until all the butter is off your hands and on the bread. Put bread cubes on the top of the casserole and add the remaining cheese. Bake at 350°F for 45 minutes. Option: Melt butter and pour it on the bread cubes instead of using your hands. It will work, but trust me, it is better to use your hands because they coat the cubes better.

"Both of my brothers married their high school sweethearts! They are great husbands and fathers to their families. My sister works for Collard Valley Cooks. She mails all cookbooks. She has a son that has cerebral palsy and is dependent on her. The Lord blessed her with a large son who helps her lift and move him. She works hard and has been his caregiver since 1997. She is an amazing mother of three. My older brother has 2 children and 6 grandchildren. My younger brother has 3 children. My sister's daughter is expecting a baby in March. She is super excited to be a Maw Maw! "-Tammy

308) Chicken Biscuit Casserole

- → 1-1/2 cups chopped cooked chicken
- → 1 small onion, chopped
- → 2 stalks celery, diced
- → 2 medium carrots, chopped
- → 1/2 cup chicken stock
- → 2 boiled eggs, chopped
- → 4 oz. jar chopped pimentos, drained
- → 1 can of green peas, drained

Preheat a large skillet on medium heat. Add 2 tbsp. butter, onion, celery, carrots (and other fresh or frozen vegetables you desire). Add stock – cover and cook until vegetables are fork-tender. In a large mixing bowl add all ingredients listed above.

For Homemade Chicken Gravy:

- → 5 Tbsp salted butter
- → 1 cup half & half (or 1/2 cup whole milk with 1/2 cup cream)
- → 3 heaping Tbsp cornstarch
- → 1 cup rich chicken stock
- → 1 Tbsp chicken bouillon granules

In a small bowl whisk together the cornstarch, bouillon, and half & half. Place butter in a preheated skillet. Add stock and cream and bring to a boil. Cook until bubbly. Pour gravy (or soup) over the chicken, vegetables, and mix. Pour chicken mixture into a well-greased casserole dish. Then top with biscuits.

For Biscuits, Mix:

- → 2 cups self-rising flour
- → 1/4 tsp McCormick poultry seasoning
- → 1/2 cup mayonnaise
- → 1 cup milk

Drop by tablespoons onto top of casserole. Bake 45 minutes at 350°F.

 OPTION: Instead of making homemade gravy heat 2- 10.5-oz. cans cream of chicken soup.

Instead of making homemade biscuits use canned or frozen biscuits.

309) Chicken Burrito Skillet

- → 1 lb. boneless skinless chicken breasts cut into 1-1/2-inch pieces
- → 1/8 tsp salt
- → 1/8 tsp pepper
- → 2 Tbsp olive oil
- → 1 cup uncooked long grain rice
- → 15 oz. black beans, rinsed and drained
- → 14.5 oz. petite diced tomatoes
- → 1 tsp ground cumin
- → 1 tsp onion powder
- → 1/2 tsp garlic powder
- → 1/2 tsp chili powder
- → 2 1/2 cups chicken stock or broth
- → 1 medium tomato, chopped
- → 3 green onions, chopped

In a large cast iron or heavy skillet (I used a braiser), heat 1 Tbsp oil and cook chicken until browned about 2 minutes. Salt and pepper chicken while browning. Put chicken in a shallow dish and set aside. Add rice into the skillet with another tablespoon of oil. Brown rice until lightly browned and you can start to smell the aroma. Add broth, spices, and beans. Mix well and bring to a boil. Once boiling reduce it to simmer and add chicken on top of mixture. Cover and simmer 20 minutes. Sprinkle with Cheese cover until it melts. Serve along with chopped tomatoes and onion. Serve with Tortilla chips, as burritos or as a main dish. Enjoy!

310) Chicken Noodle Casserole

→ 2 cups macaroni noodles, cooked
→ 1 small green pepper, chopped
→ 1 small onion, chopped
→ 1/4 cup salted butter
→ 1/4 cup all-purpose flour
→ 2 cups milk
→ 1 Tbsp chicken bouillon granules
→ 1/2 tsp salt
→ 1/2 tsp black pepper
→ 2 cups chicken, cooked, diced, or shredded
→ 4 oz. can diced mushrooms, drained
→ 2 oz. can diced pimentos, drained
→ 4 large eggs, hard boiled
→ 1 cup shredded cheese

Cook noodles and eggs in boiling water (add a dash of salt) for 10 minutes. Remove eggs and place them in a small pot with enough hot water to cover. Drain the remaining water from pasta. After eggs sit for 2 minutes rinse with cold water, add ice and peel. Mix bouillon into milk and set aside. In a large skillet, Sauté pepper and onion in butter until soft. Remove most of vegetables making sure to let the butter drain from them so butter stays in skillet to make gravy. Add flour to skillet and mix well with a whisk. Add salt and pepper. Add milk with bouillon and cook until thick like gravy. Turn off and remove from stove element. Add mushrooms, vegetables, and pimentos. Mix gravy with pasta in a large bowl. Coat a 13x9x2 baking dish with cooking spray, Pour half the noodle mixture into casserole dish. Top with 3 sliced eggs, then remaining noodles. Slice the last egg on top and sprinkle with cheese. Bake at 350°F for 30 minutes or until bubbly.

"This would be great with chicken, turkey or tuna and it is delicious. It is one of the best casseroles I have ever made, but you must like boiled eggs or omit them!"-*Tammy*

311) Chicken Spaghetti Casserole

→ 1 lb. package spaghetti
→ 2 Tbsp olive oil
→ 1/3 cup celery, minced
→ 1/3 cup onion, minced
→ 1/4 cup bell pepper, minced
→ 1/4 cup red bell pepper, minced
→ 10.5 oz can cream of mushroom soup
→ 2-10.5 oz can cream of chicken soup
→ 2 oz. jar diced pimientos
→ 1 tsp ground black pepper
→ 1 cooked, boned rotisserie chicken (or 1-1/2 cups cooked diced chicken)
→ 1 cup shredded mozzarella cheese
→ 1/2 cup parmesan cheese

Break pasta in half and cook as directed, drain. Sauté celery, onions, and bell pepper in olive oil. In a bowl, combine sautéed vegetables, soups, pimiento, and black pepper. Spray a 13"x9"x2" casserole dish with cooking spray. Layer half the pasta, add chicken, then half the soup mixture, and cover with Parmesan. Repeat layers, ending with both the parmesan and mozzarella. Bake at 350°F for 1 hour.

"Both Malissa and I enjoy this casserole. It is flavorful and works well as leftovers." – *Tammy*

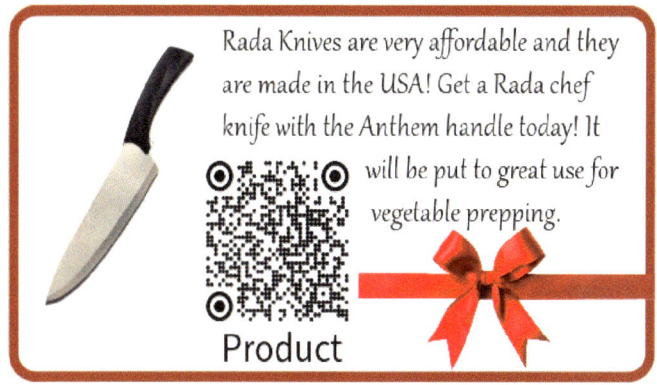

312) Chicken Spectacular

→ 3-4 cups cooked chicken (bite size)
→ 6 oz. box uncle ben's wild rice, (or 8.8 oz. packet of ready rice)
→ 10.5 oz cream of celery or chicken soup
→ 1 cup sour cream
→ 1/2 cup mayonnaise
→ 2 oz. jar diced pimentos, drained
→ 1 medium onion, chopped
→ 15 oz. can French green beans, drained
→ 8 oz. can water chestnuts, drained
→ 1 to 2 cups shredded cheese (optional)
→ 6 oz. container French fried onions for top
→ 13x9x2 baking pan, spray with cooking oil

Rice cooked as directed with seasonings. Chop chicken, onion, pimento, and water chestnuts. Mix all ingredients (DO NOT ADD FRENCH FRIED ONIONS). Pour into a greased casserole dish. Top with French fried onions. Bake for 60 minutes at 350°F. Let casserole sit for 15 minutes before serving.

Do not cook if you intend to freeze.

Option: Use regular green beans in place of French style.

313) Get out of the Kitchen, Chicken

THE BEST Chicken & Rice Recipe

→ 2-10.5 oz. cans cream of mushroom soup
→ 1/3 cup cooking sherry
→ 1 cup orange juice
→ 1/2 cup water
→ olive oil for browning chicken
→ 6-8 chicken legs (skin on)
→ 1-1/2 cups uncooked rice
→ 1 envelope Lipton onion soup mix

Grease a 13x9 casserole dish with oil. Add the soup, sherry, orange juice, and water to a medium bowl. Add olive oil and chicken legs to a hot skillet with a lid. Brown legs on all four sides with the lid on the skillet to prevent oil from splattering. Once the chicken is brown, turn off the heat. Pour drippings into the soup mixture and whisk until smooth and creamy. Add rice to soup, mix well, and immediately pour into casserole dish. Try to distribute the rice as evenly as possible across the bottom of the dish. Lay chicken on the top of the mixture and sprinkle with the soup mix. Bake covered in a 350°F oven for 1.5 hours. Casserole must be covered to prevent the loss of moisture. All moisture is needed to cook rice, so do not bake uncovered.

OPTION: You can use raw chicken without browning if you cook it in the oven for 2 hours. Crockpot: Use the same recipe above, cover, and cook on low for 4 hours.

314) Easy Green Bean Casserole

→ 2-10.5 oz cans cream of mushroom soup
→ 1 cup milk
→ 1 Tbsp soy sauce
→ 4-14.5 cans French style green beans, drained
→ 6 oz. French Fried Onions

Mix Soup, milk, soy well. Mix in green beans and 1 cup of fried onions. Place it in a well-greased baking dish and top with remaining fried onions. Bake for 45 minutes at 350 degrees.

315) Green Bean Casserole

- → 1 onion, chopped
- → 1 pint sliced mushrooms, chopped
- → 3/4 cup salted butter, divided
- → 2- 16 oz. packs frozen French style green Beans, thawed
- → 1/2 cup all-purpose or self-rising flour
- → 1 tsp salt
- → 1 tsp black pepper
- → 1 cup water mixed with 2 tsp beef bouillon granules
- → 1 cup milk
- → 1 cup sour cream
- → 1 Tbsp Worcestershire sauce
- → 1/4 cup soy sauce
- → 6 oz. French's fried onions

Sauté onions and mushrooms in 1/4 cup butter until soft. Combine with green beans in a large bowl. In the skillet, melt remaining butter, whisk in flour, salt, and pepper, then cook until browned. Add broth and milk, whisk over high heat until thickened. Pour sauce over beans. Stir in sour cream, Worcestershire, and soy sauce. Transfer to a greased 13"x9"x2" baking dish. Top with fried onions and bake at 350°F for 40 minutes.

"This is a green bean casserole I created using a homemade gravy instead of canned soups. It is delicious and perfect for your Thanksgiving table." -Tammy

316) Ground Beef Rice Casserole

- → 6 oz. box long grain wild rice
- → packet of rice seasoning from box
- → 1 cup milk
- → 1 cup hot water
- → 4 oz. can sliced mushrooms
- → 10 oz. can cream of chicken
- → 10 oz. can cream of mushroom

- → 3 1/2 cups ground beef browned and
- → drained
- → 1 medium onion chopped butter, room temperature
- → oyster crackers half of 9 oz. package

Combine the rice seasoning pack, milk, and water in a large bowl. Add mushroom liquid, cream of chicken and cream of mushroom soups, then mix in rice, onion, mushrooms, and ground beef. In another bowl, toss crackers with 1/2 stick softened butter. Grease a 9x13 pan, pour in the beef mixture, and top with buttered crackers. Bake at 325°F for 1 hour.

"Everyone is sure to love this delicious beef casserole. It is great, and you can always add a can of mixed vegetables for a one-pot meal!" -Tammy

317) Hashbrown Casserole

- → 2 lb. bag frozen shredded hash browns
- → 10.5 oz. can cream of celery soup
- → 10 oz. shredded cheddar cheese
- → 1/4 cup salted butter, melted
- → 8 oz. sour cream
- → 1 tsp salt
- → 1/2 tsp black pepper

Combine all ingredients together well and place in greased 13x9x2-inch baking dish. Bake at 350 degrees for 60 minutes

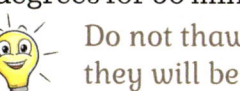 Do not thaw hashbrowns , if you do they will be the consistancy of mashed potatoes.

Make casseroles for potlucks in throw away aluminum pans for easy disposal.

"This is a nana special! Chris' mama brings this to all the potlucks when we gather for family meals and reunions." - Tammy

121

318) Italian Meats Lasagna

Sauce:

→ 3 Tbsp fresh parsley washed & chopped.
→ 1/2 medium onion, chopped.
→ 2 tsp rosemary, ground.
→ 1/2 lb. Italian sausage
→ 4 oz. prosciutto sliced
→ 2-8 oz. can crushed tomatoes
→ 14.5 oz. can petite diced tomatoes
→ 1 cup red wine
→ 2 garlic cloves, pressed.

Brown Italian sausage and prosciutto in a skillet. Sautee' onion, parsley, and rosemary for 5 minutes. Add wine. Cook 3 minutesmedium/high heat. Add both cans of tomatoes. Simmer 20 minutes. Add pressed garlic right before you take off heat. Cook pasta per package directions (al dente). Do not use "no boil" pasta. Add 1 tsp. salt to water while boiling!

→ fresh mozzarella, grated.
→ fresh parmesan, grated.

Spray a 13 x 9 baking dish with cooking spray. Layer: Sauce/Noodles/parmesan/mozzarella until all is in pan. Bake at 350°F for 50 minutes or until bubbly. Serve with garlic bread.

"Absolutely amazing Lasagna, even if you love lots of cheese, this is a must try! It is my favorite lasagna!" -*Tammy*

Rom 3:23,24

"For all have sinned, and come short of the glory of God; Being justified freely by his grace through the redemption that is in Christ Jesus:" KJV

Rom 3:28

"Therefore we conclude that a man is justified by faith without the deeds of the law." KJV

319) Tammy's Winner Lasagna

Sauce:

→ 1/2 medium onion, chopped
→ 1 lb. ground chuck, browned & drained
→ 8 oz can tomato sauce
→ 14.5 oz can petite diced tomatoes
→ 2 garlic cloves, pressed
→ 2 tsp Italian seasoning, McCormick
→ 2 tsp roasted garlic powder, Badia
→ no boil lasagna noodles

Brown hamburger with onion, then drain off excess grease. Add tomatoes, tomato sauce, garlic, Italian seasoning, and garlic powder. Cook on low/medium heat for 10 minutes. I cook pasta even when using "oven ready" type. Just cook it for 5 minutes and add 1 tsp salt to water while boiling!

Cheese Layer:

→ 16 oz. Romano cheese
→ 1 cup fresh mozzarella cheese, shredded
→ 1-1/2 tsp Italian seasoning, McCormick

Mix well. Spray a 2.5 qt. baking dish with cooking spray. Add a little sauce to bottom of dish, then a layer of noodles, then cheese, and repeat. Top with fresh grated mozzarella and Italian seasoning. Bake in oven 350°F for 60 minutes.

 OPTION: Use half lb. of ground beef and half lb. of Italian sausage browned instead of a whole lb of ground beef for more Italian flavor.

Tip: If you are not going to boil the noodles add a cup of water to your sauce.

Rom 5:1

"Therefore being justified by faith, we have peace with God through our Lord Jesus Christ:" KJV

320) Mac' N' Cheese Pizza

→ 1 box Kraft mac' n' cheese dinner with cheese packet
→ 1/2 cup milk
→ 4 Tbsp salted butter
→ 2 eggs
→ 8 oz tomato sauce
→ pizza or Italian seasonings
→ 2 cups mozzarella cheese, shredded
→ 1/4 cup bell pepper, chopped
→ 1/4 cup onion, chopped
→ 8 oz. canned sliced mushrooms, drained
→ 3 oz. pepperoni slices

Cook pasta as directed, drain (no rinsing). Mix in milk, cheese packet, margarine, then the beaten eggs. Transfer to a greased 13"x9"x2" dish. Bake at 375°F for 10 minutes. Raise oven to 425°F, add tomato sauce, and layer seasonings, cheese, pepper, pepper, onion, mushrooms, pepperoni, and more seasonings on top. Bake at 425°F until pepperoni is crisp and edges are brown and bubbly.

"I LOVE this casserole. This would freeze well and it's great warmed in the air fryer!"
-*Tammy*

321) Macaroni Delight

→ 8 oz. macaroni noodles
→ 1 cup mayonnaise
→ 1/4 cup onion, finely chopped
→ 1/4 cup green pepper, chopped
→ 10.5 oz cream of mushroom soup
→ 2 oz. jar diced pimentos, drained
→ 8 oz. sharp cheddar cheese (grated)

Boil macaroni as directed and drain. Sauté onions and peppers in olive oil until soft. Stir in soup, pimentos, and mayonnaise, heat through. Combine with noodles, add cheese, and transfer to a 2-qt. casserole. Bake at 350°F for 45 minutes. Double ingredients if using a 13x9 pan.

"My Maw Maw made this for Thanksgiving! Getting a taste of it now brings back memories."
-*Tammy*

322) Napoli Casserole

→ 1 lb. Italian sausage, Swaggerty's Farm
→ 1/4 cup onion sliced
→ 1 cup squash or zucchini
→ 1/4 cup flour
→ 1/4 cup butter
→ 2 cups milk
→ 1/2 tsp black pepper
→ 1 cup mozzarella cheese
→ 1/4 cup fresh grated parmesan
→ 1/2 cup diced tomatoes, drained
→ 2 cups cooked pasta, drained

Brown sausage in a skillet, breaking it into small pieces. After 5 minutes on high heat, add onions and cook for 3 more minutes. Stir in sliced squash or zucchini and simmer on low for 4 minutes. Transfer the mixture to a greased 13x9x2 casserole dish.

In the same skillet, melt butter, then stir in flour and pepper until browned. Add milk, cooking until thickened and bubbly, then mix in 1/2 cup mozzarella. Add tomatoes and pasta, combine well, and pour over the sausage mixture in the casserole. Top with the rest of the mozzarella and 1/4 cup shredded parmesan. Bake at 350°F for 50 minutes. Serve with garlic bread.

323) Old Fashioned Mac n Cheese

→ 1/2 cup salted butter
→ 1/4 cup sifted flour
→ 1/2 tsp. black pepper
→ 1 tsp salt
→ 4 cups milk
→ 4 cups shredded cheese, divided
→ 3 cups cooked macaroni noodles

Melt butter in a saucepan, add salt, pepper, and flour, and whisk until smooth. Brown over high heat, then add milk and cook until thick and bubbling. Remove from heat, stir in 3 cups shredded cheese, and mix with cooked macaroni. Transfer to a casserole dish, top with remaining cheese, and bake at 350°F for 40 minutes. Serve warm.

"This recipe is so creamy and cheesy. The macaroni absorbs the sauce since the butter is incorporated in the cheese sauce. If you oil pasta on its own, it causes the pasta to be slick, and sauce does not stick to it as well."-Tammy

324) Shipwreck Beef Casserole

→ 1.5 lb. lean ground chuck
→ 4 medium potatoes
→ 3 medium onions
→ 2-15.5 oz. cans kidney beans, drained
→ salt, pepper, chili powder
→ 10.5 oz. can tomato soup
→ 8 to 10 oz. shredded cheese

 OPTION: Seasonings of your choice can be added. If omitting onion, use onion powder

Preheat oven to 350°F. Layer thinly sliced potatoes in a 9x13" casserole dish, season with salt, pepper, and chili powder. Add half the onions, beans, more chili powder, and evenly distribute raw beef on top, seasoning with steak rub. Top with remaining onions and bake for 1 hour. Sprinkle shredded cheese over the dish and bake for an additional 30 minutes. Serve with crusty bread.

325) Simple Skillet Spaghetti

→ 1-1/2 lbs. ground beef, browned & drained
→ 14 oz. can diced tomatoes
→ 1 can of hunt's pasta sauce
→ 1 cup water
→ 1/2 lb. thin spaghetti noodles

Combine all ingredients except the spaghetti noodles thoroughly. Simmer over low heat for 10 minutes. Add 1/2 pound of thin spaghetti noodles to the sauce, ensuring they are fully covered; add more water if necessary. Cover and continue to simmer over low heat until the pasta is cooked, about 15 minutes. Top with slices of mozzarella cheese and sprinkle with Kraft parmesan. Replace the lid until the cheese melts, then serve.

"This method provides a quick way to prepare spaghetti and is cost-effective due to the lower price of canned sauce. For additional flavor, a clove of pressed garlic can be included. Ensure that the pasta is fully submerged during cooking." -Tammy

326) Summer Squash Casserole

→ 1 1/2 cups squash
→ 2 Tbsp bell pepper, chopped
→ 3 cups pepperidge farms cornbread dressing mix
→ 2 eggs
→ 1 can cream of chicken soup
→ 1/2 cup onion, chopped
→ 1/2 cup milk
→ 1/2 cup mayonnaise
→ 8 oz. shredded cheddar cheese
→ paprika

Cook and drain squash. Combine with remaining ingredients and mix thoroughly. Transfer to a baking dish, top with paprika, and bake at 350°F for about an hour until bubbly and golden brown.

327) Old Timer Squash Casserole

→ 5-6 yellow summer squash
→ 1 onion, chopped
→ 1 banana pepper (if available from garden)
→ 1 clove of garlic, sliced
→ 1/2 cup salted butter
→ 3/4 cup evaporated milk
→ 3 eggs
→ 1 tsp salt
→ 3/4 tsp black pepper
→ 6 oz. mild cheddar cheese, grated
→ 1 sleeve of ritz crackers

Clean and chop the squash, then place it in a saucepan along with onion, garden pepper, and garlic. Cover the ingredients with water and cook over medium heat for 20-30 minutes until they are soft and tender, then drain. Melt a stick of butter in the microwave and add it to a 13"x9"x2" glass casserole dish or a round deep baking dish. Add the drained squash. Whisk together milk, eggs, salt, and pepper, then pour the mixture into the dish and stir to combine. Top with grated cheese and crushed crackers, then bake at 350°F until

golden brown and bubbly, 50-60 minutes.

"This is a simple old fashioned squash casserole like granny made with no canned soups. Amazingly a simple fresh taste." -*Tammy*

328) Sweet Potato Soufflé

→ 1 cup sugar
→ 3-4 cups steamed sweet potatoes
→ 1/4 cup salted butter
→ 2 eggs
→ 1/2 cup evaporated milk
→ 1 tsp vanilla extract
→ 1/4 tsp cinnamon

Mix potatoes with whisk in stand mixer. Add sugar, butter, eggs, milk, vanilla, and cinnamon. Spray baking dish with Pam and add potato mixture. Top with:

Topping:

→ 1/4 cup salted butter
→ 1 cup brown sugar
→ 1/8 cup self-rising flour
→ 1 cup chopped pecans

Blend butter, brown sugar, and flour with a pastry fork or blender until its crumbly. Mix in chopped pecans. Sprinkle over the potato mixture and bake at 350°F for 45-60 minutes until set.

"This dish has always been a family favorite. Even as a child, I recall the women at Thanksgiving enjoying it instead of dessert and talking about how delicious it was. As a child I thought not for me, but now I feel just like they did."-*Tammy*

329) Tater Tot Casserole

→ 1-1/2 pounds ground chuck
→ olive oil
→ 1 medium onion, diced
→ 1 Tbsp dale steak seasoning
→ 1/2 tsp complete seasoning, Bidia
→ 1/2 tsp black pepper
→ 14.5 oz. can mixed vegetables, drained
→ 10.5 oz. cans cream of mushroom
→ 1/2 cup milk
→ 1 bag frozen tater tots

Brown and drain ground chuck in a skillet; set aside. Sauté onion in oil until tender, then stir in seasonings, veggies, cream of mushroom soup, and milk. Layer beef in a 13x9 dish, pour soup mixture over, and top with tater tots standing upright around the edges. Bake at 350°F for one hour. For fussy eaters, skip the veggies. Substitute Complete Seasoning with 1/2 tsp onion powder and 1/4 tsp garlic powder if needed.

"This is a kid pleaser, and if you have a picky eater, you can use cream of chicken in place of cream of mushroom." -*Tammy*

330) Creole Tuna Casserole

→ 3 Tbsp dehydrated or fresh chopped onion
→ 10.5 oz. cream of celery
→ 1-1/2 cup milk
→ 3 cups egg noodles, cooked and drained
→ 2 tsp creole seasoning, used Tony Chachere's or seasoning of your choice
→ 14.5 oz. can mixed vegetables, drained
→ 5 oz. can tuna, drained
→ 1 cup shredded cheese (your preference)
→ 1 sleeve Ritz crackers

Boil noodles. In a bowl, combine onion, soup, milk, seasoning, vegetables, tuna (including juice), and cheese; mix well. Add cooked noodles and stir. Transfer to a casserole dish, top with crushed Ritz crackers, and bake at 375°F for 35 minutes. Check after 20 minutes—if the crackers brown too much, reduce heat by 25°F for the last 10 minutes. Serve hot.

331) Veg All Casserole w/ Chicken

→ 4 chicken breasts, cooked & chopped
→ 3 cans veg-all, drained
→ 1 large onion chopped
→ 2-10.5 oz cans cream of chicken soup
→ 1 cup sour cream
→ 1 cup mayonnaise
→ 8 oz. can water chestnuts, drained and chopped
→ 1/2 tsp black pepper
→ 2 sleeves of ritz crackers

Combine all ingredients except the crackers in a large bowl. Transfer the mixture to a casserole dish and sprinkle the crushed crackers evenly over the top. Bake at 350°F for 40 minutes. Serve immediately.

"This is a picture of our 2024 Thanksgiving. We had macaroni and cheese, creamed potatoes, turkey, green bean casserole, granny green beans, sweet potato souffle, dinner rolls and giblet gravy!" -*Tammy*

Recipe 336

Recipe 351

Recipe 357

Recipe 352

ORANGE SLICE COOKIES

332) Apple Cookies

- → 1/4 cup salted butter
- → 1 cup brown sugar
- → 1 large egg
- → 1 tsp vanilla extract
- → 2 cups all-purpose flour
- → 1 cup quick oats, optional
- → 1/2 tsp baking soda
- → 1/2 tsp salt
- → 1/4 tsp ground nutmeg
- → 1/2 cup evaporated milk or heavy cream
- → 1 cup nuts, chopped
- → 1 cup apples, peeled, chopped

Beat butter, sugar, egg, and vanilla together in a mixing bowl. Mix dry ingredients in a separate bowl. Add dry ingredients alternately with milk. Stir in nuts, apples, and oatmeal. Drop by tsp onto a greased cookie sheet. Bake at 375°F for 10-12 minutes, or until cookies are light brown around the edges. Remove cookies and let cool slightly.

 Make this frosting before baking cookies. Frost with Recipe #333, Cookie Vanilla Frosting, while the cookies are still warm.

333) Cookie Frosting, Vanilla

- → 2 cups powdered sugar
- → 3 Tbsp salted butter, melted
- → 1 tsp ground cinnamon
- → 2-3 Tbsp milk
- → 1/2 tsp vanilla extract

Glaze is made by mixing powdered sugar, melted butter, cinnamon, vanilla, and milk.

334) Blondie Brownies

- → 2 large eggs
- → 1 cup granulated sugar
- → 1/2 cup light brown sugar, packed
- → 1/4 cup salted butter, room temperature
- → 1 tsp vanilla extract
- → 1-1/2 cups self-rising flour (If using all-purpose flour, add: 1 Tbsp baking powder & 1/2 tsp salt)

Mix the eggs, sugars, and butter, then add extract and flour. (The batter will be thick!) Transfer to a well-greased 11x7-inch or 9x9-inch pan and bake at 350°F for 35 minutes. Let cool on a cookie sheet and frost with the Recipe #335, Brownie Frosting.

335) Brownie Frosting, Vanilla

- → 1/2 cup salted butter, room temperature
- → 1 tsp vanilla extract
- → 3 cups of powdered sugar
- → 3-4 Tbsp milk or cream
- → 1/2 cup mini chocolate chips or grated chocolate for garnish, optional

Cream butter, then add vanilla, milk & powdered sugar. Spread over bars before cutting. Garnish if desired. Cut bars into squares and store them in an airtight container.

Rom 5:8,9,11

"But God commendeth his love toward us, in that, while we were yet sinners, Christ died for us. Much more then, being now justified by his blood, we shall be saved from wrath through him."

And not only so, but we also joy in God through our Lord Jesus Christ, by whom we have now received the atonement." KJV

336) Chewy Oatmeal Bars

→ 1/2 cup salted butter
→ 1/2 cup dark brown sugar, packed
→ 1/4 cup corn syrup, Karo brand used
→ 1 tsp vanilla flavoring
→ 2 cups quick oats
→ 1 cup chocolate chips microwaveable glass brownie pan (9"x9" or 7"x11")
→ Use a 1100-watt microwave (reduce cooking time for higher wattage microwaves)

Place butter in a microwave-safe dish and heat for 1 minute. Remove and add sugar, syrup, and vanilla extract, stirring until well combined. Add oats and mix thoroughly. Press mixture evenly into base of dish. Microwave on high for 2 minutes. Carefully remove dish and sprinkle chocolate chips evenly over surface. Return and heat for 1 minute. Cool to room temperature before cutting into squares and serving.

337) Carrot Cake Cheesecake Bars

Cake:

→ 1 cup all-purpose flour
→ 1 cup granulated sugar
→ 1 1/2 tsp ground cinnamon
→ 1 tsp baking soda
→ 1/2 tsp ground nutmeg
→ 1/4 tsp salt
→ 2/3 cup vegetable oil
→ 2 large eggs, room temperature
→ 2 tsp vanilla extract
→ 1 1/2 cups of finely grated carrots

Preheat oven to 325°F. In a large bowl, combine dry ingredients. Add oil, eggs, and vanilla; beat for 2 minutes on medium. Stir in carrots. Transfer batter to a greased 13x9x2-inch pan.

Cream Cheese Swirl:

→ 2 - 8-oz. cream cheese, room temperature
→ 2 Tbsp all-purpose flour
→ 1 cup granulated sugar
→ 1/4 cup milk

Mix the swirl ingredients until smooth. Drop spoonfuls onto the pan, then swirl with a flat utensil in both directions. If unsure, check the YouTube tutorial. Bake for 40 minutes or until a toothpick comes out clean. Cool, cut into squares, and serve.

338) Chocolate Chip Cookies

→ 2 sticks salted butter, room temperature
→ 3/4 cup granulated sugar
→ 3/4 cup light brown sugar, packed
→ 2 large eggs
→ 1 tsp baking soda
→ 1/4 tsp salt
→ 2 tsp vanilla extract
→ 2 1/2 cups all-purpose flour
→ 1/2 bag semi-sweet chocolate chips
→ 1/2 bag mini semi-sweet chocolate chips (or 1 full bag of the same type of chips)

Preheat oven to 375°F. Beat butter and sugars in a mixer until fluffy. Add eggs and mix well. Mix in baking soda, salt, vanilla, and flour gradually. Scrape bowl, then stir in chocolate chips on low. Drop tsp onto a prepared cookie sheet, 1-1/2 inches apart. Bake 8-10 minutes.

339) Chocolate Chip Cookie Bars

→ 1 lb. light brown sugar; 2 1/8 cup packed
→ 2/3 cup salted butter
→ 3 large eggs
→ 1 tsp vanilla extract
→ 2 3/4 cup self-rising flour
→ 1/2 cup mini semi-sweet chocolate chips
→ 1/2 cup milk chocolate chips
→ 1 cup chopped pecans, optional

Mix brown sugar and butter thoroughly. Beat in eggs until fluffy, then add vanilla and flour. Stir in chips. Spread in a greased 13x9x2" pan and optionally top with pecans. Bake at 325°F for 30 minutes, increase to 350°F, and bake 10 minutes more. Cool on a wire rack and cut into 24 pieces.

340) Chocolate Oatmeal No Bakes

→ 2 cups granulated sugar
→ 1/4 cup unsweetened cocoa powder, Hershey's
→ 1/4 tsp salt
→ 1/4 tsp cream of tartar
→ 4 Tbsp salted butter
→ 1/2 cup whole milk, warm
→ 1/2 cup creamy peanut butter
→ 1/2 teaspoon vanilla extract, optional
→ 2 cups 1-minute Quick-cooking oats
→ 12 tablespoons whole milk

Whisk sugar, cocoa powder, and cream of tartar in a large bowl until smooth; set aside. Melt butter in a deep non-stick skillet over medium-low heat. Stir in milk, salt, then add sugar mixture and cook, stirring, until dissolved. Raise heat to a rolling boil, stirring constantly. When boiling, set a timer for 2 minutes; insert a thermometer and cook until 230-234°F (about 2 minutes), without stirring. Remove from heat and quickly mix in peanut butter and vanilla, then oats. Add 1-2 tablespoons milk for creaminess. Drop by mini cookie scoop onto prepared pans (two scoops per cookie). Let set at room temperature for 30-45 minutes. Wrap cooled cookies in plastic wrap and store in an airtight container.

341) Chris's Favorite Cookies

→ 1 cup salted butter
→ 3/4 granulated sugar
→ 3/4 cup light brown sugar, packed
→ 2 large eggs
→ 1 tsp baking soda
→ 1/2 tsp salt
→ 1 tsp vanilla extract
→ 2 1/2 cups all-purpose flour
→ 1 cup 1-minute Quick-cooking oats
→ 1/2 bag semi-sweet chocolate chips
→ 1/2 bag mini semi-sweet chocolate. chips
→ 1 cup chopped pecans

Preheat oven to 375°F. Beat butter and sugars until fluffy. Add eggs, then mix in soda, salt, and vanilla. Gradually add flour, 1/2 cup at a time, mixing well. Turn off mixer, scrape bowl, and mix for 1 minute. Stir in oatmeal, chocolate chips, and pecans. Drop heaping teaspoons onto a greased or parchment-lined sheet, 1.5 inches apart. Bake 8 minutes for chewy, 10 for crunchy. Cool on wire rack. Yields 48 cookies.

342) Coconut Macaroons

- → 2 large egg whites
- → 2/3 cup granulated sugar
- → 1/4 tsp cream of tartar
- → 1 tsp vanilla extract
- → 1/4 tsp almond extract
- → 1/4 tsp salt
- → 14 oz. sweetened flaked coconut

Preheat oven to 350°F. Combine sugar and cream of tartar in a bowl. In another bowl, beat egg whites on high until stiff peaks form, about 3–4 minutes, gradually adding the sugar mixture. Mix in vanilla, almond extract, and salt. Gently fold in 3/4 bag of coconut.

Spoon onto a greased or parchment-lined baking sheet. Bake for 25 minutes until lightly golden. Cool on a rack; enjoy immediately or store in an airtight container.

"These cookies are a family favorite and are best served the day you make them." -*Tammy*

343) Cowboy Cookies

- → 1 cup salted butter or butter-flavor shortening
- → 1 cup granulated sugar
- → 1 cup light brown sugar, packed
- → 2 large eggs
- → 2 cups 1-minute Quick-cooking oats
- → 1 tsp vanilla extract
- → 1 3/4 cup all-purpose flour
- → 1 tsp baking soda
- → 1/2 tsp salt
- → 1/2 tsp baking powder
- → 1/2 package of mini semi-sweet morsels
- → 1/2 package of milk chocolate chips

Add shortening or butter to the mixing bowl. Mix with sugars until fluffy. Add eggs and beat well. Stir in soda, salt, and baking powder; mix well. Next, add flour, oats, vanilla, and finally the chips; mix thoroughly. Drop by tsp onto a greased cookie sheet and bake at 375°F for 10 minutes. Remove from oven and cool for 3-4 minutes. Place cookies on a cooling rack.

344) Krinkle Cookies, Easy

- → 1 box chocolate cake mix
- → 1/2 cup vegetable oil
- → 2 large eggs

Combine ingredients thoroughly. Spoon onto a greased cookie sheet and bake for 8-10 minutes at 350°F.

 Use Lemon Cake Mix, Red Velvet Cake Mix, or Chocolate Cake Mix for different types of cookies. The possibilities are endless!

345) Fruitcake Cookies

- → 1 cup salted butter, room temperature
- → 3/4 cup light brown sugar, packed
- → 1 large egg
- → 1 Tbsp vanilla extract
- → 1-1/2 cups of all-purpose flour, rounded
- → 1/2 tsp salt
- → 1/2 tsp baking soda
- → 1 tsp ground cinnamon
- → 1 1/2 cups of dates, purchase chopped
- → 4 oz. red candied cherries, chopped
- → 4 oz. candied pineapple, chopped
- → 1 cup pecans, chopped
- → 1/2 cup walnuts, chopped

Preheat oven (see temperatures below). Cream butter, sugar, egg, and vanilla. Mix in salt, baking soda, and cinnamon. Gradually add flour. Stir in fruit and nuts by hand if using a hand mixer; add with stand mixer.

 For flat cookies: Bake at 325°F for 15 min, then increase to 375°F for 3—4 min.

For round cookies: Bake at 350°F for 15 min.

"These are the best cookies I have ever tasted!" – *Tammy*

346) Hershey Brownies

- → 1 cup salted butter, melted
- → 4 large eggs
- → 2 tsp vanilla extract
- → 2 cups granulated sugar
- → 1/2 cup all-purpose flour
- → 1 cup cocoa, Hershey's
- → 1/4 tsp salt
- → 1/2 tsp baking powder

Whisk flour, cocoa, salt, and baking powder in a bowl. Melt butter in a glass bowl, add sugar, then whisk in eggs and vanilla. Combine wet and dry mixtures; mix well. Pour into a greased 7x11 or 9x9-inch pan, sprinkle pecans on top if you like, and bake at 350°F for 35 minutes. Enjoy fudge brownies!

"This is the Hershey's Brownie recipe. They are fudgy and delicious! I hope you try them. We sure love them." -Tammy

 Option: For a cake like brownie use 1 cup of flour instead of 1/2 cup.

347) Mincemeat Cookies

- → 1 cup vegetable shortening
- → 1-1/2 cups granulated sugar
- → 3 large eggs
- → 1 tsp vanilla extract
- → 1 1/2 cups mincemeat, jar, not block type
- → 1/2 tsp salt
- → 1 tsp baking soda
- → 3 1/4 cups of all-purpose flour

Cream shortening and sugar, then beat in eggs one at a time. Add vanilla and mincemeat, mixing well. Stir in 2 cups flour, blend, then add baking soda, salt, and remaining flour. Drop by teaspoon onto a prepared cookie sheet and bake at 400°F

for 12 minutes. Dough can be frozen or refrigerated.

348) Hum-dings

- → 10 oz. package of mini marshmallows
- → 1/2 cup of salted butter
- → 2 cups of Rice Krispies cereal
- → 1 cup chopped pecans
- → 8 oz. pack of chopped dates

Put cereal, pecans, and dates into a large bowl. In a medium saucepan, melt butter, then add marshmallows. Stir constantly over medium/low heat. Once marshmallows melt, whisk or use a slotted spoon to whip the mixture until it turns into a glossy, candy-like consistency. Pour over the ingredients in the bowl and stir thoroughly. After cooling, transfer the mixture onto parchment paper. Butter your hands and ensure everything is well mixed before shaping them into walnut-sized balls. Roll each ball in powdered sugar, then place all in a gallon zipper bag and shake to remove excess sugar. Store in an airtight container. Enjoy— these are delicious!

"Everyone loves these timeless desserts. I enjoy baking these cookies every Christmas."-Tammy

 Option: These Mincemeat cookies are soft cookies. For a crunchy cookie, add 2 tsp of cream of tartar to the batter when you add the soda. Use this trick in other recipes if desired.

349) Lemon Bars

Pre-Bake Crust:
- → 1/2 cup salted butter, room temperature
- → 1/4 cup powdered sugar
- → 1 cup all-purpose flour
- → 1/2 tsp vanilla extract
- → zest of one lemon
- → 1 large egg & 1/4 tsp salt

Filling:
- → 2 large eggs
- → 1 cup sugar
- → juice of two lemons
- → zest of one lemon
- → 2 Tbsp all-purpose flour & 1/4 tsp salt
- → powdered sugar and extra lemon for later

Cream the crust ingredients together, then spread into a 7x11 or 9x9 pan. Bake at 350°F for 20 minutes. Set aside. Mix the filling thoroughly, beating well to prevent sugar from settling. Pour over the crust and bake for 25 minutes. Cool. To serve, soften a lemon, poke a hole, and drizzle lemon juice over the bars. Sprinkle with powdered sugar. Store in an airtight container; no refrigeration is needed. Best within 2 days, up to 1 week refrigerated.

350) Lemon Teacake Cookies

- → juice of one large lemon
- → 1-1/2 tsp lemon extract

- → 1 tsp vanilla extract
- → 1 cup shortening
- → 2 cups granulated sugar
- → 1/2 tsp salt
- → 3 large eggs
- → 4 1/2 cups self-rising flour

Preheat oven to 375°F. Beat shortening and sugar until fluffy, then mix in extracts, lemon juice, and salt. Add eggs one at a time, mixing well. Stir in flour. Drop tablespoonfuls of dough onto a greased or parchment-lined baking sheet, spacing them 1-1/2 inches apart. Bake for 12 minutes for lighter cookies or 13-14 minutes for darker ones.

Optional: Add the zest of a lemon and beat it into the batter. You can also put cookies in a gallon storage bag and shake in powdered sugar. Store in a sealed container.

"Warning: you won't stop eating these until they are gone, but the upside is they are low in sugar." -*Tammy*

351) Oatmeal Cookies

- → 1/4 cup shortening
- → 3/4 cup salted butter, room temperature
- → 1 cup light brown sugar, packed
- → 1/2 cup granulated sugar
- → 2 large eggs
- → 1 tsp vanilla extract
- → 1/4 tsp baking soda
- → 1/2 tsp salt
- → 1 tsp baking powder
- → 1 tsp cinnamon
- → 1/4 tsp cloves, optional
- → 2 cups 1-minute Quick-cooking oats
- → 1-1/2 cups all-purpose flour
- → pecans and/or raisins, optional

Preheat oven to 375°F. Beat together shortening, butter, and sugars until fluffy, then mix in eggs and vanilla. Add baking soda, salt, baking powder, cloves (optional), and cinnamon. Stir in oatmeal, then gradually add flour. Drop by teaspoon onto a greased or lined baking sheet and bake for 12 minutes. Makes 3 dozen cookies.

"These are simple oatmeal cookies. We love them just like this, but without the cloves! It is hard not to eat this cookie dough!" -*Tammy*

352) Orange Slice Cookies

- → 1-1/4 cups light brown sugar, packed
- → 1 cup shortening
- → 3 large eggs
- → 1 tsp vanilla extract
- → 2 1/2 cups all-purpose flour
- → 1/2 tsp salt
- → 1 tsp baking powder
- → 1 tsp baking soda
- → 1 cup nuts
- → 1 cup chopped orange slice candy

Add sugar and shortening and beat until creamy. Add eggs and mix well. Add vanilla, salt, baking powder, and soda, then mix well. Gradually add flour (1/2 cup at a time), mixing after each addition. Stir in nuts and candy. Drop by tsp onto a greased cookie sheet and bake at 375°F for 12 minutes. Remove from oven and cool for 3-4 minutes. Transfer cookies to a cooling rack.

"This is one of my all-time favorite Christmas cookies. Chris's mama, Virginia, makes them every Christmas."- *Tammy*

353) Peanut Butter Bars

- → 2 large eggs
- → 1 cup granulated sugar
- → 1/2 cup light brown sugar, packed
- → 1/4 cup peanut butter, used Jif brand
- → 2 Tbsp salted butter, room temperature
- → 1 tsp vanilla extract
- → 1-1/2 cups self-rising flour (if using plain flour, add 1 Tbsp baking powder & 1/2 tsp salt)

Mix eggs, sugars, and butter; add peanut butter, extract, and flour to form a thick batter. Spread into a greased 11x7 or 9x9-inch pan and bake at 350°F for 35 minutes. Cool on a cookie sheet and frost with Recipe #354, Peanut Butter Frosting.

354) Peanut Butter Bar Frosting

- → 1/2 cup salted butter, room temperature
- → 1 tsp vanilla extract
- → 1/4 cup peanut butter, used Jif brand
- → 3 cups powdered sugar
- → 3-4 Tbsp milk or cream

Cream butter, add vanilla, milk & powdered sugar. Spread over bars before cutting. Cut bars into squares and store them in an airtight container.

"These peanut butter bars remind me of the ones we had in school growing up! They are a family favorite. They are also very chewy especially around the edges."- *Tammy*

355) Peanut Butter Cookies, Jif

- → 3/4 cup Jif creamy peanut butter
- → 1/2 cup Crisco all-vegetable shortening
- → 1-1/4 cups firmly packed light brown sugar
- → 3 Tbsp milk
- → 1 Tbsp vanilla extract
- → 1 large egg
- → 1 3/4 cups of all-purpose flour
- → 3/4 tsp salt
- → 3/4 tsp baking soda

Preheat oven to 375°F. Mix peanut butter, shortening, brown sugar, milk, and vanilla in a bowl; beat on medium speed. Add egg, then flour, salt, and baking soda. Blend well. Drop teaspoonfuls of dough 2 inches apart on a baking sheet and press with a fork. Bake for 8 minutes, cool on a wire rack.

"Still to this day this is one of my all-time favorite desserts, and you cannot beat the Jif recipe y'all. The flourless peanut butter cookies are popular; however, I think these are the best!" - *Tammy*

356) Peanut Butter Krispy Treats:

- → 1/2 cup salted butter
- → 10 oz. mini marshmallows
- → 1/4 cup creamy or chunky peanut butter
- → 6 cups Kellogg's Rice Krispies cereal

In a large non-stick skillet or saucepan, melt butter with marshmallows over medium heat. Meanwhile, pour cereal into a large bowl. Mix the butter and marshmallows until smooth and evenly colored. Add peanut butter and stir well. Pour the mixture over the cereal. Press into a 13x9x2-inch pan or muffin pan to mold the shape. Yields 18-20 muffin-sized treats. Store in a sealed container.

357) Rice Krispies Treats

- → 1/2 cup salted butter
- → 10 oz. mini marshmallows
- → 6 cups of Kellogg's Rice Krispies cereal

In a large non-stick skillet or saucepan, melt butter and marshmallows over medium heat. Meanwhile, pour cereal into a large bowl. Mix the butter and marshmallows until smooth and uniformly colored. Pour over the cereal. Press mixture into a 13x9x2-inch pan or muffin tin, shaping as needed. Makes 18-20 muffin-sized treats. Store in a sealed Container.

358) Snickerdoodles

- → 1/2 cup shortening
- → 1/2 cup salted butter, room temperature
- → 1-1/4 cup granulated sugar
- → 2 large eggs
- → 1 tsp vanilla extract
- → 2 3/4 cups of all-purpose flour
- → 2 tsp cream of tartar
- → 1/4 tsp salt
- → 1 tsp baking soda

Sugar Topping:

- → 2 Tbsp sugar
- → 1 Tbsp cinnamon
- → 1 tsp nutmeg, optional

Cream sugar, shortening, and butter. Add eggs and vanilla, blend. In another bowl, mix flour, cream of tartar, salt, and baking soda. Combine with wet mixture, then chill dough for at least 2 hours.

Mix sugar for topping in a separate bowl. Shape 1 tsp chilled dough into balls, roll in sugar, place 2 inches apart on ungreased sheets, and flatten. Bake at 375°F for 10 minutes.

"These are my daughter, May's favorite cookie."
- Tammy

359) Sugar Cookies

- → 1/2 cup salted butter, room temperature
- → 1/2 cup shortening
- → 2 cups granulated sugar
- → 1/2 tsp salt
- → 1/2 tsp baking soda
- → 2 large eggs
- → 1 Tbsp vanilla extract
- → 1/4 tsp butter extract
- → 3 cups all-purpose flour

Cream butter and shortening until smooth. Mix in sugar, salt, soda, eggs, and extracts; beat until fluffy. Gradually add flour. Chill dough for cutout cookies, roll thin, cut, and bake at 375°F for 10 minutes.

For sugar cookies, drop small teaspoons onto a greased sheet, bake at 375°F for 12 minutes until edges brown. Optionally, top with sugar crystals.

"For even crunchier cookies, refrigerate dough. Use refrigerated dough and bake..." -Chris

360) Tea Cakes: Maw Maw's

→ 1 cup Crisco vegetable shortening
→ 1-1/4 cup granulated sugar
→ 3 large eggs
→ 1 tsp vanilla extract
→ 3 cups self-rising flour

Cream shortening with sugars, then mix in eggs and other ingredients for 2 minutes. Spray baking sheet, place dough 1-1/2 inches apart, and bake at 350°F for 12 minutes.

"Cook these until they are nice and brown on the bottom. They will be crunchy and taste just like the ones your granny used to make when you were a kid. You will still have a hard time keeping your hands out of the cookie jar." - Tammy

361) Triple Chocolate Cookies

→ 1 cup salted butter, room temperature
→ 2 cups all-purpose flour
→ 2/3 cup cocoa, Hershey's
→ 1/2 tsp salt
→ 1-1/2 cups granulated sugar
→ 2 large eggs
→ 1 tsp vanilla extract
→ 1/2 cup white chocolate chips
→ 1/2 cup semi-sweet chocolate chips

Combine flour and cocoa using a wire whisk and set aside. Beat butter until creamy. Add sugar and continue mixing until well combined. Add eggs individually, followed by the dry ingredients. Stir in vanilla and chocolate chips. Place tablespoon-sized portions onto greased cookie sheets and bake at 350°F for 12 minutes. Serve with milk if desired.

 Optional: White chocolate chips can be substituted with peanut butter chips or milk chocolate chips.

Meet Maw Maw

Tammy's Maternal Grandmother!

Maggie Lee Howard

I can vividly remember maw maw in her kitchen, lovingly preparing chocolate icing for those scrumptious teacakes on the stove top. During that time, as a pastor's wife, she resided in the parsonage of High Schoals Baptist Church in Paulding County, Georgia. I can't wait to hug her in heaven when we meet again. Maw Maw had lupus and died in her 60's.

"My Maw Maw was always laughing. I don't remember her frowning or complaining. I just remember her being so happy all the time. She was the kind of person you wanted to be around. Her husband, my PawPaw, was always telling jokes. We LOVED being at their house. This is my favorite picture of MawMaw. She was looking up at Paw Paw laughing. It is how I remember her. I hope you are a loving and laughing person. If you are, that is how you will be remembered!"-Tammy

Recipe # 362

Try Chocolate Pudding in your Banana Pudding for a change up!

Once, I was hanging out with my Granny B in the kitchen. She shared this cool tip about preventing bananas from browning in banana pudding. She was insistent that I should scoop out the middle part, you know, the part with the black specks—she called them seeds. Can you believe she was right! Those are just undeveloped seeds, and removing them really does keep the banana from turning brown!

Use a strawberry huller or the end of this 1/4 teaspoon measuring spoon to scoop it out! Your puddings and pies will be a step above all the rest. Thanks to Granny!

Lucile

Shop Utensils

In an 8-cup glass batter bowl, add sugar, self-rising flour, and salt. Whisk well. Add egg yolks and milk, whisk thoroughly. Microwave on high for 3 minutes. Remove, whisk vigorously to incorporate, scraping flour from bottom and sides. Continue microwaving for 2-minute intervals until the pudding is THICK. Whisk in butter and vanilla.

Important Pudding Tips:

*Pudding will not thicken later, so cook it until it is THICK! **For banana pudding, it should be pourable, like gravy,** so it doesn't become too dry. **For pudding pies and other pudding recipes, cook until it is THICK.**

*For Vanilla Pudding without the need for meringue. Use two large eggs instead of using only the yolks of 5 eggs.

362) Banana Pudding

→ box of Nabisco Nilla wafers
→ 4 ripe bananas
→ Vanilla Pudding Recipe #363
→ Tammy's Meringue recipe#446

Start with half of pudding, add 3/4 box wafers, all bananas (sliced thin) then the rest of the pudding. Top with meringue, seal edges (push meringue to the edge), arrange remaining cookies around the perimeter (see page 137 image), sprinkle crumbs on meringue, and bake at 325°F for 25 minutes. Enjoy!

363) Vanilla Pudding

→ 1/2 cup sugar
→ 1/3 cup self-rising flour
→ 1/4 tsp salt
→ 5 egg yolks, beat well with whisk
→ 2 1/4 cups milk
→ 4 Tbsp salted butter
→ 1 tsp vanilla extract

364) Caramel Corn, Grandma Pearl's

→ pop 1 cup popcorn (plain no oils)
→ 2 cups light brown sugar, packed
→ 1 cup salted butter
→ 1/2 cup light corn syrup
→ 1 tsp salt
→ 1/2 tsp butter flavoring
→ 1 tsp burnt sugar flavoring
→ 1/2 tsp baking soda

Melt butter in a saucepan, add sugar, syrup, salt, and bring to a boil. Boil for 5 minutes, then take off heat and stir in flavorings and soda. Pour over popcorn, toss, and bake in a 13-quart bowl at 250°F for 1 hour, tossing every 15 minutes.

"This recipe was given to me by Chris's friend, Paul Horsley. It was his grandma's recipe, and it is delicious!" –*Tammy*

Tammy's Kitchen Helps

The Wonderful Batter Bowl!

"Mama taught me to make puddings in the microwave. She was a cake decorator and wedding caterer. This is great for grits, puddings, and oatmeal. It is also great for mixing batters. Visit our website by scanning this code with your smart phone's camera." ...Tammy

365) Chocolate Pudding

- → 1 cup granulated sugar
- → 5 Tbsp cocoa, leveled
- → 1/2 tsp salt
- → 3 Tbsp corn starch (or 1/3 cup flour)
- → 1 cup evaporated milk
- → 1 cup water
- → 2 large eggs
- → 1/4 cup salted butter
- → 1 tsp vanilla extract

Whisk sugar, salt, cocoa, and cornstarch/flour in a glass bowl. Add milk, water, and eggs; whisk well. Microwave on high for 4 minutes, then whisk thoroughly. Heat at 1-minute intervals, whisking each time, *until THICK*. Stir in vanilla and butter, cool, then refrigerate in an airtight container before serving.

 Tip: For a dark chocolate pudding, use Hershey's Dark Cocoa. Pudding will not thicken later, cook until thick!

366) Banana Split Cake

Layer 1: Mix
- → 2 cups graham cracker crumbs
- → 1/2 cup salted butter, melted
- → 1/8 cup granulated sugar

Press into a 9x13 inch pan, freeze 10 minutes.

Layer 2:
- → 2-8 oz. cream cheese, room temperature
- → 1/2 cup granulated sugar

Beat well, spread over crust.

Layer 3:
- → 20 oz. can crushed pineapple, drained

Layer 4:
- → 3 - 4 ripe bananas, de-seed & slice thin

Layer 5:
- → 2-3.4 oz. instant vanilla puddings
- → 2 cups of milk

Whisk together and set aside until set (about 5 min.) then fold in
- → 8 oz. carton cool whip topping

Layer 6:
- → 8 oz. carton cool whip topping

Toppings:
- → 1 cup chopped pecans or almonds, sliced maraschino cherries, sliced bananas, hot fudge, chocolate syrup, chocolate chips

 Slice bananas in half, and remove the middle portion of banana that has the seeds. Scoop it out with a 1/4 tsp measuring scoop or strawberry huller.

367) Butter Toffee

- → 1 cup of toasted almonds, chopped
- → 1/2 cup **mini semi-sweet chocolate chips**
- → 1 cup salted butter
- → 1 cup granulated sugar
- → 1 Tbsp corn syrup
- → 3 Tbsp cold water
- → 1/4 tsp salt

In a greased or parchment lined 15 x 10 x 1 jelly roll pan or 13x9x2 pan, distribute nuts and chocolate evenly on pan. In a saucepan, heat butter, sugar, syrup, salt, and water to 290°F, stirring occasionally, then pour over the nut and chocolate. Once candy is room temperature, break into pieces, and enjoy.

 Caution: Candy is hot - use a spatula to spread and do not touch until cooled.

If you do not have a candy thermometer cook candy until its golden in color. As shown in picture below.

I do not recommend doubling this recipe.

368) Chocolate Covered Cherries

→ 20 maraschino cherries **(stems on)**
→ 4 Tbsp salted butter
→ 2 cups powdered sugar
→ 1/4 tsp salt
→ 3-4 Tbsp white corn syrup 10 oz. package of **100% mini chocolate chips** (milk or semi-sweet your choice)
→ 1 Tbsp vegetable shortening

Drain cherries for 3 hours on a paper towel. Mix butter, sugar, salt, and syrup until it is packed solid. If needed, add an additional Tbsp of corn syrup. Wrap each cherry with 1/2 tsp of the powdered sugar mixture, pressing it evenly to mold around the cherry. Place them in the refrigerator and chill for 3 hours before dipping.

Chocolate:

Melt chocolate in a 1 cup liquid measuring cup. Cook for 30-second intervals, mixing in between being careful not to burn chocolate. Dip each cherry into the chocolate to coat it. Make sure the chocolate seals around the stem. You may need to reheat the chocolate because chilled cherries will cool chocolate quickly.

Place the dipped cherries on parchment paper. Chill in the refrigerator until set, then place in a sealed container. Keep refrigerated until the day you serve them. When ready, remove and place on a serving platter. Enjoy them, they are delicious!

"My daddy loves chocolate covered cherries! They were always a must have during the Christmas season at our house." -*Tammy*

369) Chocolate Delight

Bottom Crust:

→ 1 cup all-purpose flour
→ 1 cup chopped pecans
→ 1/2 cup salted butter, room temperature

Blend the flour and butter until butter is in about pea-sized pieces. Add pecans and place it in a 2.75-quart container baking dish. Bake at 450°F for 15-20 minutes, until golden brown around the edges. Take out and cool completely before proceeding.

2nd Layer:

→ 8 oz. cream cheese, room temperature
→ 1 cup powdered sugar
→ 16 oz. Tub whipped topping

Mix cream cheese & sugar together until creamy, then add 1 cup of whipped topping- beat well. Layer on the cooled bottom crust.

Pudding Layer:

→ 4.2 oz. Oreo instant pudding mix or use two chocolate pudding mixes
→ 3.4. oz. chocolate instant pudding mix
→ 4 cups milk

Separately mix each pudding with 2 cups of milk each. Layer the chocolate pudding first, then the Oreo pudding, and top with whipped topping. Garnish top with chopped pecans.

"This dessert can be made with Key Lime, Butterscotch, Hazelnut, Pistachio, and more— any pudding and nut combination your family loves! Enjoy this Pudding Delight Dessert." - *Tammy*

370) Coconut Pudding

→ 1/2 cup granulated sugar
→ 1/3 cup flour or 3 Tbsp corn starch
→ 1/4 tsp salt
→ 2 large eggs
→ 2 1/2 cups milk
→ 1/4 cup salted butter
→ 1 tsp vanilla extract
→ 1 cup flaked coconut, toasted

In an 8-cup glass batter bowl, add sugar, flour, and a dash of salt. Whisk the ingredients well. Add eggs and milk, then whisk thoroughly. Microwave on high for 3 minutes. Remove, then whisk, making sure to scrape the flour from the bottom and sides of the bowl. Continue microwaving for 2-minute intervals until the mixture is **THICK**. Remove, then add butter, vanilla, whisking well. Fold in coconut. Pour into serving dishes, or storage container. Once the pudding has cooled to room temp., transfer it to the refrigerator.

371) Dirt Cake

- → 8 oz. cream cheese, room temperature
- → 1/2 cup powdered sugar
- → 8 oz. Cool whipped topping
- → 5 oz. (large) instant vanilla pudding mix
- → 2 cups cold milk
- → 10 oz. Oreo cookies, crushed
- → 8x8 or 9x9 glass dish

Cream the cream cheese and sugar together until creamy. Mix in whipped topping. Set aside. Whisk the milk and instant pudding well. Start with the cream cheese mixture and spread evenly over the bottom of the dish. Add vanilla pudding and spread it out evenly. Top with the crushed Oreos.

"This dessert should be kept in the refrigerator. Enjoy it because it will not last long." -*Tammy*

372) Divinity

- → candy thermometer
- → 1-1/2 cups light brown sugar, packed
- → 1/2 cup water
- → 1 tsp white vinegar
- → 1/4 tsp salt
- → 1 large egg white, room temperature

Combine sugar, water, and vinegar in a saucepan over low heat; simmer, then boil for 2 minutes with the lid on. Meanwhile, beat one egg white

and salt in a mixer until stiff peaks form. Remove pan lid and brush sides with cold water to avoid crystallization. Continue boiling the syrup to 245°F or firm ball stage. With the mixer running, slowly pour syrup into egg whites. Mix in vanilla and nuts, then drop spoonfuls onto parchment when thick and sticky. Cool and store airtight.

Option: Use white granulated sugar for white divinity. This is an old-fashioned recipe without using corn syrup.

Option: Drained and chopped maraschio cherries can be added to divinity with nuts.

373) Martha Washington Balls

- → 3/4 lb. confectioners' sugar, sifted
- → 1/2 of 14 oz can Sweetened condensed milk
- → 7 oz. sweetened flaked coconut, Baker's
- → 1/4 cup salted butter
- → 1 cup pecans, chopped
- → 1 tsp vanilla extract
- → 1/4 tsp salt

Mix ingredients above. Roll into small balls and place on a greased cookie sheet. Insert toothpicks into balls for easy dipping and chill.

- → 12 oz. **mini semi-sweet chocolate chips** (or milk chocolate)
- → 1 Tbsp shortening

Melt chocolate in a 1 cup liquid measuring cup. Cook for 30-second intervals, mixing in between being careful not to burn chocolate. Dip the balls into chocolate, then place on parchment paper to dry.

Option: Roll the balls in toffee pieces or other chopped nuts if desired.

"Mama made divinity every Christmas season! My daddy loved it rolled in chopped pecans." -*Tammy*

374) Fudge, Old Fashioned

- → 3 cups granulated sugar
- → 3 heaping Tbsp cocoa, Hershey's
- → 1/2 tsp salt
- → 1/2 cup salted butter
- → 1 Tbsp corn syrup
- → 1/4 cup peanut butter, Jif
- → 12 oz can evaporated milk
- → 1 tsp vanilla extract
- → 1-1/2 cups parched peanuts (or pecans)

Combining Ingredients: Mix sugar, cocoa, and salt well and set aside. Add butter to a non-stick pot. Use a fork to pick up butter and coat the sides of the pot well. Once the butter is melted, add dry ingredients, syrup, and milk. Keep on low heat until the mixture simmers. Careful with sugar granules: Wash utensils to prevent transfer of sugar crystals into the fudge.

Boiling Fudge: Bring to a gentle simmer (until most of sugar has melted). Cover and cook on high heat. Set a timer for 2 minutes. Check candy with a candy thermometer. The temperature should reach the softball stage, around 234°F238°F. Remove from heat let sit 5 minutes.

Beating Fudge: Pour candy into a mixing bowl. Do not scrape the sides of the saucepan when transferring the candy. Add peanut butter and mix on high, then add vanilla. Beat until the candy begins to thicken. Add nuts and turn the mixer off. Quickly pour into a buttered 9x9 or 11x7 pan until set. Cut the fudge and store it in an airtight container at room temperature.

11 cup Pyrex Dish for Lemon Lush

Shop with Tammy through Amazon Affiliates by scanning the qr code, to shop through our Amazon Associates Account!

375) Lemon Lush

1st Layer Is Bottom Crust:

- → 1 cup all-purpose flour
- → 1/2 to 1 cup pecans, chopped
- → 1/2 cup salted butter, room temperature

Blend flour and butter until combined. Add pecans and press into a 2.75-quart baking dish or a 13"x9"x2" pan. Bake at 350°F for 25 minutes, until edges are golden brown. Cool completely before adding 2nd layer.

2nd Layer:

- → 8 oz. cream cheese, room temperature
- → 1 cup powdered sugar
- → 8 oz. whipped topping
- → 1 lemon, zest is optional

Mix cream cheese and sugar until smooth. Then, add 1 cup of whipped topping and mix well. Spread on the cooled crust. Zest your lemon over the cream cheese layer (reserve the zest for topping).

Top Layer Is Pudding Layer:

- → 2-3.4 oz. boxes lemon instant pudding mix
- → 3 cups milk
- → A Lemon's juice, optional

Mix the pudding with milk. Add lemon juice and stir. Pour the pudding over the cream cheese layer, then top with the remaining whipped topping. Garnish the top with lemon zest.

"The photo above shows lemon lush in an 11-cup Pyrex rectangular baking dish. It measures approximately 10 x 8 x 3 inches in height. It is available to buy through our website Amazon Affiliate link by scanning the QR code on the left!" -*Tammy*

376) Orange Balls

- → 1 box vanilla wafers, crushed
- → 1/2 cup frozen orange juice concentrate, thawed
- → 1/2 cup salted butter, melted
- → 1 cup chopped pecans
- → 2 1/2 cups powdered sugar
- → 8 oz sweetened flaked coconut, Baker's

An Old-Fashioned Christmas Cookie!

Place wafer crumbs in a large mixing bowl. Add juice concentrate, butter, and pecans, then beat until well blended. Mix in powdered sugar until fully incorporated.

Drop by tsp (or use a cookie scoop if you have one) onto parchment paper. Roll each cookie in sweetened flaked coconut.

I used Nabisco vanilla wafers, Minute Maid orange juice, and Baker's flaked coconut. Store in an airtight container in the refrigerator until ready to serve; leftovers can be frozen.

"When you pop these in your mouth, it is a strong burst of orange that is creamy and so delicious! The coconut is just a bonus. I hope you love them as much as I do!"-*Tammy*

377) Peanut Butter Buckeyes

- → 2 cups powdered sugar
- → 1/4 tsp salt
- → 1/2 cup salted butter, room temperature
- → 1/2 cup creamy peanut butter, Jif brand
- → 1 tsp vanilla extract
- → 1-1/2 cups **mini semi-sweet chocolate chips**
- → 1 Tbsp shortening

Mix sugar, salt, butter, and peanut butter until smooth, then blend in vanilla. Shape into balls, insert toothpicks, and freeze on parchment paper. Melt chocolate in a 1 cup liquid measuring cup. Cook for 30-second intervals, mixing in between being careful not to burn chocolate.

Dip frozen balls in chocolate, leaving some exposed, let excess drip, and dry on parchment. Reheat chocolate as needed. Use a cookie scoop to dip out balls prior to rolling for uniform size.

"My peanut butter balls stand out because I use butter, unlike most recipes. They taste amazing." -*Tammy*

378) Peanut Butter Cornflake Candy

- → 1/2 cup granulated sugar
- → 1/2 cup corn syrup, used Karo brand
- → 3/4 cup peanut butter
- → 2 1/2 cups of cornflakes, Kellogg's brand
- → 1/4 tsp salt

Boil sugar and corn syrup for 2 minutes. Add a dash of salt, remove from heat, and stir in peanut butter until melted. Mix in cornflakes; the mixture will be stiff. Drop onto waxed paper to cool.

 Note: For softer candy, boil candy for only 1 minute, then add peanut butter, mix well, add corn flakes, and pour into a brownie pan. Cut into squares.

Romans 5:12

"Wherefore, as by one man sin entered into the world, and death by sin; and so death passed upon all men, for that all have sinned:"

143

379) Potato Candy

→ 1 medium baked potato, room temperature
→ 1 tsp vanilla extract
→ 1/4 tsp salt
→ 1 lb. powdered sugar (may need extra)
→ creamy peanut butter, Jif brand
→ powdered sugar (for dusting)

Cook the potato thoroughly. Peel, remove dark spots, then blend with vanilla, salt, and 2 cups powdered sugar until smooth. Gradually add remaining sugar until dough forms and pulls away from the bowl; adjust as needed. Dust the counter with powdered sugar, roll the dough into a 1/4-inch-thick rectangle, spread peanut butter on top, and roll into a pinwheel. Wrap, chill for 1 hour, then slice. Store in an airtight container in the refrigerator for up to 2 weeks.

 Tammy's tip: roll out the candy while it is still just out of the mixer, making it easier to mold. Use the sides of the scraper to loosen the candy from the surface while rolling. Let it refrigerate before slicing, and wipe the blade clean for neater candy spirals.

380) Peanut Brittle

→ 1/2 cup salted butter
→ 1/4 tsp salt
→ 1/2 cup light corn syrup
→ 1 cup granulated sugar
→ 1 heaping cup raw peanuts, skins on.
→ 1 tsp vanilla extract
→ 1-1/2 tsp baking soda

Prepare a 13x9 sheet pan and line it with parchment paper or lightly butter it. In a large skillet or medium saucepan, melt butter over low heat. Next, add salt, syrup, and sugar to the saucepan with butter and cook until reaching crack stage (300°F-310°F. When the mixture

reaches the crack stage, it will have turned golden brown. Quickly add baking soda and vanilla, stirring well. The candy should get fluffy looking as you stir is vigorously. Pour it onto the prepared sheet pan. Caution: Candy is very hot. Use a spatula to spread it out and let it cool completely on a cooling rack. Once cooled, break into small pieces and store in an airtight container.

 It is essential to use raw peanuts when making peanut brittle. As candy cooks on stove peanuts will parch and develop a desirable flavor. **Dry-roasted peanuts are not recommended,** as they do not yield the same authentic taste as raw peanuts.

381) Microwave Peanut Brittle

Use the Same Ingredients As Recipe # 380

Peanuts: Roast peanuts on a cookie sheet at 350°F for 8-10 minutes or in an air fryer at 300°F for 6 minutes. Do not cook peanuts too dark but cook them long enough to taste toasty. Cook times for roasting peanuts will vary with different appliances.
Prepare a 13x9 sheet pan and line it with parchment paper or lightly butter it.

Candy: In a glass batter bowl, stir together butter, salt, syrup, and sugar.

 IMPORTANT: Microwave wattages vary. Once the candy starts to turn golden brown, it should be ready. Do not burn it. Cooking times can differ. Lift the spoon out of hot candy and see if it forms a thread.

1000-watt microwave: Cook on high for 3 minutes. Remove and stir well, then microwave for 3 more minutes. Stir in peanuts, and vanilla, then microwave for 2 minutes more. Add baking soda and quickly stir vigorously until light and foamy. Immediately pour onto a parchment lined or lightly buttered cookie sheet.

382) Peanut Butter Chocolate Delight

1st Layer Is Bottom Crust:

- → 2/3 cup dry roasted peanuts
- → 1 cup all-purpose flour
- → 1/2 cup salted butter, room temperature

Use a pastry cutter to blend flour and butter, stir in chopped peanuts, press into a 9-inch cheesecake pan, bake at 350°F for 20 minutes, then cool completely.

2nd Layer:

- → 1/3 cup peanut butter, Jif brand
- → 8 oz. cream cheese, room temperature
- → 1 cup powdered sugar
- → 1 cup whipped topping

Cream together peanut butter and cream cheese. Add powdered sugar and mix well. Fold in the whipped topping. Spread over the cooled crust.

3rd Layer:

- → 3 cups milk
- → 3.4 oz. vanilla instant pudding mix
- → 3.4 oz. Chocolate instant pudding mix

Combine ingredients and mix well. Spread over layer 2.

4th Layer:

- → 1 cup whipped topping
- → Hershey's chocolate bar
- → 1/3 cup chopped peanuts

Top with whipped topping. Shred a Hershey bar over the top. Sprinkle with peanuts. Refrigerate overnight before serving. Remove the outer cover of the springform pan and comb the sides as shown in the image above if desired.

383) Pecan Pralines

- → 6 Tbsp salted butter
- → 1 1/2 cups light brown sugar, packed
- → 1 1/2 cups granulated sugar
- → 1 Tbsp corn syrup
- → 1/4 tsp salt
- → 1 cup heavy cream or evaporated milk
- → 1 tsp vanilla extract
- → 2 cups chopped pecans

Measure all ingredients before you begin. Line a large pan with parchment paper. Start melting butter in a saucepan. Use a fork to pick up butter and coat sides of pot well. Once butter is melted, add sugars, syrup, salt, and cream. Bring to a slow boil over medium heat, stirring with a wooden spoon. When boiling, cover pot with a lid and time for 2 minutes. Do not reuse spoon without washing off all sugar first. After 3 minutes, insert a candy thermometer into pot, making sure it's end does not touch sides. Cook until candy reaches 234°F (soft stage). Remove from heat and let sit 5 minutes. Pour candy into a bowl, then add pecans and vanilla. Mix until slightly creamy. Quickly drop spoonfuls onto the parchment while the candy is shiny.

Tips: If candy becomes flat-looking before you can drop it, heat it up in the microwave for 1 minute, stir, and continue the cycle until it is glossy again. You can also heat it on the stovetop.

For Chocolate Pralines, add 4 oz. of baker's chocolate (finely cut) when adding vanilla.

Rom 5:18

"Therefore as by the offence of one judgment came upon all men to condemnation; even so by the righteousness of one the free gift came upon all men unto justification of life."

384) Stuffed Strawberries

→ fresh strawberries
→ 1/4 cup salted butter, room temperature
→ 4 oz. cream cheese, room temperature
→ 1 tsp vanilla extract
→ 1/2 lb. Powdered sugar (about 2 1/4 cups)
→ 1/4 tsp salt

Mix cream cheese and butter until smooth, then add vanilla. Gradually blend in powdered sugar, whipping for 4 minutes to make it fluffy. Wash, dry, and core strawberries after removing their tops; trim the tips flat so they stand upright. Fill each strawberry with the cream using a pastry bag. Garnish with a leaf from the cut tops. Refrigerate stuffed strawberries.

Now That is a Banana Split for sharing!

385) Vanilla Custard Ice Cream

→ 5 Tbsp cornstarch, leveled
→ 6 cups whole milk (icy)
→ 2 2/3 cups sugar
→ 4 large eggs
→ 3/4 tsp salt
→ 12 oz. can evaporated milk
→ 1 pt. whipping cream (icy)
→ 3 1/2 Tbsp vanilla extract
→ crushed ice and lots of ice cream salt
→ Put milk in the freezer one hour before mixing.

Put whipping cream in the freezer 20 minutes before adding.

In a batter bowl, whisk together the sugar, cornstarch, and salt. Whisk well. In a separate bowl, beat the eggs. Add the eggs and evaporated milk to the batter bowl with the sugar and whisk very well—microwave on high for 3 minutes.

 Make sure to whisk cornstarch from the bottom and sides of the bowl, or it will form lumps in the pudding.

Take it out and whisk well. (You can use a hand mixer if needed.) Continue to cook on high in 2-minute intervals—whisking well between each—until it becomes thick and gravy-like in texture.

Important: *if the creamy mixture has lumps, pour it through a mesh strainer.*

Add milk, whipping cream, and vanilla. Fill the ice cream freezer container two-thirds full. Freeze according to the ice cream freezer manufacturer's instructions. Enjoy, y'all! The ice cream should be creamy with a soft-serve texture. Yields: 5 quarts

 Important: *milk and whipping cream must be icy to help cool down the hot pudding. Make sure to put them in the freezer before adding them to the ice cream.*

Fish & Seafood Recipes

Fresh Fish Favorites & Seafood Recipes

Chris, my husband and camera operator, loves fishing, so we always have fresh fish at home. That means fish shows up in our meals all the time! The fish in the Recipe picture is speckled trout—it is light, flaky, and has a mild taste. We like it best with along with flounder and red fish.

Here you will find all recipes for speckled trout, but you can use these ideas for other kinds of fish too. After trying Shrimp and Grits on a trip to Pensacola, Chris got hooked and now we make it ourselves at home, it is budget-friendly and honestly just as good as eating out. There are other recipes here too, like our favorite fish and chips, plus some tips (like whipping up your own tartar sauce). Have fun trying them out as you go through the cookbook!

Chris holding a Red Fish

386) Catfish Nuggets Pan-Fried

- → catfish (pat dry with paper towels)
- → salt & black pepper
- → soul food seasoning

1st pie plate:
- → 1/2 cup all-purpose flour

2nd pie plate:
- → beaten large egg

3rd pie plate:
- → 1 cup cornmeal mix (self-rising)
- → large skillet with 1/4" cooking oil

Season fish with salt, pepper, and seafood seasoning. Lightly dredge the fish in flour. Dip in egg (shaking off excess), then into cornmeal. Fry in hot oil for 2 minutes per side. Serve with Recipe # 610 Tartar sauce

"When frying fish, make sure the oil is hot before adding fish for a crunchy crust..." -*Chris*

387) Crab Cakes

- → 16 oz. crab meat, chopped
- → 2 Tbsp lemon juice, fresh
- → 1/3 cup mayonnaise
- → 1/4 cup minced onion or shallots
- → 3 large eggs
- → 1/2 tsp salt
- → 1/2 tsp black pepper
- → 1 tsp soul food seasoning
- → 2 tsp yellow mustard
- → 1 Tbsp No salt salad blend
- → 1 Tbsp fresh chopped parsley
- → 1/3 cup self-rising flour
- → 1/2 cup breadcrumbs

Mix all ingredients thoroughly. Gently pack mixture to form cakes. Heat 1/4" corn oil in a skillet; test readiness by dropping in a

smallpiece—when it sizzles, add cakes. Fry on medium heat for about 3 minutes per side, flipping only once, until golden brown. Serve with lemon wedges.

 For a sturdy cake, mix the ingredients, form them into patties, and refrigerate or freeze. If you freeze them, thaw completely in the refrigerator before frying.

388) Fish and Chips

Fish Batter:
- → 1 1/2 cups self-rising flour
- → 1/4 cup corn starch
- → 1 tsp onion powder
- → 1/2 tsp garlic powder
- → 1/2 tsp cayenne pepper
- → 1/2 cup water
- → 1/2 cup milk

Mix the above ingredients with a wire whisk and set aside.

- → 1/2 cup self-rising flour
- → corn oil

Cut fish into 1-inch strips, coat with flour, and heat oil in a skillet. Test oil with a bit of batter; if it sizzles and floats, it is ready. Keep oil at medium heat, dip fish in batter, and fry for two minutes per side until golden. Drain on paper towels. Make crunchies by drizzling extra batter into hot oil. Serve with homemade potato chips.

> **Rom 5:19,20**
> "For as by one man's disobedience many were made sinners, so by the obedience of one shall many be made righteous. Moreover the law entered, that the offence might abound. But where sin abounded, grace did much more abound." KJV

389) Salmon Patties

- → 14.75 oz. can Alaskan pink salmon
- → 2 green onions, minced
- → 1 large egg
- → 1/2 tsp salt
- → 1/4 tsp pepper
- → 1/2 cup self-rising flour
- → 1/8 cup self-rising cornmeal mix

Open a can of salmon and drain the juice. Put the salmon in a large bowl. Remove the bones and skin, discarding them. Now add the remaining ingredients and mix well.

- → skillet
- → cooking oil (canola or vegetable)

Heat the skillet to a medium-high and add 1/2 inch of oil. When the oil is hot (a test piece floats and sizzles), lower the heat to medium. Drop 1/8 cup batter per patty into the skillet, fry for 3 minutes, then flip and flatten; cook two more minutes until browned. Remove with tongs and drain on paper towels. Makes 6-8 servings.

"Mama made these all the time, and they are great. It is great to have a can in the pantry for a quick meal." -*Tammy*

390) Double Dip Fried Fish

- → 1 cup self-rising flour
- → 1 tsp onion powder
- → 1/2 tsp garlic powder
- → 1 tsp seafood seasoning
- → 1/2 tsp salt, omit if seafood seasoning is salty
- → 1 cup carbonated beverage

Mix the above ingredients with a wire whisk. Batter should be thin. Set batter aside.

- → corn oil
- → 2 cups self-rising cornmeal mix

Pat fish dry with a paper towel. Dip fish into batter and place into the cornmeal. Press the cornmeal onto the fish so it adheres well. Try not to push it or the liquid batter will slide off the fish. Batter should sit on the fish around 10 minutes before frying for a good solid crust. Preheat a skillet with 1" oil. Put a little bit of batter into skillet and once it sizzles and floats the oil is ready. Keep oil at a medium temperature. Place battered fish in the skillet carefully with tongs or meat hook. Turn in two minutes and cook on the other side for another 2 minutes. The batter will be golden. Put fish on a plate lined with paper towels.

391) Mustard Fried Fish

- → 3-4 fish fillets (1/2" thick)
- → seafood seasoning
- → yellow mustard
- → 1 cup self-rising cornmeal mix
- → salt & black pepper
- → 1/2" corn oil

Pat fillets dry and sprinkle them with seasoning, salt, and pepper. Coat them evenly with mustard. Place cornmeal mix in a shallow dish, like a pie plate, and coat each fillet, pressing the cornmeal into the fish. Let the battered fish rest for 5 minutes before frying to develop a good crust. Fry in 1/2-inch-deep hot oil for 2 minutes per side or until golden brown.

392) Fish Francese

→ 1 1/2 stick salted butter
→ 1 pint sliced white mushrooms
→ salt & black pepper
→ onion powder
→ fish fillets, 1/2-inch-thick
→ roasted garlic powder, Badia brand
→ onion powder
→ 2 large eggs
→ 1-1/2 cups of self-rising flour
→ 2 lemons

Place butter in a saucepan with mushrooms over medium heat. Sprinkle mushrooms with salt, pepper, and onion powder. Cook on medium-low heat without a lid until juices from mushrooms evaporate, leaving only butter in the pan. Do not cook mushrooms on high heat to prevent burning the butter. Rinse fish and pat it dry with a paper towel. Season fish with salt and pepper, then sprinkle with garlic powder and onion powder. Beat eggs and pour over fish to coat well. In a shallow pan, coat fish evenly with flour. Fry fish for about 3 minutes per side until golden brown. Place fish on a serving plate and pour hot mushrooms and butter over it. Squeeze two lemons over fish and mushrooms. Garnish with lemon slices.

"This dish is a local favorite that is made with Chicken. We love it so much that we make it with fish as well." – *Tammy*

Rom 6:14
"For sin shall not have dominion over you: for ye are not under the law, but under grace." KJV
Rom 6:18
"Being then made free from sin, ye became the servants of righteousness." KJV

393) Salmon Steaks (Glazed)

→ salmon steak
→ 3 Tbsp olive oil
→ 3 Tbsp salted butter
→ 1/4 cup golden eagle table syrup, (or white corn syrup)
→ 2 tsp smoky barbecue seasoning

Rinse and pat the salmon steaks dry. (Cut into 2-inch-wide pieces if needed.) Preheat the skillet to medium-high. Add olive oil, then place the salmon steaks in the skillet. Cook on high for 2 minutes to sear, then cover, reduce the heat to low, and simmer for 8 minutes with the lid on. Remove the lid, flip the steaks, add butter, and cook for an additional 2 minutes. Mix the syrup and BBQ seasoning. Glaze the salmon and cook until the glaze thickens. Be careful not to burn the glaze. Remove from heat and serve.

394) Salmon Steaks w/red chili sauce

→ Asian sweet chili sauce

Make salmon as described in Recipe # 393 but use sweet chili sauce instead of the glaze. This is now my favorite way to eat salmon! Cook it in the air fryer, adding chili sauce at half the cooking time. Use the Air-Fryer Fish setting.

395) Fish Tacos

→ soft taco shells
→ fresh fish
→ 1/4 cup salted butter
→ seafood/Cajun seasoning

Place the skillet on medium-high heat and add butter. Add the fish and sear both sides until the fish is golden brown, like a scallop. Cook just enough to get a great sear. Enjoy tacos!

396) Shrimp, Fried

→ fresh shrimp, peeled, deveined
→ seasoning of your choice
→ whole buttermilk
→ 1 cup self-rising flour
→ salt & black pepper
→ corn oil

Pat dry the shrimp and sprinkle with seasoning, salt, and pepper. Lightly coat them with buttermilk. Place flour in a shallow dish, like a pie plate, and coat the shrimp, pressing the flour into them. Let the battered shrimp rest for 5 minutes before frying to achieve a good crust. Fry in 1/2-inch-deep hot oil for 2 minutes per side or until golden brown.

397) Butterfly Shrimp

→ 1 lb. size 26-30 fresh shrimp, peeled & deveined
→ 1 cup whole buttermilk

For Coating Mix:
→ 1 cup self-rising flour
→ 11 /2 tsp seafood seasoning
→ 1/2 tsp black pepper

Slice shrimp right down the middle of back to butterfly. Use a sharp knife and a cutting board, being careful not to slice all the way through the shrimp. Once they are opened, take a flat spatula and place it on top of each shrimp, then use the palm of your hand to mash it so that it spreads out. Place the shrimp in a bowl and toss them in buttermilk. Let them soak for 15 minutes. Shake off any excess buttermilk from each shrimp and dip them in the flour mixture on both sides, pressing firmly to ensure a good coating. No need to double dip! Preheat the skillet to Medium/High. Add about 1/2 inch of oil to the skillet. The oil must be hot. Fry about a minute per side until golden brown. Place on a towellined plate.

398) Shrimp & Grits

→ 1 cup quick white grits
→ 1/2 tsp salt
→ 1/4 tsp black pepper
→ 1/4 cup salted butter
→ 4 oz. shredded cheese
→ 2 1/2 cups milk
→ 1-1/2 cups water

In a tall batter bowl (to prevent spills while cooking), combine the grits, milk, water, salt, and pepper. Microwave on high for 4 minutes, then remove and stir. Continue microwaving at 1-minute intervals until the mixture is creamy. Add butter and cheese.

→ 1 cup salted butter
→ 1 small onion, peeled and sliced thin
→ 1/2 sweet red bell pepper, sliced thin
→ 1 lb. shrimp raw, peeled and deveined
→ 1 tsp. Soul seasoning from Dollar General (or your favorite seafood seasoning)

Melt butter in a skillet over low heat. Wait for the grits to cook before increasing the heat. Sauté pepper and onion until soft, then add shrimp with your preferred seasoning. Cook for 2-4 minutes until shrimp curl and change color. Serve shrimp and veggies over grits with drippings. Avoid overcooking. Enjoy!

"The first time Chris had these was in Apalachicola, Florida. He really loves this dish."
– Tammy

Rada pairing knives are great to use for things like peeling potatoes or butterflying shrimp! Get the anthem handles!

Product

151

Frostings, Fillings & Toppings

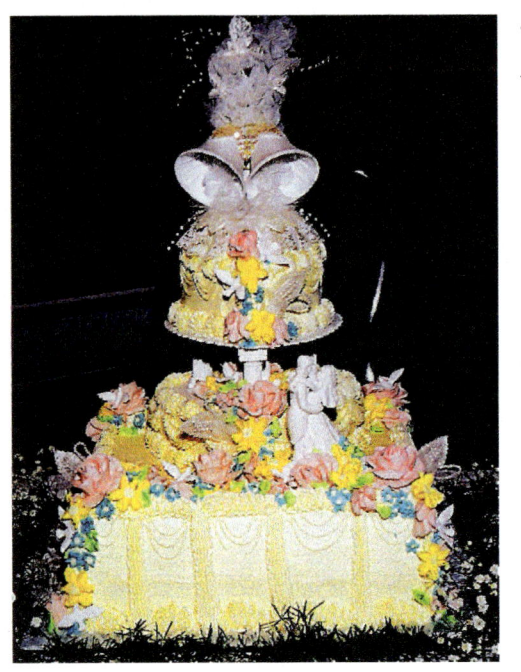

"Meet my mama, Iva Howard Benefield East! Born in 1944 to Rev. J.T. and Maggie Howard, she grew up in a loving but strict pastor's home. She married my daddy in high school and later had four children.

Mama was an incredible cook, and in her 30's, she began baking and decorating cakes professionally. I started helping her at Agan's Bakery in Cartersville, Georgia, where we would prepare nearly 100 cake orders every Saturday. I cherish those early mornings driving from Cedartown, stopping for biscuits, and the hectic Christmas Eves working at Agan's Bakery. I miss her deeply, but I treasure the memories of her incredible cake-making and the pride she took in her work. She was beautiful inside and out!"

-Tammy

399) 7 Minute Icing

→ 1-1/2 cups granulated sugar
→ 1/4 tsp cream of tartar
→ 1/2 tsp salt
→ 1/3 cup water
→ 2 tsp light corn syrup
→ 2 large egg whites
→ 1 tsp vanilla extract

In a medium saucepan, bring 6 cups of water to a boil. While it heats, combine all ingredients (except vanilla) in a large glass bowl and mix with an electric hand mixer until thoroughly combined.

Place the glass bowl with blended ingredients on top of the saucepan with boiling water and set a timer for 7 minutes. Beat with a hand mixer on the highest setting for the entire 7 minutes. Remove the icing from the heat when the timer goes off, add vanilla, and then beat for an additional 2 minutes. Ice the cake immediately. Do not do this without a timer!

"This icing is delicious, light, and fluffy. It is so creamy and so delicious on fresh coconut and devil's food cakes!" – *Tammy*

400) Black Walnut Stovetop Icing

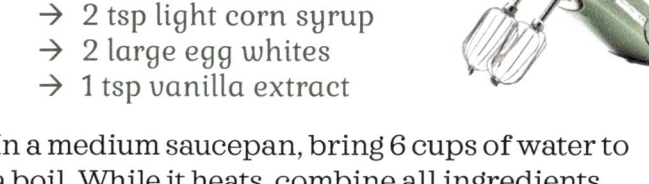

→ 1/2 cup salted butter
→ 3/4 cup packed brown sugar
→ 3/4 cup granulated sugar
→ 1 Tbsp corn syrup
→ 1 cup evaporated milk
→ 1/4 cup crushed black walnuts
→ 1 cup powdered sugar
→ 1 tsp vanilla extract
→ 1/2 tsp salt

In a saucepan, melt butter over low heat. Fork the butter and butter sides of pot. Add brown and granulated sugar, syrup, and milk. Bring to a gentle simmer on medium/low heat. Do not rush the melting of the sugar. All granules must be dissolved before the icing boils entirely. (Cook on simmer for about 4 minutes.) Once the sugar is melted, increase the heat, cover and bring to a full boil. Cook until icing reaches 234°F (soft stage). Remove from heat and let sit 5 minutes. Transfer mixture to a stand mixer and beat at high speed while adding the extract, walnuts, salt, and powdered sugar. Spread the icing on the cake immediately. Enjoy, and remember to chop or crush the walnuts to release oils and flavor!

"My daddy loves black walnuts. He always wanted Mama to buy black walnut ice cream. He absolutely loved the icing on the cake and enjoyed the walnuts in the layers too."
– *Tammy*

401) Browned Butter Frosting

→ 5 cups confectioner's sugar (sift if lumpy)
→ 1/2 tsp salt
→ 1 cup browned salted butter
→ 1/2 cup half and half (half milk, half cream)

Add butter to a saucepan or skillet and cook over medium heat until browned. Remove from heat and let cool for 20 minutes. Add the butter to a stand mixer with powdered sugar, salt, and milk, then beat until creamy. Add 1 Tbsp milk if you want it to be more spreadable.

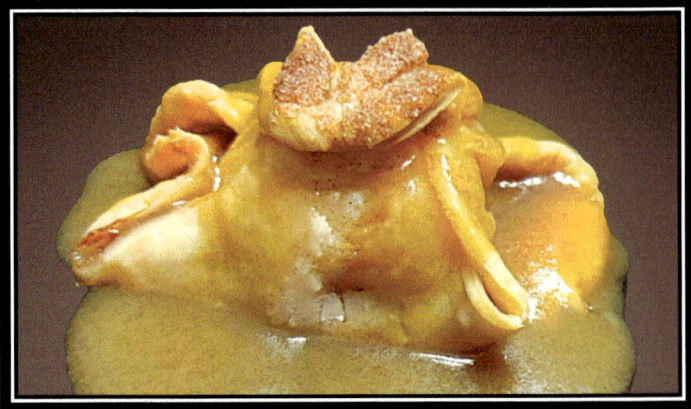

402) Buttermilk Glaze

- → 1 cup granulated sugar & 1/4 tsp salt
- → 1/2 cup buttermilk
- → 1/2 cup salted butter
- → 1 Tbsp clear corn syrup
- → 1/2 tsp baking soda
- → 1 tsp vanilla

Combine all ingredients except vanilla in a saucepan; bring to a boil for 5-6 minutes until thick like syrup—then add vanilla. To glaze a cake, poke holes in the top, and then pour the glaze over. If it is a Bundt cake, pour the glaze on top and let it drizzle down the sides.

"This is not like a traditional glaze. It is more like caramel. It is sticky and delicious!"
– *Tammy*

403) Buttercream Frosting

- → 1 cup salted butter, room temperature
- → 4 1/2 cups powdered sugar
- → 2 tsp vanilla extract
- → 1/2 tsp salt
- → 1-1/2 Tbsp cream (evaporated milk)

In a stand mixer's mixing bowl, add butter and beat with the whisk attachment on high speed until it becomes white and fluffy. Slowly add 2 cups of powdered sugar. Add cream and vanilla. Continue adding powdered sugar. Finish by adding a dash of salt.

404) Penna Colada Buttercream

Omit cream and vanilla in Recipe #403. Add 1/2 cup more powdered sugar, then 2 tsp of rum flavoring. Add 1 cup of crushed pineapple, drained, and 1 cup of toasted coconut.

405) Chocolate Buttercream

Whisk 1/2 cup cocoa with the powdered sugar in Recipe 403.

406) Caramel Topping

- → 1/2 cup salted butter
- → 1/2 cup evaporated milk or whipping cream
- → 3/4 cup light brown sugar, packed
- → tsp corn syrup
- → 1 tsp vanilla extract & 1/2 tsp salt

Melt butter in small saucepan, add brown sugar and corn syrup. Mix until well blended on low until sugar has begun to melt. Add milk, and salt and whisk well. Turn up heat and bring to a boil. Once boiling, turn down to a lower temperature for a low boil and set timer for 3 minutes. Take off heat and add vanilla. Whisk well. Pour into a pint size mason jar for serving.

Our visit to Saint Mary's, Georgia city park.

154

407) Chocolate Buttercream, Sour Cream

- → 1 lb. powdered sugar
- → 1/3 Cup cocoa powder, Hershey's
- → 1/2 cup salted butter, room temperature
- → 1/3 cup shortening
- → 1/2 cup sour cream
- → 1/2 tsp salt
- → 1/2 tsp butter extract
- → 1 tsp vanilla extract

Whisk powdered sugar and cocoa together in a separate bowl. Using an electric mixer, whisk together butter and shortening until fluffy. Then, add sour cream and mix. Gradually add dry ingredients in 1/2 cup increments until thoroughly combined. Beat on high for 2-3 minutes until light and fluffy. Enjoy!

"This is my favorite chocolate icing for cakes! My kids and Chris still like Recipe #417 best. I like this because it is fluffy and not as rich."
– Tammy

408) Chocolate Ganache

- → 2 oz. baker's unsweetened chocolate
- → 2 Tbsp vegetable shortening

Melt shortening in a small non-stick skillet. Add chocolate and heat very low. Mix until smooth.

How to Ice Brownies with Ganache:

Pour melted chocolate over the icing while it is hot. Tilt the pan to cover the entire brownie surface with chocolate. Do not touch it; tilt the pan back and forth until it is evenly spread.

Rom 8:10
"And if Christ be in you, the body is dead because of sin; but the Spirit is life because of righteousness." KJV

409) Caramel Icing, Stovetop

- → 1/2 cup salted butter
- → 2 cups dark brown sugar
- → 1 Tbsp corn syrup
- → 1 cup evaporated milk
- → 1 cup powdered sugar
- → 1 tsp vanilla extract
- → 1/2 tsp salt

In a saucepan, melt butter over low heat. Fork the butter and butter sides of pot. Add sugar, syrup, and milk. Bring to a gentle simmer on medium/low heat. Do not rush the melting of the sugar. All granules must be dissolved before the icing boils entirely. (Cook on simmer for about 4 minutes.) Once the sugar is melted, increase the heat, cover and bring to a full boil. Cook until icing reaches 234°F (soft stage). Remove from heat and let sit 5 minutes. Transfer mixture to a stand mixer and beat at high speed while adding the extract, salt, and powdered sugar. Spread the icing on the cake immediately.

 Essential Tips: Pour caramel out of the saucepan without scraping. Use clean utensils without sugar granules every time you stir.

 Note: If it hardens, use a stainless-steel spoon and scrape from the sides of the bowl, and then add a drop of cream.

"The original recipe had 3 cups of brown sugar and did not have corn syrup or powdered sugar. I have changed it because it is so hard to make the old-fashioned way. If you want to, you can use these ingredients instead but be aware that it is hard to keep this icing from turning back to sugar! Adding the corn syrup and powdered sugar makes is much easier to make successfully. The picture above shows it made without the powdered sugar." – Tammy

410) Cream Cheese Frosting

See Recipe#208 for Cream Cheese Frosting, Italian Cream, Red Velvet, Banana Bread, & More.

411) Crumble Topping.

→ 1/2 cup light brown sugar
→ 2/3 cup all-purpose flour
→ 1 cup old-fashioned oats
→ 4 Tbsp salted butter, sliced thin
→ 3/4 tsp ground cinnamon
→ 1/2 cup finely chopped pecans

Place sugar, flour, and butter in a bowl and using a blending fork, blend well until it is crumbly. Now add oats, cinnamon, and pecans and mix well.

412) Decorator's Frosting

→ 1 cup Crisco shortening
→ 5 cups of powdered sugar
→ 1 tsp clear vanilla extract
→ 1 tsp clear butter extract
→ 1/2 tsp of salt
→ 1 1/2 Tbsp canned cream

In a stand mixer, add shortening and mix on medium speed until creamy (about 3 minutes). Slowly add 2 cups of powdered sugar. Add the cream and extracts. Finish adding sugar. Add a dash of salt.

"This icing is made with white shortening and clear flavorings for a beautiful white color. It makes your mixed colors turn out gorgeous as well! Almond extract can be substituted for Vanilla, but I prefer vanilla and butter for cake decorating."- *Tammy*

If you use it for borders, make it a little thinner. For making roses (make sure it is stiff for the petals to hold up). Adjust the thickness by adding or removing powdered sugar.

413) Clear Fruit Glaze

→ 1/2 cup granulated sugar
→ 1/2 cup apple juice
→ 1/2 cup water with 2 Tbsp cornstarch

Whisk water and cornstarch together until well combined. Place sugar and juice in a saucepan and cook over medium heat. Add the water and cornstarch mixture, then bring to a boil until thick and bubbly. Cool slightly and use it to glaze fresh fruit on a cake topping or tart!

"This is great on a Fresh Fruit Topped Cake with a whipped cream icing. Just beautiful and delicious." -*Tammy*

414) Clear Lemon Glaze:

For a clear lemon glaze, add

→ 1/4 cup fresh lemon juice

To Recipe #413 when cooking.

415) Vanilla Glaze

→ 2 cups sifted powdered sugar
→ 1/3 cup milk
→ 1 tsp vanilla extract

Combine the above ingredients with a whisk until smooth and creamy.

May & Amy in the tree of our front yard. Chris built them a platform, and they called it their tree house. They had so much fun in that tree!

416) Fudge Icing, Stovetop

- → 3 cups granulated sugar
- → 3 heaping Tbsp cocoa, Hershey's
- → 1/2 tsp salt
- → 1/2 cup salted butter
- → 1 Tbsp corn syrup
- → 1/4 cup Jif peanut butter, optional
- → 12 oz. can evaporated milk
- → 1 tsp vanilla extract
- → 1/2 cup pecans, chopped, optional

NOTE: Make at least 1 1/2 recipes to frost a 3-4 layer cake.

Combining Ingredients: Mix sugar, cocoa, and salt well and set aside. Add butter to a non-stick pot. Use a fork to pick up butter and coat the sides of the pot well. Once the butter is melted, add dry ingredients, syrup, and milk. Keep on low heat until the mixture simmers.

Careful with sugar granules: Wash utensils to prevent transfer of sugar crystals into the fudge.

Boiling Fudge: Bring to a gentle simmer (until most of sugar has melted). Cover and cook on high heat. Set a timer for 2 minutes. Check candy with a candy thermometer. The temperature should reach the softball stage, around 234°F-238°F. Remove from heat let sit 5 minutes.

Beating Fudge Icing: Pour icing into a mixing bowl. Do not scrape sides of saucepan when transferring icing. Add peanut butter (optional) and mix on high, then add vanilla. Beat until it is blended. Add nuts if using and turn the mixer off. Quickly frost the cake because icing will harden as it cools.

 If icing becomes hard and unspreadable, warm it in the microwave. DO NOT add liquid. Warm and mix until it is a good spreadable consistency.

417) Favorite Fudge Frosting

- → 8 cups powdered sugar
- → 3/4 cup Hershey's cocoa
- → 3/4 cup water
- → 1 1/2 sticks salted butter
- → 1/2 tsp salt
- → 2 tsp vanilla extract

Combine powdered sugar, salt, and cocoa in a mixing bowl. In a measuring cup, mix water and butter, and microwave until boiling. Pour the hot mixture into the dry ingredients and mix on medium speed, then add vanilla extract.

 Note: Ice the cake immediately because the icing thickens as it cools. If it sets before use, reheat in the microwave until spreadable.

Milk Chocolate Frosting: Use evaporated milk in place of water for a milk chocolate frosting.

418) Lemon Glaze

- → 2 cups sifted powdered sugar
- → 1/3 cup lemon juice
- → 1 tsp vanilla extract

Combine the above ingredients with a whisk until smooth and creamy.

Thin & Tart Lemon Glaze

- → 1/2 cup sifted powdered sugar
- → 1/3 cup lemon juice
- → 1 tsp vanilla extract

Whisk until the mixture is smooth. The desired consistency is pourable. If it is too thick, microwave for approximately 20 seconds. Enjoy!

419) Lemon Curd

- → 2 large lemons (zest and juice)
- → 1 cup granulated sugar
- → 2 Tbsp corn starch
- → 1/4 tsp salt
- → 1/2 cup water
- → 6 large egg yolks
- → 1/2 cup salted butter

Zest the lemons carefully, avoiding the white pith, and set aside. Juice the lemons and combine with the zest in a small bowl. In an 8-cup glass batter bowl, whisk together sugar, corn starch, and salt. Add water, egg yolks, zest, and lemon juice; whisk well. Microwave for 1 minute, then whisk. Continue microwaving in 30-second intervals, whisking thoroughly each time to prevent lumps, until thick and creamy. Add butter and whisk until it is smooth. Store in a pint mason jar and refrigerate.

 Note: Use as a spread on breads or as a filling in cakes and pies

420) Peach Topping

- → 1 lb. frozen peaches
- → 1/4 cup salted butter
- → 1/4 tsp salt
- → 3/4 cup granulated sugar (use more if desired)

Microwave frozen peaches, butter, and sugar in a bowl on high for 4 minutes. Stir, microwave another 4 minutes, then stir in a pinch of salt. Cool on a pie plate. Serve over cakes with whipping cream or use as peach cobbler filling. If refrigerated, reheat to melt the butter before serving.

"You will be amazed at how good peach cobbler is using these peaches instead of canned ones." – *Tammy*

421) Strawberry Topping

- → 16 oz. fresh ripe strawberries
- → 3/4 cup granulated sugar
- → pie plate or shallow dish
- → microwavable bowl
- → 1 Tbsp strawberry gelatin, optional

Rinse strawberries well under cold water. Remove stems. Slice strawberries into a medium-sized microwave-safe bowl. Add sugar on top of the sliced berries—microwave on high for 3 minutes. Remove and mash the strawberries with a hamburger separator to combine the juices with the sugar. Add gelatin if desired. Mix well. Pour strawberries into a shallow pie plate or pan and cool. Refrigerate the topping in an airtight container or use it in a dessert once it is chilled.

 This topping freezes well, so buy strawberries while in season and freeze the topping for quick desserts in the fall and winter.

422) Vanilla Cream Sauce

- → 1 cup half & half
- → 1/2 cup light brown sugar, packed
- → 1/4 tsp salt
- → 1 Tbsp corn starch
- → 1 large egg

Whisk ingredients well - microwave on high for 3 minutes. The pudding should be thick; if not, microwave it until it thickens. Add:

- → 1/2 cup half & half
- → 1 tsp vanilla extract
- → 2 Tbsp salted butter

Whisk until smooth and serve over warm bread pudding or baked apples.

Pie & Cobbler Recipes

A Pie or Cobbler tastes even better because of its simplicity.

If you are looking for a little homey comfort, nothing hits the spot quite like a pie or cobbler fresh out of the oven. Let us kick things off with a classic: egg custard. It is smooth, sweet, and super simple—just a few everyday ingredients come together in a flash to make a creamy filling that is at the heart of so many favorite pies.

What you might not expect is that making a pie is easy. Forget the idea that you need a special occasion or hours in the kitchen—these recipes are perfect for busy days. You can whip up a pie while dinner's cooking, and most of these cobblers and custard pies use pantry basics and straightforward steps anyone can manage.

Whether you are in the mood for the rich flavor of egg custard or the sunny sweetness of a fruit cobbler, these classic desserts are simple enough for any night of the week. Just let your oven do its thing, and before you know it, you will have a cozy dessert ready to top off your meal with a little taste of nostalgia.

423) Easy Apple Cobbler

- → 5 medium apples, Golden Delicious or Honeycrisp
- → 1/2 cup salted butter, melted
- → 1 cup brown sugar, divided into 1/4 cups
- → apple pie spice
- → ground cinnamon
- → 1 cup milk
- → 1 cup of self-rising flour
- → 1/4 tsp salt

Preheat oven to 350°F and butter a casserole dish. Pour the remaining butter in the dish: Peel, core, and thinly slice the apples. Mix flour with milk and set aside. Layer apples in the dish, sprinkling 1/4 cup brown sugar, cinnamon, pie spice, and a little salt over each layer. Pour the milk-flour mixture on top, add the rest of the sugar, and bake for 1 hour. Serve warm with vanilla ice cream.

424) Apple Crumble

- → 7 medium apples (Granny Smith, Winesap apples, or Golden Delicious), peeled and chopped
- → 1 Tbsp brown sugar
- → 1 Tbsp all-purpose flour
- → Fresh Lemon juice
- → 1/4 tsp salt

Preheat oven to 350°F. Grease a 2-3 qt baking dish. Place all ingredients in a bowl and toss well. Place it in baking dish. Make Recipe #425. Add the topping. Bake 45 minutes until apples are soft, checking after 30 minutes as some types of apples soften faster.

425) Cinnamon Oatmeal Crumble

- → 1/2 cup brown sugar
- → 2/3 cup all-purpose flour
- → 4 Tbsp salted butter, sliced thin
- → 1 cup old-fashioned oats
- → 3/4 tsp ground cinnamon
- → 1/2 cup finely chopped pecans

Combine sugar, flour, and butter in a bowl. Use a fork to blend until the mixture is crumbly. Stir in oats, cinnamon, and pecans; mix thoroughly. Bake per dessert instructions.

426) Apple Pie, Tammy's

- → 1 deep-dish pie crust (baked for 15 min. at 375°F)
- → 1 refrigerated pie crust for top
- → 5-6 large Golden Delicious apples, peeled
- → and sliced.
- → 1 cup granulated sugar & 1/2 tsp salt
- → 1/2 tsp apple pie spice, more if desired.
- → 4 Tbsp flour
- → 1/4 cup salted butter, melted

Pre-Bake the crust. Toss apples with sugar, salt, spices & flour, then mound into crust, 1-2 inches above edge. Pour half butter, top with rolled dough slits, and crimp edges. Add remaining butter, sprinkle cinnamon sugar. Bake at 300°F for 90 min. Serve warm with vanilla ice cream!

 OPTIONAL: Don't have apple pie spice? Add 1/2 tsp cinnamon & 1/4 tsp cardamom, or just cinnamon if that is all you have!

Option: Add 1/4 cup of Recipe 592, caramel sauce to the pie before baking.

"Think Granny Smith is the best apple for pie? Just give the Golden Delicious a try!" - *Tammy*

427) Apple Pies, Fried

- → 5 oz. bag dried apples, chopped
- → water
- → 1/4 cup salted butter
- → 1 cup granulated sugar
- → 1/2 tsp salt
- → Cinnamon sugar
- → Recipe#429, Fried Pie Dough

Place apples in a non-stick saucepan with enough water to cover them. Add butter and sugar. Bring to a boil, then cook on medium heat until the water is reduced and apples resemble preserves (thick syrup forms). Observe to avoid burning. Make Fried Pie Dough, Recipe #429.

Place a heaping tbsp of cooked apples in the center of each circle, wet the edges, fold into half-moons, and seal with a fork. Preheat a 10-inch skillet over medium heat, add 1 inch of corn oil, then four tablespoons of butter just before cooking. Fry the pies until golden, flipping as needed. Drain and roll in cinnamon sugar while still warm.

Tip: Grease should be on medium heat so the dough has time to cook; do not keep the grease too hot. Use a test piece of dough if needed.

428) Cinnamon Sugar Ratios:

- → The popular ratio is four parts sugar to one part cinnamon. Example: four cups of sugar to one cup of cinnamon.
- → Another popular ratio is three parts sugar to one part cinnamon.

429) Fried Pie Dough:

- → 1 1/2 cups self-rising flour
- → 4 Tbsp shortening
- → 1/2 cup milk

Mix flour with shortening until they reach a pea-sized consistency, then add milk. Flip the dough

6-7 times on a floured surface and roll it out thin. Incorporate enough flour so you can lift it in a sheet without tearing. Cut out circles with the bottom of a rotary sifter.

430) Apple Dumplings

- → 1 refrigerated pie crust dough
- → 3 small to medium Gala apples or Golden Delicious, peeled, and cored, cut into wedges
- → 1 sifter (for cutting rounds only)
- → 1/4 cup sugar mixed with 1 tsp cinnamon
- → salted butter, room temperature
- → 1/4 tsp salt

For Dumplings:

Roll out the dough and cut into six rounds using the bottom of a crank sifter. Use leftover dough, roll it thin, and cut leaves with a paring knife or small cutter. Roll the remaining dough into six parts. Spread room-temperature butter on a round, add 1 tsp of cinnamon sugar, a dash of salt, and place one or two apple wedges in the center. Gather dough over the apple, using extra dough to seal, and top with a leaf brushed with butter and sprinkled with cinnamon sugar. Bake at 350°F until golden. Serve hot, accompanied by Recipe #406, Homemade caramel topping.

"It It took me years to figure out that I could use the bottom of my sifter to cut out circles for fried pies! When I was young, I would find a bowl big enough in diameter to work, instead of just using the sifter right in front of me. The things we learn from experience are great to know without having to learn the hard way. I hope you know this tip!" - Tammy

431) Banana Cream Pie

- → 2 med/large ripe bananas
- → 2 1/2 cups milk
- → 2 large eggs
- → 1/2 cup granulated sugar
- → 1/3 cup all-purpose flour
- → 1/4 tsp salt
- → 3 Tbsp salted butter
- → 1 tsp vanilla extract
- → 1 cup graham cracker crumbs
- → graham cracker crust, Recipe #452

Whisk eggs, then add milk, sugar, flour, and salt well. Microwave on high for 2 minutes, then remove and whisk thoroughly. Return to the microwave for an additional 3 minutes, then remove and whisk again. If it is not yet thick, microwave for an additional 2 minutes or until it has thickened. Remove and stir in vanilla and butter. Pour half of the pudding into the shell. Thinly slice bananas and lay over the pudding. Sprinkle with graham cracker crumbs. Pour in the remaining pudding. Chill and top with whipped cream before serving. Note: When microwaving puddings, continue cooking until they thicken.

 Microwaves have different wattages, and some take longer to cook. **Pudding will not thicken in the refrigerator.**

432) Buttermilk Pie

- → 1/2 cup salted butter, melted.
- → 1 cup granulated sugar
- → 1/4 tsp salt
- → 3 large eggs, beaten
- → 1 tsp vanilla extract
- → 1/4 tsp nutmeg or cinnamon
- → 1 cup whole buttermilk
- → 3 Tbsp flour

Melt butter in a batter bowl, then add sugar, salt, and eggs -whisk. Add flour, buttermilk, vanilla, and spices, and whisk once more. Place the uncooked pie shell on the oven rack and pour the filling into it (it is best to do this in the oven to prevent spilling). Bake at 325°F for 55 to 60 minutes. If possible, cover the edges of the pie crust while it bakes to prevent overbrowning.

433) Butterscotch Pie

- → 3/4 cup dark brown sugar, packed
- → 1/3 cup self-rising flour
- → 1/4 tsp salt
- → 4 large egg yolks
- → 1 can evaporated milk
- → 1/2 cup water
- → 1/4 cup salted butter
- → 1 tsp vanilla extract

Whisk flour and sugar together. Add salt, milk and water, whisk, and then add eggs, whisking very well. Microwave on High for 3 minutes, take out and whisk along bottom well to reach flour that settles. Put it back in microwave and cook two more minutes on high. Continue cooking for 2-minute intervals until it is thick! Add butter and vanilla. Mix well and pour into a pre-baked pie crust! 9-inch or 8-inch-deep dish pie crust. Refrigerate and top with fresh whipped cream.

Whipping Cream Topping Beat 16 oz. whipping cream with 1/2 cup powdered sugar; add nutmeg if desired. Refrigerate and serve with pie.

434) Blackberry Cobbler

- → 2 pints fresh blackberries
- → 1 1/2 cups granulated sugar
- → 3 cups water
- → 1/4 cup salted butter
- → 1/2 tsp salt
- → 1 cup evaporated milk
- → 2 Tbsp corn starch
- → Make Recipe #466 Biscuit Topping
- → Make Dumplings Recipe #162.

Bring berries, sugar, water, butter, and salt to a boil and cook for 10 minutes (do not add cream yet), then keep simmering. Increase the heat on the berries until they boil. Drop dumplings into the boiling blackberry juice. Cover the pot with a lid and simmer on low heat for 5 minutes. Add cold milk with starch in a separate bowl and mix well - then add to berries. Pour the filling into a sprayed Pyrex dish. Top with biscuit topping. Sprinkle with 1/8 cup sugar. Cut pieces of butter and place them on top. Bake at 400°F for 35 minutes.

"This is my favorite Cobbler. It always reminds me of childhood."- *Tammy*

435) Chess Pie

- → 3/4 cup granulated sugar
- → 1 Tbsp all-purpose flour
- → 2 Tbsp self-rising cornmeal mix
- → 1/4 tsp salt
- → 2 large eggs, beaten.
- → 1/2 cup evaporated milk
- → 1/2 Tbsp white vinegar
- → 1 tsp vanilla extract
- → 1/4 cup salted butter, melted.

Whisk all ingredients well. Pour into an unbaked pie crust and bake at 375°F for 30-35 minutes, or until set and golden brown. Remove from the oven and cool on a wire rack.

436) Chocolate Cream Cheese Pie

- → 8 oz. cream cheese, room temperature
- → 1/4 cup salted butter, room temperature
- → 1/4 cup granulated sugar
- → 1/2 cup milk chocolate chips
- → 1/4 cup semi-sweet chocolate chips
- → 1 tsp vanilla extract
- → 1/4 tsp salt
- → 16 oz. whipped topping
- → Recipe #437 Oreo Pie Crust

Add cream cheese, butter, and sugar in a mixing bowl, blend well with a mixer. Microwave chips at 30 second intervals. Use a rubber spatula and mix chips after each interval until it is melted. Add chips to cream cheese mixture. Add vanilla and salt. Scrape sides and bottom of mixing bowl and mix well. Add 8 oz. of whipped topping and mix until creamy. Place it in Recipe #437. Top with remaining whipped topping.

Garnish with miniature chocolate chips, cookie crumbs, or shaved chocolate if desired. Enjoy!

437) Oreo Chocolate Pie Crust:

- → 20 Oreo cookies
- → Or 24 if using cheesecake pan
- → 4 Tbsp. salted butter, melted Or 5 Tbsp if using cheesecake pan

Crush cookies and add butter. Add to a pie plate. Pack it into the bottom and along the sides. For a no bake crust (pie or cheesecake), you can refrigerate it for 30 minutes before adding you are filling. If you are going to bake it, bake at 350°F for 8-10 minutes.

Crust Shortcut:

 If you are using a microwavable pie plate, you can place the crust in the microwave and cook on high for 1 minute instead of baking it. Cool completely before adding pie filling.

438) Cheese Surprise Pie

→ 2- 8 oz. packages of cream cheese
→ 3 large eggs
→ 2/3 cup granulated sugar
→ 1/2 tsp almond extract
→ 1/4 tsp salt

Cream the cheese and sugar together. Add eggs, extract, and salt and beat for 5 minutes with an electric mixer. Pour into a 9" pie crust. Bake at 325°F for 50 minutes. Top with Sour Cream Pie Topping and bake an additional 15 minutes.

439) Sour Cream Pie Topping

→ 1 cup sour cream
→ 1 tsp vanilla extract
→ 3 Tbsp granulated sugar

Combine sour cream, sugar, and vanilla. Spread on the pie. Bake the pie for an additional 15 minutes.

440) Chocolate Chess Pie

→ 1 1/2 cups of granulated sugar
→ 3 Tbsp all-purpose flour
→ 2 Tbsp self-rising cornmeal mix
→ 3 Tbsp Hershey's cocoa
→ 1/4 tsp salt
→ 1/4 cup salted butter, melted
→ 2 large eggs, beaten
→ 1/2 cup evaporated milk
→ 1 tsp vanilla extract
→ 1/2 Tbsp white vinegar

Preheat the oven to 350°F. In a medium-sized bowl, whisk together the sugar, flour, cornmeal, cocoa, and salt. Add the butter and eggs and beat well. Then, add the milk, vanilla, and vinegar, and beat until smooth. Pour the mixture into a pricked unbaked pie shell, then bake at 350°F for 40-45 minutes until the center is set. Allow to cool completely before slicing.

441) Cherry Pie

→ 3 cups of fresh cherries (wash, remove pits)
→ 1 1/2 cups of granulated sugar
→ 1 stick salted butter
→ 1/4 cup cold water
→ 3 Tbsp corn starch
→ 1/2 tsp salt
→ 2 ready-made refrigerated pie crusts
→ 1/2 tsp cinnamon
→ 1/2 cup sugar
→ Lemon or orange zest, optional

Preheat the oven to 325°F. Place cherries, sugar, and butter in a saucepan; cook for 8-10 minutes. Mix water and cornstarch, then pour into the cherries. Add salt; cook until the starch becomes clear and the juice thickens like gravy. Remove from heat. Fill the pie crust with the mixture. If desired, cut a pattern in the top crust. Cover with the top crust and seal the edges. Lightly sprinkle with cinnamon and sugar. Bake for 1 hour. Serve hot with ice cream or whipped cream.

 Option: add zest of an orange or lemon to filling.

intervals until the mixture is thick and creamy. Whisk after each interval. After microwaving, add vanilla & butter, mix until butter has completely melted. Pour into pie shell and use extra to make pudding cups! Top with whipping cream or a topping if desired. Enjoy!

"This is my favorite chocolate pie. It is fudgy and richer than Granny's chocolate pie. Give them both a try and put a star next to your personal favorite!" – *Tammy*

442) Chocolate Brownie Pie

- → refrigerated pie crust
- → 1 cup granulated sugar
- → 4 Tbsp self-rising flour
- → 6 Tbsp Hershey's cocoa
- → 1/3 cup salted butter
- → 2 large eggs
- → 1/4 tsp salt
- → 1 tsp vanilla extract

Preheat oven to 375°F. Place the pie crust on a 9-inch standard pie plate. Crimp the edges to create a border. Prick the crust with a fork and bake for 20 minutes or until golden brown. Remove from oven and reduce the temperature to 350°F.

In a bowl, whisk together sugar, flour, and cocoa. Add butter, eggs, salt, and vanilla, then whisk until smooth. Pour the mixture into the Pre-Baked pie crust and bake at 350°F for 30 minutes. Serve with whipped cream!

"This pie is so easy and so unbelievably delicious! It is my youngest daughter's favorite pie." -*Tammy*

443) Chocolate Cream Pie

- → 1/3 cup cornstarch
- → 1 1/4 cup granulated sugar
- → 1/4 tsp salt
- → 1/2 cup Hershey's cocoa
- → 1 cup of evaporated milk
- → 2 cups milk
- → 4 Tbsp salted butter
- → 1 1/2 tsp vanilla extract
- → whipped topping or sweetened whipping cream
- → No-bake pie crust Recipe #437 Oreo or Recipe #452 Graham Cracker Crust.

In a glass batter bowl, using a wire whisk, mix dry ingredients (cornstarch, sugar, salt & cocoa) well. Add milk & whisk well. Place it in microwave on high setting for 3 minutes. Take out-whisk well. Microwave again at 2-minute

444) French Coconut Pie

- → 1/2 cup salted butter
- → 3/4 cup sugar
- → 1/4 tsp. salt
- → 3 large eggs
- → 1/4 cup buttermilk
- → 1 tsp vanilla extract
- → 1 1/2 cups of flaked coconut.
- → standard pie crust

Preheat the oven to 325°F. In a glass bowl, melt a stick of butter in the microwave. Add sugar and salt, whisk together. Add eggs, buttermilk, and vanilla, then whisk well. Place coconut at the bottom of your unbaked pie shell. Pour the mixture over the coconut. Bake for 1 hour.

For Deep Dish or 9 "Pie:

- → Use four eggs instead of 3
- → use 1/2 cup buttermilk instead of 1/4 cup

"This has always been my daddy's favorite pie. It is so easy to make and is so delicious." – *Tammy*

Rom 8:14
"For as many as are led by the Spirit of God, they are the sons of God."

445) Chocolate Meringue, Granny's

→ refrigerated pie crust
→ 1 cup granulated sugar
→ 1/2 cup Hershey's cocoa
→ 3 Tbsp corn starch
→ 1/4 tsp. salt
→ 1 cup evaporated milk
→ 1 cup water
→ 5 large eggs, separated
→ 3 Tbsp. salted butter
→ 1 tsp vanilla extract

Preheat the oven to 375°F. Place the pie crust in a 9-inch standard pie dish. Crimp the edges to form a border. Prick the pie crust with a fork and bake for 20 minutes or until golden brown. Remove from oven and reduce temperature to 325°F. In a glass batter bowl, whisk together sugar, cocoa, cornstarch, and salt. Add milk, water, and egg yolks, then whisk well— microwave on high for 4 minutes. Remove and whisk thoroughly, ensuring that you whisk along the sides and bottom to incorporate any starch that has settled. Continue to cook for 2-minute intervals until the filling is thick and creamy. Remove from the microwave and whisk in vanilla and butter. Pour the filling into the Pre-Baked pie crust. Top with Meringue recipe #446. Seal the meringue around the edges of the crust, leaving no holes. Bake at 325°F for 25 minutes or until golden.

446) Meringue, Tammy's

→ 1/4 cup granulated sugar
→ 1/2 tsp cream of tartar
→ 2 tsp corn starch
→ 5 large egg whites, room temperature

Combine sugar, cream of tartar, and cornstarch in a small bowl. Mix well. In a mixing bowl, beat egg whites on high until frothy. Add 1 Tbsp of dry mixture, wait for foam, then add remaining dry ingredients one tablespoon at a time, beating

until glossy and peaks form. Check every 30 seconds; do not overbeat. For pie, place meringue on hot filling. Bake at 325°F for 25 minutes, ensuring at least 20 minutes of cooking time.

💡 For a simple old fashioned meringue omit the cornstarch and/or cream of tartarWhen cooling the pie, it must stay at room temperature until completely cooled.Do not place a warm pie in the refrigerator with meringue, or it will weep.Meringue is best served the day you make it.

Pudding will not thicken as it cools!

Use monk fruit sugar in the meringue for a beautiful meringue with a crispy crust! It is delicious this way.

"This is better than my old favorite way (using powdered sugar). It results in a shiny meringue that still looks glossy after baking."
– *Tammy*

447) Egg Custard

→ refrigerated pie crust
→ 1 cup granulated sugar
→ 1/4 tsp salt
→ 5 large eggs
→ 1 tsp vanilla extract
→ 1 can evaporated milk
→ 1/2 tsp ground nutmeg
→ deep dish pie crust

Preheat oven to 375°F. Fit pie crust in a 9-inch pie plate and crimp edges (see video). Prick with a fork and bake 14 minutes until golden. Remove and increase temperature to 425°F. Whisk sugar, salt, eggs, vanilla, milk, and nutmeg; pour into crust. Bake at 425°F for 20 minutes, then reduce to 350°F and bake 20 more minutes until the center rises fully, which may take up to 1 hour.

448) Coconut Cream/Meringue

- → 1 1/2 cup sweetened flaked coconut
- → pie crust
- → 1/4 cup salted butter
- → 12 oz. can evaporated milk
- → 1/2 cup water
- → 5 large eggs, separated
- → 3/4 cup granulated sugar
- → 1/4 tsp salt
- → 1/2 cup cold water
- → 3 Tbsp corn starch or 6 Tbsp flour
- → 4 Tbsp salted butter
- → 2 tsp vanilla extract

Toast coconut at 350°F until golden, tossing occasionally. Pre-bake pie crust for about 20 minutes at 375°F until golden after the coconut browns.

Melt butter in the microwave, then whisk in milk and 1/2 cup water. Beat egg yolks separately and add them with salt and sugar; whisk again. Whisk starch (or flour) with cold water, add to the pudding, and whisk thoroughly.

Microwave on high for 4 minutes. Remove and whisk thoroughly, ensuring that you whisk along the sides and bottom to incorporate any starch that has settled. Continue to cook for 2-minute intervals until the filling is thick and creamy. Remove from the microwave and whisk in vanilla and butter. Reserve 2 tbsp. toasted coconut to garnish the pie and mix the remaining coconut into the pudding. Pour the filling into the pre-baked pie crust. Top with Meringue Recipe #446. Seal the meringue around the edges of the crust, leaving no holes. Bake at 325°F for 25 minutes, or until golden brown. Garnish with coconut.

 Do not add coconut to top of pie until 10 minutes of baking time has passed. This will ensure the coconut doesn't overbrown.

449) Coffee Cream Pie

- → 2/3 cup granulated sugar
- → 5 Tbsp cornstarch
- → 1/4 tsp salt
- → 1 cup evaporated milk
- → 1 cup strong black coffee, room temperature
- → 1 large egg
- → 2 tsp vanilla extract
- → 2 Tbsp butter, salted.

Combine sugar, cornstarch, and salt in a microwaveable glass bowl. Whisk together well. Add coffee and milk and whisk well. Add egg and whisk VERY WELL, making sure to incorporate the cornstarch from the bottom of the bowl.

Microwave on high for 3 minutes. If your microwave is powerful (over 1100 watts), use 2 minutes instead.

Take the pudding out of the microwave and whip well, incorporating ingredients from the bottom of the bowl. Beat until smooth.

Return to the microwave and cook at 2-minute intervals, whisking until smooth between each cook.

Once the pudding is thick, remove it, add the extract and butter, and whisk until smooth. Pour the mixture into a pre-baked pie shell or a graham cracker crust, Recipe #452.

Cool at room temperature. Cut and serve with whipped cream.

For A Creamy Filling:

 Use a graham cracker crust and omit the egg, replacing it with three large egg yolks. Decrease the amount of cornstarch to 4 Tbsp and refrigerate overnight before serving.

450) Georgie Porgy Pie

Chocolate Brownie Layer for Pie:

→ 1/2 cup granulated sugar
→ 3 Tbsp Hershey's cocoa
→ 2 Tbsp self-rising flour
→ 1/2 stick salted butter, melted
→ 1 large egg
→ 1/4 tsp salt
→ 1/2 tsp vanilla extract

Preheat oven to 350°F. Mix sugar, cocoa, and flour. Whisk, add butter, eggs, salt, and vanilla; mix well. Pour into unbaked pie crust.

Cake Batter for Pie:

→ 1/4 cup shortening
→ 1/2 cup granulated sugar
→ 1/4 cup light brown sugar, packed
→ 1 large egg
→ 1/3 cup buttermilk
→ 3/4 cup self-rising flour
→ 1 tsp vanilla extract

Mix shortening and sugar until creamy, then add egg and beat until fluffy. Add remaining ingredients in order, mix 2 minutes. Spread 1/2-inch layer on brownie. Bake 40 minutes, ensure done before removing. Cool pie to room temperature.

German Chocolate Icing for Pie:

→ 2 large eggs
→ 1 1/3 cups evaporated milk
→ 1 1/3 cups granulated sugar
→ 1/2 cup salted butter, melted
→ 1/4 tsp salt
→ 1 tsp vanilla extract
→ 3/4 cups pecans, chopped
→ 7 oz. Sweetened flaked coconut

Crack eggs into a large microwave-safe bowl. Add milk, sugar, and melted butter, whisk. Add salt and vanilla; whisk well. Microwave for 2 mins, then whisk. Repeat in 2-minute intervals, whisking after each, until smooth and creamy, about 6-7 mins in a 1100-watt microwave. Avoid overcooking to prevent curdling. Stir in coconut and pecans. Once cooled, spread evenly over the pie.

Fudge Frosting for Pie:

→ 2 cups powdered sugar
→ 3 Tbsp cocoa, Hershey's
→ 1/4 tsp salt
→ 1 Tbsp evaporated milk
→ 1/4 cup salted butter
→ 1 tsp vanilla extract

Whisk dry ingredients together. Heat milk and butter in the microwave until hot. Pour into dry ingredients and mix until smooth and creamy. Dollop fudge across top of pie.

"Mama and I worked at a bakery in Cartersville, Georgia, in the late 80s. They made these pies, and our family loved them!"

– *Tammy*

451) French Raisin Pie

→ 1/2 cup salted butter
→ 1/2 cup granulated sugar
→ 1/4 tsp salt
→ 1 cup sugar
→ 3 large eggs
→ 1 cup chopped pecans
→ 1 cup raisins
→ 1 Tbsp apple cider vinegar
→ 1/2 tsp cinnamon
→ 1/4 tsp cloves

Cream together first 3 ingredients, then add remaining ingredients, mix well. Preheat oven to 350°F. Fill a 9-inch unbaked pie shell with mixture. Bake for 40 minutes. The center will look soft but will firm up as it cools.

452) Graham Cracker Pie Crust

→ 1 1/2 cups graham cracker crumbs
→ 1/3 cup granulated sugar
→ 1/4 cup salted butter

Place crackers in a gallon zip lock bag, crush with a rolling pin. Melt butter in a bowl, add sugar and cracker crumbs, and mix. Press onto a pie plate and bake 10 minutes at 350°F. Cool before filling:

 Option: instead of baking, microwave it 90 seconds then chill before filling.

Cinnamon Pie Crust:

For a cinnamon crust, use Cinnamon graham crackers or add 1/2 tsp cinnamon to recipe.

453) Japanese Pie

→ 1/3 cup salted butter, melted
→ 1 cup granulated sugar
→ 3 large eggs
→ 1 dash salt
→ 1 tsp vanilla extract
→ 3/4 cup chopped pecans
→ 1/2 cup golden raisins
→ 1/2 cup flaked coconut

Mix melted butter, sugar, eggs, salt, and vanilla with a wire whisk. Add pecans, raisins, and coconut. Mix well, pour into a 9" pie crust, and bake at 325°F for 1 hour. Cool on a wire rack to prevent sweating. No refrigeration needed, ideal for holidays!

454) Key Lime Pie

→ Graham cracker or Pre-Baked pie crust
→ 5 limes-- 3/4 to 1 cup key lime juice
→ 3 large eggs
→ Dash of salt
→ 2-14 oz. cans sweetened condensed milk
→ whipping cream for topping
→ zest from one lime for topping
→ 2 Tbsp salted butter

In a bowl, combine the lime juice, eggs, salt, and condensed milk, and whisk until well blended.

For Stovetop directions: Place in a double boiler or non-stick pan and whisk until thick. Add butter and whisk. Pour into pie shell, chill, then top with whipped cream and lime zest.

For Microwave: Place filling in a microwave-safe bowl and whisk well. Microwave in 1-minute intervals, whisking after each, until total of 4

minutes. Add butter and whisk. Cool, then top with whipping cream and lime zest.

For Oven: Add butter to filling, whisk, place in pie shell, and bake at 350°F for 20 minutes. Cool, chill, and top with whipping cream and lime zest.

455) Lemon Cream Pie

→ 8 oz. cream cheese, room temperature
→ 14 oz. can sweetened condensed milk
→ 1/2 cup fresh-squeezed lemon juice
→ 2 tsp lemon Jell-O
→ lemon zest
→ 8 oz. whipped topping
→ Recipe #456 Vanilla Wafer Crust

Mix cream cheese and condensed milk until smooth. Zest lemons onto a paper towel before squeezing. Add lemon juice, lemon Jell-O, and stir well. Incorporate half of the whipped topping and mix thoroughly. Pour the filling into a vanilla wafer crust. Top with the remaining whipped topping and sprinkle with lemon zest.

456) Vanilla Wafer Crust

→ 1 1/2 cups vanilla wafer crumbs
→ 1/3 cup granulated sugar
→ 6 Tbsp salted butter

Mix the above ingredients and press into a 9-inch pie plate and up the sides as well. Bake in a 350°F oven for 15 minutes. Take out and cool completely before filling.

 Option: instead of baking, microwave it 90 seconds then chill before filling.

457) Lemon Icebox Pie

- → Recipe #452 Graham Cracker Crust
- → 2-14 oz. cans sweetened condensed milk
- → 3 large egg yolks*
- → 1/2 to 3/4 cup fresh lemon juice

Mix the juice, milk, and eggs* well with an electric mixer on high speed for 2-3 minutes. Pour into a graham cracker crust and chill overnight. Slice and enjoy!

Raw Egg Consumption*

Option: to cook eggs bake the pie at 350°F for 20 minutes, then chill.

458) Lemon Lush Pie

- → Recipe #452 Graham Cracker Crust
- → 1/3 cup whole pecans, toasted then chop
- → 4 oz. cream cheese, room temperature
- → 1/2 cup powdered sugar
- → 1 cup whipped topping
- → lemon zest

Toast pecans in a 350°F oven for 7 min, then chop and set aside. Mix cream cheese & sugar together until creamy, then add 1 cup of whipped topping-mix well and place in the pie shell. Spread evenly. Zest your lemon over this cream cheese layer. Reserve a portion of zest for topping.

For the Pudding layer

- → 3.4 oz. box lemon instant pudding mix
- → 1 cup milk
- → 1 lemon, juiced

Mix pudding with milk. Add lemon juice and stir. Pour pudding over the cream cheese layer, then cover with the remaining whipped topping. Garnish the top with lemon zest and toasted pecans.

Options: You can use different flavors of pudding and change up this pie if you would like! Just omit the lemon juice and zest.

In the video tutorial, I put pecans on the crust, then spread cream cheese. The crust wanted to break up underneath the nuts, so in this recipe, I have you add the pecans to the top of the pie.

459) Lemon Meringue Pie

- → 1 cup granulated sugar
- → 6 Tbsp corn starch
- → 2 cups water
- → 1/2 cup lemon juice
- → 4 large egg yolks
- → 3 Tbsp salted butter
- → Lemon zest
- → 1/4 tsp salt
- → Recipe #446 Meringue
- → Pre-Baked pie crust

In a glass batter bowl, using a wire whisk, mix dry ingredients (cornstarch, sugar, & salt) well. Add water, lemon juice, & egg yolks- whisk well. Place it in microwave on high setting for 3 minutes. Take out-whisk well. Microwave again at 2-minute intervals until thick and creamy. Whisk after each interval. After microwaving add butter, mix well until butter has completely melted. Pour into pre-baked pie shell! Top with Meringue and bake at 325°F for 25 minutes.

460) Maple Cream Pie Or Meringue

→ refrigerated pie crust
→ 1 cup maple syrup
→ 3 Tbsp corn starch
→ 1 cup evaporated milk
→ 1/4 tsp salt
→ 1 cup water
→ 5 large eggs, separated
→ 1/4 cup salted butter
→ 1 tsp vanilla extract
→ 1 tsp maple extract
→ Recipe #446 Meringue

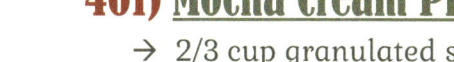

Preheat oven to 375°F. Place pie crust in a 9-inch pie plate, crimp edges, and prick with a fork. Bake for 20 minutes or until golden; then remove and lower oven temperature to 325°F. In a glass bowl, whisk syrup, cornstarch, milk, salt, water, and egg yolks. Microwave on high for 4 minutes, whisking well after.

Take the pudding out of the microwave and whip well, incorporating ingredients from the bottom of the bowl. chocolate. Beat until smooth. Return to the microwave and cook at 2-minute intervals, whisking until smooth between each cook.

Once the pudding is thick, remove it, add the extract and butter, and whisk until smooth. Pour the mixture into a pre-baked pie shell or a graham cracker crust. Finish with meringue or whipped cream. If using meringue, follow the baking directions on the Meringue Recipe.

When microwaving pudding filllings for pies, make sure and cook it until it is thick! **Pudding will not get thicker in the refrigerator.**

Rom 8:16 KJV
"The Spirit itself beareth witness with our spirit, that we are the children of God:"

461) Mocha Cream Pie

→ 2/3 cup granulated sugar
→ 5 Tbsp cornstarch
→ 1/4 tsp salt
→ 1 cup evaporated milk
→ 1 cup strong black coffee, room temperature.
→ 2 oz of baker's chocolate, unsweetened
→ 1 large egg
→ 2 tsp vanilla extract
→ 2 Tbsp butter, salted.
→ Pre-Baked pie shell

Combine sugar, cornstarch, and salt in a microwaveable glass bowl. Whisk together well. Add coffee and milk and whisk well. Add egg and whisk VERY WELL, making sure to incorporate the cornstarch from the bottom of the bowl. Add chocolate and microwave on high for 3 minutes. If your microwave is powerful (over 1100 watts), use 2 minutes instead.

Take the pudding out of the microwave and whip well, incorporating ingredients from the bottom of the bowl and melted chocolate. Beat until smooth. Return to the microwave and cook at 2-minute intervals, whisking until smooth between each cook.

Once the pudding is thick, remove it, add the extract and butter, and whisk until smooth. Pour the mixture into a pre-baked pie shell or a graham cracker crust. Cool at room temperature. Refrigerate pie. Serve with whipped cream.

For A Creamy Filling:

Use a graham cracker crust and omit the egg, replacing it with three large egg yolks. Decrease the amount of cornstarch to 4 Tbsp and refrigerate overnight before serving.

462) Millionaire Pie

- → 4 oz. cream cheese, room temperature
- → Half of 14 oz. can sweetened condensed milk
- → 8 oz. can crushed pineapple, drained well
- → 1/3 cup pecans, chopped
- → 1/3 cup maraschino cherries, chopped
- → 8 oz. cool whip topping
- → 1/2 cup flaked coconut, toasted
- → juice of 1/2 large lemon juice
- → Graham cracker crust, Recipe #452

In a mixing bowl, blend the first two ingredients well with a hand mixer until creamy. Add pineapple, pecans, cherries, lemon juice, and half of the Cool Whip. Gently fold everything together and pour into a 9-inch graham cracker crust. Use a decorating bag to pipe the remaining Cool Whip on top of the pie. Sprinkle toasted coconut over the top and refrigerate for at least 4 hours before serving. Since it contains cream cheese, keep the pie refrigerated. Enjoy!

 Tammy's tip: coconut can be toasted in the air fryer, the oven, and even in a non-stick skillet on the stovetop.

463) Tammy's Mile High Pie

- → Vanilla Wafer crust Recipe #456
- → 3.4 oz. box vanilla pudding, prepared per box instructions
- → 16 oz. whipped topping
- → 1/4 cup chopped milk chocolate
- → 1/4 cup pecans
- → 8 oz. can crushed pineapple, drained.
- → 1/4 cup maraschino cherries, halved
- → 2 bananas, sliced & seeded
- → 1/4 cup flaked coconut, toasted.

Layer the pudding at the bottom of the crust, then add a 1/2-inch layer of whipped cream. Next, top with chocolate, pecans, pineapple, cherries, and bananas. Top with more whipped

cream and sprinkle toasted coconut. Ripe, sliced strawberries can be added with other fruits if desired.

"My granny liked to de-seed her bananas!"
– *Tammy*

464) Peach Cobbler Classic

- → 2 15 oz. cans of sliced peaches in syrup
- → 3/4 cup self-rising flour
- → 3/4 cup granulated sugar
- → 1/4 tsp salt
- → 3/4 tsp vanilla extract
- → 3/4 cup milk
- → 1/2 cup salted butter
- → 1/8 cup chopped pecans, optional
- → Ground nutmeg, optional
- → Ground cinnamon, optional

Preheat oven to 375°F. Melt butter in the microwave and pour it into a 2-quart casserole dish. Spray dish edges. Mix the flour, sugar, salt, vanilla, and milk, then pour the mixture into a dish. Add canned peaches with syrup, sprinkle with cinnamon and nutmeg, and add pecans. Bake until golden and bubbly, for about 45 minutes. Serve with ice cream!!

Substitute: Other canned fruit can be used.

465) Fruit Cobbler

→ Recipe #468 Fruit for cobblers
→ 1 cup granulated sugar
→ 1/4 tsp salt
→ 2 Tbsp self-rising flour
→ 1/2 cup milk
→ Recipe #466, Cobbler Biscuit Topping
→ Recipe #467, Cobbler Cinnamon Topping

Prepare fruit with Recipe #468 and set aside. Mix flour in milk, whisk it very well, and put in the peaches and stir. Place prepared fruit on a well-greased deep pie plate or a 2-quart round casserole. Cover with the dough. Melt 1/4 cup of butter and pour it over the dough. Top with Cinnamon Topping and Bake at 375°F until bubbly and brown, about 30-40 minutes.

"Oh my, this is so good and is my favorite peach cobbler." - *Tammy*

466) Cobbler Biscuit Topping

→ 1 cup self-rising flour
→ 4 Tbsp salted butter, room temperature
→ 1/2 cup milk

In a medium bowl, combine the flour with butter. Use a fork to blend until the butter is pea sized. Add milk and mix until all the flour is incorporated into the dough. Place the dough on a floured surface and knead it 4-5 times. Roll out to 1/4 inch thick.

467) Cobbler Cinnamon Topping

→ 1/2 cup granulated sugar,
→ 1/2 tsp ground cinnamon
→ 1/8 cup finely chopped pecans

Mix and top the cobbler and bake.

> **Rom 8:28 KJV**
> "And we know that all things work together for good to them that love God, to them who are the called according to his purpose."

468) Frozen Fruit for Cobblers

Use **16 oz. bag of frozen fruit** and place it in a saucepan or pot with **3/4 cup sugar** and a **dash of salt**. Cook on medium heat for about 12 min or microwave in a bowl for 10 minutes on high.

469) Peanut Butter Pie

→ 8 oz. cream cheese, room temperature
→ 1/2 cup peanut butter, Jif
→ 1/2 cup granulated sugar
→ 1/4 tsp salt
→ 1 tsp vanilla extract
→ 16 oz. container cool whip topping
→ Recipe #437 Oreo Pie Crust

Using an electric mixer, blend cream cheese and peanut butter until smooth. Add sugar, salt, and vanilla, and mix until well combined. Scrape down the sides and bottom of the bowl to ensure all ingredients are incorporated into the filling. Fold in 1/2 of the Cool Whip (4 oz.), mixing on high speed for 1 minute. Pour the filling into the pie crust. Top with the remaining whipped topping

Pick A Garnish For Top Of Pie:

→ crumbs from the edges of your Oreo crust.
→ pipped hot fudge
→ minichocolate chips
→ chocolate curls

"This was my mother's favorite pie! She absolutely loved it and so do most people that try it. It is one of my personal favorites as well." – *Tammy*

> **Rom 8:17 KJV**
> "And if children, then heirs; heirs of God, and joint-heirs with Christ; if so be that we suffer with him, that we may be also glorified together.

470) Tammy's Pecan Pie

→ 2 Tbsp salted butter, melted
→ 1 cup granulated sugar
→ 2 large eggs
→ 1/2 cup dark corn syrup
→ 1/2 cup light corn syrup
→ 1 tsp vanilla extract
→ 1/4 tsp salt
→ 1 1/2 tsp flour
→ 1 regular pie crust
→ 1 1/2 cups of pecans (whole or chopped)

For A Deep-dish Or 9" Pie Crust Pie Use:

→ 3 eggs instead of 2
→ 2 tsp flour instead of 1 1/2 tsp

Preheat the oven to 325°F. Melt butter in a microwave-safe bowl. Mix in sugar and eggs, then whisk. Add remaining ingredients (except pecans) and whisk again. Spread pecans on the pie crust bottom. Place pie on the oven rack, pour filling over pecans, then slide into the oven. Bake for 60 minutes.

"I prefer to use a pie crust shield and over bake mine 20 extra minutes because it gets a little chewy like I like it."– *Tammy*

471) Pie Crust, Shortening

→ 1 1/2 cups all-purpose flour
→ 1/2 cup shortening (or lard)
→ 1/4 tsp salt
→ 5-7 Tbsp cold water

Cut shortening and salt into flour using a pastry blender or fork, until all flour is incorporated into the shortening. Add cold water until the dough comes together when pressed. Knead briefly, form into a ball, wrap, and chill for 30 minutes. After chilling, knead lightly on a floured surface, then roll into a circle 1 1/2 inches wider than the pie plate. Place the upside-down pie plate on the dough to check the size, then lightly flour and roll the dough onto a rolling pin and unroll it over the dish. Press into the dish and crimp the edges. Prick the crust with a fork if pre-baking. Bake at 375°F for 20 minutes for a pre-baked crust.

472) Pie Crust, Butter

→ 1 1/2 cups of all-purpose flour
→ 1/4 tsp salt
→ 1/2 cup salted butter, room temperature
→ 5-7 Tbsp ice cold water

Cut shortening and salt into flour with a pastry blender or fork until the flour is incorporated. Gradually add water, 1 Tbsp at a time, until dough comes together. Shape into a circle, wrap in plastic, and chill for at least 30 minutes. Roll dough out on a floured surface, turning often, until it is about 1 1/2 inches larger than the pie plate. Place the upside-down pie plate on the dough to check the size, then lightly flour and roll the dough onto a rolling pin and unroll it over the dish. Place it on a pie plate, fold edges under, and crimp.

For pre-baking, prick the crust with a fork. Bake at 375°F until golden, which is about 20 minutes.

473) Pineapple Cream Cheese Pie

→ Recipe #452 Graham Cracker Crust
→ 1 cup cubed fresh pineapple or 8 oz. can crushed pineapple, drained
→ 8 oz cream cheese, room temperature
→ 3 tsp pineapple-flavored gelatin
→ 1/4 tsp salt
→ 1/4 cup granulated sugar
→ 16 oz. cool whipped topping, divided
→ fresh pineapple for garnish, optional

Drain canned pineapple using a mesh strainer. Blend cream cheese, sugar, salt, and gelatin until smooth, then add 2 cups Cool Whip and mix well. Fold in chopped pineapple and pour into a graham cracker crust. Top with whipped topping and pineapple. Refrigerate until set; serve the same day. Avoid pureeing the fruit to prevent a runny pie.

 Options: This pie can be made with any fruit and fruit-flavored gelatin. (Blueberry, strawberry, etc..)

"So easy, so delicious, and tastes like cheesecake! This is amazing, y'all." – *Tammy*

474) Pineapple Meringue Pie

→ 1 deep dish pie crust (Pre-Baked)
→ 1 cup sugar
→ 6 Tbsp corn starch
→ 1/4 tsp salt
→ 1 1/2 cups of evaporated milk
→ 3/4 cup water
→ 5 large eggs, separated
→ 1 tsp vanilla extract
→ 2 Tbsp salted butter

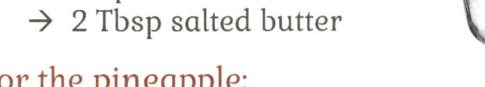

For the pineapple:
→ 15.5 oz. crushed pineapple, strained
OR- 8 oz. crushed pineapple plus 8 oz. pineapple tidbits, strained

Bake the pie crust at 350°F until golden. In a bowl, whisk sugar, salt, cornstarch, then add milk, water, and egg yolks; whisk again. Microwave on high for 3 minutes, stir, and repeat in 2-minute intervals until thick. Stir in vanilla, butter, and pineapple, then pour into crust. Top with Recipe #446 meringue while hot and bake at 325°F for 25 minutes. Cool fully before refrigerating.

475) Sweet Pot Cheesecake Pie

→ 2 cups of cooked sweet potatoes
→ 3/4 cup brown sugar, packed
→ 3/4 cup granulated sugar
→ 1/4 tsp salt
→ 8 oz. cream cheese, room temperature
→ 1/4 cup salted butter, room temperature
→ 3 large eggs
→ 1/2 cup milk or whipping cream
→ 1/2 tsp cinnamon
→ 1/4 tsp nutmeg, optional

Use a whisk attachment to beat the potatoes until creamy, then set aside. In the mixer, beat sugars, salt, cream cheese, and butter until fluffy. Add eggs, potatoes, milk, cinnamon, and nutmeg, whisking well. Pour into a 9-inch unbaked pie shell and bake 50 minutes at 325°F.

476) Pumpkin Pie, Tammy's

→ 1 1/2 cups of freshly cooked whipped pumpkin or canned pumpkin
→ 1/4 cup salted butter
→ 3/4 cup evaporated milk
→ 4 large eggs, beaten
→ 1 tsp baking spice, used Penzey's or 1/2 tsp pumpkin pie spice
→ 1 tsp ground cinnamon
→ 1/2 cup packed brown sugar
→ 1/4 cup of granulated sugar
→ 1/4 tsp of salt

Combine ingredients in a large bowl, mix well, then pour into an uncooked pie shell. Bake at 350°F until set, about 45 minutes. Serve with whipped cream or Cool Whip.

477) Pumpkin/Sweet Potato Pecan

→ 1 1/2 cups of freshly cooked whipped pumpkin or canned pumpkin, or sweet potatoes cooked & whipped
→ 1/4 cup salted butter
→ 3/4 cup evaporated milk
→ 4 large eggs, beaten
→ 1 tsp baking spice, used Penzey's or 1/2 tsp pumpkin pie spice
→ 1 tsp ground cinnamon
→ 1/2 cup light brown sugar, packed
→ 1/4 cup of granulated sugar

→ 1/4 tsp of salt

Combine the ingredients in a large mixing bowl. Mix well with a wire whisk, then pour into the uncooked pie shell. Top with Recipe #478, Pecan pie topping. Bake at 350°F for 40-45 minutes, or until set.

478) Pecan Pie Topping

→ 4 Tbsp salted butter
→ 1/2 cup light brown sugar
→ 2 Tbsp all-purpose flour
→ 1/2 cup pecans, chopped

Use a pastry fork or a blender to mix the butter, brown sugar, and flour until the mixture is crumbly. Stir in chopped pecans. Sprinkle over pie filling and bake the pie's recipe directions.

479) Sweet Potato Cobbler, Bruce's

→ 40 oz. Can Bruce's yams, with juice.
→ 1/2 cup salted butter
→ 3/4 cup self-rising flour
→ 3/4 cup granulated sugar
→ 1/4 tsp salt
→ 3/4 cup milk
→ 1/2 cup brown sugar
→ ground cinnamon
→ 2 or 2.5 qt. casserole dish

Preheat the oven to 350°F. Melt butter and pour it into the bottom of a casserole dish. In a bowl, whisk together flour, sugar, salt, and milk. Place yams with their juice in the casserole dish. Break yams into smaller chunks using a spoon. Sprinkle yams with brown sugar. Lightly dust yams with cinnamon. Pour the flour mixture over the yams in the casserole. Bake at 350°F for 40 minutes or until golden brown and bubbly. Enjoy!

 Options: Sprinkle with chopped nuts before baking if desired. If you want a sweet potato cobbler without all the fuss this is the recipe for you!

480) Sweet Potato Cobbler

→ 4-5 medium/large, sweet potatoes, peel and chop into 1/4-inch slices.
→ 2 cups water
→ 1/2 cup whole milk
→ 1/2 cup canned or whipping cream
→ 1/4 tsp salt
→ 1 cup granulated sugar
→ 1/2 cup light brown sugar
→ 1/4 cup salted butter
→ 1/4 tsp ground cinnamon
→ 1 tsp vanilla extract

Boil potatoes in water and cream for 12 minutes, then add salt, sugar, butter, and cinnamon. Cover and cook on low to medium heat for 5 minutes until the sugar dissolves. Remove from heat, stir in vanilla, and transfer to a greased round baking dish. Prepare Cobbler Biscuit Topping (Recipe #466), roll it out, and place it over the filling. Cut slits into the dough and top with butter. Bake at 350°F for 40 minutes or until golden brown.

 If Recipe #162, dumplings are added to a cobbler, water must be added to provide enough juice for dumplings to cook in.

481) Sweet Potato Pie-Granny's

→ 2 cups cooked sweet potato, whipped
→ 1 1/2 cups granulated sugar
→ 1/4 tsp salt
→ 3 large eggs
→ 1/2 cup salted butter
→ 1 tsp vanilla extract
→ 1/2 cup canned evaporated milk

Begin by creaming or mashing the sweet potatoes thoroughly. Incorporate the remaining ingredients and mix until well combined. Pour the mixture into an unbaked pie shell. Bake at 350°F for approximately 45 minutes, or until the

filling is set. Bake this pie until the center rises even in height with the sides. Serve with whipped cream or Cool Whip topping as desired.

"This is my granny's, Lucile Benefield, recipe! She grew her own sweet potatoes every year. She would bake her sweet potatoes and mix this pie up by hand with a fork." – *Tammy*

482) Sweet Potato Pie-Tammy's

→ 1/4 cup salted butter, melted
→ 3/4 cup sugar
→ 3 large eggs
→ 2 cups cooked, mashed sweet potatoes
→ 3/4 cup evaporated milk
→ dash of salt
→ 1 tsp vanilla extract
→ 1/2 tsp ground cinnamon
→ pie crust

Preheat oven to 350°F. Melt butter in a microwave-safe bowl. Add sugar and eggs, then whisk. Mix remaining ingredients and whisk again. Pour into the pie crust. Bake for 40 minutes, until the pie has swelled and risen in the center, like the edges. Do not remove it too soon. Make sure it cooks until the center rises. Cool on a wire rack to avoid sweating.

 Do not remove until center of pie has risen as high as the sides.

483) Sweet Potato Pies, Fried

→ 2 large, sweet potatoes, cook & whip
→ 1/4 cup salted butter
→ 1/2 cup granulated sugar
→ 1/4 tsp cinnamon, optional
→ Recipe #429 Fried Pie Dough
→ 1/2 cup butter for frying

Whip sweet potatoes with butter, sugar, and cinnamon. Place a large heaping tablespoon of sweet potato filling in the center of the dough. Fold to make a half-moon shape. Wet the edges of the dough, then press the edges closed with a fork. Fill a skillet with 1 inch of corn oil, preheat, then add butter. Carefully add the pies to the skillet. Flip when browned and roll in (or sprinkle) with cinnamon sugar while still warm. Place on a cookie cooling rack. These are great warmed in an air fryer!

484) Strawberry Glaze Pie

→ 1 pie crust
→ 2 lb. strawberries, clean and dry

Pre-Bake the crust for 25 minutes at 350°F until golden. Remove stems from strawberries and chop into 3/4" pieces, saving a few for garnish.

Glaze:

→ 1 cup strawberries
→ 1/2 cup granulated sugar
→ 3/4 cup water
→ 4 Tbsp cornstarch
→ 1 tsp cornstarch
→ 1/4 tsp salt
→ 1 cup granulated sugar
→ 10 drops red food coloring
→ 1 tsp vanilla extract, optional

Blend strawberries and sugar in a blender or with a stick blender to make a strawberry puree. Whisk together water, cornstarch, salt, and sugar, then add the strawberry puree. Microwave the mixture in a glass bowl for 2 minutes. Carefully remove from the microwave and whisk well, ensuring any cornstarch that may have settled at the bottom is mixed in. Return the bowl to the microwave and cook on high for an additional 2 minutes, or until it becomes a thick glaze. Whisk in vanilla and food coloring. Chill the glaze before adding it to the pie. Place strawberries into a pre-baked crust and pour the chilled glaze over them. Garnish with whipped cream or Cool Whip and extra strawberries. Keep refrigerated until ready to serve.

485) Strawberry Cheesecake Pie

→ Recipe #452, Graham Cracker Crust 1 cup cut strawberries, cut into cubes, do not mash strawberries
→ 8 oz cream cheese, room temperature
→ 1/4 cup salted butter, room temperature
→ 2 tsp strawberry flavored gelatin
→ 1/4 cup granulated sugar
→ 16 oz. Cool Whip topping, divided
→ 1 cup sliced strawberries for garnish

Cream butter and cream cheese together until creamy. Add sugar and fluff. Add gelatin and mix well, then add 2 cups of cool whip topping. Fold in the cut strawberries, then place in the graham cracker crust. Garnish with whipped topping. This pie must be refrigerated. It sets up well and can be served the same day. Do not smash the berries or your pie will become runny. Enjoy!

Use different fruits and Jell-O flavors for new flavor profiles.

Use less than 2 teaspoons of flavored gelatin to maintain the cheesecake flavor in your pie.

"Wow... It is so easy, so delicious, and tastes like cheesecake! This is amazing, y'all."
– Tammy

486) Toll House Pie

- → 2 large eggs
- → 1/2 cup all-purpose flour
- → 1/2 cup sugar
- → 1/4 tsp salt
- → 1/2 cup light brown sugar, firmly packed
- → 3/4 cup salted butter, softened
- → 1 cup walnuts, chopped
- → 6 oz. pkg. (1 cup) Nestle Toll House semi-sweet chocolate morsels
- → 9-inch pie shell, unbaked
- → whipped cream or ice cream, optional

Preheat oven to 325°F. Beat eggs in a large bowl until foamy (about 3 minutes). Mix in flour, sugar, salt, and brown sugar until blended. Add softened butter, walnuts, and chocolate morsels. Pour into a pie shell. Bake 55-60 minutes until a knife comes out clean and top is golden. Cool on a wire rack. Serve with whipped cream or ice cream if desired.

"Our Wedding Day was the best day of my life! I am so thankful for my husband. He is the best husband and father, and I know he loves me as much as I love him! I love you, Chris Nichols!"
- Tammy

487) Watergate Pie

- → 3.4 oz. pistachio instant pudding mix
- → 8 oz. can crushed pineapple, with juice
- → 1/4 tsp salt
- → 1/2 cup sour cream, optional
- → 10 maraschino cherries, chopped
- → 8 oz. cool-whip topping
- → mini marshmallows, for topping
- → 1/2 cup chopped pecans, divided

Toast whole pecans at 350°F for 5 minutes and then chop them. In a large bowl, combine pudding, pineapple, salt, and sour cream, mixing thoroughly. Add cherries, half of the pecans, and half of the whipped topping, then mix well. Place the mixture into a Recipe #452, graham cracker pie crust and garnish with the remaining pecans, whipped topping, and a few whole cherries.

 It is best to make this a day ahead and serve cold!

Rom 8:31 KJV
"What shall we then say to these things? If God be for us, who can be against us?"

Pork Recipes

I first discovered Swaggerty's Farm sausage at Sam's Club, a wholesale store. From the moment I tasted it, the familiar flavors instantly transported me back to childhood memories.

As a child, growing up on a farm meant tending to a busy hog barn filled with hundreds of pigs alongside cattle, with our own beef and pork stocked in the freezer—meat from animals we raised ourselves. After months of caring for the animals, it was rewarding to enjoy the fruits of our labor each morning at breakfast. The sausage was so flavorful, and I can still picture my mama cutting open those tubes of sausage, shaping the savory meat into patties, and frying them alongside strips of bacon in the skillet. The aroma filled our kitchen and made every morning feel warm and comforting, filling me with a sense of belonging and gratitude for those simple yet meaningful moments.

The Swaggerty's sausage was the closest thing that I had ever tasted that brought that flavor of our fresh sausage growing up and yes, I was hooked! I often showed the box of sausage in my YouTube videos and to my surprise the company's representative called me up and offered to sponsor our channel.

Even before being sponsored, Swaggerty's Farm breakfast sausage was a staple at our house. I encourage you to try this sausage because it is delicious! Use it to make your favorite recipes and of course for your breakfast. We thank Swaggerty's Farm for bringing a taste of home back into our kitchens. I have also included a picture of my favorite breakfast syrup; it is buttery and so good!

488) Baby Back Ribs

→ Rack of Baby Back Ribs, unmarinated
→ Recipe #598 Chris's Rib Rub
→ Recipe #591 CVC BBQ Sauce

Rinse ribs and trim them with kitchen shears. Using a spoon to start, pull back the membrane from the back of the rib rack and grasp it with a paper towel – pull to remove it from the back of the rack. Rub the ribs with Recipe # 598, Chris's Rib Rub. Place the ribs in a preheated smoker at 300°F. Smoke for 6 hours.

489) Boston Butt, Crockpot

→ Boston butt roast
→ Crock pot liner
→ 1-1/2 tsp salt
→ 1 tsp black pepper
→ No salt added salad spice blend
→ 1 tsp liquid smoke, optional
→ 3/4 cup hot water
→ onion, cut into quarters

Place roast in a lined crockpot, and season with salt, black pepper, and a salad blend. Fresh sage or herbs can be added if available. Add onion around the roast. Mix liquid smoke with hot water and pour it around the edges without knocking off the seasonings. Cook on low for 8 to 10 hours.

"Pork pairs well with sweet potatoes. Leftover pork can be diced and combined with Recipe # 591, barbecue sauce to create sandwiches for another night's meal Serve it alongside Recipe #571, potato salad and Recipe #555, coleslaw."
– *Tammy*

490) Holiday Ham, Processed

→ I typically buy a butt portion instead of a shank. It has a smaller bone and more meat
→ unwrap ham
→ ham is preseasoned
→ discard the glazing packet, if desired

Spray the roasting pan with cooking spray for easy cleanup. Use heavy, wide aluminum foil in both directions and extend it 3 feet past each side of the pan. Place the ham on the foil, then wrap and cover the ham. Bake covered at 325°F for 20 minutes per pound. Let cool, carve, and pour drippings over the ham for added flavor.

 Serve leftover slices by frying them in butter on both sides for breakfast! Keep fattier portions and freeze for making dried beans.

KEEP THOSE LEFTOVERS:

"Refrigerate drippings for up to two weeks to make gravy. Make my ham salad or ham spread with leftover ham. Prepare my butterbean soup and add chopped ham."

– *Tammy*

491) Hamburger Steak With Sausage

→ 1 lb. 90/10 ground chuck
→ 1 lb. breakfast sausage, Swaggerty Farms
→ 1/4 cup onion, chopped
→ 1/4 cup bell pepper, chopped
→ 3 Tbsp salted butter
→ 1 tsp onion powder
→ 1/2 tsp salt
→ 1/2 tsp black pepper
→ 1 tsp steak seasoning, Weber Steak N Chop

Combine the hamburger, sausage, onion, and peppers, mixing until evenly incorporated. Shape into 6 hamburger steaks. Add the patties to a preheated skillet with a little oil. Season with salt, pepper, and steak seasoning. Cook over medium/high heat for 4 minutes on each side until browned. Reduce the heat to medium/low, cover, and cook until the patties are no longer pink inside. Never eat raw ground beef or pork sausage. Serve with Recipe # 59 Easy Mushroom Gravy

492) Pork Chop & Potatoes

→ braiser or Dutch oven
→ pork chops, bone-in or pork steaks will be more tender
→ potatoes, 1 medium for each chop
→ sweet onion, 1/3 cup sliced for each chop
→ 1/2 cup butter
→ salt & black pepper

In A Braiser or Dutch Oven Peel and slice potatoes into thick chips. Slice the onion into thin rings. Preheat a braiser or Dutch oven on the stovetop, add 1/4 cup of butter to the braiser, and brown the pork on each side. Add the potatoes, onion, remaining butter, and salt and pepper to taste. Cover with a non-vented lid. Simmer on low for 1 hour. Serve with cornbread and pinto beans.

Tip: Near the end of cooking, increase the heat briefly to brown the potatoes and chops being careful not to burn them.

To Bake: Brown chops in 1/4 cup butter, then place in a baking dish. Add another 1/4 cup butter, potatoes, and onion. Season well, bake at 350°F for 1.5 hours covered.

For Skillet: Use a large non-stick skillet with a non-vented lid, following braiser instructions. If Making a lot of Chops: After 30 minutes, remove the chops and vegetables, place chops on the bottom, and cook for another 30 minutes so chops absorb some moisture.

493) Pork Chops, Fried

→ 1/2-inch-thick bone in pork chops
→ Steak seasoning, Weber Steak n Chop
→ ground black pepper
→ salt
→ roasted garlic seasoning, Bidia
→ 1-1/2 cups self-rising flour
→ corn or vegetable oil for frying

Preheat a large skillet. Season chops without rinsing. If rinsed, dry thoroughly. Season one side, dip in beaten egg, then coat in flour from a shallow dish. Coat both sides, set on a platter, and rest for 10 minutes. Add 1/2 inch of corn oil to skillet. Fry for 3 minutes per side on medium-high, or 5 minutes for thicker cuts, adjusting heat to prevent browning too fast.

Tip: Pork chops should reach a minimum of 150°F internal temp..

If you do not rinse the chops, you do not need the egg wash, because they have fat on the ouside and flour will cling to them.

494) Pork Chops, Fried Cereal

→ 6 thick pork chops
→ salt and pepper
→ 2 cups corn flakes, crushed
→ 1 cup self-rising flour
→ 1/2 tsp pepper
→ 3/4 tsp salt
→ 2 eggs, beaten
→ oil, Mazola corn oil

Combine flour, salt, and pepper in a shallow dish. Beat eggs in another dish. Add crushed cornflakes to a third dish. Lightly coat the chops with the flour mixture, dip in eggs, then in cornflakes, pressing flakes into the chops. Let them sit for 5 minutes. Fry in 1/2-inch oil until browned. Transfer to a baking dish, cover, and bake at 350°F for 30 minutes or until tender.

For Thinner Chops — There is no need to bake thin chops in the oven. Brown them for 3-4 minutes per side and serve.

Tip: Pork chops minimum of 150°F.

495) Pork Chop Hashbrown Bake

→ 7 boneless pork chops
→ 1/2 cup salted butter
→ 1/2 cup sour cream
→ 1 cup milk
→ 2-10.5 oz. cans cream of mushroom
→ 1/2 tsp salt & 1/2 tsp black pepper
→ 30 oz. package frozen hashbrowns
→ celery salt, or regular salt
→ medium onion, cut into thin rings
→ Lipton Onion Soup Mix
→ 2 cups shredded cheese

In a medium bowl, whisk together sour cream, milk, one cream soup, onion soup mix, salt, and pepper; set aside. Spray a baking dish with cooking spray. Place the chops in the bottom of the dish. Cut butter into tablespoons and place on top of the chops. Add onions. In a bowl, add

one can of soup with a can of water and whisk together. Pour over the chops. Add half of the hashbrowns and season well with salt and pepper. Sprinkle with 1 cup of shredded cheese. Add half of the sour cream soup mixture. Repeat with remaining hashbrowns, salt and pepper, remaining soup, and top with cheese. Cover with foil and bake at 350°F for one hour. Uncover, add more cheese, and bake for another hour. Keep warm until serving. Longer cooking makes the chops more tender; ensure they are fully cooked, especially if they are 1/2-inch thick.

This original recipe used cream of chicken, but it was too boring. I changed it to mushroom and added onion soup mix. It needed a bolder flavor. -Tammy

496) Pork Chops, Lodge Grilled

→ 1/2" thick bone in pork chops
→ lodge grill cast iron pan
→ steak seasoning, Weber Steak 'n Chop
→ olive oil

Remove pork chops from the fridge an hour before cooking and season with steak seasoning. Preheat a cast iron pan in the oven or on the stove for at least 10 minutes until it is fully hot. While preheating, rub chops with olive oil. Place on the hot grill without moving; cook 4 minutes per side for 1/2" chops. Rest for 5 minutes, then serve.

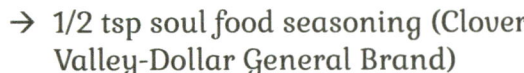

- → 1/2 tsp soul food seasoning (Clover Valley-Dollar General Brand)
- → 1 tsp Roasted Garlic Powder, Bidia
- → 4-5 shakes Worcestershire sauce
- → 2 Tbsp light brown sugar
- → 1 Tbsp white vinegar
- → 1 tsp salt
- → 1/2 tsp black pepper
- → 1/2 cup water
- → 1 medium head of cabbage
- → red pepper flakes (to taste)

497) Simple Fried Cabbage

- → 1 package of link pork sausage, Kielbasa or Smoked
- → 1 medium cabbage, cut into large chunks
- → 1 medium onion, sliced
- → 1 tsp salt
- → 1/2 tsp black pepper

Slice sausage into 1/4-inch-thick disks. Cook in a preheated skillet with onions until golden. For lean sausage, add 2 Tbsp olive oil. Once browned and onions are soft, remove and set aside. Drain excess grease if needed, then add cabbage. Cook for 5 minutes, then return sausage and onions, and cook until cabbage softens.

"I like the cabbage to still hold its shape a little and not be cooked until it is mushy. Enjoy with my cream potatoes and crunchy cornbread."
– Tammy

498) Southern Fried Cabbage

- → 6 oz bacon, chopped
- → 1 smoked sausage
- → olive oil if lean sausage
- → 3/4 cup bell pepper, mixed colors if available, slice into strips
- → 1 large onion, slice into strips
- → 1 tsp onion powder
- → 2 tsp Chicken bouillon granules

Chop cabbage into 1-inch-wide pieces. Preheat a large wok or skillet. Add bacon and smoked sausage, cook until golden brown over medium heat. Remove the meat from the skillet, leaving the drippings. Add onion and peppers, cooking until soft. Stir in seasonings, then add water to deglaze the skillet. Add cabbage and cook until tender. Return the meats to the skillet, stir, and serve immediately with cornbread! Enjoy. So very Good

499) Pork, Tenderized & Fried

- → 1/4" thick tenderized pork chops
- → 1-1/2 cups of self-rising flour
- → Steak seasoning, Weber Steak N Chop
- → salt
- → 2 eggs

Place flour on a shallow pie plate. Whisk eggs in another. Sprinkle chops with steak n chop, pepper, salt. Dip chops in eggs, then flour, pressing to coat. Fry in 1/2" hot oil: 3 mins first side, 2 mins other side, adjusting heat to prevent burning. Use drippings and make Recipe #613 White Milk Gravy to serve over chops! Pork chops: 150°F internal temp. minimum!

"We eat this regularly at our house. I like tenderized pork better than cubed beef steaks."
–Tammy

500) Ribs, Baked

→ boneless ribs or.... BONE in ribs!
→ Recipe #598 Chris's Rib Rub
→ 2 tsp Liquid Smoke
→ 1 medium onion, cut in quarters

Remove ribs from the package (do not rinse). Cut if needed, then season with rib rub or a mix of salt, pepper, and onion powder. Line a half sheet pan with foil, set a rack inside, and broil ribs for 10 minutes per side. Wrap ribs and pan with foil, add liquid smoke, seal, and cook to an internal temperature of 160°F. Also see Recipe # 591 for our BBQ sauce.

Boneless Ribs: Bake 280°F for 4 hrs.

Bone in Ribs: Bake 280°F for 6 hours

 Use salt, pepper, onion powder, fresh or dried sage, and fresh rosemary inside foil for more flavor. This is optional.

501) Pork Ribs with Vegetables

→ kosher salt & black pepper
→ 2 lb. country-style boneless pork ribs

Mix and set aside:

→ 2 cups water with
→ 1 tsp beef bouillon granules

Wash and prep these vegetables and herbs:

→ 3 carrots, peel & cut into chunks size
→ 4 green onions, chopped
→ 4-5 red potatoes, quartered
→ 2 stalks of celery, chunk size
→ 1 tsp fresh rosemary (or 2 tsp dried rosemary)
→ 1 tsp Fresh thyme (or 2 tsp dried thyme)
→ 1 tsp fresh basil (or 2 tsp dried basil)
→ 4 cloves of garlic (or 3 tsp garlic powder) press or smash cloves to release flavor

 Note: For more flavor, crush dried herbs in a spice mill or heat them briefly before adding them to the pot.

Salt & Pepper Ribs. Brown all sides of the ribs in a Braiser or large skillet with a lid. After all sides have a brown sear, add 1/2 cup of bouillon water. Add herbs, onion, and garlic, and simmer for 10 minutes. Add carrots, celery, and potatoes. Cover with a lid and cook on low heat for 30 minutes. Remove the lid and cook for 15 minutes or until the liquid is reduced.

502) Smoked Sausage Simmer

→ Smoked sausage, sliced into circles
→ 15 oz. can diced tomatoes
→ 1 medium cabbage, chopped
→ 1 medium onion, sliced into strips
→ olive oil
→ 4 Tbsp salted butter
→ 1/2 tsp salt
→ 1/2 tsp black pepper

Optional:

→ 1 tsp Cajun or sausage seasoning

In a large saucepan or skillet, sauté the onion and sausage with a bit of olive oil. Add tomatoes and cabbage. Salt and pepper well and add the butter. Simmer until cabbage is soft.

Serve with cornbread or over rice if desired.

"I like to fry potatoes or okra to go with this recipe!"- *Tammy*

503) Ribs & Beans -Crockpot

- → 4 lbs. bone in ribs cut apart
- → pork rub, your choice
- → onion cut into 1-inch pieces
- → 15 oz. pork n' beans
- → 15 oz. black beans
- → 15 oz. kidney beans
- → 1-1/2 cup BBQ sauce, your choice
- → 1/2 tsp liquid smoke
- → 1 cup hot water

Remove ribs from the package; I prefer not to rinse mine. If needed, cut the ribs apart. Rub with pork rub. Line a half-sheet pan with foil, place a rack inside if available. Broil ribs 10 minutes each side. Line crockpot with a liner, place ribs at bottom. Chop onion and mix with remaining ingredients, then pour over ribs. Cook on low for 8 hours.

Note From Cook: skim fat off the top of the meal when it is done with a deep spoon or ladle and discard before serving.

This can be made in a dutch oven as well. Cover the dish in a dutch oven and place in a 350°F oven and bake for 4 hours.

"This meal is a family favorite for sure! It may sound boring, but it is delicious!" – *Tammy*

Rom 8:38,39

"For I am persuaded, that neither death, nor life, nor angels, nor principalities, nor powers, nor things present, nor things to come, Nor height, nor depth, nor any other creature, shall be able to separate us from the love of God, which is in Christ Jesus our Lord." KJV

504) Roasted Pork Loin

- → large pork loin
- → 1 onion
- → 1 bell pepper
- → 13"x9"x2" pan (minimum of 2" deep)
- → heavy duty aluminum foil
- → Chris's rib rub Recipe #598 (or sprinkle roast well with salt, white pepper, cayenne pepper, Dollar General Soul Food Seasoning (clover valley), Badia roasted garlic powder & weber steak 'n chop)
- → 2 cups chicken broth

Place the roast fat side down on 2 or 3 pieces of heavy-duty aluminum foil. Foil will be folded up around the roast creating a perimeter wall, so pull off several pieces that are much longer than the roast. Season well on all sides, then position fat side up in the center of the foil. Place wrapped roast in a 13x9x2" baking pan. Pour broth into the pan without disturbing the seasonings. Surround the roast with bell pepper and onion. Roast at 350°F for 25-30 minutes per pound, ensuring the internal temperature reaches at least 155°F before removing. Let rest 15 minutes before slicing against the grain.

Make a Pan Sauce:

Create a pan sauce with drippings if desired— melt 3 tbsp salted butter in a skillet. Add 3 tbsp flour and mix well. Brown the flour slightly, then add 1 cup of broth or juices from the pan. Bring it to a boil and serve over pork. If the gravy is too thick, just add a little water and whisk.

Rom 11:24

"For if thou wert cut out of the olive tree which is wild by nature, and wert graffed contrary to nature into a good olive tree: how much more shall these, which be the natural branches, be graffed into" their own olive tree?" KJV

505) Smoked Sausage Hash

→ 1 pack smoked link sausage, sliced into rounds
→ 1 large onion, chopped
→ 4 medium potatoes, chopped into 1/2" cubes
→ 3 large carrots, chopped into 1/2" cubes
→ salt & pepper
→ 1/4 cup chopped sweet pepper, optional
→ 1/2 tsp red pepper flakes, optional

In a large non-stick pot, skillet, or braiser (make sure it has a lid), add the sausage only and cook on medium heat while prepping the vegetables.

First, cut the onion and add it to the pot with the sausage. Next, cut the carrot and add it to the pot with the lid on, cooking for 5 minutes.

While waiting, chop the potatoes. When the carrot timer goes off, add the potatoes and peppers. Place the lid on and cook on medium-low for 5 minutes.

Open and stir, then put the lid back on and cook for another 5 minutes. When the potatoes have been in for a total of 10 minutes with the lid on, the hash is ready to serve. Enjoy with summer vegetables and cornbread!

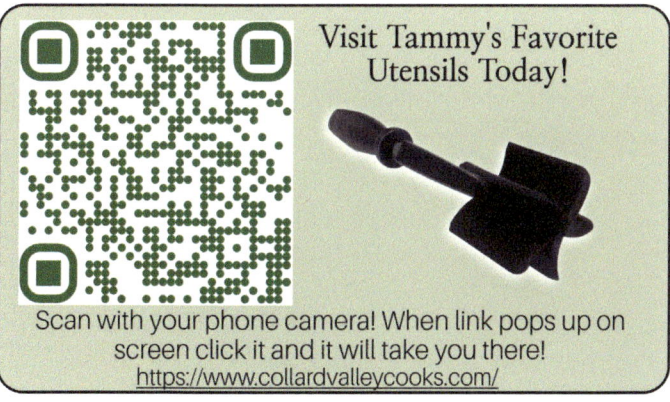

506) Sausage Beans & Rice

→ 1 lb. red beans (or pinto beans)
→ 1 lb. hot breakfast sausage (Swaggerty's breakfast sausage)
→ 1 lb. diced ham, optional
→ 1 large onion chopped
→ 1 large bell pepper chopped
→ garlic diced, if desired
→ salt to taste
→ hot sauce, if desired

Wash and rinse the beans. Cover with water until water is two inches above the beans. Bring to a boil and boil for 10 minutes. Remove from heat and soak overnight on the stovetop. (Only water should be added to the beans if soaking at room temperature, NO MEAT!)

Next day: Scramble and brown the breakfast sausage. Remove the sausage from the skillet, then add onion and peppers, cooking them in the sausage drippings. Mix all ingredients with the presoaked beans (excluding hot sauce) and cook over medium heat until the beans are tender. Watch closely and add water as needed. Serve on a bed of rice. Add hot sauce to taste.

Slow Cooker: A crockpot can be used to finish cooking beans with other ingredients, but it could take 10-12 hours.

Instant-pot: Cook beans and remaining ingredients in an instant-pot on multigrain setting. Highest pressure for 38 minutes.

507) Settler's Beans or Cowboy Beans

Brown And Drain:

- → 1/2 lb. ground beef
- → 1/2 lb. bacon, chopped
- → 1 onion, chopped

Add:

- → 1/3 cup brown sugar
- → 1/4 cup ketchup
- → 1 Tbsp mustard
- → 1/4 cup BBQ sauce
- → 1 tsp salt
- → 1/2 tsp black pepper
- → 1/2 tsp chili powder
- → 15 oz. can pinto beans
- → 15 oz. can pork n' beans
- → 15 oz. can butter beans
- → 15 oz. can kidney beans

Mix well, put in an oven-safe baking dish, and bake for 2 hours at 350°F. We enjoy this with homemade cornbread or garlic toast.

 For a change up, Swaggerty's Farm breakfast sausage could be used in place of beef!

508) Smothered Pork Chops

- → thick-sliced bacon
- → Pork Chops
- → 2 cups milk
- → 1 clove garlic, peel, and slice
- → 1 small onion, chopped

- → asparagus spears, optional
- → 1/4 cup self-rising flour

Fry bacon on medium heat in a skillet (large enough to cook chops in). While bacon is cooking salt and pepper chops then rub with flour. When the bacon is nearly done, add half of the chopped onion. Remove the bacon and add asparagus spears to the skillet with onion, garlic, and bacon drippings. Cook the asparagus and onion until fork tender.

Remove and cover to keep warm. Add the chops to the skillet with drippings and enough olive oil for browning. Cook 3/4-inch-thick chops for 4 minutes on medium, then flip. Add remaining chopped onion. Cook second side for 4 minutes or until internal temperature reaches 160°F. Remove the chops. Do not cook on high heat, or drippings will burn.

Top chops with Recipe #509, Sage & Garlic Milk Gravy.

509) Sage & Garlic Milk Gravy

- → 1/4 cup salted butter
- → 2 cloves garlic, peel, and slice
- → 1/2 tsp salt
- → 1/4 tsp black pepper
- → 1/4 tsp ground sage
- → 1/4 cup flour
- → 2 cups milk

 Option: use olive oil in place of butter for gravy if desired

Add butter to a skillet with fresh garlic. Cook for 1 minute. Then add salt, black pepper, ground sage, and flour, whisking until the mixture is well blended. Continue cooking until the flour begins to brown, then add the milk. Heat until it boils and thickens. Pour the mixture into a serving bowl or a glass measuring cup. Season with salt to taste.

Our chickens eating fresh cabbage and strawberries.

Poultry Recipes

I have always loved chickens since I was a child. The way they laid eggs fascinated me so much. I would stand and watch through the cracks of our barn. Their laying areas were against the back wall so I could get a great look at them. I just thought it was so cool how they cackled after laying an egg. I spent hours watching in amazement. We now have chickens for egg laying, and they are pictured above. I love going out and wishing them a good day each morning as I let them out to scratch and find bugs and worms. The white one loves to have dirt baths as you can see by how dingy she is. Living on a farm was a great experience for me. I wish that my kids had had chores growing up. I think it taught me how to be responsible and I for one took great pride in making the adults in my life happy. I was always a people pleaser. I did not give my kids chores, as a cancer survivor, I had a housekeeper that I went to church with. She was a great friend, and I loved her so much. Her name was Kim Gamblin, and she was a hard worker and a beautiful redhead. She did not clean the kids rooms; I did at least make them do that.

She had a large family, and the money helped them get extra things they might not otherwise be able to afford. They were workers in the church and a tithing family as well. Many families that tithe do not have the extra money that others have to treat their families with. They sacrifice for the cause of Christ. God takes care of them and has his hand upon them as they are good stewards of faith. Even through having cancer, we never were in a place where we had to ask for help. God always took care of us, and you could bet, if we needed extra money for something, He always provided. God even laid it on my heart during a church service one day to tell Chris that I felt we should add cancer insurance to his work plan when it came up for renewal. Within two years, I was diagnosed with stage 3c breast cancer, and the plan was a HUGE blessing for our family. I was out of work, but the benefits of the plan paid us lump sums for each chemotherapy and radiation treatment. The money was also tax free! Wow, God has always showed up and even showed out for us, and we give Him all the glory! — *Tammy*

510) 6 Spice Chicken

- → Olive oil
- → 1 whole young fryer chicken (cut into parts, split breast into 4 pieces)
- → coriander
- → ground cumin
- → white pepper
- → curry powder
- → rubbed sage
- → ground mustard
- → salt
- → onion (sliced)
- → 2 garlic cloves
- → large braiser or Dutch oven
- → 2 cups chicken stock
- → 1/4 cup salted butter

Heat olive oil in a large pot, add chicken, cover briefly, then season with six spices and salt. Brown on high, flip, add onion and garlic, and season again. Brown chicken pieces, pour in chicken stock and butter, cover, and simmer on low for 20 minutes. Serve with the pan sauce—perfect for potatoes.

511) Butter Fried Chicken

- → boneless skinless chicken breasts or thighs
- → 1/2 cup salted butter
- → chicken seasoning, if salty go light on table salt
- → 1/2 onion, chopped
- → salt
- → black pepper
- → flour

Score chicken pieces with a crisscross pattern, about 1/2 inch deep. Season with salt and pepper. Coat the chicken lightly with flour. Melt butter in a preheated skillet. Fry chicken on medium heat for 4 minutes per side. Increase heat, add chopped onion and an optional seasoning, and brown for 1-2 minutes per side. Total cooking time is 10-12 minutes. Let chicken rest for 5 minutes before serving. Use a meat thermometer to ensure the chicken's internal temperature reaches 165°F in the center of the breast.

512) 30 Min. Chicken Gravy Dinner

- → non-stick braiser (required) or Dutch Oven
- → olive oil
- → 2 large chicken breasts, skin on
- → salt & black pepper
- → 1 pack Lipton onion soup mix
- → 1 cup water
- → large cut vegetables: carrots, red potatoes, red bell pepper, onion, celery, squash & zucchini
- → seasoning salt or Goya vegetable salad seasoning
- → salt & black pepper

Heat a non-stick braiser (4-quart or larger, with an unvented lid) on high. Add olive oil, then place chicken skin-side down to brown for 2-3 minutes. Add a soup mix packet, water, and all vegetables except squash and zucchini, then sprinkle with seasoning salt. Cover and simmer on low for 10 minutes. Flip chicken breast side up, add squash and zucchini, cover, and cook for another 10 minutes. Remove the lid, increase heat to medium-high, and turn chicken breast side down. Continue simmering until the liquid reduces to a gravy consistency. Use a meat thermometer to ensure the chicken's internal temperature reaches 165°F in the center of the breast. Serve the chicken with vegetables and gravy right away. A quick, tasty dinner to enjoy.

513) Brown Sugar Baked Chicken

→ chicken pieces, your choice
→ 1/2 cup light brown sugar
→ 1 tsp onion powder
→ 3 Tbsp yellow mustard
→ salt & pepper
→ 1 Tbsp smoked paprika
→ 2 cups chicken broth
→ 1/2 cup salted butter, melted

Rub the chicken well with the mustard, then place it in a 13x9x2-inch baking dish. Sprinkle with brown sugar, salt, and pepper. Add broth and melted butter. Then sprinkle with paprika and onion powder. Bake uncovered in a 350°F oven for 1 hour or until the chicken is cooked through. The internal temperature of the chicken must reach at least 175°F.

 Other Options: Regular paprika can be used instead of smoked. If you use regular paprika, put a little liquid smoke in the baking dish if desired.

Garlic: Add some fresh garlic or garlic powder if desired.

If you prefer to take the skin off of the chicken, it will still be delicious!

514) Chicken Burrito Skillet

→ 1 lb. boneless skinless chicken breasts, cut into 1" cubes
→ 1/8 tsp salt
→ 1/8 tsp black pepper
→ 2 Tbsp olive oil
→ 1 cup uncooked long-grain rice
→ 15 oz. black beans rinsed and drained
→ 14.5 oz. petite diced tomatoes
→ 1 tsp ground cumin
→ 1 tsp onion powder
→ 1/2 tsp garlic powder
→ 1/2 tsp chili powder
→ 2 1/2 cups chicken stock or broth

→ 1 medium tomato, chopped
→ 3 green onions chopped

Heat 1 tablespoon oil in a heavy skillet and brown chicken for about 2 minutes, seasoning with salt and pepper. Set aside. Add rice and another tablespoon of oil; cook until lightly browned and fragrant. Stir in broth, spices, and beans, then bring to a boil. Reduce heat, return chicken to the pan, cover, and simmer for 20 minutes. Top with cheese and cover until it melts. Serve with tomatoes, onions, and tortilla chips, or use as a burrito filling or main dish.

515) Chicken & Rice (Asian)

→ 2 cups cooked rice, cold
→ 4 scallions/green onion, sliced thin
→ 2 tsp peeled & grated fresh ginger
→ 1 large carrot, grated thin
→ 3 Tbsp olive oil
→ 1 Tbsp sesame oil, optional
→ 2 Tbsp sherry
→ 4 Tbsp soy sauce
→ 1 tsp granulated sugar
→ 1 lb. chicken cut in thin strips
→ 4 tsp corn starch
→ 1 tsp salt

Rice: Prepare the day ahead, and it should be cold out of the refrigerator for good fried rice.

Chicken: Toss the chicken in salt and cornstarch, then set it aside.

Heat the wok, then add sesame oil and olive oil, followed by the veggies. Sauté for 1 minute. Add chicken and sauté for 2 minutes. Add sherry, soy, and sugar. Mix well. Take it out of work and set it aside. Add cooked rice to the hot wok and cook on high heat, tossing until hot. Put chicken and vegetables back in, toss and cover for 10 minutes. This will make four servings. Sesame oil is optional, but it adds great flavor to the dish.

516) Chicken Francese

- → Four 1/2 inch thick chicken breasts
- → salt & black pepper
- → Onion powder
- → 3 lemons
- → Badia roasted garlic powder
- → 2 eggs
- → 1-1/2 cups self-rising flour
- → 1 pint sliced white mushrooms
- → 1-1/2 cups salted butter

Place butter in a saucepan with mushrooms over medium heat. Sprinkle the mushrooms with salt, pepper, and onion powder. Cook on medium heat until the juices go from cloudy to clear. Do not cook on high, or the butter will burn.

Salt and pepper the chicken, then thinly slice the breasts to ensure thorough cooking, especially if they are thicker, as they need to reach a safe internal temperature of 175°F. Sprinkle garlic powder and onion powder on top. Beat the eggs and coat the chicken well. In a shallow pan, coat the chicken in flour until completely coated. Fry for about 3 minutes on each side until golden brown. Allow chicken to cool on a drying rack for 3 minutes before placing it on a serving dish. Pour hot mushrooms and melted butter over the chicken. Squeeze the juice of two lemons into the dish and garnish with lemon slices. Serve with a lemon wedge for optional added flavor.

"This dish is my version of a Cedartown, GA. Favorite that is served at our local Petros and Zorbas Restaurants." – *Tammy*

517) Chicken Fried Chicken

- → 2 boneless skinless chicken breasts
- → 1-1/2 cups self-rising flour
- → black pepper & salt
- → 1/4 cup buttermilk (whole, if not available use sour cream)

→ oil (corn or peanut)

Cut each breast lengthwise into two thinner, equal pieces. Place in a gallon bag and pound flat to about 1/2". Remove, then season one side with salt and pepper. Pour buttermilk over and coat well. Coat in flour placed in a shallow dish. Fry in 1/2" preheated oil over medium/high heat for 3 minutes per side until golden brown. Use drippings and prepare Recipe #169 to serve over the chicken!

Tammy's tip: don't let drippings burn or the gravy won't be good! If the drippings burn, clean out the skillet before making butter gravy. It will still be delicious!

When you batter the chicken, let it rest 10 minutes before frying.

518) Chicken Wings, Baked

- → 3 dozen wing pieces
- → olive oil
- → chicken spice blend
- → Dry Ranch Dressing Mix
- → 3 Tbsp salted butter
- → ranch dressing
- → wing sauce, use your favorite

Cut wing pieces with kitchen shears or a knife, discarding tips. Sprinkle wings with spices evenly, then toss 12-15 wings in 1/8 cup olive oil.

Line a baking sheet with parchment paper and place a cookie rack on top. Spray the rack with cooking spray for easy cleanup. Arrange wings on the rack. Bake at 350°F convection or regular bake for 45 minutes, then increase the heat to 400°F and cook for an additional 30 minutes. Flip the wings, and bake another 30 minutes, for a total of 1 hour and 45 minutes.

Melt 3 tablespoons of butter, toss hot wings in the butter and 1/8 cup wing sauce, and serve with ranch dressing. Using an air fryer will reduce cooking time.

519) Chicken Legs, Crusty

- → 2 cups self-rising flour
- → 1 Tbsp poultry seasoning, McCormick
- → 2 tsp salt
- → 1 tsp pepper
- → 2 cups of breadcrumbs
- → 1/2 cup salted butter, melted

Bowl One: Melt butter in a bowl large enough to dip drumsticks into.

Bowl Two: Mix flour and seasonings well with a whisk.

Bowl Three: Place crumbs on a pie plate. Dip each piece of chicken in the melted butter (shake off excess), then in flour (shake off excess), and finally roll in breadcrumbs. Press the crumbs into the chicken to coat well.

Line a baking sheet with parchment paper or foil. Place a cooling rack on top of the sheet and spray it with cooking spray. Place the chicken on the rack. Bake the chicken at 425°F for 20 minutes. Then turn the oven down to 400°F and bake for another 40 minutes.

Using the convection setting is preferred if available. If not, use the regular bake setting. Remove from the oven and let cool for 10 minutes before serving. Enjoy! This recipe should coat 8 drumsticks; if you need more, double the recipe.

 When chicken has 30 minutes left on the timer, remove it and spray well with cooking spray. Return to oven to finish cooking to make it turn golden in color.

520) Delicious Drumsticks

- → 1 cup self-rising flour
- → 2 tsp salt
- → 1/2 tsp black pepper
- → 1 tsp paprika
- → 1/4 cup salted butter, melted
- → 6-8 chicken legs

First, remove chicken 1 hour prior to cooking. Combine the first four ingredients in a gallonsized storage bag. Do not rinse the chicken; it will bake at a high temperature, so that is unnecessary. Coat the drumsticks well with melted butter. Put them in the flour-filled bag, shake to coat, then shake off extra flour. Bake on foil at 425°F for 1 hour. The legs may not be fully brown and might have some flour left on them. Do not worry, they may not be pretty, but they are outstanding!

 When chicken has 30 minutes left on the timer, remove it and spray well with cooking spray. Return to oven to finish cooking to make it turn golden in color.

521) Citrus-Baked Cornish Hens

- → 4 Cornish hens

Sauce:
- → 1/4 cup apricot preserves
- → 2 Tbsp grated onion
- → 1 Tbsp salted butter
- → 1 Tbsp Dijon or regular mustard
- → 1 garlic clove, minced
- → 1 lemon, grated and peeled
- → 1 orange, grated and peeled

Remove giblets and necks from hens, then tie the legs of hens together and turn wing tips under the backs.

In a saucepan, combine all sauce ingredients and simmer for 5 minutes. Brush hens with sauce and arrange breast side up on a rack in a roasting pan.

Bake at 350°F for 60 minutes. Brush occasionally with sauce during cook time. Enjoy!

"This is also a great sauce to use on other poultry as well!" – *Tammy*

522) Chicken Pot Pie

Recipe # 116 Boil a Chicken

Recipe #613 White Milk Gravy

- → 2 refrigerated premade pie crusts
- → 2 cups of cooked chicken, chopped
- → 2-14.5 oz. cans of mixed vegetables, drained
- → salt & black pepper
- → round casserole or 10" cast iron 3" deep skillet

Preheat oven to 375°F. Place a crust in the casserole dish. Pour the gravy into a bowl, then add the drained vegetables and chicken. Taste, then season with salt and pepper if needed. Mix and pour into the crust. Cover the dish with the remaining crust. Cut at least five 2" long slits in the crust. Bake at 375°F for 45-60 minutes.

 Do not use frozen vegetables unless you pre-boil them first, or they won't get done.

If using cast iron or a dark baking pan, the casserole may get nice and brown in 45 minutes; however, if using glass, it will take longer. It is so delicious with a dark brown crust.

When making gravy, you can substitute a cup of the milk with the chicken broth; however, Tammy likes it best with milk only for a creamy sauce.

"I make this in my 3" deep cast iron skillet. The crust gets golden brown" - *Tammy*

523) Orange Chicken Stir Fry

- → 1/8 cup olive oil
- → 2 Tbsp sesame oil
- → fresh vegetables, prepped
- → 1/2 tsp ground ginger
- → 1 Tbsp fried rice seasoning, Badia

Heat the wok, add olive and sesame oils. Cook vegetables, ginger, and seasonings until tender, then transfer to a large bowl. Keep the wok juices boiling.

Orange Sauce for Stir Fry:

- → orange zest
- → orange, peeled & chopped
- → 2 Tbsp honey or sugar
- → 1/8 cup soy sauce

Add chopped orange to the wok. Add soy sauce and mash the oranges to release some juice. Add zest.

- → 2 Tbsp cornstarch
- → 1 cup cold water

Mix cornstarch with water and add to the sauce. Cook until it becomes clear and thickens. Add sugar/honey. Stir, then pour over the vegetables.

Chicken:

- → 2 boneless chicken breasts, cut very thin for stir fry

Clean the wok and preheat it. Add olive oil and sesame oil. Add chicken and sprinkle with fried rice seasoning. Cook until the chicken is no longer pink. Serve with vegetables and white rice.

 This is not an Orange Chicken dish that is traditionally served at places like Panda Express. It is a stir fry with vegetables and a homemade orange sauce that isn't spicy. Red Pepper flakes can be added for heat.

524) Chicken Wings (Deep fry)

- → 1/2 cup all-purpose flour
- → Recipe #597 Chris's Special Seasoning
- → 1/2 cup salted butter, melted

Do not wash wings. Cut with shears! Preheat fryer to 250°F. Season wings generously. Shake wings with melted butter in a bag. Coat wings with flour, then shake off excess after 5 minutes. Fry at 250°F for 8 min, then rest. Increase to 375°F, fry 10 min. Serve or hold in oven.

 Note: Wings can be frozen after first fry. This will enable you to eat great wings on another day without a lot of prep work.

Serve wing sauce on the side to prevent wings from getting soggy.

525) Fried Chicken Bone-in

→ 1 young fryer chicken (not a hen)
→ whole buttermilk

Chicken tends to be more affordable when bought on the bone. Cut your chicken into pieces, splitting each breast into two for frying. Then, soak the chicken in buttermilk overnight, or at least a couple of hours.

→ 2 cups self-rising flour
→ 1-1/4 tsp pepper
→ 1 3/4 tsp salt
→ 2 1/2 tsp paprika
→ 1 Tbsp Hidden Valley Ranch mix

Mix the dry ingredients thoroughly in a shallow dish or pie plate. Coat each piece evenly with flour, pressing the flour onto the chicken with your fingers. Let the coated chicken rest for 10 minutes before frying.

→ 3" deep iron skillet, wok, or deep large skillet
→ cooking oil (peanut, canola, or corn oil)

Pour oil into a skillet, about 2 inches deep, and heat until very hot. Test the temperature by adding a small piece of crust; if it floats and sizzles loudly, the oil is ready. Fry the chicken for 10 minutes on each side over medium-high heat. Remove with tongs and place on a wire cooling rack with parchment paper underneath or paper towels to catch the oil. Adjust the heat while cooking as needed to prevent the chicken from becoming too dark. For deep-frying, maintain an oil temperature between 300°F and 325°F for optimal results.

 Note: Drain chicken directly on a wire rack instead of paper towels for a crunchy crust.

165°F is the minimum temp. for poultry to be done. Juices should run clear when

opened. If there is pink, cook for a longer time.

526) Fried Chicken, Covered Skillet

→ whole fryer chicken, cut into pieces
→ salt & black pepper
→ Crisco or vegetable shortening
→ 3" deep iron skillet, (with lid)

Add to a Pie Plate:

→ 1-1/2 cups of self-rising flour

Rinse chicken pieces and pat dry. Cut each breast into two pieces. Salt and pepper the chicken well. Beat eggs and pour over the chicken. Coat each piece with the flour mixture, then let it sit for 10 minutes before frying.

Put shortening in a deep iron skillet. The oil should be 1/2 inch high. Preheat the oil until hot, then add the chicken pieces. Fry on both sides until golden brown. Place a lid on the skillet, ensuring it has a steam hole to allow steam to escape. Cook with the lid on for 5 minutes. Flip each piece and cover with the lid for 10 minutes. Flip the chicken, reduce the temperature slightly, and cook covered for an additional 5 minutes.

Remove the chicken and place on a wire cooling rack with parchment paper underneath or paper towels to catch the oil. Do not rest the chicken directly on paper towels. Let the chicken rest and cool before serving.

 Tammy's tip: chicken juices should run clear when done. If there is pink or red in the juices, the chicken should cook longer.

The internal temperature of the chicken must reach at least 175°F.

"If it has been a long time since granny cooked you chicken, this is the recipe for you! The chicken is so soft it tastes like it was pressure-cooked. So delicious!" – Tammy

527) Fried Chicken, Famous

- → 1 young fryer chicken (not a hen)
- → cut into parts & half each breast
- → Recipe #597 Chris's Special Seasoning
- → 2 shallow pie plates or cake pans

Prepare one plate with:

- → 1 cup self-rising flour
- → 2 tsp Chris's seasoning

Prepare 2nd plate with:

- → 2 eggs
- → 1/2 cup milk

Sprinkle each chicken piece with Chris' seasoning, dip into the egg, then into the flour, pressing it on well. Let them sit 10 minutes before frying to help the coating stick.

Add oil to a deep fryer until it reaches the line and preheat to 350°F. Fry chicken for 20 minutes, then cool on a wire rack with parchment or paper towels underneath to catch oil. Rest before serving. For pan-frying, cook 10 minutes per side, ensuring the internal temperature hits 175°F.

528) Fried Chicken, Mustard

- → peanut oil
- → chicken pieces (bone-in, skin on) if using breast piece, half each one in half

Add the following to a Pie Plate and whisk well:

- → 1-1/2 cups self-rising flour
- → 2 tsp Chris's Special Seasoning, Recipe 597

- → 2 tsp ground mustard
- → Add the following to Gallon Zip Lock Bag:
- → chicken pieces and plenty of yellow mustard

Let chicken sit in mustard at room temp. for one hour. Then coat each piece with a flour mixture and let it sit for 10 minutes before frying. Pour peanut oil into a deep iron skillet or wok, filling it about 3 inches deep so the chicken can fry in deep oil. If you do not have a deep enough skillet or wok, use a large pot. Preheat the oil to 350°F. Drop the chicken in and fry for 18 minutes for thighs. I prefer to flip them after the first 8 minutes and reduce the temp. a bit for the second fry so they do not get too brown. Remove the chicken and place it on a wire cooling rack with parchment underneath or paper towels to catch the oil.

💡 Do not rest the chicken on paper towels. Let the chicken rest and cool before serving.

529) Mexican Style Chicken

- → olive oil
- → 1 red sweet pepper, sliced in strips
- → 1/3 onion, sliced in strips
- → 1 Tbsp salted butter
- → Badia Fajita Seasoning
- → 4-5 chicken tenders (3/4" thick maximum)
- → 3 Tbsp chopped fresh cilantro

Preheat a skillet and add the olive oil, peppers, onions, and butter. Sprinkle well with seasoning and cook until soft. Take veggies out of the skillet and set aside. In the same skillet, add about 1/8 cup olive oil. When hot put in chicken and sprinkle well with fajita seasoning. Cook on a high heat for 3-4 minutes. Turnover and while second sides are browning, add peppers and onion back in and add fresh cilantro. After second side is cooked 4 minutes, take out and serve with Recipe # 682, Cheesy Potato Hash.

530) Chicken Nuggets or Tenders

→ chicken breast
→ whole butter milk

Chicken is cheaper on the bone. Buy it when it is on sale and cut the breast meat from the bone. Cut into 1" strips. If making nuggets, cut into 1" pieces. Soak chicken in buttermilk for 20-30 minutes at room temperature before frying.

→ 1-1/2 cups of self-rising flour
→ 1 tsp black pepper
→ 1-1/2 tsp salt
→ 2 tsp paprika
→ 1-1/2 Tbsp Hidden Valley Ranch mix

Add the dry ingredients to a shallow dish and whisk thoroughly to combine. Place the chicken in the dish and turn to coat it evenly with flour and seasonings. Press flour onto chicken well. Let it rest for 10 minutes before frying. This helps the crust adhere better. Put oil about 1" deep in the skillet. Heat until a small piece of crust floats and sizzles.

Fry tenders: 3 minutes each side.

Fry nuggets: Cook for 4 minutes if deep frying, or two minutes per side. If you cut larger nuggets, cook longer.

Remove the chicken and place it on a wire cooling rack with parchment paper or paper towels underneath to catch the oil.

 Serve with Recipe #603 Honey Mustard or Recipe #599 Dippen Chicken Sauce

Do not rest cooked chicken on paper towels, as this will cause it to sweat and become soggy.

"These are the best chicken tenders you will ever taste! Everyone raves about how good they are." – *Tammy*

531) Catalina French Chicken

→ 1 bottle of French dressing, used Catalina
→ 1 can of cranberry sauce
→ 1 Lipton Onion Soup Mix Packet
→ 3 lb. Chicken, your choice

Mix dressing, sauce and soup mix in a medium microwave-safe bowl and microwave on high for 3 minutes. Stir with a whisk until combined. For large chicken breasts, remove skins and halve, keeping ribs attached. Spray a 13x9-inch dish with cooking spray. Place chicken with bones up, pour sauce over, flipping to coat both sides. Spoon more sauce if needed. Cover tightly with foil without venting and bake at 350°F for 30 minutes. Poke holes for steam release, remove foil, then bake another 60 minutes. Serve with cream potatoes, rice, or noodles. The sauce is sweet, like BBQ sauce with a twist.

"There are so many kitchen gadgets that have been mailed to me by viewers over the years! One of my very favorites is the pig tail food hook. I absolutely love this thing. It is super sharp and will pick up meats without knocking off the crispy batter. Scan the code below with your phone's camera for a link to this product. If you cook, it will be one of the best tools you have ever been introduced to! - Tammy

SHOP TAMMY'S KITCHEN TOP SELLERS

Scan with your phone camera!
collardvalleycooks.com

GET A FOOD HOOK TODAY!

532) Linguinie Positano, Tammy's

→ 1 lb. linguine pasta
→ 10 Roma tomatoes (or 12-8 oz. can diced tomatoes, drained)
→ 3/4 cup salted butter
→ 1/4 to 1/2 cup fresh basil, chopped
→ 6 large cloves garlic, peel- slice thin
→ 112 oz. can marinated artichoke hearts, chopped & drained, reserved liquid
→ 1/2 tsp salt & pepper
→ 1 large lemon
→ chicken or protein of your choice

Bring a pot of water to a boil. Make shallow crosswise slits at the bottoms of the tomatoes and place them in boiling water until the skins loosen. Remove with a slotted spoon and set aside to cool. Add pasta to the boiling water along with 1/2 teaspoon salt and cook according to package directions. While the pasta is cooking, peel the tomatoes, remove the stem ends, and place them in a large skillet or wok. Chop the tomatoes, then add butter to the pan along with basil, garlic, artichokes, and 1/4 cup reserved artichoke juice. Simmer for 5 to 6 minutes as the pasta boils. After draining the pasta, rinse briefly and separate. Combine the pasta with the tomato mixture and toss thoroughly. Season with salt as needed. Serve with grilled or seared chicken (thinly sliced) or another preferred protein. Top each serving with a squeeze of lemon. So very yummy!

533) Lemon Garlic Chicken

→ 1 lb. chicken cutlets, skinless, boneless
→ salt and black pepper
→ oregano
→ 1/4 cup salted butter
→ 1/4 cup olive oil
→ juice of one lemon
→ 1 cup water
→ 2 garlic cloves, pressed

Season chicken with salt, pepper, and oregano. Fry in butter and olive oil until browned on both sides. Remove and use the crockpot or oven method below to finalize the cook.

Crockpot: Place chicken in the bottom of the crockpot. Add lemon juice & water and deglaze the pan. Add garlic and simmer for 1 minute. Pour the juice over the chicken. Cook 2.5 hours on high or 5-6 hours on low. Baste the chicken with juice when serving.

Oven: Place chicken in a baking dish. Add lemon juice & water and deglaze the pan. Add garlic and simmer for 1 minute. Pour the juice over the chicken and bake at 350°F for 35-40 minutes. Baste the chicken with juices when serving.

To zest a lemon, use a microplane or fine grater to gently scrape the outer yellow layer of the lemon peel, avoiding the bitter white pith underneath.
Hold the lemon firmly and move it across the grater until you have the desired amount of zest, which can add a bright, citrusy flavor to your dish.

534) Lo Mein Noodles

→ 10 oz. lo Mein noodles (egg white only)
→ 3 Tbsp soy sauce (or 4 tbsp. light soy)
→ 2 tsp sesame oil
→ 1 tsp ground ginger
→ 4 tsp sugar
→ 1 tsp sriracha sauce (or 2 tsp red chili sauce)
→ 3 Tbsp salted butter
→ 3 Tbsp olive oil
→ 1 large chicken breast, small thin slices
→ 3 green onions, washed & chopped
→ 1 medium onion, cut in chunks or slices
→ 1 red bell pepper, cut into chunks or slices
→ 1 or 2 carrots, cut into chunks or slices

Bring a large stockpot of water to a boil. (Put a lid onto boil quicker). Pre-heat a large Wok. Add olive oil (about 3 tbsp.) and cook veggies until tender. Drop pasta and cook per package directions. Put veggies out on a plate or platter when tender and set aside. Add butter to wok, then add chicken and cook until no pink is left (about 2 minutes while turning well). Make sure you cut chicken VERY THIN, so it cooks through quickly. Drain pasta, then add pasta to wok with vegetables and sauce! This makes approx. 6 servings.

"This is best reheated the next day, y'all." – *Tammy*

535) Marry Me Chicken

→ 3 Tbsp extra-virgin olive oil, divided
→ 4 boneless, skinless chicken breasts
→ kosher salt
→ freshly ground black pepper
→ 2 cloves garlic, finely chopped
→ 1 Tbsp fresh thyme leaves
→ 1 tsp crushed red pepper flakes, optional

→ 3/4 cup chicken broth
→ 1/2 cup chopped sun-dried tomatoes
→ 1/2 cup heavy cream
→ 1/4 cup finely grated parmesan
→ torn fresh basil, for serving

In a large non-stick skillet with a lid over medium-high heat, add chicken with a little oil. Generously season chicken with salt and black pepper and cook, turning halfway through, until golden brown, about 5 minutes per side. Transfer chicken to a plate. In the same skillet, over medium heat, heat remaining 2 Tbsp oil. Stir in garlic, thyme, and red pepper flakes. Cook, stirring, until fragrant, about 1 minute. Stir in broth, tomatoes, cream, and Parmesan, and season with salt. Bring to a simmer, return chicken and any accumulated juices to skillet.

Place the lid on the skillet, turn the heat to low, and cook until the chicken is cooked through and the juices run clear when pierced with a knife, about 10 to 12 minutes. Arrange chicken on a platter. Spoon sauce over. Top with basil.

Marry Me Chicken became a popular dish around 2016. The name originated from a playful comment made by a video producer who tasted the dish and exclaimed, "I'd marry you for that chicken!" This reaction was to Lindsay Funston's creamy, herb-filled skillet chicken, which she had just cooked. The dish quickly gained popularity due to its delicious flavors and the charming, romantic notion that it could inspire a marriage proposal.

Its popularity soared with the rise of social media, where it became a viral sensation, frequently appearing in recipes across the web. The name "Marry Me Chicken" has since become synonymous with a meal that is both romantic and unforgettable.

Cookbook Citation: Microsoft 365 Copilot. (2025). *Marry Me Chicken*.

536) Mexican Chicken, Crockpot Recipe

- → crockpot liner, optional
- → 2 or 3 chicken breasts, boneless, skinless
- → 2 or 3 chicken thighs, boneless, skinless
- → 1/2 cup chopped onion
- → 1/2 bell pepper, chopped
- → 1 Tbsp chicken bouillon granules
- → 1 Tbsp fajita seasoning, Bidia
- → 1/2 cup médium salsa, Herdez
- → 1/2 cup salsa verde, Herdez
- → 1/2 cup water
- → 1/3 cup original queso cheese, optional

Line crockpot with crockpot liner for easy cleanup and storage. Place chicken in bottom of pot. Add remaining ingredients in order listed. Mix up a little. Cover and cook on high for 4 hours or low for 8 hours. Use a fork to separate chicken (shred it). Once it has cooled, pick it up (bag and all) and transfer it to a plastic storage container if you have leftovers.

 This recipe is similar to Recipe #537, however, this recipe uses boneless chicken because it's cooked in the crockpot. It will be better with bone-in chicken, removing bones before serving. Boneless breasts tend to be dryer and less flavorful. See tip below on adding queso.

537) Mexican Shredded Chicken

- → Recipe # 116 Boil a Chicken

You only need half of the chicken for this recipe. Refrigerate the broth and leftover chicken to make another dish.

- → 1 chopped onion
- → 3/4 bell pepper, chopped
- → 1/8 cup olive oil
- → 1/2 tsp salt

- → 1/2 tsp black pepper
- → 1/2 cup medium salsa, Herdez
- → 1-1/2 tsp fajita seasoning, Badia
- → 1/3 cup original queso cheese, optional

In a skillet, combine onion, pepper, olive oil, salt, and pepper. Cook until onions are soft. Pull cooked chicken apart, shredding it. Add it to the skillet. Add salsa, cheese and fajita seasoning. Mix well and simmer for 5 minutes.

 To Serve: Use for nachos, tacos, or burritos.

Tip: Adding the queso puts this dish in another league. It is a must if you have it.

538) Garlic Chicken (Pan Seared)

- → 2 or 3 green onions, chopped
- → 2 Tbsp minced garlic
- → 6 Tbsp olive oil, divided
- → 1 1/2 lb. boneless chicken breast
- → poultry seasoning blend
- → 2 Tbsp sherry

Butterfly chicken breasts. In a hot skillet, combine the onions, garlic, and 3 tbsp. olive oil and cook, stirring constantly, until the garlic is light golden brown. (Do not overbrown the garlic, or it will taste bitter.) Place in a bowl to use later.

Rub chicken breasts well with olive oil. Add chicken to a hot skillet. Sprinkle dried herbs on the chicken and cook for 5 minutes over medium-high heat. Flip the chicken and cook for 4 minutes. Add the garlic/scallion mixture. Add 2 Tbsp sherry. Cook for another minute. Turn heat on lowest setting, cover with a lid, and let the chicken simmer for 5 minutes before serving. Serves 4-5. Chicken must reach 170°F internally.

539) Pan-Seared Chicken Breasts

→ boneless chicken breasts

Slice Chicken breasts in half. When I say half, I mean the depth of the chicken (full length sliced in half or butterfly). This reduces cooking time.

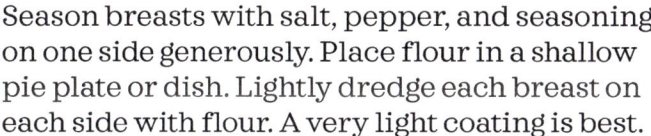

→ Skillet with lid
→ salt
→ black pepper
→ steak seasoning, Weber Steak-n-Chop
→ 1/2 cup all-purpose flour

Season breasts with salt, pepper, and seasoning on one side generously. Place flour in a shallow pie plate or dish. Lightly dredge each breast on each side with flour. A very light coating is best.

→ 3 Tbsp salted butter
→ 3 Tbsp olive oil

Heat skillet on medium heat. Once hot, add butter/oil and turn element temp. to medium-high. Pick up skillet and move it around so entire bottom is coated with oil. Add chicken breasts. Cover and cook 3 minutes per side. Set timer to ensure cooking time. Take out of skillet and place on platter Chicken should rest 5 minutes before carving. Serve with salad or as an entrée.

 CAUTION: Cooking time is for chicken no thicker than 1/2".

The chicken must be cut thin for this recipe. Do Not Overcook the chicken, or it will be dry.

Rom 12:3

"For I say, through the grace given unto me, to every man that is among you, not to think of himself more highly than he ought to think; but to think soberly, according as God hath dealt to every man the measure of faith." KJV

540) Parmesan Chicken

→ thin sliced chicken breast (buy thin sliced chicken breasts or freeze breast 1 hour prior to slicing)
→ 1 lb. spaghetti noodles (cook per package directions and drain)
→ 1 cup self-rising flour
→ 1 pack Italian-style croutons, crushed
→ 1 egg, beaten
→ 1 Tbsp Italian Seasoning, not salt
→ 2 jars Bertolli Marinara & 1 cup water
→ 8 oz. grated parmesan
→ 8 oz. grated mozzarella, or sliced if baking
→ cooking oil

Preheat oven to 350°F. Slice chicken 1/2 inch thick. Place the flour and seasoning in one dish, and the crushed croutons in another. Dip the chicken in egg, then dredge it in flour, and place it in croutons, pressing them into the chicken. Rest for 10 minutes. Preheat the oil in a skillet until small test piece sizzles. Fry chicken for 3 to 4 minutes per side. Drain on paper towels.

To Bake: In a 13x9 dish sprayed with cooking spray, layer noodles, marinara, and cheese, top with fried chicken. Place mozzarella slices on the chicken and sprinkle with Parmesan. Bake until bubbly.

Quick No-bake: Mix marinara sauce with cooked noodles and shredded mozzarella cheese. Plate the noodles, then top with fried chicken. Grate fresh mozzarella over the chicken. Enjoy!

 Tammy prefers the no-bake for a crispier chicken.

"This is a family favorite!" – Tammy

541) Take It Easy Chicken

- → 2 bone-in, skin on chicken breasts
- → deep round casserole, Dutch oven, or skillet
- → cooking spray
- → 10.5 oz. cream of mushroom
- → 4 oz. can mushroom stems and pieces, drained
- → 2 oz jar diced pimentos, or 1 heaping Tbsp of diced pimentos
- → 1 cup chicken bone broth option: use 1/2 cup for a thicker gravy
- → 1 packet Lipton onion soup mix seasoning

Preheat the oven to 350°F. Spray your baking dish with cooking spray. If breasts are thick, use a knife and butterfly them so they will lay flatter. Place them in baking dish meat side down and bone side up. In a medium bowl combine the soup, mushrooms, pimentos, broth, and soup mix. Mix well. Pour over chicken. Cover the dish with foil or an oven safe lid and bake for 1 hour. Remove the lid/foil and bake for an additional 30 minutes. Chicken should reach an internal temp. of 170°F.

 If using large breasts without splitting them, use a meat thermometer.

Serve chicken with gravy poured over it. This is super easy and VERY GOOD!

"Chris produced a name for this recipe! I thought it sounded catchy and used it. I hope you enjoy this easy recipe on a night you are just feeling lazy!"– *Tammy*

542) Roasted Turkey Breast

- → boneless turkey breast
- → 1 tsp poultry seasoning, Bidia
- → 1 tsp steak seasoning, Weber Steak-n-Chop
- → 1 tsp McCormick poultry seasoning
- → 1 tsp garlic salt
- → olive oil

Preheat oven to 450°F. Place seasonings in a pie plate. Rinse and dry the turkey breast, then rub with olive oil and coat with seasonings. Insert a digital thermometer in the center.

Oven Directions: Put breast on a rack, bake 20 minutes at 450°F. Reduce to 350°F and bake until internal reaches 170°F. Use a pop-up thermometer or package instructions for time, and let stand 15-20 minutes before carving.

Crockpot Directions: place seasonings in a pie plate with 1/2 cup flour. Roll the breast in the seasonings and flour until it is well-coated. Put it in a crockpot with a crockpot liner. Add:
- → 1/2 cup salted butter
- → 2 cups chicken broth

Cook on low for 8-10 hours. Slice and serve with drippings.

 Tammy's Tip: Use fresh herbs if available. Thyme, rosemary, and fresh garlic are great for roasting turkey and prime rib. Just chop finely and put it on a plate with other seasonings.

543) Turkey Crockpot Dinner

→ Thick sliced turkey breast
→ 8 oz. Pepperidge Farm stuffing mix, Traditional
→ 8 oz. Pepperidge Farm stuffing mix, Cornbread style
→ 1 onion chopped
→ 3/4 cup chopped celery
→ poultry seasoning, McCormick
→ black pepper
→ Thick sliced turkey breast
→ 2-6 oz. can cream of chicken (or 2-10.5 oz. cans)
→ 2 tsp chicken bouillon granules
→ 2 1/2 cups hot water
→ 2-14.5 oz cans sliced potatoes
→ 2-14.5 oz. cans green beans
→ 2-14.5 oz cans sliced potatoes
→ 1/2 cup salted butter
→ oval-shaped large crockpot

Spray the crock with cooking spray. Place half of each pack of stuffing mix in the bottom of the crockpot starting with traditional. Mix well.

Add diced onion, celery, poultry seasoning and black pepper on top of the stuffing. Place sliced turkey on top of the celery in center of crock pot.

Spread cream of chicken soup evenly over the turkey & stuffing. Add the remaining stuffing on top, distributing each evenly.

Dissolve the bouillon in hot water and whisk it. Pour this mixture over the stuffing.

Drain the potatoes and green beans. Move ingredients from one side of the pot and pour the green beans into that side, then do the same for the potatoes on the opposite side.

Slice the butter and place it on top of the stuffing & veggies. Cook on low for 8-9 hours, or High for 6 hours.

 Serve with a can of cranberry sauce or Recipe #562 : Cranberry Relish.

"In order to serve 6 people and less stuffing, reduce stuffing to 1 1/2 bags (18-oz.) and add 3 cans of vegetables instead of 2. Great dish for small gatherings, singles, or couples." – *Tammy*

Rom 12:20
"Therefore if thine enemy hunger, feed him; if he thirst, give him drink: for in so doing thou shalt heap coals of fire on his head." KJV

544) Thanksgiving Turkey

- → 2 lemons, for full roasting
- → Whole turkey, thawed
- → fresh rosemary
- → fresh thyme
- → fresh garlic (5 cloves)
- → 1 large onion
- → fresh green onions (1 bunch)
- → 1/2 cup salted butter
- → salt & pepper
- → poultry seasoning, McCormick
- → pork belly, optional
- → 1 cup apple juice
- → 1/2 cup water

Unwrap the turkey—remove the neck and giblets from the cavity. Rinse the bird and dry it with paper towels. Rub the cavity with lemon and insert fresh herbs, garlic, and onion. Rub the outside with butter, salt, pepper, and poultry seasoning, then place on a rack breast side down. Put the pork belly on top of the bird. Pour apple juice and water into the roasting pan, cover with foil, and place in a preheated oven to slow roast.

Use a roasting chart for cooking time based on the bird's weight and bake at 325°F covered. It is best to use a thermometer if your bird does not have an automatic pop-out. Insert the thermometer deep into the breast.

Once you have slow-roasted the turkey for the full bake time, and the thermometer reaches 170°F, remove the pan from the oven.

Poke holes in the foil to release steam, then remove the foil, rotate the bird to breast side up, and place the pork belly on top of the breast. Increase the oven temperature to 400°F to brown. When the bird is golden brown, remove it from the oven. Let it stand for 20 minutes before carving. Do not overbake. Carve the turkey and baste the slices with juices from the roasting pan. pan

 Use two large spoons to rotate the turkey breast, and get help if needed.

Ensure the turkey is fully out of the oven before rotating.

If carving before dinner, there's no need to increase the oven temp. and turn it for browning. I personally prefer that the turkey be sliced prior to dinner so guest don't have to wait for someone to carve the turkey.

Save drippings and pour over sliced turkey.

Keep all juices to pour over leftover meat before refrigerating to keep it from drying out.

Using pork belly is optional.

Serve with Recipe #562 Peggy's Cranberry Relish.

Salad Recipes

Do you ever get a craving for a delicious salad?

The salad section features a variety of fresh and flavorful recipes designed to complement any meal. These salads incorporate a range of fruits, vegetables,

Recipe #546 Avocado Salad

Recipe #545 Apple Salad

Recipe #560 Cucumber Salad

and creative ingredients, offering both classic and unique combinations. Ideal for those seeking a refreshing side dish or a light, satisfying option, each recipe is easy to prepare and perfect for gatherings or everyday enjoyment.

545) Apple Salad

→ 20 oz. can crushed pineapple
→ 1/3 cup granulated sugar
→ 3 oz. lemon flavored gelatin
→ 8 oz. cream cheese, room temperature
→ 8 oz. whipped topping, Cool whip
→ 2 cups of chopped apples
→ 1/2 lemon
→ 1/2 cup purple seedless grapes, halved
→ 1 cup chopped pecans

Combine pineapple (juice and all), sugar, and gelatin in a saucepan and bring to a boil for 2-3 minutes or until sugar has dissolved. Pour into a shallow dish and cool to room temperature. Peel and chop apples. Squeeze a half lemon over apples and mix well. After the gelatin has cooled, mix it with cream cheese using a hand mixer. Gently fold in whipped topping, apples, grapes, and pecans with a large spatula until everything is evenly combined. Keep the dish refrigerated.

 Use other fruits and Jell-O flavors for different profiles, however, make sure fruit is drained.

546) Avocado Salad

→ 3 ripe avocados, cubed
→ 1/2 chopped onion
→ 1 Tbsp fresh cilantro, chopped
→ 1 medium tomato, chopped
→ 1 lime or lemon, juiced
→ 1/4 tsp black pepper
→ 1/2 tsp salt

 2 tsp chili lime seasoning can be used as a replacement for black pepper and salt.

Mix above ingredients and serve with fish tacos or tortilla chips and enjoy!

547) Bean Salad

→ 2-14.5 oz. cans kidney beans, drained
→ 1 onion, chopped small
→ 1 green pepper, chopped small
→ 4 stalks celery, chopped small
→ 3 boiled eggs, chopped small
→ 1/2 cup sweet (or dill pickles) your choice
→ 1/4 cup mayonnaise
→ 1/2 tsp granulated sugar
→ 1/4 tsp salt & black pepper

Add drained beans, chopped vegetables, eggs, pickles, and mix well. Add mayonnaise, a small pinch of sugar, a dash of salt & pepper, and mix. Put in a covered dish & refrigerate for 2 hours. Serve & enjoy

548) Broccoli Salad

→ 4 cups of fresh broccoli florets
→ 1/4 cup granulated sugar
→ 1/2 cup pecans, chopped & toasted
→ 1/2 cup red onion, chopped
→ 3/4 cup mayonnaise
→ 2 Tbsp apple cider vinegar
→ 1/2 cup golden raisins, soaked in orange juice overnight
→ 68 slices of bacon, cooked till crisp
→ 2 or 3 Tbsp bacon grease

Drain the orange juice (off raisins) and put it into a small bowl; set both aside. In a large bowl, combine 1/4 cup of the orange juice, sugar, onion, mayonnaise, vinegar, and bacon grease. Until well blended. Add broccoli and toss well. Keep refrigerated until ready to serve. Before serving, add chopped toasted pecans and crumbled bacon to the top of the salad. Seedless grapes, halved, can be added.

549) Carrot Raisin Salad

→ 1 lb. carrots, peel, and grate
→ 1/4 cup raisins
→ 8 oz. can crushed pineapple
→ 2 Tbsp mayonnaise
→ 1/4 tsp salt

Add pineapple juice and all to the grated carrots. Add raisins, mayonnaise, and salt. Mix well. The mayonnaise should be evenly distributed. Put in a serving dish and cover. Refrigerate for up to 5 days.

"This is so delicious. It reminds me of the carrot raisin salad from Chick-fil-A. So, Good Y'all!" – *Tammy*

Tammy's tip: do not use a larger grate typically used for cole slaw. Grate with a small grater on a hand grater. This small grate breaks down the carrot pieces, making them smaller and juicier for enhanced flavor.

550) Caesar Salad

→ 2 romaine hearts
→ 1/2 red onion sliced thin
→ Caesar croutons
→ 1 large carrot, peel, and grate
→ Recipe #551 Caesar Dressing
→ Black pepper

Wash Romaine Hearts and dry them in a salad spinner. Place on paper towels, roll up, and store in the refrigerator to prepare salad later. Tear (or cut) lettuce, add sliced onion, & shredded carrots. Toss in chilled Caesar dressing. Top with croutons, black pepper, and shaved parmesan cheese.

551) Caesar Dressing

→ 1 cup plain yogurt (or 1 cup mayo)
→ 1 raw egg yolk, optional
→ 4 cloves garlic pressed

→ 1 Tbsp Dijon mustard
→ 2 tsp Worcestershire
→ 1 Tbsp anchovy paste
→ 1/2 tsp salt
→ 1/2 cup grated parmesan
→ 1/2 cup shaved parmesan (for topping)

Combine ingredients, blend well with whisk and toss in greens.

"This is best when you mix it and chill it in the refrigerator before serving."– *Tammy*

552) Cherry Jell-O Salad

→ 2-3 oz. cherry fruit-flavored gelatin
→ 1/4 tsp salt
→ 2 cups of boiling water
→ 8 oz. can crushed pineapple
→ 20 oz can pie filling flavor is your choice

Mix all the ingredients and pour into a dish. Chill in the refrigerator until set.

Topping:

→ 8 oz. cream cheese, room temperature
→ 1/2 cup granulated sugar
→ 1 cup sour cream

Mix cream cheese with sugar and sour cream and spread over the top of the congealed fruit. Keep refrigerated until serving. Enjoy!

553) BLT Chicken Salad

→ 5 slices bacon
→ 3/4 cup mayonnaise
→ 2 Tbsp green onion, minced
→ 1 Tbsp chopped fresh parsley
→ 2 tsp lemon juice
→ 3 dashes Worcestershire sauce
→ salt and ground black pepper, to taste
→ 3 cups of diced cooked chicken
→ 1 cup tomato, chopped
→ 1 stalk celery, thinly sliced
→ 1 large avocado, sliced, optional
→ butter croissants, for serving
→ Romaine lettuce leaves, optional

Cook the bacon until crisp in a skillet over medium-high heat. Drain on paper towels and crumble once cooled.

In a large bowl, whisk the mayonnaise, green onion, parsley, lemon juice, Worcestershire sauce, salt, and pepper until creamy and well combined. Add chicken, tomato, and celery. Add the crumbled bacon and toss gently to coat.

Cover and refrigerate for at least 30 minutes to let the flavors enhance. Spoon the chilled salad onto split butter croissants or crisp salad leaves to serve.

Add bacon pieces and tomatoes the day that it is served, or they will become soggy.

554) Chicken Salad, Rotisserie

→ 1 rotisserie chicken
→ 1/2 medium onion, minced
→ 1/8 cup chopped celery
→ 1/2 tsp dill weed, chopped
→ 1/4 tsp pepper
→ 1/2 cup mayonnaise or more

 Use dehydrated or sauté onions for a milder flavor.

Chicken: If refrigerated, remove it from the refrigerator and let it sit at room temperature for 1 hour before mixing. Take off skin, bones, and cartilage. Chop the chicken into 1/2-inch cubes.

Combine the above ingredients in a large bowl and mix with a metal spoon so you can break up the chicken chunks. I prefer to hand mix.

 Options: Omit Dill if preferred. Add additional ingredients, such as chopped pecans and grape halves, for special occasions.

Some like to warm and serve with toasted almond slices in salad.

Appetizers: Bake small phyllo cups according to the package directions, 20 minutes before guests arrive. Fill each cup with a dollop of chicken salad. People love these!

Sandwich: Best on sourdough (untoasted) with a thinly sliced cucumber and a little mayo. Delicious!

555) Cole Slaw

- → 1/3 head green cabbage
- → 1/3 cup mayonnaise
- → 1/4 tsp pepper
- → 1 Tbsp sweet pickle juice
- → 2 Tbsp pickle relish, optional

Shred the cabbage using a box grater. Add mayonnaise, pepper, pickle juice, and relish. Mix everything thoroughly. Add extra mayo if you like.

556) Cole Slaw, Carrot

- → 1 small head green cabbage
- → 1 large carrot or 2 medium carrots
- → 1/2 cup mayonnaise, Blue Plate or Dukes
- → 1 1/2 tsp apple cider vinegar
- → 1 Tbsp sugar
- → 1/2 tsp black pepper

Grate the cabbage using a hand grater or a mandolin. Peel the outer layer of the carrots with a vegetable peeler or scrape it off with a knife. Grate the carrots using a hand grater or mandolin, then add both the cabbage and carrots to a bowl. Add mayonnaise, vinegar, sugar, and pepper, then mix well. If you use more cabbage, you might need to add an extra 1/4 cup of mayonnaise!

- → Do not use organic raw vinegar

557) Cole Slaw, German

- → 1 head cabbage, grated
- → 2 medium onions, sliced thin then half
- → 1/4 cup sugar for slaw
- → 1 cup vinegar, apple cider
- → 1 tsp salt
- → 1 tsp dry mustard
- → 3/4 cup salad oil
- → 1 tsp celery seed
- → 1/4 cup sugar for dressing

In a bowl, layer cabbage and onions alternately. Sprinkle 1/4 cup sugar on top. In a saucepan, bring vinegar, salt, dry mustard, salad oil, celery seed, and 1/4 cup sugar to a boil for 2-3 minutes. Pour over the cabbage and let stand for 24 hours or overnight in the refrigerator. Keeps up to 2 weeks in the fridge.

 Best after sitting in the refrigerator overnight.

558) Cole Slaw, KFC Style

- → 1 head cabbage, grated
- → 1 or 2 Tbsp grated onion
- → 1 carrot, shredded
- → 1/3 cup sugar
- → 1/2 cup mayonnaise
- → 1/2 cup buttermilk
- → 1/2 cup milk
- → 2 1/2 Tbsp lemon juice
- → 1-1/2 Tbsp white vinegar
- → 1/2 tsp salt
- → 1/2 tsp pepper

Grate cabbage, onion, and carrot and set aside. In a bowl whisk together the remaining ingredients. Whisk well and pour over grated cabbage. Mix well and refrigerate in an airtight container overnight for the best flavor. Enjoy y'all!

559) Cornbread Salad

→ 2 lbs. tomatoes, peeled
→ salt & black pepper
→ wine vinegar
→ 5 medium green peppers, chopped fine
→ 4 ribs of celery, chopped fine
→ 2 or 3 cups cooked cornbread, crumbled
→ 3 cups kernel corn
→ buttermilk ranch dressing, or your choice
→ 1/3 cup chopped fresh parsley, optional
→ 6 slices crumbled crisp cooked bacon

Chop tomatoes and drain if they are juicy. Wash and prepare all vegetables. Use a clear truffle bowl and start by putting half of your cornbread on the bottom. Top with 1/2 of your onion, then peppers, celery, tomatoes. Salt and pepper and sprinkle with vinegar. Add corn, then drizzle with dressing. Repeat layers, ending with layer of dressing. Top with bacon and parsley. Refrigerate 23 hours, covered. Toss before serving.

Optional Ingredients: chopped boiled eggs, chopped green onion, shredded cheese, sour cream, pinto beans

Optional dressings: Italian dressing, buttermilk dressing, or ranch dressing

560) Cucumber Salad

→ 2 cups cucumber sliced thin
→ 1/4 cup sliced onion, sliced thin
→ 2 Tbsp white vinegar
→ 2 Tbsp sugar
→ 2 Tbsp oil, olive oil recommend
→ 1/2 tsp dill weed, optional

Mix the above ingredients together well. Let salad sit out refrigerator for 2 hours for sugar to dissolve. Serve with dinner and store leftovers in the refrigerator. Enjoy, y'all!

561) Crab Salad Tarts

→ 1/2 cup mayonnaise
→ 2 Tbsp diced onion
→ 1/4 cup diced red bell pepper or pimentos
→ 1/2 tsp black pepper
→ 8 oz. crab meat, chopped
→ 1/2 lemon juice
→ seasoned croutons, half 5 oz. bag crushed
→ 2 boxes of 15 phyllo tart shells
→ Parsley, chopped small for garnish

In a bowl mix mayonnaise, onion, bell pepper, and black pepper well. Squeeze lemon juice over mixture, add crab meat and croutons - mix well. Refrigerate until ready to serve. Just before company arrives:

Air Fryer : Heat the shells at 350°F for 3 minutes.

Conventional oven: Heat shells at 350°F for 8 minutes.

Remove shells and fill them with salad. Sprinkle with garnish and serve.

"These are AMAZING and best when served fresh, so croutons do not get soggy. Enjoy!"
– *Tammy*

562) Cranberry Relish, Aunt Peggy's

→ 1 lb. fresh cranberries, chopped
→ 1/2 cup diced celery
→ 1/2 cup chopped pecans
→ 20 oz. can crushed pineapple, reserve juice
→ 1-1/2 cups boiling water
→ 1/4 tsp salt
→ 1 cup sugar (or sweetener of choice)
→ 1 navel orange, peeled and chopped
→ lemon zest, optional
→ 3 oz. pack of strawberry flavored gelatin
→ 3 oz. pack of cranberry flavored gelatin

Prepare all ingredients first. Bring water to a boil. In a large bowl, combine water, sugar, salt, and gelatins. Stir until fully mixed, then add the remaining ingredients. Pour the mixture into a dish and refrigerate to set. Keep it refrigerated in an air-tight container. Enjoy with your delicious turkey dinner!

Lower Sugar Option: Substitute water with sweetened fruit juice and omit 1/2 cup of sugar! Use sugar-free gelatin.

563) Egg & Olive Salad

- → 6 hard-boiled eggs
- → 1/2 cup mayonnaise
- → 1/4 tsp black pepper
- → 2 Tbsp sliced green olives
- → 1 tsp olive juice

Chop eggs using an egg slicer (both directions) or a pastry blender. Add the remaining ingredients and stir well with a fork. Serve with crackers or bread for sandwiches. Refrigerate. Makes 3 generously stuffed sandwiches. Enjoy!

564) Fruit Salad Surprise

- → 8 oz. cool whip topping
- → 16 oz. 2% small curd cottage cheese
- → 1/4 tsp salt
- → 3 oz. lime flavored gelatin, Jell-O
- → 1/4 tsp lemon extract
- → 1/4 tsp coconut extract
- → 15 oz. can fruit cocktail, drained
- → 8 oz. can crushed pineapple, drained well
- → 1/3 cup sweetened flaked coconut
- → 1/3 cup chopped pecans, optional
- → sugar sprinkles, optional

In a large bowl, add whipped topping, cottage cheese, salt, Jell-O packet, and flavorings, then mix well. Add drained fruit cocktail, pineapple, coconut, and pecans, then mix again.

Tammy's tip: Try strawberry or cherry Jell-O with red sugar sprinkles or cherries for Christmas. Use lime Jell-O with green sprinkles for saint patrick's Day!

"This is absolutely my favorite fruit salad. The extract makes it so delicious! This is a must try!" – *Tammy*

565) Fruit Salad

- → 6-7 fresh strawberries
- → 1 orange, peeled and cut into wedges
- → 2 slices cantaloupe, raspberries, or other fresh fruit
- → 1/8 cup golden eagle table syrup or honey
- → 2 Tbsp powdered sugar
- → salt

After cleaning and peeling the fruit, cut it into bite-sized pieces (leaving smaller berries whole). Place the fruit in a bowl, sprinkle with salt then drizzle syrup or honey over it and mix well. Lightly sift powdered sugar over the fruit before serving.

566) Fruit Salad, Yogurt

- → 16 oz. plain yogurt
- → 3 oz. sugar-free flavored gelatin, Jell-O
- → 1/2 lb. assorted color seedless grapes
- → 3 assorted color apples, chopped
- → 1/2 cup golden raisins
- → 1/2 cup chopped walnuts or pecans
- → 1/2 lemon, juiced
- → 15 oz. can mandarin oranges, drained
- → 10 oz. can pineapple chunks, drained
- → 1/4 tsp salt

First, drain pineapples and oranges through a strainer and let them continue to drain while making salad. Then, place yogurt, salt, and gelatin in a large bowl and whisk well until it is distributed evenly with yogurt. Cut grapes in half and place them in the bowl with gelatin & yogurt. Add remaining ingredients and toss to coat well. Best served immediately!

Leave skin on apples on for color

Use a different Jell-O flavor to create different colors for holiday themes.

Tammy's Tips: Do not make this a day ahead, and do not use strawberries, bananas, or any soft fruits in this salad

567) Ham Salad or Spread

→ 4 oz. cream cheese, room temperature (or 1/2 cup shredded mild cheddar)
→ 2 green onions, diced
→ 2 Tbsp dill relish
→ 1 tsp Worcestershire sauce
→ 2 boiled eggs, diced
→ 1/4 cup mayonnaise
→ 1 celery stalk, diced
→ 1 tsp mustard
→ 2 cups ham, diced

Combine all ingredients except ham in a mixing bowl. Using a hand mixer, mix ingredients well. Mix in ham and serve on sandwich bread or crackers. Keep refrigerated in an air-tight container.

Instead of mixing in ham, use the combined ingredients as a spread. Spread on sandwich bread and top with sliced ham and lettuce.

568) Macaroni Salad, Creamy

→ 16 oz. elbow macaroni
→ 12 oz. frozen baby green peas, optional
→ 1 zucchini, chopped, optional
→ 2 radishes, sliced and halved, optional
→ 1 squash, chopped, optional
→ 1 sweet onion, chopped
→ 4 oz. jar pimientos
→ 1/2 jar mayonnaise
→ 1 tsp black pepper
→ 1 tsp celery seed
→ 2 Tbsp pickle relish
→ 3/4 tsp salt
→ 1 tsp onion powder
→ 1 tsp Mrs. Dash original
→ 1 cucumber, chopped
→ 8 oz. cream cheese, room temperature

Wash and trim vegetables. Chop vegetables into cubes (except radishes). Set half of chopped onion and cucumber aside. Boil pasta in boiling water with 1 tsp salt added - 8 minutes. Immediately add peas, zucchini, radishes, squash, and half of onion to boiling pasta, boil two minutes. Drain pasta and vegetables, rinse under cold running water. In a large bowl add chopped cucumbers to pasta with remaining uncooked onion. In a separate bowl, mix pimentos, mayo, black pepper, celery seed, pickle relish, salt, onion powder, Mrs. Dash, and cream cheese with a hand mixer and pour creamy mixture into pasta bowl, mix, and enjoy. Add more salt and pepper if desired. Refrigerate pasta salad!

569) Pasta Salad, Italian

→ 1 box bowtie pasta
→ 2 radishes, slice thin, optional
→ 1 cucumber, wash, slice thin, and quarter
→ 2 bell peppers, 1 yellow and 1 red
→ 1 sweet onions, sliced thin
→ 1 small package mini pepperoni
→ salami, cut into bite-sized pieces
→ jar of marinated mushrooms, sliced thin
→ 2-4 oz. cans of black olives, rinse & drain
→ Bertolli balsamic sauce or other marinade
→ 1/4 cup olive oil
→ salt & pepper to taste
→ cheddar cheese, sliced or cubed

Prepare pasta per package directions adding 1 tsp salt while pasta boils. Drain pasta and put it in a large bowl. Add radishes, cucumber, peppers, onions, pepperonis, salami slices, mushrooms, and olives. Add olive oil, toss, and mix well. Add balsamic glaze to pasta. Mix and taste, adding more balsamic glaze, per your own taste preference. Salt and pepper salad to taste. Allow you to marinate at room temperature. Add cheese and toss just before serving. A red onion can be used instead for additional color.

570) Pizza Salad

→ 3 romaine lettuce hearts, sliced
→ 1 lb. Italian sausage, Swaggerty's farm
→ 1 pk. small grape tomatoes, halved
→ 1/2 cup mushrooms, fresh sliced
→ 1/2 cup pepperoncini, sliced rings
→ 12 oz. jar artichoke hearts, chopped
→ 1/2 cup black olives, sliced
→ 2 Tbsp red onions, chopped
→ 1/4 cup colored bell peppers, chopped
→ 1/2 cup pepperoni, sliced or small size
→ 1 cup pearl mozzarella balls
→ 1/2 cup pineapple chunks, optional
→ 2 Tbsp fresh basil, chopped
→ parmesan cheese, grated
→ Italian-style croutons

Note: all ingredients are optional except for lettuce. Brown the Italian Sausage, drain on paper towels, and set aside. Chop the Romaine lettuce into small pieces and place the lettuce in a large bowl. Add tomatoes, mushrooms, pepperoncini, olives, onion, peppers, pepperoni, pineapple, and Italian sausage. Toss ingredients together well. Top with mozzarella, parmesan, basil, and croutons. This is a great Party Salad!

571) Potato Salad, Mama's

→ 2 Tbsp bell pepper, diced
→ small onion, diced
→ 3 Tbsp olive oil
→ 3 large eggs, boiled hard and chopped
→ 6 medium russet potatoes
→ 1 cup mayonnaise
→ 1/3 cup sweet pickle relish
→ 1 tsp yellow mustard
→ 1 tsp granulated sugar
→ 1/2 tsp pepper
→ 1/2 tsp salt
→ 1 large red tomato, optional

Sauté bell pepper and onion in olive oil on low/ medium heat for 10 minutes. Peel and cut potatoes into walnut size hunks. Boil on high for 10 minutes. Boil eggs separately, placing cold eggs in boiling water with spoon- boil 12 minutes. Peel eggs and chop. Drain Potatoes and place in large bowl. Add mayonnaise, pickles, mustard, sugar, pepper, salt, peppers, onions, & chopped boiled eggs. Mix well then fold in chopped tomato for color! Makes 8 servings.

Must refrigerate after 3 hours!

"This potato salad is creamy with some hunks of potatoes. Sautéing the onion and peppers is optional!" – *Tammy*

572) Potato Salad, Simple

→ 6 medium russet potatoes, peel and cut into walnut size pieces.

Boil potatoes on high for 10 minutes. Drain potatoes and place them in large bowl.

→ boil 3 large eggs, placing cold eggs in boiling water with spoon- boil 12 minutes. Peel eggs and chop.

place eggs in large bowl with potatoes. In a separate bowl mix together:

→ 1 cup mayonnaise, Blue Plate or Dukes
→ 1/3 cup sweet pickle relish
→ 3 Tbsp dehydrated onions, McCormick
→ 1 tsp yellow mustard
→ 1 tsp granulated sugar
→ 1/2 tsp pepper
→ 1 tsp salt

Mix dressing into the potatoes. Refrigerate leftovers and don't leave out over 4 hours.

"The dehydrated onions add an onion flavor without being overpowering. I make this version for Chris's family because they don't like onions and bell pepper. They love it!" -*Tammy*

573) Tomato Mozzarella Salad

- → 2 pints cherry tomatoes, mixed colors
- → 1/2 cup red onion sliced thin
- → 1-1/2 cups of Italian marinated mozzarella balls, use juices
- → balsamic vinegar

Slice the tomatoes in half and add to a mixing bowl. Add onion and mozzarella. Drizzle with vinegar, toss, and serve! DELICIOUS!

574) Vinaigrette, Master

- → 3 Tbsp red wine vinegar
- → 1/2 cup extra virgin olive oil
- → 1/2 tsp black pepper
- → 1/2 tsp salt

Combine the above ingredients in a dressing container or small canning jar. Place lid on and shake well before serving. Makes about 8 servings.

575) Sweet Master Vinaigrette

Use recipe above but substitute

- → 1/2 cup cider vinegar in place of red wine vinegar.

Add:

- → 2 Tbsp sugar
- → 1 clove garlic, sliced thin

Let it sit for a few hours, shake, and serve.

"My favorite loaf bread is Nature's Own Perfectly Crafted Thick sliced multigrain bread. This bread is pictured in the Tuna Salad recipe above. I love Starkist's new tuna fish packed in evo (extra virgin olive oil). I mix one in oil and one in water together for a great tuna salad." – *Tammy*

576) Tuna Salad

- → 5 oz can tuna in water, drained
- → 5 oz can tuna in oil, drained
- → 1/4 cup mayonnaise
- → 2 Tbsp sweet pickle relish
- → 1/4 tsp black pepper
- → hard-boiled egg, chopped
- → thick sliced loaf bread
- → crisp lettuce & pickles for garnish

Deluxe Salad:

- → 1/4 cup diced celery
- → 1/4 cup diced onion

Mix all ingredients together. Serve as a sandwich or piled on a crisp lettuce leaf.

Family Food Fight on ABC

In 2018 my brother, Chris and I competed in a televised cooking show called "Family Food Fight" by ABC. We stayed in Los Angeles three weeks while the filming took place. We came in 2nd place and enjoyed watching it with our family in the summer of 2019. This is the final show party at my brother Eddie's home. The judges on the show were Graham Elliot, Cat Cora, and Ayesha Curry. It was quite an experience. Ayesha was the host.

577) Watergate Salad

→ 3.4 oz. package pistachio pudding mix
→ 20 oz. can crushed pineapple
→ 1/4 tsp salt
→ 1/2 cup sour cream, optional
→ 10 oz. bag mini marshmallows
→ 1/2 cup chopped pecans, toasting optional
→ 10 maraschino cherries, chopped
→ 8 oz. whipped topping, Cool Whip

IMPORTANT: toasting pecans. Toast WHOLE pecans at 350°F for 5 minutes. Toast before chopping.

In a large bowl, combine the pudding, pineapple, salt, and sour cream. Mix well. Add 1/2 bag of the marshmallows, pecans, cherries, and cool whip topping and mix well. Put into a serving dish & garnish with chopped pecans and a few whole cherries! It is best to make this a day ahead and serve cold! Enjoy this delicious light salad and keep leftovers refrigerated.

"You cannot have a family reunion in the South without this being on the table. I used to wonder why the old people loved it so much. Now I am older and can understand why they do." – *Tammy*

"I remember this day so well. Chris and I were fishing in Saint George Island, Florida. We used to go there for every family vacation. Look closely, you will see that I was completely flat-chested. This picture was taken during my four years of recovery from breast cancer. I did not have reconstruction surgery until 4 years after my double mastectomy. I am very grateful that God allowed me more time to spend with Chris. I love him so very much. Looking at this brings back many happy memories that we have shared."
– *Tammy*

578) Wilted Lettuce Salad

Salad:

combine the following:

→ 1 head iceberg lettuce, washed & drained
→ 1/2 large red onion, sliced (or 4 green onions, chopped)
→ salt and pepper to taste

In a skillet fry:

→ 6 slices of bacon chopped in small pieces reserving the bacon grease

Dressing:

→ reserved bacon grease
→ 1/2 cup white vinegar
→ 1/4 cup water
→ 1 Tbsp sugar (add extra tsp if desired)

Combine the warm or hot grease with the dressing ingredients. Cook over low heat until the sugar dissolves. Mix thoroughly and pour over the greens. Add bacon on top and serve immediately with crusty bread.

 Option: Add slices of tomato or other garden vegetables if desired

Sandwich Recipes

A Delicious Sandwich is always an option for any time of day!

Ahh, the wonderful sandwich! It is something many of us enjoy multiple times a week. Peanut butter and jelly will always be a classic for Chris and me, especially when we are out fishing. Just a heads up, though—if you are superstitious, do not bring a banana on the boat!

Mama used to make lots of peanut butter and banana sandwiches. Daddy mashed them up, while Mama added mayonnaise. Recently, I tried a banana boat sandwich with peanut butter and mayo in a hot dog bun, and it was surprisingly delicious! Give it a go next time you are craving a banana sandwich.

Don't forget, salads can make great sandwich fillings too! Think pimento cheese, tuna salad, or even potato salad. There is a coffee shop that serves a toasted sandwich with cornbread dressing, turkey, and cranberry salad. This goes to show the possibilities are endless!

Oh, and if you want a taste of the Big Mac at home, I got that sauce recipe from a friend during Covid. It is a total game-changer! — *Tammy*

579) Big Mac Style Burger

- → 1 cup mayonnaise
- → 1/4 cup sweet pickle relish
- → 1 1/2 Tbsp yellow mustard
- → 1 tsp white wine vinegar
- → 1/2 tsp paprika
- → 1/4 tsp onion powder
- → 1/4 tsp garlic powder

Mix above ingredients. Let it marinate at least 2 hours (I prefer overnight) in the refrigerator.

Serve it like this: Put sauce on two bottom hamburger buns. Both get freshly diced onion and shredded lettuce. Now put an American cheese slice on one and pickles on the other. Then place your hamburger patties (cooked, thin), stack and ENJOY!!

580) BLT Sandwich

- → 2 bacon slices
- → black pepper
- → 2 slices of loaf bread
- → iceberg lettuce
- → slice of tomato
- → mayonnaise

Cut bacon slices in half and fry on medium heat. Fry until bacon is golden brown. Spread

mayonnaise on both pieces of bread. Place slices of tomato on top of the mayo and sprinkle with black pepper. Put fried bacon on one piece of bread. Add lettuce on top of the bacon. Close the sandwich and cut diagonally into two triangleshaped pieces. Serves one.

581) Deluxe Grill Cheese Sandwich

- → 2 pieces of loaf bread
- → Room temperature butter
- → Cream cheese, room temperature
- → Sliced cheddar cheese
- → Sliced American cheese

Butter both slices of bread on one side, including edges. Place them butter side together and spread cream cheese on the outside on one piece. Place bread butter side down in a pre-heated skillet. Add cheddar to one side and American to the other. Cook for a few minutes open, then close sandwich and cook until bread browns, and cheese melts. Remove, cut diagonally, and enjoy warm.

582) Cheesesteak Hoagies

→ 1" thick ribeye or tri-tip steak or packaged shaved steak
→ 1 onion sliced thin
→ bell pepper, sliced in strips
→ 1 clove garlic, minced or pressed
→ 1 1/2 cups of sliced mushrooms
→ 1/4 cup water
→ 1 tsp beef bouillon granules
→ 1 tsp cornstarch
→ 1 Tbsp Dale Steak Seasoning
→ olive oil & salted butter
→ 8 oz ole queso cheese dip, original
→ butter for buns

Flash Freeze Steak for 1 hour, take out, slice into very thin strips across the grain.

In a liquid measuring cup, combine water and bouillon. Microwave on high until boiling – remove and whisk. Whisk in corn starch.

Preheat an iron skillet, griddle, or wok, then add 2-3 tablespoons of olive oil. Quickly add the onion & mushrooms, cooking on medium-high until they are soft. Place veggies on a plate.

Add 2 Tbsp each of olive oil and butter, then add sliced beef and garlic. Stir constantly on high heat for 2 minutes.

Remix the bouillon mixture with a whisk to blend in the settled cornstarch, then add it to the wok. The gravy will thicken fast. Mix it in with the beef.

Place the meat mixture on top of the hoagie buns, then the veggies, and top with cheese—place in a hot oven on broil until the sides of the bread are toasted. Take out and enjoy while hot! Makes 3-4 hoagies

583) Chili Steak Burgers

→ 1 large egg
→ 14.5 oz. Can Hormel chili with beans
→ 1 lb. ground chuck (very cold)
→ 3 Tbsp dehydrated onions

Place the ingredients listed above in a large bowl. Mix them thoroughly, then add:

→ 1 cup breadcrumbs

Mix the breadcrumbs in until well blended. Place the beef on parchment paper and press it down to about 1/2 inch thick. Cut the patties to 5 inches in diameter or shape them with your hands. The patties should be larger than your buns. Place

→ 1 cups all-purpose flour
→ 1-1/2 cups of panko crumbs

In separate shallow pans for coating patties.

Use a spatula to lift each patty off the counter and place it in flour. Gently coat the sides and edges. Then, transfer to the panko and coat well. Reshape the patty if necessary. Let the patties sit for 10 minutes before frying.

To Fry on Stovetop: Fry in a round non-stick skillet on medium heat for about 7 minutes per side. DO NOT fry at a hot temperature. or panko will brown too quickly. Patties must be no thicker than 1/2".

This recipe makes six XL 5" dia. Patties.

To Bake: Bake at 425°F for 25 minutes, or until golden brown.

Air Fryer: Bake at 350°F for 15 minutes, or until golden brown, flipping halfway through the cooking time.

Freezing: Patties can be frozen. If using a frozen patty, use the baking method and adjust the bake time to 35 minutes. Thaw before frying.

584) Fried Bologna Sandwich or BBQ Bologna

→ 2 pieces of sliced bologna, skinned
→ 1/2 small onion, sliced, optional
→ yellow mustard
→ 2 slices of loaf bread
→ 2 Tbsp salted butter
→ iceberg lettuce
→ slice of tomato
→ mayonnaise
→ black pepper

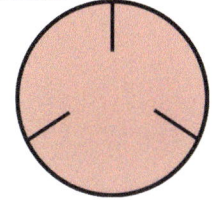

Bologna Cuts Example

Stack bologna pieces and cut three 1" slits from the outside toward the center to prevent the bologna from bowing when fried. Melt butter in a skillet, then fry the bologna and onions together. Spread mayo on one bread slice and mustard on the other. Add onions and bologna to the bread, sprinkle with black pepper, then add lettuce and tomato. Close the sandwich, cut diagonally into two triangles. Serves one.

BBQ Bologna: Fry six pieces of bologna (cut into bite-sized pieces) with a whole onion sliced, then pour in 1/2 cup BBQ sauce, stir, and simmer for 10 minutes. Serve with fried potatoes and fresh bakery bread (such as sourdough, rye, or French bread). Serves 3-4.

585) Fried Spam Sandwich

→ 1 can spam
→ Yellow mustard, optional
→ 2 slices of loaf bread
→ 3 Tbsp salted butter
→ iceberg lettuce
→ slice of tomato
→ mayonnaise
→ black pepper

Take spam out of can, rinse, pat dry. Cut into 1/4" thick slices. Melt butter, fry spam until golden,

flip and cook other side. Place on plate. Spread mayo on one bread slice, mustard on the other. Add spam, pepper, lettuce, tomato, and close sandwich. Cut diagonally into two triangles. Serves one.

Option: Toast bread if desired. We typically use untoasted bread.

586) Meatloaf Hamburgers

→ 1-1/2 lb. ground beef
→ 2 eggs
→ 1/2 sleeve Saltine crackers
→ 5-6 shakes Worcestershire sauce
→ 1/2 tsp salt
→ 1/2 tsp black pepper
→ 1 pkg onion soup mix, Lipton
→ 1/2 tsp roasted garlic powder, Badia

Mix all ingredients above well - shape into 6 hamburger patties. Preheat the skillet on medium heat. Add 1/4" of oil. Fry patties until no pink is left in center. Time varies due to size and thickness of burgers. Ground beef should be cooked until well done. Butter and Toast Buns. Top burgers with topping below.

Meatloaf Topping: 3/4 cup ketchup, 3 Tbsp brown sugar, 1/2 tsp onion powder. Whisk all the ingredients well, then microwave for 1 minute. Serve on burgers

587) Open-Faced Tuna Loaf

→ 1 large loaf of Italian bread
→ salted butter, softened
→ 6-8 oz. Monterey Jack cheese, sliced thin
→ two 6 oz. cans of tuna, drained
→ 1/3 to 1/2 cup mayonnaise
→ 1/4 cup chopped parsley (1 Tbsp reserved for garnish)
→ dash pepper
→ Fresh Lemon juice

Slice bread in half lengthwise and butter both halves. Place the bread, buttered side up, on a baking sheet. Cover both halves with cheese slices. Mix remaining ingredients, adjusting mayonnaise to taste. Spread on top of cheesecovered bread. Broil 3" from the heat for about 10 minutes or until lightly browned. Recipe makes 8 servings. This recipe can be halved using only half a loaf and 1 can of tuna.

 As you can see in the picture above, loaf bread works great for this sandwich! I adjusted the cheese to go on top instead of the bottom.

588) Sloppy Joes

→ 1-1/2 lb. ground chuck, brown & drain
→ 1 medium onion, chopped
→ 1/2 bell pepper, chopped

→ 2 garlic cloves (or 1/2 tsp garlic Powder)
→ 2 tsp onion powder
→ 1/4 tsp chili powder
→ 1 tsp black pepper
→ 1 tsp salt
→ 3 shakes Worcestershire
→ 8 oz. can tomato sauce
→ 8 oz. ketchup
→ 1 Tbsp yellow mustard
→ 1/4 cup sweet pickle relish

In a large skillet, brown ground beef with onion and peppers. Drain grease off the meat, then add the remaining ingredients. Simmer on low heat for 10 minutes. Serve on hamburger buns. Great for a quick supper with Lays Potato Chips!

"You are never too old to enjoy a good sloppy joe! They are so exceptionally good with potato chips and good Coca-Cola."– *Tammy*

589) Turkey Parmesan Sandwich

→ deli smoked turkey slices
→ 2 slices of thick-sliced loaf bread
→ marinated mushrooms
→ sliced or shredded mozzarella
→ pizza sauce or marinara
→ grated parmesan, optional

Evenly butter bread pieces. Flip and spread marinara on the non-buttered side, then add turkey and cheese. Place it in a non-stick pan with butter side down. Sauté mushrooms in the pan. Cook until bread is golden. Remove from the heat, add the mushrooms, and then close the sandwich. Cut diagonally into two triangles. Serves one.

 There should be enough exposed surface in the pan to cook mushrooms with the sandwich.

Recipe#602

Sauces, Gravy & Spice Recipes

Essential Sauces, Gravy, and Seasonings for Every Kitchen

This section features a variety of recipes and tips for creating flavorful sauces, rich gravies, and essential spice blends to elevate any meal. From classic pasta sauces to creative condiments, you will find simple instructions and ingredient lists designed to help both beginners and seasoned cooks add delicious depth to their dishes. Giblet gravy plays a crucial role in enhancing chicken and dressing,

Recipe#605

providing both moisture and a rich, savory flavor that elevates the entire dish. The deep, meaty notes from the gravy complement the tender chicken and seasoned dressing, creating a harmonious blend that is a staple at traditional meals. Without giblet gravy, the dish may lack the depth and comfort that make it so beloved, especially during holidays and family gatherings.

590) Alfredo Pasta & Sauce

- → 12 oz. pasta
- → 1/2 cup salted butter
- → 1 clove garlic, pressed
- → 2 cups heavy cream
- → 2 cups fresh grated parmesan
- → 1/2 tsp. salt
- → 1/2 tsp. black pepper
- → pinch of nutmeg

Cook pasta according to package instructions minus 2 minutes, then drain. In a medium saucepan over medium heat, melt the butter. Add garlic and cook, stirring often, until fragrant, for about 2 minutes. Stir in cream and bring it to a simmer. Cook, stirring occasionally, until the sauce thickens slightly, about 10 minutes. Remove the pot from heat. Gradually whisk in the Parmesan until the sauce is smooth and creamy. Mix in salt, pepper, and nutmeg.

"Do not pay the high prices at the Restaurant. Simple and so delicious." – *Tammy*

591) C.V.C. Barbeque Sauce

- → 2/3 cup apple cider vinegar
- → 1/2 cup dark cane syrup, or molasses
- → 1 tsp coarse black pepper or use 1/2 tsp. black pepper for mild sauce
- → 1/2 tsp cayenne pepper, omit for mild sauce
- → 1/2 tsp roasted garlic powder
- → 1 tsp yellow mustard
- → 1 cup tomato sauce
- → 1 tsp salt
- → 1 tsp onion powder
- → 1 cup water
- → 1 cup light brown sugar, packed
- → 1 tsp smoked paprika
- → 1-1/2 cups of ketchup

Bring all ingredients to a boil and then simmer for 20 minutes. Store in a Mason jar in the refrigerator for up to 6 months.

 Omit cayenne and half of the black pepper for a milder sauce.

Having a gravy whisk is very helpful when making sauces and gravies. Get yours today by scanning the QR code on the right.

"As an Amazon Associate, I earn from qualifying purchases."

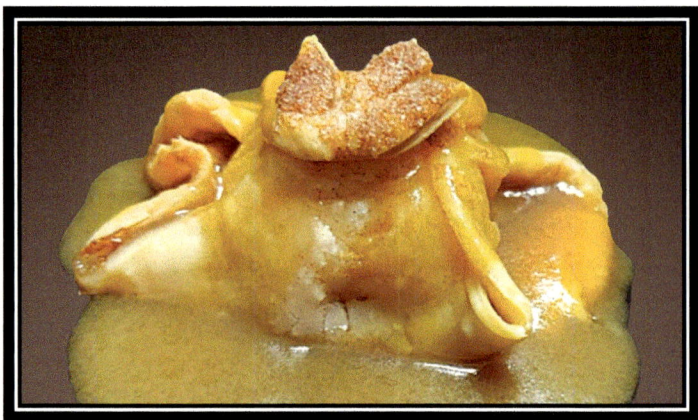

592) Caramel Sauce

- → 1/2 cup salted butter
- → 1/2 cup evaporated milk or whipping cream
- → 3/4 cup light brown sugar, packed
- → 2 tsp corn syrup
- → 1 tsp vanilla extract.

Melt butter in a small saucepan, then add brown sugar and corn syrup. Stir until well combined over low heat until the sugar begins to melt. Add milk and whisk thoroughly. Increase the heat and bring to a boil. Once boiling, reduce the heat to a low simmer and set a timer for 3 minutes. Remove from heat and stir in vanilla. Whisk well, then pour into a pint-sized mason jar for serving.

593) Cheese Sauce

- → 2 cups of shredded Mexican blend cheese
- → 3/4 cup half and half
- → 1/4 cup water

Microwave on 1-minute intervals and mix with a fork or whisk until creamy. Put in a liquid measuring cup for easy pouring. Note: Cheese will be creamier if you grate fresh cheese instead of using the pre-grated cheese

594) Chicken Broth Gravy

→ 1/2 cup flour in a sifter
→ 1/2 cup shortening (or 1/2 cup salted butter)
→ 1/2 tsp pepper
→ 1 tsp salt
→ 3 cups of chicken broth

Melt the shortening in a large skillet over medium heat. Once melted, turn up to medium/high. Add butter and sift flour quickly into the shortening. Use a wire whisk to blend thoroughly, season with pepper, then brown slightly. Add broth and stir constantly, scraping the skillet. Whisk to prevent lumps. Pour out when it thickens; it will thicken more after. If it is too thick, add milk and whisk to desired consistency. Add salt if needed.

 Option: Replace the chicken broth with 3 cups of water mixed with 1 Tbsp Knorr chicken bouillon granules, delete salt.

595) Chocolate Gravy

→ 1/2 cup granulated sugar
→ 3 Tbsp Hershey's cocoa
→ 1/8 cup flour
→ 1 cup milk
→ dash of salt
→ 1 tsp vanilla
→ 1/8 cup salted butter

Melt butter in a skillet, then whisk in the flour. Combine the sugar and cocoa and add to the skillet. Whisk in milk and keep whisking constantly until it becomes smooth and creamy. Remove from heat once it thickens and transfer to a glass bowl. (You can add more milk and whisk if it gets too thick). Add vanilla and enjoy gravy with hot biscuits!

596) Chocolate Sauce

→ 1 cup granulated sugar
→ 1/2 cup cocoa, Hershey's
→ 1/2 cup cold milk
→ 1/8 tsp salt
→ 1 tsp vanilla extract
→ 1 Tbsp salted butter

In a dry saucepan, whisk together the cocoa and sugar until all lumps are gone. Add the salt and milk, then bring to a boil over medium-high heat. Reduce to a gentle simmer, stirring constantly. Simmer for about 30 seconds, then remove the pan from the heat. Add the vanilla and butter. Pour into a glass jar and let cool. {The chocolate sauce will be very thin when it finishes boiling, but it will thicken quite a bit as it cools.

597) Chris's Special Seasoning

→ 2 tsp cayenne pepper
→ 2 tsp black pepper
→ 2 tsp white pepper
→ 4 tsp paprika
→ 4 tsp salt

Place seasonings in a small container with a lid and shake well. Put the seasoning in a saltshaker and label it for frying foods. This is amazing in our Famous Fried Chicken!

"Enjoy my special blend of spices." – *Chris*

598) Chris's Rib Rub Recipe

→ 1/2 cup granulated sugar
→ 1/2 cup light brown sugar
→ 2 Tbsp cayenne pepper, omit for mild rub
→ 1/2 cup paprika
→ 2 Tbsp onion powder
→ 1/2 cup kosher salt
→ 1/2 cup coarse ground black pepper

Blend spices well and store in an air-tight container.

599) Dippen Chicken Sauce

- → 1/2 cup mayonnaise
- → 1/2 tsp pepper
- → 1/4 cup ketchup
- → 1 tsp Worcestershire sauce
- → 1 tsp garlic powder
- → 1/4 tsp cayenne pepper, optional

In a glass bowl, combine all ingredients and blend well. Serve with chicken, pork, fish, or seafood. Best if made the day ahead. Store in the refrigerator.

600) Enchilada Sauce

- → 1/4 cup cooking oil
- → 2 Tbsp flour
- → 1/4 cup chili powder
- → large garlic clove, diced or pressed.
- → 1 Tbsp diced onion
- → 8 oz. can tomato sauce
- → 1 1/2 cup water
- → 1/2 tsp ground cumin
- → 1 tsp salt
- → 1/2 cup ketchup

Add oil to hot skillet. Add flour and whisk well. Add chili powder, garlic, onion, tomato sauce and whisk well. Add water, cumin, salt, and ketchup and whisk well. Turn down to simmer and simmer for 10 minutes. Cool down and pour in jar for refrigerator storage. Store up to 3-4 weeks.

"This is even better than what you would get in a restaurant!"– *Chris*

601) Meatloaf Topping

- → 3/4 cup ketchup
- → 3 Tbsp light brown sugar
- → 1/2 tsp onion powder

Whisk all the ingredients well and add them to the meatloaf during the last 15 minutes of baking. This is good on meatloaf, hamburger steak, and hamburgers.

 If using this sauce for something other than meatloaf, cover it and microwave for 1 minute before serving.

602) Hot Dog Chili Sauce

- → 1 lb. ground chuck
- → 1 medium onion, chopped
- → 1/4 cup bell pepper, red & green, chopped
- → 1 Tbsp chili powder
- → 1/2 tsp basil
- → 8 oz. can tomato sauce
- → 1/2 tsp salt
- → 1/2 tsp black pepper
- → 1 clove garlic, pressed

Brown ground chuck with onions and peppers. Drain off excess grease (use paper towels to absorb it). Add remaining ingredients and simmer for 10 minutes. For Hillbilly Dogs, serve over a loaf of bread instead of on a bun!

603) Honey Mustard

- → 1 cup mayonnaise
- → 1 cup sour cream
- → 3 Tbsp yellow mustard
- → 3 Tbsp honey

In a glass bowl, combine all ingredients and whisk until well blended. Serve with chicken, pork, fish, or seafood. Store in the refrigerator.

604) Smokey Honey Mustard

- → 1 cup mayonnaise
- → 1 cup sour cream
- → 3 Tbsp yellow mustard
- → 3 Tbsp honey
- → 2 Tbsp. BBQ sauce

In a glass bowl, combine all ingredients and whisk until well blended. Serve with chicken, pork, fish, or seafood. Store in the refrigerator.

"This is similar to Chick-fil-a Sauce."– *Chris*

605) Giblet Gravy, Mama's

→ giblets from a fryer chicken or turkey
→ (neck, liver, heart & gizzard)
→ 1 tsp meat tenderizer

Boil giblets per Recipe #607

Giblet Gravy:

→ 1 cup milk
→ 1 can cream of chicken soup
→ 1 cup chicken stock
→ 1 Tbsp vegetable shortening
→ 2 Tbsp salted butter

Mix milk, cream of mushroom, and chicken stock in a medium bowl or a 4-cup glass measuring cup and set aside. Melt shortening and butter in a large skillet.

→ 3 Tbsp self-rising cornmeal mix
→ 2 Tbsp flour
→ 1/4 tsp salt
→ 1/4 tsp black pepper
→ Hard-boiled egg, chopped is optional

Turn the heat to medium/high and add cornmeal, flour, salt, and pepper. Whisk constantly until browned. Pour in the milk/soup mixture and stir until slightly thickened. Mix in the giblets. Pour into a serving dish.

Option: Mama chopped up a boiled egg and put it in her gravy.

606) Giblet Gravy –Granny's

→ 1 Tbsp shortening
→ 2 Tbsp salted butter
→ 3 Tbsp self-rising cornmeal mix
→ 2 Tbsp flour
→ 3/4 tsp salt
→ 1/2 tsp black pepper
→ 1 cup chicken broth
→ 1 cup milk
→ cooked tenderized & chopped giblets

→ 1 hard-boiled egg, chopped is optional
→ Boil giblets per Recipe #606

Melt shortening and butter in an iron skillet. Add cornmeal and flour. Add salt and pepper, then whisk until well blended. Let the flour brown slightly for a better flavor! You will start to smell it as it browns. Keep cooking until it turns a golden brown. Add milk and broth, then whisk well. When it begins to thicken, add eggs and giblets. Pour into a serving bowl. Serve over cornbread dressing!

607) How to Cook Giblets:

Boil them in water with 1 tsp meat tenderizer. Boil on medium heat for 30 minutes. Add water as needed to keep them covered. Remove, discard, and chop the fat, bone, and gristle, then chop the meat.

"This is my Granny Benefield's recipe." -*Tammy*

608) Poultry Pan Sauce (Gravy)

→ 1 cup turkey or chicken stock
→ 2 Tbsp corn starch
→ salt and black pepper
→ 3 Tbsp salted butter
→ sliced turkey or chicken

Warm your poultry slices in a skillet with a little butter. Flip and warm the other side, then remove and set aside. Place butter in the pan and melt. Mix cornstarch into the stock and whisk until smooth. Pour the stock into the skillet and use a spoon to scrape up any drippings from the pan into the stock. Add salt if needed. Serve over the poultry slices!

609) Red Eye Gravy

→ 1 piece of slab ham (salt-cured or smoked)
→ 2 Tbsp salted butter
→ 6 oz. strong coffee, instant or brewed.

In an iron skillet, add pieces of ham and butter. Fry at a low/medium temp. until nice and brown. Take out and put on a serving plate. Scrape out any burn drippings and pour off excess grease, then pour the hot coffee into the skillet. Pour it into a serving bowl and serve over breakfast foods.

"I love redeye gravy on Christmas morning on top of my grits!" -*Tammy*

610) Tartar Sauce

→ 2 Tbsp minced onion
→ 1 Tbsp sweet pickle relish
→ 1/2 cup mayonnaise
→ 1/8 tsp roasted garlic powder, Bidia
→ 1/4 tsp black pepper

In a glass bowl, combine all ingredients and mix well. Serve with fish or seafood. It is great, but even better if made a day ahead. Store in the refrigerator.

611) Tomato Gravy

→ 1/2 large onion, chopped
→ 15 oz. can petite diced tomatoes
→ 6 oz. can tomato paste
→ 2 cups hot water
→ 2 tsp beef bouillon granules
→ 2 Tbsp shortening
→ 2 Tbsp salted butter
→ 1/4 cup self-rising flour
→ 1 tsp salt
→ 1/2 tsp black pepper
→ 1 cup milk
→ 1/4 tsp salt

Cook the onion and tomatoes in a saucepan on medium heat until soft. Blend tomato paste with hot water, then add bouillon and whisk well. In a large deep skillet, add shortening. Place the skillet on medium/high heat until the shortening is melted, then add butter. Sift the flour into the skillet and whisk until well blended. Add salt and pepper. Cook until golden brown. Add the tomato/water mixture, milk, and sugar. Whisk until creamy, then add the diced tomato/onion mixture. Remove from heat and serve over homemade, open-faced buttermilk biscuits.

"Some people enjoy this with meatloaf, hamburger steaks, or serving it with rice and fish. Many also love eating it for breakfast alongside biscuits." – *Tammy*

612) A Healthier Tomato Gravy

→ 3 Tbsp olive oil
→ 1/2 medium onion, peeled, chopped
→ 2 Tbsp margarine spread (Smart Balance or other equivalent)
→ 15 oz. can petite diced tomatoes Or 2 fresh tomatoes, cut up
→ 1 cup hot water
→ 2 tsp beef bouillon, better than bouillon, low sodium if needed
→ 5 oz. can tomato sauce
→ 1/2 cup cold skim milk
→ 3 Tbsp corn starch
→ 5 oz. can tomato sauce
→ salt & black pepper to taste

Sauté onions in oil and butter until soft. Add tomatoes and simmer 2 minutes. Mix hot water, tomato sauce, and bouillon; whisk well. Pour broth into tomatoes. Whisk cornstarch and cold milk; add to gravy. Cook 5-8 minutes on medium until thickened and clear.

"Serve over Biscuits, Meatloaf, or Hamburger Steaks." – *Tammy*

613) White Milk Gravy

→ 1/2 cup self-rising flour, in sifter
→ 1/2 cup shortening or salted butter
→ 1 tsp salt
→ 1/2 tsp black pepper
→ 3 cups milk

Start with a large skillet, at least 10 inches (larger if available). Melt shortening or butter over medium heat. Turn to medium-high. Sift flour quickly into the melted fat. Mix thoroughly with a wire whisk. Add salt and pepper. Let the flour brown to golden, then add milk; you will smell a great aroma as it browns. Stir constantly, scraping bottom and sides, to prevent lumps. Pour when it thickens; it will continue to thicken. If it is too thick, add a bit of milk and whisk until desired consistency.

Summer Supper: Serve over biscuits with sliced cantaloupe. "Family Favorite"

"Mama used shortening instead of butter. Over the years, I have replaced it with butter and now prefer the butter gravy. You can choose which to use or mix half and half. Margarine will not work as well as butter, as it contains water." – *Tammy*

Soup & Stew Recipes

I want to share a family favorite of ours: Benefield Chicken. Since my maiden name is Benefield, it feels special to talk about this dish that Mama made for us until she couldn't cook anymore due to her health. When we were kids, one night she surprised us with this meal, and we loved it so much that we begged her to tell us what it was called. To our delight, she decided to name it Benefield Chicken, and we were all thrilled! The idea of a recipe carrying our family name was just amazing to us. We constantly asked her to whip it up for us; it was that good.

Mama's kitchen was always busy. The stovetop was built right into the countertop, and the oven was in the wall. There was a little pass-through into the dining room where we could stand and watch her cook. We spent so much time hanging out there, and I honestly think that's why all of us turned out to be great cooks.

Watching her flip bacon, roll biscuits, and make dinner felt like a hands-on masterclass, and she didn't even realize it! Most kids didn't have the chance to see their mamas cooking from this angle. I even made a little illustration to show how our kitchen was set up back in 1975 so you can see how we could stand and see from the other side.

Our kitchen had oak cabinets with yellow countertops and olive green appliances. I wish I had a picture, but the place was remodeled by my younger brother, Eddie, who lives there now. The original house was about 1450 square feet. The girls shared a room, and the boys shared another. So many memories and delicious meals came out of that kitchen!

I can still see mama standing in that corner you see there. She is standing over her biscuit tupperware bowl and mixing up biscuits by hand. She would then pinch off a piece, roll it, and put it in the pan. She made biscuits daily.

Some of my favorite things that she made include old-fashioned fudge, chicken and dumplings, blackberry cobbler, spaghetti served with biscuits, waffles, homemade cinnamon rolls, and so much more! All the recipes are included in this cookbook for you to share with your family. She also made blackberry preserves and blackberry candy! The list goes on and on in my head, and I now realize how blessed I was to have a mom who could cook! Just think, with these recipes and my video tutorials, you can learn to cook just like my mom did! - *Tammy*

614) Benefield Chicken

→ Recipe #116, boil a chicken
→ 10.5 oz. can cream of chicken
→ 1/2 tsp black pepper
→ 1/2 tsp salt
→ 1/2 tsp garlic salt
→ 5 large carrots, wash & peel
→ 5 med/large potatoes, wash & peel
→ 1 whole onion, peel & chop

Bring the reserved chicken and broth from boiling the chicken to a boil. Add cream of chicken, salt, pepper, and garlic salt. Stir the spices into the broth. Cut the carrots in half, then quarter, and add them to the broth. Cut the potatoes into quarter pieces and add them to the broth. Add the onion. Simmer on medium-high heat until the vegetables are tender. Thicken the broth with:

→ 1/3 cup flour mixed with 1-1/2 cups of cold milk

Whisk the flour and milk together thoroughly, ensuring no lumps remain. Add the mixture to your pot and turn up the heat to thicken the broth. Once thickened, it is ready to serve. We love this served over open-faced homemade biscuits.

"Mama made this Benefield Chicken when we were little. We asked her what it was when she served it to us. She said, "I do not know, I just created it tonight. We told her she had to name it. She named it our family name, and we thought that was the coolest thing ever!"– *Tammy*

615) Beef Stew, Dutch Oven

→ 1/2 cup salted butter
→ 2-3 lb. meat stew beef
→ 5 6 red potatoes washed and cut
→ 3 stalks celery, cut small
→ 1 medium onion, cut into 1" pieces.
→ 1 lb. carrots, peel, cut into 1" pieces
→ 14.5 oz. can stewed tomatoes, not Italian
→ 14.5 oz. can diced tomatoes
→ 3 Tbsp soy sauce
→ 4 Tbsp corn starch
→ 1 can water

Preheat oven to 350°F. In a Dutch oven on medium heat, melt a stick of butter. Add stew meat and brown, then turn off heat. Add both cans of tomatoes. Add potatoes, celery, onion, and carrots.

Fill one of the cans with water, about 1/2 inch below the top. Add cornstarch and beat well with a whisk or fork. Add soy sauce and stir, making sure the starch is off the bottom of the can. Pour into the Dutch oven and add a little more water to the stew if the vegetables are not covered. Put the lid on the Dutch oven, slide it into the preheated oven, and cook for 3 hours.

Crockpot Instructions:

Same as above but add the butter to the bottom of the crock pot before adding the other ingredients. Cook on low for 8 hours. (Roast and beef tips should be cooked on low to stay tender.)

Using a slow cooker liner is recommended for easy cleanup and leftovers storage.

616) Butterbean Soup

- → 16 oz. butterbeans, dried
- → 2 tsp chicken bouillon granules
- → 1 package of cubed ham or leftover ham, chopped
- → 1/4 onion, sliced thin
- → 1 tsp salt
- → 1/4 tsp black pepper
- → 1/4 tsp white pepper
- → 1/2 tsp dill
- → 1/4 tsp ground mustard

Cover the beans in a large saucepan with water, ensuring the water level is 2 inches above the beans. Add all the listed ingredients, stir them, and bring them to a boil. Boil for 20 minutes. Then, add more water to cover the beans and put the lid on the pot. Reduce the heat to low and simmer until the beans are fork tender. Turn off the heat until you are ready to serve. Serve with Recipe #125.

"Enjoy on a cold night in front of a burning fireplace. Delicious!"– *Tammy*

617) Beef Stew, Hardy Tomato

- → 2.5 to 3-lb. sirloin or chuck roast, cubed
- → 1/2 cup self-rising or plain flour
- → 1/8 cup olive oil
- → 1 large onion, chopped
- → 2 bay leaves
- → 2-8 oz. can diced tomatoes
- → 7 oz. can tomato paste, optional
- → 1 tsp Penzey's beef roast spice or use 1/8 cup brown gravy mix
- → 2 tsp steak seasoning, Weber Steak n Chop
- → 4 shakes Worcestershire sauce
- → 3/4 cup frozen or canned green peas
- → 1 lb. bag baby peeled carrots
- → 3-4 large potatoes cubed into 1" pieces
- → 1 cup frozen shoe peg corn

→ 1 packet onion soup mix

Toss the beef in flour and brown in a Dutch oven with olive oil over medium-high heat. Remove beef and set aside. Add onion, bay leaves, some tomato juice (from diced tomatoes), spice or gravy mix, and simmer 4-5 minutes. Return beef, add remaining tomatoes, steak n chop, Worcestershire, and 1 cup water. Lower heat or use crock pot, simmer for 4 hours, stirring occasionally. Add 2 cups water, peas, carrots, potatoes, corn, soup mix, and tomato paste (optional), and simmer 2 hours. Serve with cornbread! ENJOY!

618) Chicken Bone Broth Stock

- → young fryer chicken, not a hen
- → 1 large carrot cut into four sections
- → 2 stalks of celery (cut into large sections)
- → 1 stick of salted butter
- → 2 Tbsp chicken bouillon granules
- → 1 onion (peeled & quartered)

Boil the chicken with the ingredients above, breast-side down, on a low simmer for 2 hours to flavor the stock. Remove chicken with two large spoons and place on a platter. (Remove from bones after cooling.) Discard bones and fat; strain the broth into a large pot or bowl to remove any floating vegetable pieces and skin.

 NOTE: When you boil a chicken this long, the broth is "bone broth". This means that when cooled, it will resemble a gel instead of a liquid. This is because the gelatin in the bone is transferred into the broth.

Pour stock into quart mason jars, place lids, and wipe with soapy water. Refrigerate. The chicken and butter fat create a seal on top. With a good airtight seal (from fat), store in the fridge for up to 4 months.

Once the seal is broken, use it within 3 days.

619) Irish Beef Stew
- → olive oil
- → 2 lb. boneless beef chuck roast, cut in 1" pieces
- → salt & black pepper
- → 1 medium onion, chopped
- → 3 medium carrots, peel, cut into 1" pieces
- → 3 medium parsnips, peel, cut into 1" pieces, optional ingredient
- → 8-10 oz. white mushrooms, sliced
- → 2 cloves of garlic, pressed
- → 1 tsp dried thyme
- → 1 tsp dried rosemary
- → 2 bay leaves
- → 12 to 15 oz. Guinness stout beer, stout beer
- → 2 1/2 cups of beef broth
- → 1 Tbsp Dijon mustard
- → 1 Tbsp tomato paste
- → 1 Tbsp Worcestershire sauce
- → 1 lb. small yellow potatoes, halved
- → chopped fresh parsley, optional

Heat 2 Tbsp oil in a Dutch oven. Season beef with salt and pepper; cook 5 minutes, browning all sides. Remove. Add 2 Tbsp oil and onions; cook 3 minutes. Add carrots, parsnips, and mushrooms; season and cook 8 minutes until mushrooms release liquid. Add garlic, thyme, rosemary, bay leaves, Guinness, broth, mustard, tomato paste, and Worcestershire; bring to boil, scraping browned bits. Return beef, lower heat, cook 1.5 hours. Add potatoes, add water if needed, cook 30 minutes until tender. Serve with parsley.

620) Brunswick Stew, Easy
- → Recipe #116 Boil a chicken
- → 1 large onion chopped
- → 6 potatoes, chopped small
- → 2 tsp chicken bouillon granules
- → 2 tsp beef bouillon granules
- → Worcestershire sauce 5-6 dashes
- → 28 oz can crushed tomatoes
- → 14.5 can green lima beans, drained or

frozen lima beans
- → 1/2 tsp liquid smoke
- → 2 ears fresh corn cut off cob (or can kernel corn drained)
- → salt and pepper to taste
- → 4 cups chicken stock
- → 1/2 cup tomato ketchup

Add ingredients above to a stockpot and simmer slowly all day until thick. Serve over loaf bread.

621) Chicken & Dumplings
- → Recipe #116 Boil a chicken
- → Recipe #162 Dumplings, double Recipe
- → 2-10.5 oz. cans cream of chicken
- → 1 tsp salt & 1/2 tsp black pepper
- → Water

Read Recipe #162 entirely before starting this recipe.

In a large stockpot, bring broth with 4 cups water to a boil. Add canned soup, salt, and pepper, and stir well. Drop the dumplings into the boiling broth. Stir occasionally with care. Once all the dumplings are in, turn the heat down to the lowest setting. Cover the pot with a lid and cook for 10 minutes. Open the lid and stir the dumplings every 2-3 minutes to prevent them from sticking to the bottom. The broth should thicken. If the broth does not thicken, add:

- → 1/3 cup self-rising flour
- → 1-1/2 cups cold milk

To a small bowl. Mix the flour and milk thoroughly with a whisk, then add them to the broth. Add the chicken and stir. Dumplings should change texture when they are finished cooking; they will look flatter. It should be ready 15 minutes after adding the dumplings.

"These are the best chicken and dumplings you will ever eat; I promise!" – *Tammy*

622) Chicken Noodle Soup

→ Recipe #116 Boil a Chicken
→ All chicken broth from Recipe #116
→ 1/3 cup salted butter
→ 10.5 oz. can cream of chicken soup
→ stalk of celery, diced
→ optional: 3 carrots, peel & dice
→ 1/4 cup chives (or sliced green onions)
→ add 1/2 lb. to 1 lb. of chopped chicken, chop chicken in small pieces
→ 1 lb. spaghetti noodles or other pasta

Add stock, butter, soup, celery, onion, and chicken to a large stockpot. Add carrots if you use them. Bring it to a boil and cook for 20 minutes. Stir the soup well. Add pasta to the pot and bring to a boil. Cook for 10 minutes. Serve the soup with crackers. Add additional salt and pepper if desired. Garnish with fresh parsley if desired.

"This has always been our go-to chili recipe! It has the perfect balance of spices. Hot sauce can be added to your bowl if you like it HOT!"– *Tammy*

623) Chili

→ 3 Tbsp olive oil
→ 1 medium onion, chopped
→ 1 bell pepper, chopped
→ 1 lb. ground chuck brown & drain
→ 2 cloves garlic, pressed
→ 2 14.5 oz. cans diced tomatoes
→ 16 oz. can black beans
→ 2-16 oz. cans kidney beans
→ 15 oz. can tomato sauce
→ 2 cups water
→ 1 tsp basil
→ 1/2 tsp black pepper
→ 1 tsp salt
→ 3 Tbsp chili powder

Sauté onions and peppers in olive oil until they are soft. Add the ground beef and cook until it is browned and no pink remains. Drain excess grease from the meat. Transfer the cooked beef to a large stockpot or a slow cooker. Add the remaining ingredients and stir well.

Crock pot:

Use a slow cooker liner. Add drained beef and remaining ingredients. Cook on low for 6 hours or high for 4 hours or until very hot and bubbly. (Use your own judgement on how long to cook, depending on how hot your individual appliance gets.)

Stovetop:

Cook on medium-low heat for at least 1 hour. Serve with your favorite condiments.

 Add hot sauce or diced chilis, if desired.
Using a slow cooker liner is recommended for easy cleanup.

624) Chili for Two

→ 1/4 cup onion, chopped
→ 1/4 cup bell pepper, chopped
→ 2 Tbsp olive oil
→ 1/2 lb. ground chuck
→ 10 oz. can Rotel with mild chilies (or 14.5 oz can petite diced tomatoes)
→ 16 oz. can kidney beans with juice
→ 1 cup water
→ 8 oz. can tomato sauce
→ 1 tsp basil
→ 1/2 tsp black pepper
→ 3/4 tsp salt
→ 1 Tbsp chili powder

Sauté onions and peppers in olive oil in a stockpot, then add ground beef. Brown the ground beef and drain any excess fat.

Add beef and remaining ingredients. Stir well.

Stovetop:

Cook on medium-low heat for at least 1 hour. Serve with your favorite condiments.

Add hot sauce or diced chilis, if desired.

Crock pot: Use a slow cooker liner. Add drained beef and remaining ingredients. Cook on low for 6 hours or on high for 3-4 hours. Add hot sauce or diced chilis if desired. Serves 2-4.

Chili is great served with sour cream and fritos!

625) Chili, Double Meat

→ 1-1/2 pounds ground chuck, cook & drain
→ 2 lb. beef roast, cubed
→ 1/2 cup all-purpose flour
→ Steak seasoning, Weber steak n chop
→ 1 large onion, chopped
→ 1 bell pepper, chopped
→ 4 large garlic cloves, pressed
→ 5 Tbsp olive oil
→ 2- 15 oz. cans diced tomatoes
→ 2- 16 oz. cans kidney beans with juice
→ 16 oz. can pinto beans with juice
→ 16 oz. can black beans with juice
→ 15 oz. can tomato sauce
→ 2-8 oz. can crushed tomatoes
→ 2 Tbsp basil
→ 1 tsp black pepper
→ 2 tsp salt
→ 6 Tbsp chili powder
→ 1/2 cup ketchup

Sauté onions, garlic & pepper with olive oil in a stockpot, then add ground beef. Brown the ground beef, drain it, and set it aside. Season roast cubes with steak seasoning. Dredge with flour—Brown in stockpot with 2 Tbsp olive oil. Add ground beef. Add remaining ingredients. Stir well.

Crock pot: Cook low 6 hours or high 3-4 hours.

Stovetop: Cook on low heat for 1 hour or more. Stirring occasionally to prevent sticking.

Add hot sauce or diced chilis if desired.

626) Chili, White Chicken

→ 1 onion, chopped
→ 2 cups water
→ 2 Tbsp chicken bouillon granules
→ 10 oz. can Rotel with mild chilies
→ 14.5 oz kernel corn, drained (optional)
→ 2-16 oz. cans navy beans
→ 1 Tbsp & 1/2 tsp ground cumin

→ 1 tsp oregano
→ 1 tsp roasted garlic powder, Bidia or 1 fresh garlic clove pressed
→ rotisserie chicken's meat, chopped
→ 8 oz. block pepper jack cheese

Combine the above ingredients (except the cheese) in a medium saucepan and cook over medium-low heat for 1 hour. Add grated pepper jack cheese and serve with Frito scoops.

 Can be used as a bean dip if you reduce the water to 1 cup. Use a non-stick pot and heat it until boiling. Then, continue cooking until most of the broth has evaporated. Add cheese and serve hot.

627) Corn Chowder, Easy

→ 3 Tbsp salted butter
→ 1 large carrot, chopped small
→ 1 stalk celery, chopped
→ 1/3 cup onion, chopped
→ 1/2 lb. smoked sausage, cut bite-size
→ 1 cup cold water
→ 3 Tbsp flour
→ 1/4 tsp paprika
→ 1/2 tsp salt
→ 1/2 tsp celery salt
→ 1/4 tsp black pepper
→ 12 oz. or 14 oz can corn with peppers
→ 1 can regular or shoe peg corn, drained
→ 2 1/2 cups of cheddar cheese, shredded
→ 1/2 cup evaporated milk
→ 1/2 cup water

Sauté butter, carrots, celery, and onion with smoked sausage for 10 minutes on medium heat. In a cup, mix cold water and flour with a fork or whisk very well - add to simmered veggies. Now add remaining ingredients (minus the cheese). Turn burner down to low and mix well. Add cheese and serve!

628) Tammy's Crazy Soup

This is very similar to Mexican Soup
- → 2 chicken breasts, bone in
- → 2 tsp chicken bouillon granules

Place ingredients in saucepan. Cover with water and simmer 1.5 hours-turn off and let cool. Pick meat from bones (keep broth and meat for soup). Discard bones and skin.

- → 2 cups chicken stock
- → 15 oz. can chili with beans
- → 2-8 oz. can petite diced tomatoes
- → 2-8 oz. can pinto beans, drained
- → 7 oz. frozen shoe peg corn, white
- → medium jar of salsa
- → medium onion, chopped
- → 1 tsp onion powder
- → 1 Tbsp taco seasoning
- → 1/2 tsp black pepper
- → 1/2 tsp salt
- → 2 Tbsp fajita seasoning, Bidia
- → 15 oz. can kidney or black beans

Add above ingredients to large stockpot. Cook on medium heat for 15 minutes, then turn down to a simmer. Be careful not to let it stick to bottom of pot. Serve in a bowl with:

- → sour cream, shredded Mexican cheese, and tortilla chips!

629) Potato Soup (Simple)
- → 4-5 medium/large russet potatoes, peel and chop into 3/4-inch pieces
- → 1 tsp chicken bouillon granules
- → 1 cup half & half
- → 2 Tbsp corn starch
- → 1/4 tsp black pepper
- → 1/2 tsp salt
- → 3-4 Tbsp salted butter

Put potatoes in a medium saucepan. Add enough water to cover the potatoes. Stir in the bouillon and bring to a boil over medium/high heat. Once boiling, set a timer and cook for 12 minutes. In a glass measuring cup, combine the half and half, cornstarch, pepper, and salt. Whisk well. Add this mixture to the potatoes when the timer goes off. Turn the heat to medium/high and add the butter. Stir well. Simmer for 5 minutes and then serve.

 Optional: add cheese, crumbled bacon, and sour cream if desired.

Serves one person per potato used.

TIP: DO NOT add skim or low-fat milk into boiling base, or it will curdle! Use halfand-half or whole milk.

630) Shrimp Bisque
- → 1/4 cup diced onion
- → 1/4 cup diced celery
- → 1/8 cup diced carrot
- → 1/3 cup salted butter
- → juice of a small lemon
- → 2 cups of chicken broth
- → 1 pinch of nutmeg
- → 1 pinch of marjoram
- → half a bay leaf
- → 1-1/2 cups of chopped raw shrimp
- → 1 cup cream (half & half or evaporated milk)
- → salt & black pepper

In a medium stockpot, combine the onion, celery, carrot, butter, and lemon juice. Cook on low for 10 minutes. Add broth, nutmeg, marjoram, and bay leaf, then simmer for 15 minutes. Remove the bay leaf. Add the shrimp and cook for 4 minutes. Do not overcook the shrimp. Stir in the cream and simmer for 1 more minute. Season with salt and pepper to taste and serve immediately.

Enjoy with Recipe #128, Cornbread that's been mixed with 1 cup of shredded cheddar cheese.

632) Sizzling Rice Soup

→ 4 cups of chicken broth
→ 2 smoked dried black mushrooms chopped thin. (soak ahead)
→ 2 tsp grated ginger
→ 3 green onions, diced
→ 1 tsp salt
→ 1/3 tsp black pepper
→ 1 chicken breast sliced very thin
→ trimmed pork chop sliced thin
→ 1/2-pound medium shrimp, deveined and heads and tails off
→ Chinese crispy noodles

Place the broth, mushrooms, ginger, onion, salt, and pepper in a large stockpot. Bring to a boil. Add chicken and pork and boil for 1 minute. (use a timer) Make sure the broth is boiling, then add shrimp and sticky rice! (Boil for 1 minute) Use a ladle and serve immediately with noodles. Serves 4-5 persons.

Find dried black mushrooms and chinese crispy noodles in the international section of the grocery store!

633) Split Pea Soup

→ 8 oz. dried split peas
→ 6-7 pearl onions
→ 4 cups of chicken broth
→ 1 tsp salt
→ 1/4 tsp black pepper
→ 5 Tbsp salted butter, divided

Place split peas in a saucepan and cover with chicken broth. Add salt and pepper. Peel 6 Pearl Onions and add them to the peas. Bring it to a boil and cook for 20 minutes. Remove from heat and let cool to room temperature. Ensure the peas are covered with liquid; add water if needed, then refrigerate overnight. Next, take out the peas and heat to medium. Add water if necessary to cover the peas. Simmer until tender. Strain the mixture or use an immersion blender to make a creamy soup. Stir in 3 tablespoons of butter. Add water as needed until creamy, then serve warm.

Use a hand-held mesh strainer, or immersion blender.

631) Jambalaya

→ 1/2 lb. bacon, cut into pieces
→ 1 lb. smoked sausage, sliced
→ 1 lb. chicken breast, cut into 1/2" cubes
→ 2 bell peppers, chopped
→ 2 medium onions, chopped
→ 1/2 cup celery, sliced
→ 1/2 cup carrot, sliced into thin strips
→ 1/2 cup green onion, diced
→ 4 cloves garlic, minced or pressed
→ 22-8 oz. tomato sauce or puree
→ 6 oz. can tomato paste
→ 1 quart chicken broth
→ 1 Tbsp chicken bouillon granules
→ 1 tsp chili powder
→ 1 tsp thyme
→ 1 tsp oregano
→ 1 tsp black pepper
→ 1/2 tsp cayenne
→ 2 bay leaves
→ 1-1/2 cups of uncooked rice
→ 1 cup water
→ 1 cup sliced okra

ADDED LATER:

→ 1/2 cup minced fresh parsley,
→ 1 lb. raw shrimp, without tails, and hot sauce to taste

In a Dutch oven, fry the bacon and sausage until crisp. Add the chicken and cook until it is no longer pink. Remove the meat and set it aside. Sauté peppers, onions, celery, carrots, and green onions in the drippings until tender. Add tomato sauce, paste, broth, and rice; stir until well combined. Incorporate the remaining ingredients (except shrimp and parsley). Cover the Dutch oven and bake at 350°F for 3 hours. Remove from the oven, add shrimp and parsley. Mix well, then return the mixture to the oven (uncovered) and cook for 15 minutes.

634) Steak and Dumplings

→ Onion, chopped
→ corn or vegetable oil
→ 3 cups beef stock
→ 5 cups water
→ 3 Tbsp beef bouillon granules or 2 Tbsp Dale seasoning
→ 1-1/2 lb. cubed steak, cut 1" wide pieces
→ salt & black pepper
→ onion powder
→ roasted garlic powder, Badia
→ Recipe #162 Dumplings, double recipe

Make dumplings first and have them handy. In a large skillet, preheat 1" of vegetable or corn oil on medium heat. Add chopped onion and fry until golden brown. Take it out and set aside.

Place the bouillon, water, and stock in a large pot, then cover and bring to a boil. As the stock heats up, cut the steak into pieces and arrange them in glass pie plates. Season the steak with salt, pepper, onion powder, and garlic powder. Then, coat each piece with flour by pressing it into the flour with your fingers. Drop a test piece of steak into the skillet, and when it sizzles nicely, add the rest. Deep fry steak pieces for 4 minutes or until golden brown. Take out and put on a paper towel-lined plate. In a broth pot, drop dumplings into the boiling broth once it reaches a good boil. Add fried steak and onions. Cover and simmer for 10 minutes before serving. Stir frequently to prevent dumplings from sticking to the bottom of the pot. The broth should thicken. If the broth does not thicken, add

→ 1/3 cup self-rising flour
→ 1-1/2 cups cold milk

To a small bowl. Mix the flour and milk thoroughly with a whisk, then add them to the broth. Dumplings should change texture when they are finished cooking; they will look flatter.

It should be ready 15 minutes after adding the dumplings.

635) Tomato Soup

→ 6 large tomatoes
→ 2 tsp beef bouillon granules
→ 2 cups water
→ 1/2 tsp onion powder
→ 1 tsp salt
→ 1/2 tsp black pepper
→ 1 tsp guacamole seasoning, optional
→ 1 Tbsp cornstarch
→ 1 cup milk
→ 1 Tbsp salted butter

Boil tomatoes until the skin turns loose. Peel the skins off the tomatoes and cut out their stem. Chop tomatoes and place them in a stockpot. Add bouillon, water, pepper, herbs, salt, and onion powder.

Cook for 30 minutes over medium heat, then strain the tomatoes and collect the juice. Place the juice in a saucepan. Put cornstarch and milk in a pint jar with a lid and shake well. Then, add the mixture to the soup along with the butter.

Taste and add salt and pepper if needed. Serve with homemade croutons, Recipe #14, and sour cream. Enjoy!

 OPTIONAL: Instead of straining the tomatoes, you can use an immersion blender or a regular blender and blend them well.

2-2-8 oz. Cans of plum tomatoes can be used as a substitute for fresh tomatoes.

636) Vegetable Beef Soup

- → 2 tsp beef bouillon granules
- → 1 Tbsp Mrs. Dash original blend
- → 4 medium russet potatoes, peeled, quartered, & cut
- → 2 large carrots, peeled and cut into rounds
- → 2 cups v8, or mixed vegetable juice
- → 2 cups water
- → 14.5 oz can plain diced tomatoes
- → 1 chopped onion
- → 1-1/2 lb. ground chuck, browned & drained
- → 1-1/2 cups frozen speckled butter beans
- → 1-1/2 cups frozen butter peas
- → 1-1/2 cups frozen shoe peg corn (do not use canned or sweet corn)
- → 1 cup green peas, (or 14.5 oz. can)
- → salt & black pepper to taste

 *Add vegetables of your choice, chopped fresh cabbage, cut green beans, peas, etc., use what you have in the freezer or refrigerator!*

Combine all the ingredients and simmer at the lowest setting for at least 1 hour. Make some cornbread and enjoy! Serves 8-10.

637) Vegetable Beef Soup For Two

- → 1 tsp Mrs. Dash original blend
- → 1 russet potato, peeled, chopped
- → 1 large carrot, peeled and cut into rounds)
- → 1 cup v8 or mixed vegetable juice
- → 1 cup water
- → 14.5 oz can diced tomatoes
- → 1/4 cup chopped onion
- → 1/2 lb. ground chuck, brown & drain
- → 2 cups of frozen mixed vegetables or vegetables you have on hand frozen or fresh
- → salt & black pepper to taste

 Add vegetables of your choice, chopped fresh cabbage, cut green beans, peas, etc., use what you have in the freezer or refrigerator!

Combine all the ingredients and simmer at the lowest setting for at least 1 hour. Make some cornbread and enjoy! Serves 2-4 persons.

638) Vegetable Soup, Garden

- → 8-10 medium Roma tomatoes, skins removed, chopped (or 2-8 oz. can diced tomatoes)
- → 4 cups water
- → 1 large carrot, peeled, sliced thin
- → 1/2 chopped onion
- → 1/3 cup fresh peas, or frozen
- → 1/3 cup frozen shoe peg corn, not canned or sweet corn
- → 1/4 large cabbage, chopped
- → 1 garden sweet banana pepper, optional
- → 1 tsp original Mrs. Dash, optional
- → 1/2 tsp Goya vegetable & salad blend
- → 2 tsp beef bouillon granules
- → salt & black pepper, to taste

 *Mrs. Dash, Goya, and bouillon can be omitted. Add vegetables of your choice, chopped fresh cabbage, cut green beans, peas, etc., use what you have in the freezer or refrigerator!*

Combine all the ingredients and simmer at the lowest setting for at least 1 hour. Make cornbread and enjoy! Serves 3-4 persons.

"I remember being in Granny's kitchen when I was a kid and eating her vegetable soup that she canned every year. She would open a few quart jars and make a pan of biscuits. Granny served it on a plate, and we would sop up the juice with the biscuits. It was so good!" – *Tammy*

Southern Sides Recipes

Hearty Classics and Family Traditions

Welcome to the Southern Sides section, where beloved recipes and comforting flavors await you. Here, you will find my time-honored favorites, like Granny Green Beans. I take three simple ingredients and transform them into a delicious bite of Southern goodness. This dish is my most popular Southern side, and for good reason.

For years, I struggled to make my green beans taste like my mama's. She would often ask, "Did you cook them long enough?" I would assure her that I cooked them for what felt like an eternity.

One day, I discovered a secret ingredient that made my canned green beans taste just like Granny's! You are going to love this recipe, but it is not just a recipe; it is a technique. You must cook them as I describe or demonstrate in a video tutorial; otherwise, they will not measure up to the grand finale that is truly Granny Green Beans.

I urge you to try this recipe, even if it seems too simple or you doubt it will be good enough. Many have said this recipe has changed their lives. So go ahead and try them!

Enjoy all my Southern side dishes alongside your meals. Each dish highlights simple ingredients and easy techniques, inviting you to share the warmth and hospitality of the Southern table at your gatherings—whether it is a festive family dinner or a cozy weeknight meal.

639) Baked Beans, Stovetop

→ 1/4 cup onion, chopped
→ 3 Tbsp bell pepper, chopped
→ 4 slices bacon, chopped
→ 3 Tbsp salted butter
→ 4 Tbsp olive oil
→ 20 oz can original baked beans, no artificial pork flavoring
→ 1/2 cup BBQ sauce

Add olive oil to saucepan. Add bacon, pepper, and onions. Cook on medium/low heat and stir until bacon is crispy and brown. Add butter, beans, and BBQ sauce. Simmer for 15 minutes on low heat. Stir frequently to prevent sticking.

"I have been making my baked beans like this for years. They are delicious, get done quicker, and do not need to be baked. This keeps the heat reduced in the kitchen which is great in the summer when having picnics and cook outs." – *Tammy*

640) Black-Eyed Peas

→ 16 oz. dried black-eyed peas
→ 2 tsp beef or chicken bouillon granules season with pork ribs or ham
→ 2 tsp salt
→ 1/2 tsp pepper

Look your peas (discard discolored peas). Rinse thoroughly under running water. Place peas in a large pot. Add bouillon, salt, and pepper. Cover with water until water is 2 inches over top of peas. Bring to a hard boil for 15 minutes. After boiling make sure water is 1" over top of beans. Cover and leave on stove top soaking for 1 hour. After soaking, add seasoning meat and simmer until peas are soft. Make sure you stir occasionally and do not let them burn!

"Each New Year's Day my family serves these with Collard Greens, Creamed Potatoes, Cornbread and Ham leftover from Christmas! Daddy always said the Collards were the money he would make in the new year, and the peas were the change. He always encouraged us to eat more & more." – *Tammy*

641) Green Beans, Fresh

→ 2 lb. fresh green beans
→ water
→ 1 1/2 tsp salt
→ 1/2 tsp black pepper
→ 1/4 cup cooking oil
→ 1 1/2 Tbsp granulated sugar
→ 2 tsp chicken bouillon granules

Trim green beans and snap into 1" pieces; shell any pods that are too tough. Combine with beans in a bowl, wash, then add to a non-stick pot with enough water to cover. Add salt, pepper, oil, bouillon, and sugar; boil on medium until most water evaporates, and beans start to sizzle. Watch closely as oil and sugar caramelize; rub beans against the browned sides to deglaze. Remove from heat when glazed and aromatic. Add 1/2 cup water to finish deglazing and mix the caramelization into the beans: smash slightly if desired.

"The key to the right flavor is not how long you cook them; it is the oil and sugar caramelizing. This happens when all liquid has left beans allowing It to sit on bottom of pot and caramelize. It is also deglazing the pot and getting that flavor into your beans." – *Tammy*

642) Tammy's Granny Green Beans

→ 3-14.5 oz. cans of green beans, do not drain
→ 1/8 cup cooking oil
→ 1 Tbsp granulated sugar

This will make the best green beans you have ever tasted, but ONLY if you follow the directions carefully. Many people do not cook them down to the caramelization stage and complain that they are sweet. This is because the directions are not followed.

Add three ingredients to a non-stick saucepan. Bring to a boil and continue cooking on high. When water is almost gone, the beans will begin to sizzle. At this point you must stay in kitchen to watch them closely. The oil and sugar will then begin to caramelize in bottom of pot. You will notice the sides of pot becoming brown. Once this begins, take beans, and rub them on sides of pot that has glazing. The juice from the beans will deglaze the pot. Take them off the heat after they have formed a good glaze and you begin to smell it. Put about 1/2 cup water in pot and continue deglazing so caramelization is in beans and not on pot. Smash them a little breaking them apart if desired.

Recipe for 1 Can:

Use 1 Tbsp cooking oil and 1 tsp sugar for every can of green beans. Always use juice from can.

"Follow the directions and it is recommended to watch my video tutorial as well." – *Tammy*

643) Great Northern Beans

→ 16 oz. package dried great northerns
→ 1/4 tsp pepper
→ 2 tsp chicken bouillon granules
→ 1 cup chopped smoked pork

Examine your beans (taking out dark, discolored, or ugly beans). Rinse beans thoroughly and drain. Run water over beans

until it covers 3" above top of beans. Add pepper, bouillon, and pork. Place on stove top and bring to a high boil and boil for 10-15 minutes. Turn off and let it sit for about 1.5 hours with lid on. Place in refrigerator overnight. Get out the next day and bring to a boil adding water if needed. Turn down to medium heat and cook until tender. Enjoy! Makes 8-10 servings.

644) Bowl Of Butter Beans

→ 16 oz. dried lima beans
→ large stock pot or pressure cooker
→ 4 cups water with 2 tsp chicken bouillon granules or 32 oz. chicken stock
→ 1/8 cup of olive oil
→ 1 tsp salt
→ 1/2 tsp black pepper

When removing beans from package, take out discolored beans, rocks, debris, and clumps if present. Rinse beans well, pour off water, then cover beans with about 1 1/2 inches of water or chicken stock. If using water add bouillon listed above. Add oil, salt, and pepper.

Pressure cooker:

Bring to high pressure for 10 minutes, turn off and let sit for 2 hours. Take off cover and continue cooking until soft. Taste and add more salt if needed before serving.

Stock pot:

Bring to a boil for 15 minutes. Turn off, let beans sit on stove. Beans should be soaked for about 3 hours. Check every hour and add water to cover beans if needed during soak. Bring to a medium simmer and cook until soft. Taste and add more salt if needed before serving.

 Tammy's Tip: I love light beans cooked with chicken bouillon. They are delicious without pork fat! I prefer them this way. Try it!

645) Old Settler's Beans

In a large stock pot, skillet, or Dutch oven, brown and drain grease from:

- → 1/2 lb. ground beef
- → 1/2 lb. bacon, chopped
- → 1 onion, chopped

Preheat oven: 350 degrees. Add the following ingredients:

- → 1/8 cup brown sugar
- → 1/4 cup ketchup
- → 1 Tbsp mustard
- → 1/4 cup BBQ sauce
- → 1 tsp salt
- → 1/2 tsp black pepper
- → 1/2 tsp chili powder
- → 15 oz. can pork and beans
- → 15 oz. can pinto beans
- → 15 oz. can butter beans
- → 15 oz. can of kidney beans

Mix well, put in a well-greased oven-safe baking dish, and bake for 2 hours.

We enjoy this with homemade cornbread or garlic toast.

646) Peas, Field with Snaps

- → 1 lb. frozen field peas with snaps
- → water
- → 1/8 cup olive oil
- → 1/2 tsp salt
- → 1/4 tsp pepper
- → 2 tsp chicken bouillon granules

Put all ingredients in a medium saucepan. Add enough water to cover peas well. Bring it to a boil then turn down to medium heat. Stir well to distribute bouillon. Cook on medium heat for 30 minutes, watching and adding water to cover if needed. Add water to cover peas and put on lowest setting for 1 hour. Serve as a side. Add salt if needed.

647) Peas, Purple Hull

- → 1 quart peas, fresh purple hull
- → 4 cups of beef or chicken broth, nonsalted
- → 2 cups of water
- → 1/2 tsp salt
- → 1 Tbsp oil

Rinse peas and discard any that look discolored. Add to a pot along with broth, water, and salt. Bring to a boil then turn down on low and simmer for 1 hour. Check them every few minutes to make sure they do not burn and add water if needed. When they are done the water should still be right at top of peas. Enjoy with supper!

 Option: Chicken bouillon can be mixed with water to replace broth.

"Chris works so hard in the yard and in our garden. He loves to cut grass and keep the yard looking pristine. He has quite a green thumb. The soil down here is so much different than the red clay we grew up around in NW Georgia. I do not think we have many bees for pollinators down here either." – *Tammy*

648) Pinto Beans, Tammy's

→ 16 oz. dried pinto beans
→ large stock pot or pressure cooker
→ 4 cups water with 1 Tbsp beef bouillon granules
→ 1 large vegetable bouillon, Knorr
→ 1/8 cup olive oil
→ 1/2 tsp salt
→ 1/2 tsp black pepper

Remove any discolored beans, rocks, or debris from the package. Rinse the beans thoroughly, drain, then cover with water and bouillon, ensuring the water is 2 inches above the beans. Add oil, salt, and pepper.

Old Fashioned Pressure cooker:

Bring to high pressure for 20 minutes, turn off and let sit for 3 hours. Take off cover and continue cooking until soft. Taste and add more salt if needed before serving.

 **Stock pot:** Bring to a boil for 15 minutes. Turn off soak 2 hours. Add water to cover, place in refrigerator and soak overnight in pot. Take pot out, bring beans to a LOW boil and cook until soft. Taste and add more salt if needed before serving.

Option: Use ham pieces to flavor (I do not recommend bacon, bacon grease). If using meat do not let beans sit out without refrigeration for more than 2 hours.

649) Pinto Beans, Instapot

→ 1 1/2 cups of dried pinto beans
→ 4 cups of beef stock or 4 cups hot water mixed with 1 Tbsp. beef bouillon granules
→ 3-4 oz. country ham seasoning meat
→ 1/8 cup olive oil
→ 1/2 tsp black pepper, optional

Inspect your beans when removing them from the package by pouring them by the handful into your hand before dropping them into the pot. Take out discolored beans, rocks, & clumps if present. Rinse beans and pour off water.

Cover beans with water/bouillon or beef stock. Add oil, ham, and pepper. Water should be 2 inches higher than the beans.

Secure lid and close the pressure valve. Use the multigrain setting: 40 min. on medium.

After the time is up and the pressure valve releases, carefully remove the lid and turn your Instant Pot to the sauté setting*. Cook until the liquid is just at the top of the beans. Turn off the heat and serve hot!

*If you do not have a sauté setting, add the beans to a large pot and cook on medium/high until broth has reduced just to the top of the beans.

650) Red Beans & Rice

→ 1 lb. red beans
→ 1 lb. diced ham
→ Or 1 lb. breakfast sausage browned, used Swaggerty's Farm brand
→ 1 large onion chopped
→ 1 large bell pepper, chopped
→ garlic diced, optional
→ salt to taste
→ hot sauce, if desired

Wash and rinse beans. Pour off water. Add enough water to cover beans 2 inches. Bring to a boil and boil for 10 minutes. Take off heat and soak overnight on stovetop. Add enough water to cover them if needed. (Do not add anything to beans but water if soaking at room temperature)

Next day- In a medium skillet with olive oil, add onion, peppers, and diced ham. Cook until vegetables are soft. Combine onions, peppers, ham, garlic, and salt to presoaked beans (minus hot sauce) and cook on medium until beans are soft. Watch closely and add water as needed. Serve on a bed of rice. Add hot sauce to taste. A crockpot can be used to finish cooking beans with other ingredients, but it could take 10-12 hours.

Instant-pot: Cook beans and remaining ingredients in an instant-pot on multigrain setting. (Highest pressure for 38 minutes)

"We loved, loved, loved this recipe. It is so good you can serve it on hotdogs one night, and in a Mexican burrito another night so it stretches the dollar!"– *Tammy*

651) Red Kidney Beans

→ 16 oz. package dried red beans
→ 1/4 tsp pepper
→ 1/2 tsp salt
→ 1/8 cup olive or vegetable oil
→ 1 Tbsp beef bouillon granules

STEP 1: Examine your beans (taking out dark, discolored, or ugly beans). Rinse and pour off water. Run water over beans and cover 2" above top of beans. Add pepper, salt, oil, and bouillon.

STEP 2: Place on stove top and bring to a high boil and boil for 10-15 minutes. Turn off and let it sit for about 1.5 hours with lid on.

STEP 3: Place it in refrigerator overnight, making sure water covers the beans.

STEP 4: Get out next day and bring to a boil adding water if needed. Turn down to medium heat and cook until tender. Enjoy!

"Red or Pinto beans are great to serve with Mexican Style Dishes."– *Tammy*

652) Tammy's Refried Beans

→ 16 oz. cooked pinto beans & 2 cups of bean broth
→ 1/2 cup dehydrated onion or 1 med. onion, diced
→ 2 tsp onion powder
→ 2 Tbsp fajita seasoning, Bidia
→ 2 cups of shredded Mexican cheese blend
→ 8 oz. sour cream, or mayonnaise

Mix all ingredients together with an electric mixer until they are blended well.

 Other types of dried beans can be used to make re-fried beans.

Ready for Breakfast?

653) Hoppin John

→ 1/2 large onion, chopped
→ 2 green onions, chopped
→ 2 Tbsp cooking oil
→ 1/2 tsp black pepper
→ 1/2 tsp red pepper flakes
→ 1 bay leaf
→ 4 cups of chicken stock
→ 1 Tbsp chicken bouillon granules
→ 12-16 oz. package frozen black-eyed peas
→ 1 lb. chopped cooked ham

Serve over:
→ 1 cup cooked white or brown rice

Cook onion and scallion in a few Tbsp of oil (or chicken stock grease) until tender (about 2 minutes). Add remaining ingredients (except rice) and cook until most of water has evaporated and you are left with about a cup of liquid. Serve over rice. Best if served with a pone of Cornbread. Easy and delicious! Makes 4 large servings.

"This is great on a cold winter night or a football night with company! A nice change from chili."
– *Chris*

654) Speckled Butter Beans

→ 14 oz. dried speckled butter beans
→ water
→ 1/8 cup olive oil or cooking oil
→ 1 Tbsp beef bouillon granules
→ Salt to taste

Place beans in a medium saucepan (do not rinse beans). Add bouillon and oil. Cover with water until water is 2 inches over top of beans. Bring it to a hard boil for 10 minutes. Now make sure they have water to cover them. Cover and cook for 1 hour on low heat. Add salt if needed. Makes 4-6 servings.

 Make sure you stir occasionally and do not let them BURN!

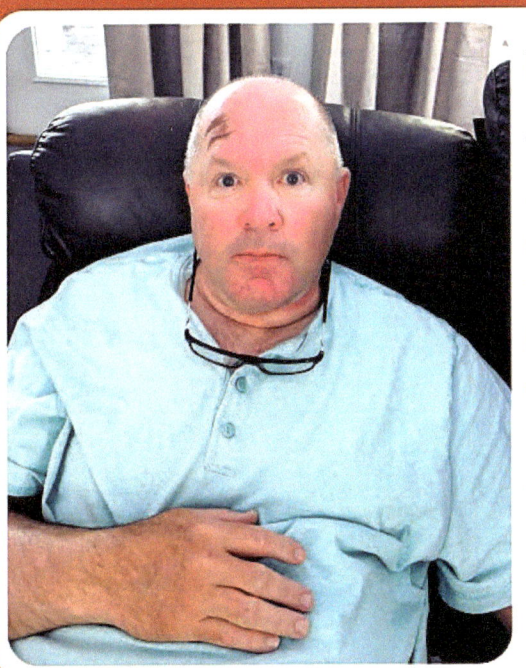

Funny Moments

Tammy: "Chris what is on your head?"
Chris: no response
Tammy: "its a big black mark
Chris in thought: "is she for real, or is she tricking me?"

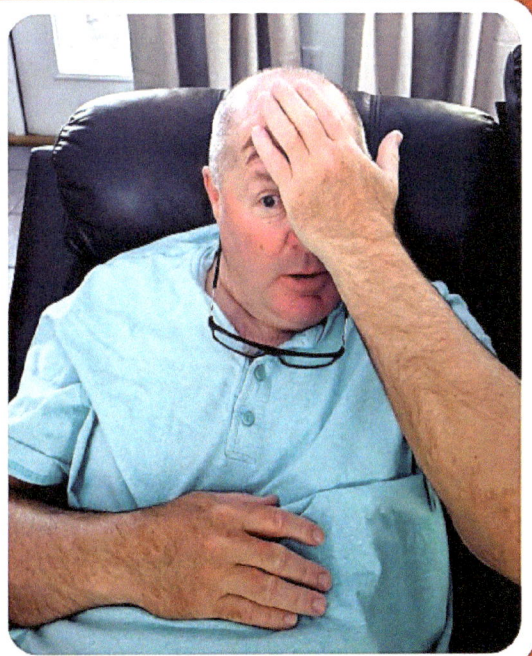

655) Corn On the Cob

- → fresh ears of corn, shuck & remove silks
- → water
- → salt & black pepper
- → salted butter
- → herb butter, optional

Corn should be room temp., so it does not cool down boiling water.

Bring a large pot of water to a rolling boil. Add corn and boil for 4 minutes. Remove corn carefully with tongs and put on a plate. Let it cool 5-8 minutes. Salt, pepper, and butter corn. Enjoy!

"This method makes the corn taste amazing and fresh." – *Tammy*

656) Corn On The Cob, Herb Butter

- → 1/4 cup salted butter, room temperature.
- → 2 Tbsp your choice of seasoning blend, no salt
- → 1 Tbsp snipped chives or sliced green onion or a fresh herb of your choice fresh corn

In small bowl, stir butter, seasoning and chives until smooth set aside.

Remove husks of each ear of corn and remove silks. Rub about 2 tsp herb butter over kernels of each ear.

For Grilling:

Wrap ear well in foil. Arrange corn directly on grill and cook, turning once. Cook for about 8 minutes.

For Air Fryer:

Wrapping corn in foil is optional. Place corn directly into air fryer basket and cook at 350 degrees for 6 minutes.

657) Corn, Mexican Street

- → 4 ears fresh corn, shuck, remove silks, dry
- → 4 Tbsp salted butter, room temperature
- → 2 Tbsp Mexican crema, or sour cream
- → 2 Tbsp mayonnaise
- → fresh-grated cotija cheese or a crumbled Mexican cheese
- → ground chipotle pepper
- → lime
- → chopped cilantro for garnish, optional

Wash corn, remove silks and dry well. Rub 1 Tbsp butter on each piece of corn. Grill for 4-6 minutes over hot coals. Remove from grill.

In a small bowl mix the cream and mayo together well. Spread on each ear of corn.

Grate fresh cheese onto each piece of corn. Sprinkle with pepper to taste.

Squeeze lime juice on each piece of corn. Garnish with cilantro if desired.

658) Corn Pudding

- → 5 ears of fresh corn, cut off the cob.
- → 1/2 cup onion, chopped
- → 1/4 cup bell pepper, chopped
- → 3 Tbsp salted butter or bacon grease
- → 1 1/2 tsp salt
- → 1/2 tsp black pepper
- → 2 cups of whole milk (or 1 1/2 cup evaporated milk & 1/2 cup water)
- → 4 eggs, beaten
- → 3/4 cup cornmeal mix, not sweet kind - use self-rising cornmeal mix
- → 1/3 cup self-rising flour
- → 10 oz grated cheese, optional

Sauté the onion and pepper in 3 Tbsp butter until soft. Add corn and cook for 4 minutes. Add salt & pepper.

In a separate bowl combine milk, cornmeal, flour, and eggs and beat well with a fork. Add to corn and mix well. Pour into a 2qt. baking dish (sprayed with cooking spray) and bake at 350 degrees for 30 minutes. Top with cheese and bake an additional 15 minutes.

OPTIONAL: Instead of using fresh corn, use one 12 to 16 oz. bag frozen shoe peg corn and one can of yellow whole kernel corn (drained).

659) Corn, Creamed & Fried

- → 6 ears fresh corn, shuck & silks removed
- → 1 1/2 cups of water
- → 1 tsp salt
- → 1/4 tsp pepper
- → 3 Tbsp salted butter or bacon grease

Cut corn off cobb with very sharp knife. Start at top and cut downward into a wide bowl while resting cobb on bottom of bowl. Rotate cobb while cutting. Try to cut thin slices so you can cut two rows. After cutting off kernels, scrape the cobb with back side of knife. Add corn, water, salt, pepper, and butter to a large wok or skillet. Turn on high and cook until water evaporates off corn. About 5-8 minutes.

For Creamed Corn:

Put 3 Tbsp cornstarch in 1 1/2 cups of cold milk. Whisk very well. After corn has been cooked for 5-8 minutes like recipe above., pour milk/starch in and cook another 5 minutes. Corn starch will turn from cloudy to clear when done. Enjoy!

Chris picking corn in Collard Valley in 2019

Field Corn:

"My family planted field corn every year to

make cornmeal with. They also used it for feeding the animals. Many farmers ate their field corn. We sure loved it. You cook and prepare it the like the recipe above except it has so much natural starch that it is very creamy on its own. The field corn is ready to pick when its tassels are light golden brown. It gets hard quick so there is a short window for picking. It does not have sugar in it, and it is so very good with fresh fried okra and sliced garden tomatoes."– *Tammy*

660) Cabbage, Stewed

→ 1 medium head cabbage
→ 2 tsp chicken bouillon granules
→ 1/4 cup salted butter
→ 1 cup water

Chop cabbage in 1-inch-wide pieces. Rinse cabbage to clean. Heat water in microwave until boiling then add bouillon. Preheat large wok or skillet. Add butter and chopped cabbage. Now add water/bouillon. Toss occasionally while most of water cooks off. Cook until there is just a little broth left in the bottom of wok or skillet and serve as a side dish. Enjoy. So very Good!

661) Collard Greens

→ 2 large bunches of collards
→ 2 Tbsp chicken bouillon granules
→ 1 tsp salt
→ 2 Tbsp sugar
→ 1/4 cup oil

Wash greens well. Tear leaves from ENTIRE stem and discard ENTIRE stem. Tear leaves into sections and place in a large stock pot. Stems are bitter and should not be cooked. Press greens down with hands as you add water. Add water until it reaches your fingers (while pressing greens down with hands). Add oil, bouillon, salt, and sugar (and ham if using). Cover and pressure cook for 30 minutes. Open and boil until most of water has evaporated and has formed a good pot liquor. Collards can be a tough green, so I prefer to pressure cook them. Use this same recipe in your instant pot.

662) Purple Cabbage, Saute

→ 1/2 small head purple cabbage
→ 3 Tbsp olive oil
→ 3 Tbsp of salted butter

Use a large sharp knife and cut the cabbage very thin. It should look like thin strips. Place cabbage in a large skillet with butter and oil on medium/high heat. Sauté it until soft. Salt and pepper to taste and serve.

663) Turnip Greens

→ 2 large bunches of greens
→ 2 Tbsp chicken bouillon granules
→ 1 tsp salt
→ 2 Tbsp sugar
→ 1/4 cup oil

Wash greens well. Tear leaves from bottom of stem and discard lower stem. Tear leaves into sections and place in a large stock pot. Press greens down with hands as you add water. Add water until it reaches your fingers (while pressing greens down with hands). Add salt, oil, pepper, sugar, and bouillon. Cook on a medium temp. until greens are soft and water has turned into a greenish brown color.

 Note: use ham to season greens if desired. We do not like the taste of bacon, smoked meats, or bacon grease in our greens. Try them my way please! -Tammy

246

664) Basmati Rice

→ 1 cup uncooked basmati rice
→ 1 1/2 cup of water

Heat rice and water to a boil. Reduce heat to low, then cover and simmer for 15-20 minutes.

665) Jasmine Rice

→ 1 cup uncooked jasmine rice
→ 1 3/4 cup of water

Heat rice and water to a boil. Reduce heat to low, then cover and simmer for 15-20 minutes.

666) Texmati Rice

→ 1 cup uncooked Texmati rice
→ 1 3/4 cup of water

Heat rice and water to a boil. Reduce heat to low, then cover and simmer for 15-20 minutes.

667) Brown Rice

→ 1 cup brown rice
→ 2 cups of water or stock
→ 1 tsp salt
→ 50-minute cooking time make ahead!!

Rinse rice well, place rice, water, and salt in a large pot. Bring to a boil and boil for 5 minutes. Reduce heat to lowest setting and cover. If you have a gas stove do not use the warming element. Simmer 40 minutes. Let rice rest 10-15 minutes before serving. Open lid and fluff to serve. Do not open lid until the entire process is finished. Enjoy!

"If you boil a chicken or cook a beef roast and have stock left, use it to boil your rice! It gives it a delicious flavor! I encourage you to eat brown rice because it is much healthier for you than white rice. It also has more texture, and I like it better."– *Tammy*

668) Parboiled White Rice

→ 1 cup uncooked parboiled rice
→ 2 1/2 cups of water

Heat liquid to boiling, then add rice. Reduce heat to low. Cover and simmer for 20-25 minutes, then remove from heat. Let stand covered for 5 minutes before fluffing.

669) How To Make The Best Rice

→ 1 cup white regular long-grain rice
→ 2 tbsp olive oil
→ 2 cups of water
→ saucepan with lid

Place rice and olive oil in a saucepan. On a medium heat stir rice until toasty (a light brown color).

Add water to rice and bring to a good boil. Cover and turn temp. to a low simmer and cook covered for 20 minutes.

When timer goes off, turn off heat and let rice sit covered and undisturbed for 5 minutes before serving. Makes 3 cups of cooked rice.

670) Mexican Rice, Authentic

→ 2 Tbsp of cooking oil
→ 2 cups of long grain rice
→ 8 oz. can tomato sauce
→ 5 cups of water
→ 3 Tbsp knorr chicken bouillon granules
→ 2 Tbsp dehydrated onion flakes
→ 1/2 tsp of cumin

Use large deep skillet with lid. Heat to med/high until skillet is warm. Add oil. Put rice in skillet and stir continually until its light brown.

Pour in tomato sauce and water then mix in chicken bouillon, onion flakes, and cumin.

Cover pan and wait until rice begins to boil then turn heat to low simmer. Do Not Remove Lid Or Stir.

Set timer for 20 minutes, but after 10 minutes jiggle the handle to move rice around to prevent from sticking and to redistribute sauce. Remove from heat do not disturb or uncover for 5 minutes. Open and serve.

"This recipe is taken from a YouTuber named Deb. Her channel name is In Deb's Kitchen on YouTube."– *Tammy*

671) White Rice

→ 1 cup white regular long-grain rice
→ 2 cups of water

Heat rice and liquid to a boil, then reduce heat to low. Cover and simmer for 15 minutes. Makes 3 cups of cooked rice.

672) Carrots, Apricot Glazed

→ 16 oz. carrot, sliced thin or mini-sized
→ 2 Tbsp salted butter
→ water
→ 1/3 cup apricot preserves
→ red pepper flakes (a few shakes)
→ dash of salt

In a skillet or saucepan add carrots and butter. Add enough water to cover the carrots. Place on Simmer and cook 20 minutes or until they are tender. Drain, add preserves, and salt and mix well. If you want to use pepper flakes, add them now. Keep on simmer (warm) until serving.

673) Potatoes, Baked

→ large russet, or sweet potato scrub potatoes clean with vegetable brush under running water-pat dry with paper towels.
→ 1/4 cup salted butter, room temperature
→ aluminum foil

Use foils large enough to wrap each potato. Lay each potato on top of foil. With hands rub butter on each potato. Salt (unless sweet potato) and wrap well. Bake at 400 degrees for 30 minutes. Rotate and bake an additional 30 min. Remove from oven & serve with butter, salt, pepper & sour cream. Serve Sweet potato with butter and cinnamon sugar! Sweet potatoes can be used in sweet potato pies!

674) Potatoes, Creamed

→ 2.5 lb. russet potatoes
→ water
→ 1 tsp salt
→ 1/4 tsp black pepper
→ 1/2 cup of milk
→ 4 Tbsp salted butter
→ 1/4 cup of sour cream

Peel potatoes, rinse, and cut into small cubes so they cook well. Place them in medium saucepan, cover with water and boil on medium heat for 20 to 30 minutes, or until fork tender. Drain, Add remaining ingredients, and use a hand or stand mixer with whisk attachment to cream until fluffy. Salt to taste! Serves 6-8.

675) Potato Cakes

→ 1 1/2 cups of leftover mashed potatoes
→ 1 small potato, washed and grated
→ 1/3 cup self-rising flour
→ 1/4 cup onion or green onion, chopped
→ 1/2 tsp black pepper
→ 1 egg

Mix ingredients listed above together well. Preheat a skillet. Add bacon grease or cooking oil. Roll dough in hands about the size of a walnut. Put in the skillet and flatten with a spatula. Fry until golden brown. Flip patties and fry until golden brown on the other side. Enjoy as a side dish.

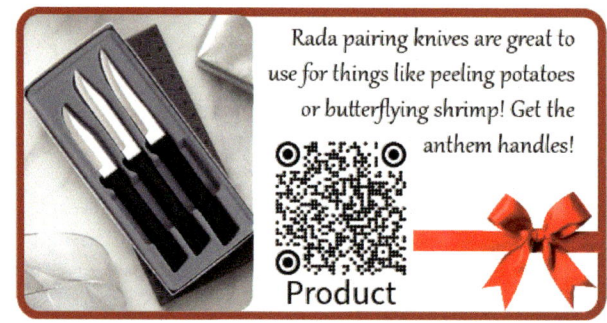

Rada pairing knives are great to use for things like peeling potatoes or butterflying shrimp! Get the anthem handles!

Product

676) Potatoes, Stewed

→ 6-7 medium/large russet potatoes, peel and chop into 3/4" – 1" size pieces.
→ water
→ 2 Tbsp corn starch
→ 3/4 cup half and half or whole milk
→ 1/2 tsp black pepper
→ 1 tsp salt
→ 4-5 Tbsp salted butter

Put potatoes in medium saucepan. Add water to cover potatoes. Put it on high heat and bring it to a boil. Once boiling, put on medium heat, set timer - boil 15 minutes.

In glass measuring cup, combine half and half, cornstarch, pepper, and salt. Whisk well. After boiling potatoes the amount of liquid should be about 1/2 inch below top of potatoes. (Pour off excess if necessary).

Add cream mixture to potatoes and fold in butter. Potatoes should be in hunks and slightly creamy. Serve warm. Serves 6-8

"The only difference in these and potato soup is that the broth is much more diluted. My mama made them both ways and called them by different names."– *Tammy*

677) Potatoes, Skillet Fried

→ 2 lb. potatoes
→ cooking oil
→ salt & black pepper
→ cut up onion if desired

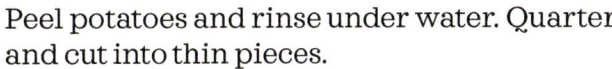

Peel potatoes and rinse under water. Quarter and cut into thin pieces.

→ iron skillet, wok, or large skillet
→ cooking oil, canola, or vegetable
→ 4 Tbsp salted butter

Put enough shortening or oil in skillet to be about 1/2" high after melting. Oil must be HOT. Put a piece of potato in oil and once it floats and sizzles the grease is hot and ready! Add butter, then potatoes. It takes a good 20 minutes to fry these up so Do Not Rush. Let potatoes fry in hot oil until they are golden brown before turning them over. You may have to rotate potatoes from edges to middle, so all will brown if using a gas stove. Fry until golden brown. Take them out with large, slotted spoon and place on a paper towel covered platter/plate. Salt and pepper to taste and serve.

"I was pleasantly surprised to find a heart shaped potato. It was so cute I had to take a picture of it. When I was growing up Granny always planted long rows of potatoes. Every year granddaddy would use the tractor with a shovel attachment to dig the earth on each row. From the sound of that you should be able to imagine how long her garden rows were. So, there were so many potatoes to gather. She called on everyone to help gather the potatoes and put them in the smoke house for storage. The girls filled up the five-gallon buckets while the boys had to pick up the bucket, take it to the smoke house, and pour them out on the floor. It was a family affair as most harvesting was in our family"– *Tammy*

678) Scalloped Potatoes

→ 5 medium potatoes, peeled and sliced thin
→ 1 3/4 cup milk
→ 2 Tbsp salted butter
→ 2 Tbsp flour
→ 1/2 tsp salt
→ 1/2 tsp pepper
→ 1 1/2 cups of shredded cheddar cheese
→ 1/4 cup diced onion

Boil potatoes until fork-tender—overcooking is better than undercooking. In a skillet, melt butter, then mix in flour and cook until golden. Add milk and stir until smooth, then blend in 1 cup shredded cheese. Place cooked potatoes in a greased 2.5 qt. casserole dish, sprinkle with diced onion, and cover with cheese sauce. Stir to coat, then bake at 350°F for 45 minutes. Sprinkle with remaining cheese, return to oven to melt, and serve hot.

679) Potatoes, Red

→ 2.5 lb. red potatoes
→ water
→ 1/2 cup sour cream
→ 1 1/2 tsp salt
→ 1/2 tsp black pepper
→ 1/4 cup salted butter

Wash potatoes. Take a knife and cut discolored parts off potatoes but leaving most of the red skin. Cut potatoes in 1" pieces and place in a medium stock pot or saucepan. Cover with water and bring them to a boil. Continue to boil for 1520 minutes, or until fork tender. Drain the potatoes. Add sour cream, salt, pepper, and butter and lightly stir them. Try not to break up the potatoes.

680) Potatoes, Hashbrowns

→ 2 Tbsp cooking oil
→ 2 Tbsp salted butter
→ 1 medium potato
→ 1/8 cup chopped onion, optional
→ shredded cheddar cheese, optional
→ salt & black pepper
→ 8" non-stick skillet

Note: if using larger skillet double recipe

Wash and scrub potato leaving skins on if desired. If not, peel potato. Dry potato with a towel or paper towel. With a hand grater, grate potato. It is best to use a safety glove while using a grater.

Add oil and butter to skillet. Carefully add potatoes to skillet. Salt and pepper potatoes. Cook on medium heat until golden brown before flipping with a large spatula. Cook both sides until done. Serve with breakfast or with a sandwich. Sprinkle with cheese if desired.

 Note: For better results soak hashbrowns in cold water and drain on paper towels to remove starch prior to frying. Make sure potatoes are dry before frying or the grease will pop!

If you omit the soaking step, the potatoes will have a slimy texture from the starch.

Option: Add a 1/8 cup diced onions to potatoes before browning if desired. Each medium potato makes 1 serving.

681) Sweet Potatoes, Candied

→ 5 Tbsp salted butter
→ 3-4 sweet potatoes
→ 1/2 tsp salt
→ 1/4 cup brown sugar total.

Peel and wash potatoes. Slice sweet potatoes in 1/4 to 1/2-inch slices. Place them in medium saucepan. Add 1/8 cup packed brown sugar, 3 Tbsp butter and salt. Add water to top of potatoes. Put on stovetop-bring to a boil. Boil until potatoes are tender (should take about 12 minutes). Add 2 Tbsp butter and 1/8 cup brown sugar unpacked. Simmer slow until sticky glaze forms. Cover until ready to serve. Serve warm.

 I also like to slice these thin and cook in a non-stick skillet so the glaze and sugar get stick and the potatoes start turning brown as shown in the picture above. They are delicious this way, but you have to watch them closely.

682) Potato Hash, Cheesy

→ 2 medium potatoes, peeled and diced
→ olive oil
→ 2 Tbsp salted butter
→ salt & pepper
→ 1 cup grated Mexican cheese blend

In a hot skillet add olive oil and diced potatoes. Then add butter. Salt, and pepper. Cook until golden brown. Once brown, sprinkle cheese and serve once the cheese is melted.

683) Rutabaga's, Glazed

→ 2 medium rutabagas (near turnips in produce section and many are coated in wax) -peel off wax and chop into 3/4-to-1-inch cubes. (chops easier if microwaved a couple of minutes)
→ 1/4 cup salted butter
→ 2 1/2 tsp granulated or brown sugar

Put rutabagas in a medium saucepan. Add water just to top of rutabagas. Put on stovetop with butter- bring to a boil. Boil until rutabagas are tender (all juices should be evaporated except for a tiny bit). Add sugar and cook until they glaze well. Make sure they sizzle for 3 or 4 minutes to form a glaze. Add a dash of salt and serve! Serves 4-6

684) Garlic Mashed Potatoes

→ 2.5 lb. Russett potatoes
→ water
→ 1 tsp salt
→ 1/4 tsp pepper
→ 1/2 cup milk
→ 4 Tbsp salted butter
→ 1/4 cup sour cream
→ 1 clove garlic wrapped in alum foil

Wrap your garlic in alum foil and place it in a 350-degree oven for 30 minutes. Peel potatoes, rinse, then cut up into small cubes so they cook well. Place in medium saucepan, cover with water and boil on medium heat for 25 minutes. Drain. Take garlic out of oven and let it cool for at least 10 minutes. Cut off end of clove with a seriated knife (using a seriated knife works better cutting through all the thin layers of peeling. Carefully squeeze out the garlic over your drained potatoes without getting the peels in the potatoes. Add the remaining ingredients and use a hand or stand mixer with whisk attachment to cream till fluffy. Enjoy!

685) Broccoli, Steamed

→ large head of broccoli
→ 1 1/2 cups water
→ salt
→ pepper
→ 4 Tbsp salted butter

Wash broccoli and cut florets off head. Place a steamer basket in a medium saucepan and add 1 1/2 cups of water. Put half broccoli in basket. Salt and pepper. Put in remaining broccoli and salt and pepper. Put lid on and bring it to a boil. Boil 4 minutes and turn off. Drain and toss broccoli in butter.

686) Asparagus, Sauteed

→ one bunch asparagus
→ salted butter or garlic spread
→ fresh garlic or garlic spread
→ Mrs. Dash original
→ 2 Tbsp olive oil
→ 2 Tbsp salted butter

Snap off ends, wash, and add to flat skillet that is preheated. Add olive oil and butter. Add minced garlic and a tsp of your favorite spice (Mrs. Dash Original salad blend works great) Sprinkle with salt and pepper to taste. Sauté on Medium heat until veggies are soft

687) Sautéed Fresh Veggies

→ 3 summer squash
→ 1 red bell pepper
→ Mixed fresh vegetables, peeled and cut into 1-inch hunks (no root vegetables)
→ 2 Tbsp olive oil
→ 2 Tbsp salted butter

Cut off ends, wash, and add to flat skillet that is preheated. Add olive oil and butter. Sprinkle with salt and pepper to taste.

Sauté on Medium heat until veggies are soft enough for your preference. If you are cooking a skillet full of vegetables add 1/2 cup water to help steam but let water evaporate before serving so you can taste the butter and spices. Enjoy with dinner!

688) Bacon Brussel Sprouts

→ 16 oz. fresh Brussel sprouts, washed & halved
→ 2-3 slices bacon, chopped
→ 1/2 small onion, sliced thin
→ 1 cup hot water
→ 1 1/2 Tbsp sugar
→ 1 1/2 Tbsp apple cider vinegar
→ salt & black pepper

Place bacon in a preheated skillet and cook on med/high until golden brown. Take out bacon & leave bacon grease in the skillet.

Combine the water, sugar, and vinegar.

Add brussels to skillet with onion and sauté for 3 minutes. Pour water over the brussels sprouts and simmer until all liquid has evaporated from them.

Let them sizzle in a skillet for a couple of minutes, then turn off heat. Crumble bacon on top of brussels, add salt, pepper, and stir. Enjoy it as a side!

Potato Tip:

 If you have potatoes that are older and are rubbery, do not use them for mashed or creamed potatoes. If you do the results will be sticky potatoes. Don't throw them out, you can use them for frying. Make skillet fried potatoes, french fries, or roasted potatoes with them. I would not use them for hashbrowns either.

689) Brussels, Sautéed

- → 1 lb. of fresh Brussel sprouts
- → 2 Tbsp olive oil
- → 3 Tbsp salted butter
- → 1/2 tsp salt
- → 1/4 tsp pepper

Wash Brussels cut stems off and half them. If they are jumbo cut them into quarters. Place oil and butter in a skillet. Add Brussels. Salt and pepper them. Cook on medium/low heat for 5 minutes. Cover and cook 5 more minutes. Turn off until ready to serve. Sprinkle with Parmesan cheese before serving if desired.

690) Brussels, Steamed

- → fresh Brussel sprouts
- → salt & black pepper
- → Mrs. dash original recipe
- → 3 Tbsp salted butter

Rinse your brussels. Cut off stem ends and half each Brussel. Place them in a steamer basket inside of a saucepan. Add water, cover, and bring to a boil to create steam. Once pot starts smoking with steam, set timer for 10 minutes. Turn off heat, drain and toss with 3 Tbsp butter. Serve as a side dish.

691) Butternut Squash, Roasted

- → 2 cups of butternut squash, peel, and cube.
- → 2 tsp olive oil
- → 1 tsp poultry seasoning
- → salt & black pepper to taste

Mix the ingredients in a small baking dish. Broil at 400°F for 25 minutes, or until edges are golden brown.

 Replace olive oil with 3 Tbsp. melted butter if desired.

Air Fryer Version:

Toss together and place in air fryer on 325°F for 6 minutes. Shake and cook 6 more minutes. If squash does not have toasty edges, cook longer (if desired).

Toaster Oven Version:

Toss, transfer to a baking sheet, and bake in a toaster oven at 350°F for 20-25 minutes.

692) Okra, Boiled

- → 1 lb. of fresh okra or 1lb. of frozen whole okra
- → water
- → 1/2 tsp salt
- → 1/4 tsp pepper
- → 4 Tbsp salted butter

Place washed okra, salt, pepper, and butter in a saucepan. Cover well with water. Boil on high until okra is soft and starts to separate and show a few seeds. You may have to add water to the pot. Rub with a little butter before serving and sprinkle with salt and pepper. Delicious!

Eph 1:5
"Having predestinated us unto the adoption of children by Jesus Christ to himself, according to the good pleasure of his will," KJV

693) Fried Okra Deluxe

→ 1 lb. fresh okra
→ 1 small Vidalia onion, cut into 1/2" to 3/4" chunks.
→ 1 large green tomato, cut into chunks
→ 1 side of bell pepper, cut into chunks
→ 1/8 cup whole buttermilk
→ 1 1/2 cups of self-rising flour
→ salt & black pepper

Wash okra and snip base and tip off. Cut okra into 1/4-inch-thick pieces. Place it in a medium bowl with other vegetables. Pour buttermilk on it and toss well.

In another bowl, sift 1/2 cup flour in the bottom. Add half of veggies, salt & pepper well. Repeat layers with remaining veggies until they have all been battered and salted/peppered well.

Melt shortening in a skillet or wok until it is about 1" deep. Oil must be HOT. Put a breaded piece of okra in oil, when it floats, and sizzles the grease is hot and ready! It takes time to fry up okra. DO NOT RUSH. Flip a maximum of three times. Let okra sit in hot grease until it is golden brown before turning it over. Add more shortening after turning once. Cook on high setting if using a gas stove or med/high for electric elements.

Take it out with a large, slotted spoon and place it on a paper towel covered platter/plate. It is so delicious, y'all!

> ### Eph 1:13,14
> "In whom ye also trusted, after that ye heard the word of truth, the gospel of your salvation: in whom also after that ye believed, ye were sealed with that holy Spirit of promise, "Which is the earnest of our inheritance until the redemption of the purchased possession, unto the praise of his glory."KJV

694) Okra, Fried

→ 1 1/2 lb. fresh okra
→ 1/8 cup whole buttermilk
→ 1 1/2 cups of self-rising flour
→ salt & black pepper

Wash okra and snip off base and tip (if desired) with a knife. Cut okra into 1/4-inch-thick pieces. Place it in a medium bowl and pour buttermilk on it. Mix it well. Put 1/2 cup self-rising flour in bottom of a pie plate. Add half of okra. Salt and pepper generously. Using a sifter with self-rising flour, coat okra well. Pour in remaining okra and repeat by adding salt, pepper, and flour.

→ iron skillet, wok, or large skillet
→ shortening

Put enough shortening in skillet to be about 1" deep after melting. Oil must be HOT. Put a breaded piece of okra in oil and once it floats and sizzles, your grease is hot and ready! It takes a good 20-30 minutes to fry up okra. Do Not Rush. Flip a maximum of three times. Let okra sit in hot grease until it is golden brown before turning it over. Add more shortening after turning once. You may have to rotate okra from edges to middle, so all will be brown if you have a gas stove. Fry okra until it is golden brown. Take it out with large, slotted spoon and place on a paper towel covered platter/plate.

Fry Frozen Okra the same way. Take frozen okra out of freezer and hit package on counter to break it up. Pour into a bowl and add 1/3 cup buttermilk. Toss to coat. Add flour to bowl and toss okra until coated well. Fry immediately using same method as above.

> ### Eph 2:4,5 KJV
> "But God, who is rich in mercy, for his Even when we were dead in sins, hath quickened us together with Christ, (by grace ye are saved;) great love wherewith he loved us,"

695) Okra Patties, Fried

→ 1 lb. okra, cut thin
→ 1 cup buttermilk, may need more
→ 1/2 cup onions, chopped
→ 1 tsp salt
→ 1/2 tsp pepper
→ 3/4 cup self-rising flour
→ 1/2 cup self-rising corn meal
→ 1 can diced tomatoes or fresh tomatoes
→ 1 cup shortening for frying

Combine okra, onions, salt, pepper, and mix well. In a separate bowl add flour, cornmeal, and diced tomatoes. Starting with 1 cup of buttermilk, add to the flour mix and mix well. Add enough milk to make it like a thick pancake batter. Fold into the okra mixture. Drop by Tbsp into hot fat, flatten slightly, and brown well on both sides. Drain on paper towels.

Option: Use sour cream in place of buttermilk.

If you cannot find buttermilk, you can use 1 cup of sour cream for the 1 cup of buttermilk and then add regular milk until the batter is thick like a waffle or pancake batter.

TIP: If you want to use frozen okra, you MUST thaw it first!

696) Spaghetti Squash

→ 1 spaghetti squash
→ 1/4 cup salted butter
→ salt and pepper

Put squash in the microwave for a couple minutes to soften and make it easy to cut. After it cools a couple minutes, use a knife and slice it in half. Place it on a shallow pie plate and microwave for 4-5 minutes. Let cool enough to handle. Scrape squash out with a spoon. Add butter, salt, and pepper to taste. Enjoy this as a side dish. You can also use it in cold salads as you would a noodle.

697) Squash, Butternut

→ 1 butternut squash
→ salt to taste
→ 3-4 Tbsp salted butter

Microwave the squash for 4 minutes. Trim both ends, halve it, and peel off the skin (a knife is recommended to remove the white layer that may cause reactions). Cut into 1" cubes, steam for 10-12 minutes, then toss with butter, salt, and pepper. Serve as a side.

698) Squash, Fried

→ 1 lb. of fresh summer squash
→ 1/8 cup whole buttermilk
→ 1 1/2 cups of self-rising flour
→ salt & black pepper
→ chopped onion if desired

Wash and trim the squash, then slice into 1/4-inch pieces and halve the rounds. In a medium bowl, mix the squash with buttermilk. Salt and pepper squash then coat with flour.

→ iron skillet, wok, or large skillet
→ cooking oil (canola or vegetable)

Heat about 1" of oil in a skillet until hot. Test with a breaded squash piece; if it floats and sizzles, the oil is ready. Fry squash for about 20 minutes, flipping no more than three times. Let each side turn golden brown before flipping. Add oil after the first turn and rotate okra as needed for even browning. Remove when golden with a slotted spoon and drain on paper towels.

> **Eph 2:8**
> "For by grace are ye saved through faith; and that not of yourselves: it is the gift of God: Not of works, lest any man should boast." KJV

699) Squash, Stewed

→ 5-6 pieces squash
→ water
→ salt
→ black pepper
→ 1/4 stick salted butter

Pick out longer skinny squash (straight neck) for less seeds. Wash squash and cut off and discard ends. Cut squash up and place in medium saucepan covered with water. Bring to a boil. Continue boiling until squash is soft. Boil at least 20 minutes. Remove from heat and drain. Add salt and pepper to taste and butter.

Note: if you want onion add them chopped before boiling.

700) Summer Squash, Ribboned

→ 3 summer squash or 2 summer squash and a zucchini
→ 2 green onions
→ 3 Tbsp salted butter
→ salt & black pepper

Wash and cut the ends off squash/zucchini. Use a vegetable peeler and cut strips off squash/zucchini until you reach the inward seeds. The strips will be thin like ribbons.

Pull the outside leaf off green onions. Cut onions into thin strips and place them in saucepan with butter, and squash. Simmer on a low temp. and stir occasionally for 10-12 minutes. Sprinkle with salt and pepper to taste. Serve warm. 4 servings.

 When picking out squash pick long neck instead of crooked neck on the end if possible. Long neck tends to yield more squash and less seeds. Do the same when choosing which variety to plant in your garden.

701) Tomato Pie

→ 1 can grand's biscuits
→ 12 sliced ripe red tomatoes
→ 3 slices bacon cooked crisp
→ 1/8 cup chopped onions
→ 1/8 cup chopped bell peppers
→ 1/2 cup mayonnaise
→ 1 cup mozzarella cheese
→ black pepper
→ Italian seasoning

Prepare Crust: Spray an 8- or 9-inch cake pan with cooking spray. Open biscuits and pull each biscuit apart into two equal thicknesses. Then put them into the bottom of the pan pushing some up the sides. You should have left over dough. Bake crust at 350 degrees F for 15 minutes.

Place bacon on two paper towels and cook for 2 minutes in the microwave or until crispy. Slice tomatoes and sauté onion and peppers in a little bacon grease while waiting on the crust to bake. Combine cheese and mayo well. Take out crust when ready and press down the center making a well for tomatoes and filling.

Place tomatoes in the crust and sprinkle with black pepper. Put the onion and peppers on and crumble bacon on top. Top with mayo cheese mixture and spread out over pie. Sprinkle with Italian seasoning. Bake at 350 degrees for 40 minutes and reduce cooking temperature to 325 for 30 minutes in a toaster oven. Cut into slices and enjoy! This is AMAZING!!

702) Succotash

→ 2-14.5 oz. cans baby lima beans
→ 14.5 oz. can corn, or fresh corn cut off cob (3 ears)
→ 1 Tbsp chicken bouillon granules
→ 1/2 tsp salt
→ 1/2 tsp black pepper
→ 2 large garden tomatoes (or 3 medium sized peeled and chopped) or 28-oz. can diced tomatoes)
→ 6-8 pods fresh okra (1/3 cup cut)
→ 2 Tbsp salted butter

Drain cans of corn and one can of lima beans and reserve juice. Drain and discard juice of 2nd can of beans. Put all vegetables into a stock pot. Put bouillon in the reserved juice and whisk well. Pour over beans in pot. Wash and cut okra and add to pot. Peel tomatoes, chop, and put into beans. Put on stove top. Add butter and cook until okra is tender. Enjoy as a side dish.

703) Tomatoes, Stewed

→ 2-8 oz. can whole tomatoes (or 3 fresh tomatoes)
→ 1 medium onion, chopped.
→ 1 cup chicken or beef broth
→ 2 tsp sugar
→ 3 Tbsp bell pepper finely chopped.
→ 1/2 tsp salt (if tomatoes are not salted)
→ 1/2 tsp black pepper
→ 2 slices of bread, cubed and toasted
→ 3 Tbsp salted butter

Put bell peppers and onions in a medium saucepan with butter and cook until soft. Chop the tomatoes into cubes (canned or fresh) and place in the saucepan. Add remaining ingredients (minus the bread). Simmer on low for 15 minutes. Place the bread in your serving bowl and spoon the hot tomatoes over the bread before serving.

 If you prefer skinless tomatoes, blanch them: Boil water, cut a small X on the stem end of each tomato, and immerse briefly until the skins loosen. Use a slotted spoon to remove them and peel off the skins. No cold bath is needed since you'll be cooking them right away.

Eph 2:14
"For he is our peace, who hath made both one, and hath broken down the middle wall of partition between us;" KJV

704) Vegetables, Roasted

→ 1 summer squash, cut into 1 1/2" pieces.
→ 1 bell pepper, cut into 1" pieces.
→ 1 red bell pepper, cut into 1" pieces.
→ 1 medium onion, cut into 1" pieces.
→ 1 medium zucchini, cut into 1" pieces.
→ 2 medium potatoes, cut into 1" pieces.
→ 4 Tbsp olive oil
→ salt & pepper
→ your favorite herb blend

In a large bowl, combine the veggies and toss in the olive oil. Spread veggies out on a cooking sheet lined with parchment or foil. Sprinkle on your favorite herb blend, salt, and pepper well.

Bake uncovered at 400°F for 45 minutes, or until the vegetables are tender when pierced with a fork. If preferred, finish by sprinkling grated Parmesan cheese over the top before serving.

705) Air Fryer Vegetables

Set the air fryer to 320°F and cook for 20 minutes until fork-tender. Reduce the temperature if vegetables brown too quickly after 10 minutes.

Eph 2:18-22
"For through him we both have access by one Spirit unto the Father. Now therefore ye are no more strangers and foreigners, but fellow citizens with the saints, and of the household of God;

And are built upon the foundation of the apostles and prophets, Jesus Christ himself being the chief corner stone; KJV

Eph 3:14,16,17,21
"For this cause I bow my knees unto the Father of our Lord Jesus Christ,

Of whom the whole family in heaven and earth is named,

That he would grant you, according to the riches of his glory, to be strengthened with might by his Spirit in the inner man;

That Christ may dwell in your hearts by faith; that ye, being rooted and grounded in love,

And to know the love of Christ, which passeth knowledge, that ye might be filled with all the fulness of God.

Unto him be glory in the church by Christ Jesus throughout all ages, world without end. Amen." KJV

Tammy's Cooking Tips

Essential Kitchen Tips Organized by Category
Practical Wisdom and Cooking Hints for Everyday Meals

General Cooking Wisdom

- **Read Your Recipe Twice:** Review the entire recipe before you begin to avoid missing ingredients or steps.
- **Prep Ingredients First:** Chop, measure, and organize all ingredients before starting to make cooking smoother.
- **Season with Confidence:** Adjust salt, pepper, and spices to taste to suit your family's preferences.
- **Use Fresh When You Can:** opt for fresh veggies and herbs to enhance flavor.
- **Embrace Versatility:** Treat recipes as guidelines; swap ingredients or add nuts and seeds for variety and texture.
- **Layer Those Flavors:** Build flavor by sautéing aromatics and finishing with cheese, nuts, or fresh herbs.
- **Taste as You Go:** Sample and adjust flavors throughout the cooking process.
- **Cleanup as You Cook:** Keep your workspace tidy for a less stressful experience and easier cleanup.
- **Enjoy the Process:** Remember, cooking is about nourishing loved ones and making memories.

Main Dishes

- **Meats:** Let steaks and roasts rest after cooking to lock in juices; marinate tough cuts for tenderness.
- **Poultry:** Pat chicken dry for crispier skin and use a thermometer for perfect doneness.
- **Seafood:** Remove fish from heat when just opaque; it will continue cooking off the pan.

Vegetables & Sides

- **Roasting:** Toss veggies in oil, season generously, and cook in a single layer for caramelized edges.
- **Steaming:** Brighten steamed veggies with a squeeze of lemon or fresh herbs.
- **Grains:** Toast rice or quinoa in a dry pan before adding liquid for a nutty flavor boost.

Baking & Sweets

- **Cookies & Bars:** Chill dough before baking for thicker, chewier treats.
- **Cakes & Muffins:** Stir batter just until dry ingredients are moistened for a tender crumb.
- **Pie Crusts:** Keep ingredients cold and handle dough minimally for the flakiest crusts.

Cooking Methods

- **Sautéing:** Preheat your pan and cook ingredients in batches for better browning.
- **Slow Cooking:** Brown meats and aromatics before adding to the slow cooker for richer flavor.
- **Grilling:** Bring meats to room temperature and let them rest under foil after grilling for juicier results.
- **Air Frying:** Shake the basket halfway through for even crisping; avoid overcrowding.

A view from the front yard of the home I grew up in.

Where is Collard Valley?

The History of Collard Valley:

Chief Collard was a leader of a Cherokee tribe who lived in what is now known as Collard Valley, located in Polk County, Georgia. Here is what we know about him:

Peaceful Coexistence: Historical accounts suggest Chief Collard and his tribe lived peacefully alongside white settlers in Cedartown, Georgia, before the forced removal of Cherokees known as the Trail of Tears in 1838.

Chief Collard & His Sons

Dispossession and Relocation: Documents from 1837 show that Chief Collard lost his land to white settlers before the official removal. He relocated to Cedar Creek and established another farm before being forced westward with his tribe.

Photographic Evidence: A rare photograph exists of Chief Collard and his sons, taken after their relocation to Oklahoma. The photo suggests they may have converted to Christianity, as they wear crosses around their necks. It is believed the sons returned to Georgia after the Civil War and presented the photograph to the Whatley family, with whom they had been neighbors.

Where to Learn More: Polk County Historical Society: The Polk County Historical Society website has a section dedicated to Chief Collard: https://polkhist.com/chief-collard-and-the-cherokee/.

The Family of Collard Valley Cooks

My granny and Grandaddy jumped into marriage quickly. Granny was just a kid, around 14, and Grandaddy was not too much older himself. They settled down in Collard Valley, Georgia, in this old, rickety shack. But Grandaddy was a hard worker and eventually built a successful construction company of his own. In his younger days, he was busy building houses—one of which he made for his family once he saved up enough. They ended up having four boys and one girl.

My daddy, William, and my Mama, Iva, met at a church event for the first time. Mama was super young, and at first, Daddy did not even notice her! But by the next time they saw each other, he was head over heels. They dated for a bit and got married during Mama's last year of high school.

After Mama graduated, they moved to Marietta, Georgia, so Daddy could go to college. He earned an associate's degree in construction from Southern Tech. Once he graduated, he built a house on a hill overlooking the valley, just a couple of pastures away from my

grandparents' home, but still on the same side of the road. In 1962, while living in Marietta, they welcomed my brother Barry. After a five-year gap, they had us three in a row! My sister, Malissa, was born in 1968. I came along in 1969, and then my younger brother, Eddie, followed in 1971. Growing up on the farm was a blast. Daddy raised cattle, and there was even a massive hog barn behind my grandparents' house—talk about a smell! But we always had plenty of beef and pork in the freezer. Mama also grew plenty of vegetables, which she canned or froze so we would have food during the winter months.

I met the love of my life, Chris Nichols, in 1999. We were set up on a blind date by my 1st cousin and his wife. I was 29, and Chris was 32. We fell in love and were married in 2000. This picture was taken a few months before we met. I was a blonde when we met, but that changed because it was expensive, and he liked my red hair! We were blessed with May in 2000 and Amy in 2001.

We moved to Paulding County in 2001 so Chris could work for the county school system. I worked for an Architectural firm drawing schools. The firm was called Chegwidden Dorsey & Holmes. Don Dorsey and Chuck Holmes were old classmates of my dad's when he attended college. I so enjoyed working as an Architectural Project Manager. I loved the detailing aspect of the work more than the design, and I guess that came from my family's background in construction.

We were very faithful and went to a local Missionary Baptist church called Grace Baptist in Powder Springs, Georgia. We attended all services and raised the girls in the faith of the Lord Jesus Christ.

In the year 2010, while the girls were in the 3rd and 4th grade, I was diagnosed with stage 3C Triple Negative Breast Cancer. It had spread, and I had two tumors in my right breast and 12 lymph nodes positive with cancer. I had a double mastectomy and did chemotherapy and radiation. The picture on the left is the Christmas after my treatments in October. By then, my hair had started growing back, and I was thrilled to have eyebrows and lashes again! Praise the Lord, I am still here today, and Collard Valley Cooks was founded in 2017. I did not have intentions of starting a social media channel, but I wanted to make videos for the girls. I wanted them to know how to cook if the cancer came back. I began using an iPad with Velcro to film. I made a Facebook channel first and followed up with a YouTube channel. The channel grew fast, and I had 100k followers on YouTube by January of 2020.

In 2020, at the beginning of the COVID-19 pandemic, we sold our home in Paulding County and our single-wide mobile home in Pensacola, Florida, and moved to Saint Mary's. We wanted to retire near the coast, and it was significantly more affordable to move there than to the Gulf. We loaded up the girls and came here, and they all enrolled in Georgia Southern that fall.

We moved to Richmond Hill from Saint Mary's in 2022 to be closer to our kids. It is much easier to eat with mama when she is 50 minutes away vs. 2.5 hours. Chris spends most of his time fishing, and you can watch him on his personal YouTube channel, Nichols Retirement Empire.

Visit
Nichols Retirement
Empire on
YouTube

♥

Scan to visit now

These images feature our children: May, our eldest daughter. Amy is our youngest and is wearing an aqua and black dress, and Kaysha is our goddaughter. All three reside in Savannah, Georgia. May and Amy are employed as therapists working with children on the spectrum, while Kaysha will graduate with a degree in Computer Engineering by the end of 2025. The picture below shows our family at Amy's College Graduation in May of 2024. She has a bachelor's degree in psychology.

Age 4

Age 9

Age 16

Age 19

Age 27

Age 28

Age 28

Age 28

Age 40

Age 42

Age 48

Age 50

Age 55

Age 55

Age 56

Merry Christmas!

Tammy's Holiday Recipes!

This Thanksgiving create a menu with our recipes and have a celebration of Southern tradition. Each recipe is crafted with love and care, ensuring that your family will enjoy a delicious and memorable meal. Gather your loved ones around the table, share stories, and create beautiful memories that will last a lifetime. Happy Thanksgiving from our family to yours! Tammy

Appetizers:

Recipe #34 Deviled Eggs

Start your Thanksgiving feast with these classic Deviled Eggs. Made with a blend of mayonnaise, mustard, and sweet pickle relish, they are topped with a sprinkle of paprika for a touch of color and flavor. These are sure to be a hit with your guests

Sausage Balls Recipe 42

These savory Sausage Balls are the perfect bite-sized appetizer for your holiday gathering. Made with a blend of sausage, cheese, and biscuit mix, they are baked until golden and delicious, making them a crowd-pleasing addition to your festive menu.

Main Courses:

Southern Fried Chicken #526 or #527

This Southern Fried Chicken is crispy on the outside and tender on the inside. The chicken is seasoned with a blend of spices, dipped in an egg mixture, and coated with self-rising flour before being fried to golden perfection. It is a comforting and delicious main dish that everyone will love

Rump Roast #75

Roasted Rump Roast is a tender and flavorful main dish. The roast is seasoned with a blend of herbs and spices, then slowly roasted to perfection. It is a hearty and satisfying addition to your holiday menu

Holiday Ham #490

This Holiday Ham is a showstopper for any festive gathering. The ham is sliced and plated before guests arrive, creating a beautiful centerpiece for your holiday table.

Southern Side Dishes:

Mama's Chicken & Dressing #118

No Thanksgiving dinner is complete without Cornbread Dressing. This recipe combines crumbled cornbread, chopped onions, celery, and a blend of seasonings, all baked to a golden brown. It is a savory and satisfying side that pairs perfectly with the fried chicken

Green Bean Casserole # 314 or 315

This Green Bean Casserole is a classic favorite. French green beans are combined with a creamy mushroom sauce and topped with crispy fried onions. It is a comforting and delicious side that adds a touch of nostalgia to your meal

Granny Green Beans # 642

Granny Green Beans are a classic Southern side dish. These green beans are cooked with a touch of sugar that caramelizes and gives them the flavor of Granny's green beans. They are a comforting and delicious addition to your holiday feast.

Creamed Potatoes 674 or Hashbrown Casserole #317

Creamed Potatoes are a creamy and indulgent side dish. Made with tender potatoes and a rich, buttery sauce, they are the perfect complement to the savory ham and green beans.

Broccoli Casserole #306

This Broccoli Casserole is a comforting and delicious side dish. Made with fresh broccoli, a creamy sauce, and topped with cheese, it is a dish that everyone will love.

Sweet Potato Souffle' Casserole #328

Sweet Potato Soufflé is a sweet and savory side dish that adds a touch of elegance to your holiday meal. The sweet potatoes are whipped to perfection and topped with a crunchy pecan streusel.

Breads:

Broccoli Cornbread #119

Add a twist to your traditional cornbread with this Broccoli Cornbread. Made with Jiffy cornbread mix, sour cream, and finely chopped broccoli, it is a moist and flavorful side dish that will complement your Thanksgiving spread beautifully

Butter Rolls #157

These soft and fluffy Butter Rolls are a classic addition to any holiday table. Baked to golden perfection and brushed with melted butter, they are the ideal accompaniment for hearty holiday meals, perfect for soaking up gravy and sauces.

Desserts:

Pumpkin Pie #476

Pumpkin Pie is a classic holiday dessert featuring a smooth, spiced pumpkin filling baked in a flaky pie crust. It has warm flavors and creamy texture make it a festive favorite, perfect for rounding out your Thanksgiving or Christmas menu.

Granny's Chocolate Meringue #445

This luscious chocolate pie features a rich, silky chocolate filling nestled in a flaky crust and is crowned with a light, golden meringue. It is an old-fashioned dessert that brings comfort and nostalgia to your holiday t{ crowdpleasing finale to you

Pecan Pie #470

This classic Pecan Pie features a sweet, gooey filling loaded with crunchy pecans, all nestled in a buttery, flaky crust. It is a timeless holiday treat that offers the perfect balance of rich, nutty flavor and satisfying sweetness for your festive table.

Carrot Cake #207

This Carrot Cake is moist, flavorful, and packed with fresh carrots, nuts, and spices. It is topped with a rich cream cheese frosting that adds the perfect touch of sweetness.

Salads:

Broccoli Salad #548

Broccoli Salad is a crisp and colorful addition to your holiday menu, featuring fresh broccoli florets tossed with savory bacon, crunchy pecans, and sweet golden raisins. It is dressed in a creamy, tangy sauce that brings all the flavors together for a refreshing side dish that complements festive meals perfectly.

Cranberry Relish #562

Cranberry Relish is a vibrant, tangy side dish made with fresh cranberries, citrus, and just the right amount of sweetness. It is a festive and refreshing complement to rich holiday fare, adding a bright burst of flavor and color to your holiday menu.

A

Air Fryer
Air Fryer Vegetables 257
Bacon 3
Baked Potato 3
Blooming Onion 2
Bread Pudding 3
Brussels Sprouts 2
Buttermilk Biscuits 3
Chicken Fries 4
Chicken Tenders 4
Chicken Wings 4
Cinnamon Toast 4
Coconut Custard 5
Corn on Cob 5
Croutons 5
Fried Chicken 8
Home Fries 6
Hot Dogs 6
Italian Meatballs 34
Nachos 5
Panko Crusted Fish 6
Peach Cobbler 7
Potato Chips 7
Potato Skins 7
Sausage Pepperoni Bread 8

Appetizers
14 Day Sweet Pickles 10
Artichoke & Spinach Dip 11
Blooming Onion 2
Cheese Ball 14
Cheese Straws 12
Chex Mix 12
Chocolate Strawberries 13
Cocktail Meatballs 13
Cream Cheese Rangoons 14
Cucumber Salad 12
Deviled Eggs 14
Dill Pickles 11
Fried Green Tomatoes 15
Fried Mozzarella Sticks 15
Fruit Dip 16
Guacamole Dip 16
Ham Spread 16
Hushpuppies 52
Nachos 5
Onion Rings 17
Pimento Cheese 17
Pizza Popovers 65
Potato Skins 7
Sausage Balls 18
Sour Cream & Onion Dip 18
Stuffed Strawberries 146

Apples
Apple Cookies 128
Apple Crumble 160

Apple Dapple Cake 80
Apple Dumplings 161
Apple Fritters 54
Apple Nut Bread 54
Apple Pie 160
Apple Salad 206
Apple Skillet Cake 80
Apple Stack Cake 81
Applesauce Cake 80
Caramel Sauce 154
Easy Apple Cobbler 160
Fried Apple Pies 161
Sausage Bread Dressing 66

Asparagus
Asparagus, Sauteed 252

Avocado
Avocado Salad 206
Guacamole Dip 16

B

Bacon
BLT Chicken Salad 208

Bananas
Banana Bread 55
Banana Bread Pudding 56
Banana Coffee Cake 71
Banana Cream Pie 162
Banana Custard 82
Banana Custard Cake 82
Banana Muffins, Brown Sugar 60
Banana Nut Muffins 60
Banana Pound Cake 81
Banana Pudding 138
Banana Split Cake 139
Easy Hummingbird Cake 112
Hummingbird Cake 91
Mile High Pie 172
Tropical Dream Cake 108
Whole Shebang Cake 113

Bars
Blondie Brownies 128
Carrot Cake, Cheesecake Bars 129
Chewy Oatmeal Bars 129
Chocolate Chip Cookie Bars ... 130
Chocolate Ganache 155
Hershey's Brownies 132
Lemon Bars 133
Peanut Butter Bars 134
Peanut Butter Krispy Treats 135
Rice Krispy Treats 135

Beans & Peas
Baked Beans 238
Bean Salad 206
Black eyed Peas 238
Butter Beans 239
Chili 231

Cowboy Beans 188
Field Peas with Snaps 240
Fresh Green Beans 238
Granny Green Beans 239
Great Northern Beans 239
Hoppin John 243
Pinto Beans 241
Pinto Beans Instant Pot 241
Purple Hull Peas 240
Red Beans & Rice 242
Red Kidney Beans 242
Refried Beans 242
Sausage Beans & Rice 187
Settler's Beans 188, 240
Speckled Butter Beans 243
Texas Hash 36

Beef
Baked Spaghetti Casserole 115
Battered Hamburger Steak 27
Beef Burrito Supreme 20
Beef Shanks 22
Beef Stew, Dutch Oven 228
Beef Tips & Gravy 22
Big Mac Style Burger 217
Braised Chuck Roast 31
Butter Basted Steak 29
Chili 231
Chili Steak Burgers 218
Chip Beef & Gravy 22
Chuck Roast, Pressure cook 31
Cocktail Meatballs 13
Corned Beef & Cabbage 24
Cottage Pie 24
Double Meat Chili 232
Fried Cubed Steak 25
Fried Round Steak 33
Hamburger Steak 26
Hamburger Steak Deluxe 26
Hardy Tomato Beef Stew 229
Hot Dogs 6
Irish Beef Stew 230
Italian Meatballs 34
London Broil Marinade 27
Mama's Chuck Roast 32
Mama's Meatloaf 28
Marvelous Meatballs 29
Mississippi Pot Roast 27
Nana's Steak Fries 25
Pepper Steak 29
Prime Rib Roast 30
Roast & Vegetables 30
Roasted Rump Roast 33
Rump Roast Dutch Oven 32
Salisbury Steak 34
Secret Spaghetti Sauce 37
Shipwreck Casserole 124

Stuffed Bell Peppers 33
Swiss Steak 35
Taco Cabbage Skillet 36
Taco Skillet 35
Texas Hash 36
Tomato Sauce Meatloaf 28
Ukrainian Goulash...................37
Vegetable Beef Soup 236
Beef Roast
Braised Chuck Roast 31
Chuck Roast, Pressure cook......31
Mama's Chuck Roast 32
Mississippi Pot Roast................27
Roast & Vegetables 30
Roasted Rump Roast................ 33
Rump Roast Dutch Oven 32
Beef Steak
Butter Basted Steak..................29
Cheesesteak Hoagies 218
Fried Round Steak 33
Pepper Steak.........................29
Prime Rib Roast 30
Steak & Dumplings 235
Berries
Berry Scones 55
Blackberry Cake 85
Blackberry Dumpling Cobbler.163
Blueberry Biscuits 43
Blueberry Muffins.....................61
Chocolate Strawberries 13
Holiday Bread Dressing 66
Strawberry Cake 113
Strawberry Cheesecake Pie.....178
Strawberry Coffeecake............72
Strawberry Glaze 178
Strawberry Topping 158
Stuffed Strawberries............... 146
Tropical Dream Cake 108
Beverages
Coffee Frappe 39
Coffee Punch 39
Egg Nog.............................39
Eggnog Pound Cakes 89
Fruit Sweet Tea 40
Georgia Sweet Tea 40
Hot Chocolate Mix 40
Lemonade 41
Orange Punch.........................41
Peach Milkshakes.....................41
Biscuit Mix
Biscuit Mix 47
Biscuit Mix Pancakes.................47
Biscuits.............................47
Dumplings 47
Biscuits
2 Ingredient Biscuits.................43

Angel Biscuits 43
Biscuit Cinnamon Rolls.............57
Blueberry Biscuits 43
Buttermilk Biscuits....................44
Cheddar & Garlic Biscuits 44
Chicken Biscuit Casserole 118
Hand Rolled............................45
Hoecake Biscuit 45
Lard Fried Biscuits....................46
Mayonnaise Biscuits.................46
Sour Cream Biscuits..................46
Spoon Biscuits 44
Stovetop Biscuits.....................47
Sweet Biscuit Glaze 43
Braising
30 min Chicken Dinner...........190
6 Spice Chicken 190
Braised Chuck Roast 31
Chicken Buritto Skillet 118
Corned Beef & Cabbage 24
Pork Chop & Potatoes.............182
Pork Ribs with Vegetables 185
Smoked Sausage Hash............187
Bread
Bread Dressing 66
Butter Rolls 62
Cheese Fritters........................63
Corn Fritters 63
Crazy Crust Pizza 63
Croutons 5
Drop Dumplings 64
Dumplings 64
Hot Cross Buns 65
Irish Soda Bread 66
Spoon Bread 62
Breads, Sweet
Apple Nut Bread.......................54
Banana Bread 55
Banana Bread Pudding 56
Banana Coffee Cake..................71
Berry Scones 55
Biscuit Cinnamon Rolls.............57
Bread Pudding 56
Bread Pudding, Granny's...........56
Buttermilk Doughnuts 58
Cherry Coffeecake 72
Cinnamon French Toast........... 74
Cinnamon Rolls 57
Cinnamon Rolls, Shortcut..........71
Cinnamon Toast 4
French Toast 74
Orange Date Nut Bread 59
Pancakes...............................75
Pumpkin Bread 59
Strawberry Coffeecake............72
Vanilla Scones.........................59

Waffles, Mamas......................76
Breakfast
1 Cup Gravy...........................69
2 Egg Omelet.........................68
Banana Coffee Cake.................71
Biscuit Cinnamon Rolls.............57
Biscuits & Gravy......................68
Breakfast Casserole 70
Breakfast Pizza........................69
Broccoli Cheese Quiche............69
Buttermilk Doughnuts 58
Cherry Coffeecake 72
Chris's Breakfast 70
Cinnamon French Toast........... 74
Cinnamon Rolls, Shortcut..........71
Creamy Grits..........................73
Egg in a Hole 71
Egg Sandwich......................... 73
Eggs over Easy 72
Fireman's Breakfast 70
French Toast 74
Hard Boiled Eggs 73
Hashbrowns............................75
Microwave Oatmeal 75
Milk & Butter Gravy 68
Pancakes...............................75
Sausage Milk Gravy 76
Strawberry Coffeecake............72
Streusel Topping 71
Waffles, Mamas......................76
Breakfast Sausage
2 Egg Omelet.........................68
Breakfast Casserole 70
Breakfast Pizza........................69
Cabbage Roll Skillet..................23
Fireman's Breakfast 70
Hamburger Steak with Sausage...
182
Holiday Bread Dressing 66
Pancakes & Sausage.................75
Red Beans & Rice 242
Sausage & Egg Pie....................76
Sausage Balls from Scratch.......18
Sausage Beans & Rice..............187
Sausage Milk Gravy 76
Sausage Pepperoni Bread 8
Settler's Beans 188
Broccoli
Broccoli Cheese Casserole 117
Broccoli Cheese Quiche............69
Broccoli Cornbread 49
Broccoli Salad 206
Broccoli, Steamed 252
Brussels
Bacon Brussels 252
Brussels, Sauteed 252, 253

Brussels, Steamed 253
Roasted Brussels 2

C

Cabbage
Cabbage Roll Skillet 23
Carrot Cole slaw 209
Cole Slaw 209
Corned Beef & Cabbage 24
German Cole Slaw 209
KFC Cole Slaw 209
Purple Saute Cabbage 246
Simple Fried Cabbage 184
Smoked Sausage Simmer 185
Southern Fried Cabbage 184
Stewed Cabbage 246
Taco Cabbage Skillet 36
Vegetable Beef Soup 236
Vegetable Beef Soup for 2 236
Vegetable Soup, Garden 236
Cake Mix Creations
Banana Nut Pd Cake 105
Better than Sex Cake 109
Black Forest Cake 105
Chocolate Chip Pound Cake ... 106
Daddy Dump Cake 106
Earthquake Cake 106
Easy Hummingbird Cake 112
Egg Nog Pound Cake 105
Fruit Bar Cakes 107
Gooey Butter Cake 107
Honeybun Cake 109
Italian Cream Cake 108
Krinkle Cookies 131
Lemon Gooey Butter Cake 107
Lemonade Cake 109
Nutmeg Cake 110
Peaches & Cream Cake 111
Pecan Upside Down Cake 112
Pie Filling Cake 110
Pig Pickin Cake 110
Pina Colada Pound Cake 112
Strawberry Cake 113
Tropical Dream Cake 108
Tunnel of Fudge Cake 111
Watergate Cake 113
Whole Shebang Cake 113
Cakes from Scratch
1 Egg Spice Cake 93
5 Flavor Pound Cake 78
Angel Food Cake 78
Apple Dapple Cake 80
Apple Skillet Cake 80
Apple Stack Cake 81
Applesauce Cake 80
Banana Custard Cake 82

Banana Pound Cake 81
Black Walnut 153
Blackberry Cake 85
Brown Beauty Cake 82
Buttery Fruitcake 86
Carrot Cake 83
Cheesecake Plain or Oreo 84
Cheesecake, Pumpkin 101
Cheesecake, Sweet Potato 101
Chocolate Pound Cake 84
Condensed Milk Pound Cake 86
Eggnog Pound Cake 89
Favorite Chocolate Cake 85
Favorite Pound Cake 94
Flaked Coconut Cake 88
Fresh Coconut Cake, Mama's ... 87
German Chocolate Cake 90
Hershey's Syrup Cake 90
Hot Fudge Pudding Cake 89
Hummingbird Cake 91
Ice Box Fruitcake 91
Japanese Fruitcake 92
Magdalenes Coconut Cake 88
Maple Pecan Pound Cake 92
Mexican meets Cola 102
Mini Cheesecakes 83
Mississippi Mud Cake 93
Oatmeal Cake 94
Orange Juice Cake 95
PB & J Cake 96
Peach Skillet Cake 95
Peanut Butter Cake 96
Peter Paul Mounds Cake 96
Pineapple Pound Cake 97
Pineapple Skillet Cake 97
Pound Cake for Layers 98
Praline Cake 100
Prune Cake 97
Pumpkin Cake 59
Red Velvet Cake 99
Snickerdoodle Spice Layers 99
Spanish Bar Cake 100
Sponge Cake 101
Sweet Potato Pound Cake 98
Tea Cakes, Maw Maws 136
Toffee Pecan Crunch Cake 102
White Cake Layers 87
Whoopie Pies 103
Yellow Cake Layers 103
Candy
Butter Toffee 139
Chocolate Covered Cherries .. 140
Divinity 141
Martha Washington Balls 141
Microwave Peanut Brittle 144
Old Fashioned Fudge 142

Orange Balls 143
Peanut Brittle 144
Peanut Butter Buckeyes 143
Peanut Butter Cornflake Candy ... 143
Potato Candy 144
Pralines 145
Caramel
Butter Toffee 139
Buttermilk Glaze 154
Caramel Corn 138
Caramel Icing 155
Caramel Sauce 154, 222
Praline Cake 100
Carrots
Apricot Glazed 248
Carrot Cake 83
Carrot Cake, Cheesecake Bars 129
Carrot Cole slaw 209
Carrot Raisin Salad 207
Casseroles
Baked Chicken Salad 115
Baked Spaghetti Casserole 115
Beefy Mushroom Mac 116
Breakfast Casserole 70
Broccoli Cheese Casserole 117
Buffalo Mac N Cheese 116
Chicken & Rice Casserole 116
Chicken Biscuit Casserole 118
Chicken Buritto Skillet 118
Chicken Noodle Casserole 119
Chicken Spaghetti Casserole ... 119
Chicken Spectacular 120
Chris's Breakfast 70
Creole Tuna Casserole 126
Easy Green Bean Casserole 120
Fireman's Breakfast 70
Get out of the Kitchen Chicken 120
Green Bean Casserole 121
Ground Beef & Rice 121
Hashbrown Casserole 121
Italian Meats Lasagna 122
Mac n Cheese Pizza 123
Macaroni Delight 123
Napoli Casserole 123
Old Fashioned Mac N Cheese .. 124
Old Timer Squash Casserole 125
Reuben Casserole 117
Shipwreck Casserole 124
Skillet Spaghetti 124
Summer Squash Casserole 125
Sweet Potato Souffle 125
Tater Tot Casserole 126
Veg-All Casseroles 126
Winner Lasagna 122

Cheese

Broccoli Cheese Casserole 117
Broccoli Cheese Quiche 69
Buffalo Mac N Cheese............. 116
Cheddar & Garlic Biscuits 44
Cheese Fritters.........................63
Cheese Sauce......................... 222
Cheesey Sausage Muffins 60
Deluxe Grill Cheese 217
Fireman's Breakfast 70
Fried Cheese sticks...................15
Hashbrown Casserole.............121
Macaroni Delight 123
Mexican Cornbread...................52
Old Fashioned Mac N Cheese ..124
Pepper Jack Mac 115
Pimento Cheese 17
Potato Skins.............................7
Sausage & Egg Pie....................76
Sausage Balls 18
Tomato Mozzarella Salad.........214
Winner Lasagna 122

Cheesecakes

Carrot Bars...............................129
Cheesecake Plain or Oreo........84
Graham Cracker Crust 101
Mini Cheesecakes....................83
Pineapple Pie 175
Pumpkin or Sweet Potato 101
Strawberry Cheesecake Pie.....178
Sweet Potato Cheesecake Pie 175

Cherries

Banana Split Cake 139
Black Forest Cake 105
Cherry Coffeecake 72
Cherry Jell-O Salad 207
Cherry Pie............................... 164
Chocolate Covered Cherries ..140
Fruitcake Cookies....................131
Icebox Fruitcake 91
Japanese Fruit Cake 92
Mile High Pie 172
Millionaire Pie 172
Pineapple Skillet Cake 97
Tammy's Buttery Fruitcake 86
Watergate Pie 179
Watergate Salad 215

Chicken

30 min Chicken Gravy Dinner 190
6 Spice Chicken.......................190
Baked Chicken Salad............... 115
Baked Chicken Wings 192
Benefield Chicken 228
BLT Chicken Salad 208
Boiled Chicken..........................48
Brown Sugar Baked Chicken ... 191

Brunswick Stew 230
Butter Fried Chicken 190
Catalina French Chicken......... 197
Chicken & Dumplings...............230
Chicken & Rice Casserole......... 116
Chicken and Rice, Asian 191
Chicken Biscuit Casserole 118
Chicken Bone Broth 229
Chicken Broth...........................48
Chicken Buritto Skillet 118, 191
Chicken Francese 192
Chicken Fried Chicken 192
Chicken Fries 4
Chicken Noodle Casserole 119
Chicken Noodle Soup 231
Chicken Pot Pie........................ 194
Chicken Salad 208
Chicken Spaghetti Casserole... 119
Chicken Spectacular 120
Chicken Tenders, Air Fryer 4
Chicken Wings Deep fry 194
Chicken Wings, Air Fryer........... 4
Chris's Special Seasonings..... 223
Citrus Baked Cornish Hens......193
Crusty Chicken Legs 193
Delicious Drumsticks 193
Famous Fried Chicken............. 196
Fried Chicken Bone-in 195
Fried Chicken Nuggets........... 197
Fried Chicken Tenders............. 197
Fried Chicken, Air Fryer 8
Garlic Chicken 200
Get out of the Kitchen Chicken ....
    120
How to Cook Giblets................225
Lemon Garlic Chicken............ 198
Linguinie Positano.................. 198
Lo Mein................................... 199
Marry Me Chicken................... 199
Mexican Chicken.....................200
Mexican Shredded Chicken...200
Mexican Style Chicken............ 196
Mustard Fried Chicken............ 196
Orange Chicken Stir Fry.......... 194
Pan Seared Chicken 201
Paremesan Chicken 201
Skillet Fried Chicken............... 195
Take it Easy Chicken...............202
Veg-All Casseroles...................126
White Chicken Chili................. 232

Chocolate

Better than Sex Cake...............109
Black Forest Cake 105
Brown Beauty Cake..................82
Brown Beauty Frosting 82
Buckeyes.................................143

Chocolate Bread Pudding 56
Chocolate Brownie Pie............. 165
Chocolate Buttercream....154, 155
Chocolate Chess Pie................ 164
Chocolate Chip Cookie Bars ... 130
Chocolate Chip Cookies...........129
Chocolate Chip Pd Cake..........106
Chocolate Covered Cherries ..140
Chocolate Cream Cheese Pie ..163
Chocolate Cream Pie.............. 165
Chocolate Delight....................140
Chocolate Ganache 155
Chocolate Gravy 223
Chocolate Meringue, Granny's ....
    166
Chocolate Oatmeal Cookies ... 130
Chocolate Pie Crust.................163
Chocolate Pound Cake.............84
Chocolate Pralines 145
Chocolate Pudding...................139
Chocolate Sauce 223
Chocolate Strawberries 13
Coffee Frappe 39
Coffee Punch 39
Cream Puffs.............................58
Dark Chocolate Pudding........... 111
Dirt Cake 141
Earthquake Cake 106
Easy Chocolate Frosting 93
Favorite Chocolate Cake 85
Georgie Porgy Pie 168
German Chocolate Cake 90
Hershey's Brownies 132
Hershey's Syrup Cake............. 90
Hot Chocolate Mix................... 40
Hot Fudge Pudding Cake..........89
Krinkle Cookies........................131
Mississippi Mud Cake...............93
Mocha Cream Pie 171
Peanut Butter Delight............. 145
Pudding Frosting 110
Sheetcake Frosting...................85
Toll House Pie..........................179
Triple Chocolate Cookies 136
Whoopie Pies 103

Chocolate Chips

Better than Sex Cake...............109
Brown Beauty Cake..................82
Brown Beauty Frosting 82
Chocolate Chip Cookie Bars ... 130
Chocolate Chip Cookies...........129
Chocolate Chip Pound Cake ...106
Chocolate Covered Cherries ..140
Chocolate Cream Cheese Pie ..163
Chocolate Strawberries 13
Chris's Favorite.......................130

270

Coffee Frappe 39
Cowboy Cookies........................131
Hot Fudge Pudding Cake...........89
Peanut Butter Buckeyes...........143
Toll House Pie 179
Triple Chocolate Cookies 136
Cobblers
Blackberry Dumpling Cobbler.163
Cobbler Biscuit Topping...........173
Cobbler Cinnamon Topping.....173
Easy Apple Cobbler 160
Frozen Fruit for Cobblers 173
Fruit Cobbler 173
Peach Cobbler Classic..............172
Sweet Potato Cobbler 176
Sweet Potatoes........................177
Coconut
Apple Dapple Cake 80
Better than Sex Cake................109
Broiled Coconut Icing...............94
Coconut Buttercream 87
Coconut Cream Pie 167
Coconut Custard 5
Coconut Filling & Topping 87
Coconut Macaroons..................131
Coconut Pudding......................140
Condensed Milk Pound Cake....86
Earthquake Cake 106
Easy Hummingbird Cake 112
Flaked Coconut Cake 88
French Coconut Pie..................165
Fresh Coconut Cake, Mama's...87
Georgie Porgy Pie 168
German Chocolate Cake 90
German Chocolate Icing 90
Italian Cream Cake 108
Japanese Pie 169
Magdalenes Coconut Cake.......88
Magdalene's Coconut Icing 88
Martha Washington Balls 141
Millionaire Pie 172
Mississippi Mud Cake...............93
Peter Paul Mounds Cake...........96
Pina Colada Pound Cake...........112
Toffee Pecan Crunch Cake...... 102
Tropical Dream Cake 108
Coffee
Chocolate Pound Cake..............84
Coffee Frappe 39
Coffee Punch 39
Favorite Chocolate Cake...........85
Coffeecake
Banana Coffeecake 71
Cherry Coffeecake 72
Strawberry Coffeecake.............72
Cookies

Apple Cookies 128
Chocolate Chip 129
Chocolate Oatmeal No Bakes . 130
Chris's Favorite........................ 130
Coconut Macaroons..................131
Cookie Frosting 128
Cowboy Cookies........................131
Fruitcake Cookies 131
Humdings 132
Lemon Teacakes 133
Mincemeat Cookies...................132
Oatmeal....................................133
Orange Balls..............................143
Orange Slice Cookies 134
Peanut Butter Cookies 134
Snickerdoodles 135
Sugar Cookies...........................135
Tea Cakes, Maw Maws 136
Triple Chocolate Cookies 136
Corn
Corn Chowder 232
Corn Fritters 63
Corn on Cob..............................5
Corn on the Cob 244
Corn on the Cob Herb Butter ..244
Corn Pudding............................245
Cream & Fried Corn..................245
Creamy Grits............................ 73
Mexican Street Corn 244
Mighty Good Cornbread 52
Cornbread
Broccoli Cornbread 49
Chicken and Dressing, Mamas.48
Corn Pones 51
Cornbread and Milk..................52
Cornbread Dressing Cakes 50
Cornbread Dressing, Granny... 50
Cornbread for Dressing 48
Cornbread for Two 49
Cornbread Fritters....................49
Cornbread Salad...................... 210
Crackling Cornbread..................51
Crunchy Cornbread 51
Hot Water Cornbread................51
Hushpuppies.............................52
Mexican Cornbread...................52
Mighty Good Cornbread 52
Oven Fried Cornbread...............53
Shortcut Dressing 50
Corned Beef
Corned Beef and Cabbage........24
Reuben Casserole..................... 117
Cream Cheese
Apple Salad 206
Banana Split Cake 139
Buffalo Mac n Cheese 116

Carrot Cake, Cheesecake Bars 129
Cheese Ball................................14
Cheese Surprise Pie 164
Cheesecake Plain or Oreo........84
Cheesey Sausage Muffins 60
Cherry Coffeecake 72
Cherry Jell-O Salad 207
Chocolate Cream Cheese Pie ..163
Chocolate Delight 140
Cream Cheese Frosting..... 83, 156
Cream Cheese Rangoons...........14
Deluxe Grill Cheese 217
Dirt Cake 141
Earthquake Cake 106
Fruit Bar Cakes 107
Gooey Butter Cake 107
Ham Salad 212
Ham Spread 16
Italian Cream Cake 108
Lemon Cream Pie 169
Lemon Gooey Butter Cake 107
Lemon Lush 142
Lemon Lush Pie 170
Macaroni Salad........................ 212
Millionaire Pie 172
Mini Cheesecakes......................83
Peach Frosting.......................... 111
Peanut Butter Chocolate Delight..
145
Peanut Butter Pie.....................173
Pimento Cheese 17
Pineapple Cream Cheese Pie .. 175
Pumpkin Cheesecake...............101
Strawberry Cheesecake Pie.....178
Stuffed Strawberries............... 146
Sweet Pot Cheesecake Pie 175
Cream Cheese Frosting
Applesauce Cake 80
Banana Bread 83
Carrot Cake...............................83
Cinnamon French Toast........... 74
Hummingbird Cake 91
Italian Cream 83
Italian Cream Cake 108
Lemonade Cake 109
Red Velvet 83
Red Velvet Cake 99
Snickerdoodle Spice Cake........99
Spanish Bar Cake 100
Crockpot
Beef Stew Dutch Oven 228
Beefy Mushroom Mac 116
Boston Butt Crockpot............... 181
Corned Beef & Cabbage............24
Get out of the Kitchen Chicken ....
120

Lemon Garlic Chicken............. 198
Mexican Chicken 200
Mississippi Pot Roast.................27
Red Beans & Rice 242
Ribs & Beans Crockpot 186
Roast & Vegetables 30
Roasted Turkey Breast 202
Sausage Beans & Rice..............187
Turkey Crockpot Dinner 203

Cucumbers
14 Day Sweet Pickles 10
Cucumber Salad 12, 210
Dill Pickles....................................11
Italian Pasta Salad 212
Macaroni Salad 212
Tuna Salad.................................214

D
Dates
Buttery Fruitcake......................86
Fruitcake Cookies 131
Hot Cross Buns 65
Humdings 132
Orange Date Nut Bread 59

Desserts
Banana Bread Pudding 56
Banana Pudding 138
Banana Split Cake 139
Bread Pudding 3, 56
Bread Pudding, Granny's..........56
Butter Toffee 139
Caramel Corn.............................138
Chocolate Pudding...................139
Chocolate Strawberries 13
Coconut Custard 5
Coconut Pudding......................140
Dirt Cake 141
Divinity......................................141
Martha Washington Balls 141
Old Fashioned Fudge...............142
Orange Balls..............................143
Peanut Brittle 144
Peanut Butter Buckeyes...........143
Peanut Butter Chocolate Delight.. 145
Peanut Butter Cornflake Candy ... 143
Potato Candy 144
Stuffed Strawberries.............. 146
Vanilla Custard Ice Cream....... 146
Vanilla Pudding........................138

Dips
Artichoke & Spinach...................11
Dippen Chicken Sauce 224
Fruit Dip 16
Guacamole Dip 16

Honey Mustard 224
Horsey Dipping Sauce.................2
Smokey Honey mustard 224
Sour Cream & Onion Dip 18
White Chicken Chili.................232

Dumplings
Apple Dumplings 161
Biscuit Mix Dumplings 47
Blackberry Dumpling Cobbler.163
Chicken & Dumplings................230
Drop Dumplings 64
Dumplings 64
Steak & Dumplings 235
Sweet Potato Cobbler 177

Dutch Oven
30 min Chicken Dinner...........190
Beef Stew 228
Hardy Tomato Beef Stew 229
Irish Beef Stew.........................230
Jambalaya..................................234
Old Settler's Beans 240
Pork Chop & Potatoes..............182
Ribs & Beans 186
Rump Roast Dutch Oven 32

E
Eggs
2 Egg Omelet.............................68
Deviled Eggs 14
Egg & Olive Salad 211
Egg Custard 166
Egg in a Hole 71
Egg Nog......................................39
Egg Nog Pound Cake, Easy.....105
Egg Sandwich............................73
Eggnog Pound Cake.................89
Eggs over Easy 72
Fireman's Breakfast 70
French Toast 74
Hard Boiled Eggs 73
Lemon Curd 158
Sausage & Egg Pie....................76
Tammy's Meringue..................166

F
Fillings
Banana Custard.........................82
Coconut Filling & Topping 87
Dark Chocolate Pudding........... 111
Frozen Fruit Filling....................95
Lemon Curd 158
Pastry Cream 58
Peter Paul Mounds Cake 96
Whoopie Pie Fluff 103

Fish
Creole Tuna Casserole 126
Fish and Chips 148

Fish Francese............................150
Fish Tacos.................................150
Fried Catfish Nuggets 148
Mustard Fried Fish...................149
Panko Crusted Fish 6
Salmon Patties......................... 149
Salmon Pie 149
Salmon Steaks..........................150
Salmon Steaks, Glazed............150
Tartar Sauce.............................226

Frosting
Brown Beauty Frosting 82
Browned Butter Frosting 153
Buttercream Frosting.............. 154
Chocolate Buttercream........... 154
Chocolate Frosting, Sheetcake.85
Chocolate Ganache 155
Coconut Buttercream 87
Cookie Frosting 128
Cream Cheese Frosting..... 83, 156
Decorator's Frosting 156
Easy Chocolate Frosting 93
Favorite Fudge Frosting 157
Fudge Icing, Stovetop.............. 157
Orange Juice Cake Frosting......95
Orange Juice Frosing 95
Peach Frosting........................... 111
Peanut Butter Bar Frosting 134
Peanut Butter Buttercream.......96
Peanut Butter Frosting.............134
Penna Colada Buttercream..... 154
Peter Paul Mounds Cake 96
Pineapple Pudding Frosting 110
Pistachio Pudding Frosting.......113
Pudding Frosting 110
Sour Cream Chocolate Frosting ... 155
Strawberry Frosting..................113
Vanilla Brownie Frosting..........128
Whipped Cream Frosting........105

Fruit
Banana Split Cake 139
Black Forest Cake 105
Buttery Fruitcake......................86
Clear Fruit Glaze 156
Fruit Cobbler............................173
Fruit Dip 16
Fruit Salad 211
Fruit Salad Surprise..................211
Fruit Salad, Yogurt 211
Fruitcake Cookies 131
Ice Box Fruitcake 91
Japanese Fruitcake 92
Mile High Pie 172
Mincemeat Cookies..................132
Prune Cake 97

Spanish Bar Cake 100
Tropical Dream Cake 108
Whole Shebang Cake 113

G

Glaze
5 Flavor Glaze 78
Butter Glaze 71
Buttermilk Glaze 154
Clear Fruit Glaze 156
Clear Lemon Glaze 156
Coconut Glaze 112
Lemon Glaze 157
Sweet Biscuit Glaze 43
Vanilla Glaze 156

Gravy
1 Cup Gravy 69
Chicken Broth Gravy 223
Chicken Fried Chicken 192
Chocolate Gravy......................223
Giblet Gravy, Granny's............225
Giblet Gravy, Mama's 225
Meatballs and Gravy 29
Milk & Butter Gravy 68
Mushroom Gravy.......................34
Mushroom Gravy, Easy............26
Poultry Pan Sauce 225
Red-Eye Gravy.........................225
Sage & Garlic Gravy 188
Sausage Milk Gravy 76
Tomato Gravy 226
White Milk Gravy 226

Green Beans
Easy Green Bean Casserole 120
Granny Green Beans 239
Green Bean Casserole 121

Ground Beef
Battered Hamburger Steak 27
Beef Enchiladas........................21
Beef Pot Pie..............................20
Beef Stroganoff 36
Beefy Mushroom Mac 116
Cabbage Roll Skillet.................. 23
Chili Steak Burgers 218
Chris's Goulash......................... 37
Cottage Pie...............................24
Cowboy Beans.......................... 188
Ground Beef & Rice 121
Hamburger Steak 26
Hamburger Steak Deluxe..........26
Italian Meatballs 34
Mama's Meatloaf......................28
Marvelous Meatballs 29
Meatloaf Hamburgers..............219
Salisbury Steak 34
Shipwreck Casserole................124

Skillet Spaghetti.......................124
Sloppy Joes 220
Stuffed Bell Peppers 33
Taco Pie 25
Taco Skillet 35
Texas Hash 36
Tomato Sauce Meatloaf 28
Vegetable Beef Soup 236
Winner Lasagna 122

Ground Turkey
Turkey Stroganoff 36

H

Ham
Butterbean Soup.....................229
Ham Spread 16

Hashbrowns
Breakfast Casserole 70
Chris's Breakfast 70
Hashbrown Casserole 121
Hashbrown Potatoes.............. 250
Hashbrowns...............................75
Pork Chop Hashbrown Bake....183

Hershey's Cocoa
Bread Pudding 56
Chocolate Brownie Pie............ 165
Chocolate Buttercream........... 154
Chocolate Chess Pie................ 164
Chocolate Cream Pie............... 165
Chocolate Frosting, Sheetcake.85
Chocolate Gravy...................... 223
Chocolate Meringue Pie.......... 166
Chocolate Oatmeal Cookies ... 130
Chocolate Pound Cake..............84
Chocolate Pudding...................139
Chocolate Sauce 223
Dark Chocolate Pudding........... 111
Favorite Chocolate Cake 85
Favorite Fudge Frosting 157
Fudge Icing, Stovetop.............. 157
German Chocolate Cake 90
Hershey's Brownies 132
Hot Chocolate Mix 40
Hot Fudge Pudding Cake...........89
Mexican meets Cola 102
Mississippi Mud Cake...............93
Old Fashioned Fudge...............142
Sour Cream Chocolate Frosting ...
    155
Triple Chocolate Cookies 136
Tunnel of Fudge Cake.............. 111
Whoopie Pies 103

Hidden Valley Ranch
Battered Hamburger Steak 27
Cheese Straws 12
Chicken Fries 4

Chicken Tenders 197
Fried Chicken Bone-in 195
Mississippi Crockpot Roast 27

I

Icing
7 Minute Icing 153
Black Wanut Stovetop Icing.....153
Broiled Coconut Icing................94
Browned Butter Icing..............100
Caramel Icing........................... 155
Chocolate Ganache................. 155
Favorite Fudge Frosting 157
Fudge Icing, Stovetop.............. 157
German Chocolate Icing 90
Japanese Fruitcake 92
Magdalene's Coconut Icing 88
Penna Colada Buttercream..... 154

Instant Pot
Chuck Roast, Pressure cook......31
Collard Greens 246
Pinto Beans Instant Pot...........241
Turnip Greens 246

Italian Dishes
Caesar Salad 207
Italian Meatballs 34
Italian Meats Lasagna 122
Italian Pasta Salad 212
Italian Pasta Sauce 34
Napoli Casserole......................123
Parmesan Chicken 201
Pizza Salad...............................213
Skillet Spaghetti.......................124
Tomato Mozzarella Salad 214
Winner Lasagna 122

Italian Sausage
Baked Spaghetti Casserole 115
Crazy Crust Pizza......................63
Italian Meatballs 34
Italian Meats Lasagna 122
Napoli Casserole......................123
Pizza Salad...............................213
Winner Lasagna 122

L

Leafy Greens
Collard Greens 246
Stewed Cabbage.....................246
Turnip Greens 246

Lemons
Chicken Francese.....................192
Clear Lemon Glaze 156
Fish Francese...........................150
Krinkle Cookies........................131
Lemon Bars 133
Lemon Curd 158
Lemon Garlic Chicken.............. 198

273

Lemon Glaze 157
Lemon Icebox Pie 170
Lemon Lush 142
Lemon Lush Pie 170
Lemon Meringue Pie 170
Lemon Teacakes 133
Lemonade 41
Lemonade Cake 109
Lime
   Key Lime Pie 169

M

Marshmallows
   Humdings 132
   Icebox Fruitcake 91
   Mississippi Mud Cake................93
   Mounds Cake 96
   Peanut Butter Krispy Treats.....135
   Rice Krispy Treats....................135
   Watergate Pie 179
   Watergate Salad 215
Meringue
   Chocolate Meringue................ 166
   Coconut Meringue 167
   Coffee Meringue..................... 167
   Lemon Meringue Pie 170
   Maple Meringue.......................171
   Mocha Meringue 171
   Pineapple Meringue Pie 175
Mexican Night
   Beef Burrito Supreme 20
   Beef Enchiladas..........................21
   Chicken Buritto Skillet 118, 191
   Enchilada Sauce 21
   Fish Tacos.................................150
   Mexican Chicken....................200
   Mexican Cornbread..................52
   Mexican Rice, Authentic.........247
   Mexican Shredded Chicken...200
   Mexican Style Chicken............ 196
   Nachos 5
   Refried Beans..........................242
   Taco Pie 25
   Taco Skillet 35
Microwave
   Banana Cream Pie 162
   Banana Pudding 138
   Butterscotch Pie 162
   Chewy Oatmeal Bars 129
   Chocolate Meringue Pie..........166
   Chocolate Pudding..................139
   Coconut Cream Pie 167
   Coconut Pudding....................140
   Coffee Cream pie 167
   Key Lime Pie 169
   Lemon Curd 158

Microwave Peanut Brittle 144
Mocha Meringue 171
Peach Topping 158
Vanilla Pudding........................138
Mississippi Mud Cake
   Easy Chocolate Frosting 93
Muffins
   Banana Muffins, Brown Sugar 60
   Banana Nut Muffins................. 60
   Blueberry Muffins.....................61
   Cheesy Sausage Muffins 60
   Pineapple Muffins.....................61
   Streusel Topping 60

O

Oatmeal
   Chocolate Oatmeal No Bakes . 130
   Cinnamon Oatmeal Crumble .160
   Cowboy Cookies.......................131
   Microwave Oatmeal 75
   Oatmeal....................................133
Okra
   Boiled Okra 253
   Fried Okra 254
   Fried Okra Deluxe 254
   Fried Okra Patties...................255
One Pot Meal
   30 min Chicken Gravy Dinner 190
   Beef Pot Pie..............................20
   Braised Chuck Roast 31
   Cabbage Roll Skillet.................. 23
   Chicken Pot Pie....................... 194
   Corned Beef & Cabbage 24
   Cottage Pie................................24
   Mama's Chuck Roast 32
   Pork Ribs and Vegetables 185
   Roast & Vegetables 30
Onion Soup Mix
   30 Min Chicken Dinner...........190
   Beef Stew 229
   Beef Stroganoff........................36
Beef Tips & Gravy 22
Beefy Mushroom Mac................116
Catalina French Chicken 197
Get out of the Kitchen Chicken 120
Mama's Meatloaf 28
Mississippi Pot Roast 27
Salisbury Steak...........................34
Take it Easy Chicken 202
Take It Easy Chicken 202
Oranges
   Orange Balls 143
   Pig Pickin Cake.........................110
   Orange Chicken Stir Fry 194
   Orange Date Nut Bread............. 59
   Orange Juice Cake 95

Orange Juice Frosing................. 95
Orange Punch 41

Orange Slice Cookies............... 134
Oreos
   Dirt Cake 141
   Oreo Pie Crust 163

P

Pasta
   Alfredo Pasta Sauce.................222
   Baked Spaghetti Casserole........115
   Beefy Mushroom Mac...............116
   Buffalo Mac N Cheese 116
   Chicken Noodle Casserole 119
   Chicken Spaghetti Casserole 119
   Chris's Goulash 37
   Creole Tuna Casserole 126
   Italian Meats Lasagna 122
   Italian Pasta Salad...................212
   Linguinie Positano 198
   Lo Mein, Chicken 199
   Mac n Cheese Pizza 123
   Macaroni Delight......................123
   Macaroni Salad 212
   Napoli Casserole 123
   Old Fashioned Mac N Cheese... 124
   Pepper Jack Mac 115
   Secret Spaghetti Sauce..............37
   Skillet Spaghetti 124
   Ukrainian Goulash 37
   Winner Lasagna........................122
Pastry
   Bear Claws............................... 55
   Cream Puffs 58
Peaches
   Peach Cobbler Classic 172
   Peach Milkshakes...................... 41
   Peach Skillet Cake 95
      Peach Topping 158
      Peaches & Cream Cake.............. 111
Peanut Butter
   Old Fashioned Fudge................142
   Peanut Butter Bars 134
   Peanut Butter Buckeyes...........143
   Peanut Butter Cake 96
   Peanut Butter Chocolate Delight..
      145
   Peanut Butter Cookies 134
   Peanut Butter Cornflake Candy ...
      143
   Peanut Butter Krispy Treats.....135
   Peanut Butter Pie....................173
   Potato Candy 144
Pecans
   Better than Sex Cake................109

Browned Butter Icing 100
Buttery Fruitcake........................86
Chocolate Delight....................140
Chris's Favorite........................130
Divinity..................................... 141
How to Toast Pecans 99
Humdings 132
Italian Cream Cake 108
Lemon Lush 142
Martha Washington Balls 141
Pecan Pie.................................174
Pecan Upside Down Cake 112
Pralines 145
Pumpkin Pecan Pie 176
Toffee Pecan Crunch Cake...... 102

Pie Crust
Butter Pie Crust 174
Graham Cracker Crust 101
Graham Cracker Pie Crust 169
Oreo Pie Crust 163
Shortening Pie Crust 174
Vanilla Wafer Crust 169

Pie Filling
Black Forest Cake 105
Cherry Coffeecake 72
Daddy Dump Cake 106
Fruit Bar Cakes 107
Pie Filling Cake 110

Pies
Apple Crumble.........................160
Apple Dumplings 161
Apple Pie 160
Banana Cream Pie...................162
Buttermilk Pie 162
Butterscotch Pie 162
Cheese Surprise Pie 164
Cherry Pie 164
Chess Pie.................................163
Chocolate Brownie Pie............ 165
Chocolate Chess Pie................ 164
Chocolate Cream Cheese Pie ..163
Chocolate Cream Pie.............. 165
Chocolate Meringue Pie.......... 166
Coconut Cream Pie 167
Coffee Cream Pie..................... 167
Egg Custard 166
French Coconut Pie 165
French Raisin Pie 168
Fried Apple Pies 161
Fried Pie Dough 161
Georgie Porgy Pie 168
Japanese Pie 169
Key Lime Pie 169
Lemon Cream Pie 169
Lemon Icebox Pie 170
Lemon Lush Pie 170

Lemon Meringue Pie 170
Maple Meringue........................171
Mile High Pie 172
Millionaire Pie 172
Mocha Meringue 171
Peanut Butter Pie.....................173
Pecan Pie.................................174
Pecan Pie Topping 176
Pineapple Cream Cheese Pie .. 175
Pineapple Meringue Pie 175
Pumpkin Pecan Pie 176
Pumpkin Pie.............................176
Sour Cream Pie Topping.......... 164
Strawberry Cheesecake Pie.....178
Strawberry Glaze 178
Sweet Pot Cheesecake Pie 175
Sweet Pot Fried Pies................178
Sweet Potato............................177
Sweet Potato Pie......................177
Tammy's Meringue................... 166
Toll House Pie 179
Watergate Pie 179

Pineapple
Apple Salad 206
Banana Bread 55
Banana Split Cake 139
Carrot Cake...............................83
Cheese Ball...............................14
Fruit Salad Surprise..................211
Hummingbird Cake 91
Japanese Fruitcake 92
Pineapple Meringue Pie 175
Pineapple Muffins 61
Pineapple Pound Cake 97
Pineapple Pudding Frosting 110
Pineapple Skillet Cake 97

Pistachio
Pistachio Pudding Frosting.......113
Watergate Pie 179
Watergate Salad 215

Pizza
Breakfast Pizza.........................69
Crazy Crust Pizza......................63
Mac n Cheese Pizza.................123
Pizza Popovers 65
Pizza Salad 213

Pork
Bacon 3
Chris's Rib Rub 223
Chris's Special Seasonings..... 223
Corn Pones 51
Ham Salad 212
Ham Spread 16
Holiday Ham 181
Hot Dogs 6
Italian Meatballs 34

Processed Ham, Spiral 181
Sausage Balls 18
Sausage Pepperoni Bread 8
Pork Chops
Fried Cereal Chops 183
Fried Pork Chops 182
Lodge Grilled............................183
Pork Chops & Potatoes............182
Smothered Pork Chops 188
Pork Loin
Roasted Pork Loin 186
Pork Ribs
Baby Back 181
Baked Pork Ribs 185
Pork Ribs and Vegetables 185
Ribs & Beans Crockpot 186
Pork Roast
Boston Butt Crockpot.............. 181
Potatoes
Baked Potato.............................. 3
Baked Potatoes........................248
Candied Sweet Potatoes..........251
Cheesy Potato Hash 251
Cottage Pie...............................24
Creamed Potatoes....................248
Hashbrown Casserole...............121
Hashbrown Potatoes.............. 250
Hashbrowns...............................75
Home Fries 6
Potato Cakes............................248
Potato Candy 144
Potato Chips 7
Potato Salad Deluxe 213
Potato Skins 7
Potato Soup 233
Red Potatoes 250
Scalloped Potatoes 250
Shipwreck Casserole................124
Simple Potato Salad 213
Skillet Fried Potatoes................249
Stewed Potatoes......................249
Tater Tot Casserole 126
Pound Cakes
5 Flavor Pound Cake 78
Banana Nut Pd Cake................105
Banana Pound Cake 81
Chocolate Pound Cake.............84
Condensed Milk Pound Cake....86
Egg Nog Pound Cake, Easy 105
Eggnog Pound Cake.................89
Favorite Pound Cake 94
Maple Pecan Pound Cake 92
Pina Colada Pound Cake..........112
Pineapple Pound Cake 97
Pound Cake for Layers 98
Sweet Potato Pound Cake........98

Pressure Cooking
  Beef Tips & Gravy......................22
  Chuck Roast, Pressure cook......31
Puddings
  Banana Cream Pie....................162
  Banana Pudding.......................138
  Banana Split Cake 139
  Butterscotch Pie......................162
  Chocolate Cream Pie...............165
  Chocolate Delight....................140
  Chocolate Meringue Pie..........166
  Chocolate Pudding...................139
  Coconut Cream Pie 167
  Coconut Pudding.....................140
  Coffee Cream pie 167
  Dark Chocolate Pudding.......... 111
  Dirt Cake 141
  Lemon Lush 142
  Mile High Pie 172
  Mocha Meringue 171
  Peanut Butter Chocolate Delight.. 145
  Vanilla Pudding........................138
Pumpkin
  Cheesecake, Pumpkin..............101
  Pumpkin Bread or cake.............59
  Pumpkin Pecan Pie 176
  Pumpkin Pie.............................176

R
Ribs
  Baby Back 181
Rice
  Basmati 247
  Brown......................................247
  Chicken & Rice Casserole......... 116
  Chicken and Rice, Asian 191
  Chicken Buritto Skillet 118, 191
  Chicken Spectacular 120
  Get out of the Kitchen Chicken 120
  Ground Beef & Rice 121
  How to Make the Best Rice 247
  Jasmine....................................247
  Mexican Rice, Authentic.........247
  Parboiled White Rice...............247
  Red Beans & Rice 242
  Sausage Beans & Rice..............187
  Texmati....................................247
  White Rice................................247
Rutabagas
  Glazed Rutabagas.....................251

S
Salads
  Apple Salad 206
  Avocado Salad 206

Bean Salad 206
BLT Chicken Salad 208
Broccoli Salad 206
Caesar Dressing 207
Caesar Salad 207
Carrot Cole slaw 209
Carrot Raisin Salad................. 207
Cherry Jell-O Salad 207
Chicken Salad 208
Cole Slaw 209
Cornbread Salad...................... 210
Crab Salad................................ 210
Cranberry Relish 210
Croutons 5
Cucumber Salad 12
Cucumbers Salad 210
Egg & Olive Salad 211
Fruit Salad 211
Fruit Salad Surprise..................211
Fruit Salad, Yogurt 211
German Cole Slaw 209
Ham Salad 212
Italian Pasta Salad 212
KFC Cole Slaw......................... 209
Macaroni Salad 212
Master Vinaigrette...................214
Pizza Salad 213
Potato Salad Deluxe 213
Simple Potato Salad 213
Sweet Master Vinaigrette 214
Tomato Mozzarella Salad 214
Tuna Salad................................214
Watergate Salad 215
Wilted Lettuce Salad................215
Sandwiches
Big Mac Style Burger................217
BLT Sandwich 217
Cheesesteak Hoagies 218
Chicken Salad 208
Chili Steak Burgers 218
Deluxe Grill Cheese 217
Egg & Olive Salad 211
Egg in a Hole 71
Egg Sandwich............................73
Fried Bologna...........................219
Fried Spam Sandwiches 219
Meatloaf Hamburgers...............219
Open Faced Tuna Loaf 220
Sloppy Joes 220
Tuna Salad................................214
Turkey Parmesan 220
Sauces......................................226
  Alfredo Pasta Sauce...............222
Big Mac Style Burger................217
Caramel Sauce.................154, 222
Cheese Sauce......................... 222

Chocolate Sauce.................... 223
CVC BBQ Sauce....................... 222
Dippen Chicken Sauce 224
Enchilada Sauce 21, 224
Honey Mustard 224
Horsey Dipping Saue................02
Hot Dog Chili Sauce................224
Italian Pasta Sauce 34
London Broil Marinade............. 27
Meatloaf Topping...................... 28
Poultry Pan Sauce 225
Secret Spaghetti Sauce 37
Smokey Honey Mustard.......... 224
Tartar Sauce............................226
Vanilla Cream Sauce 158
Sausage
  Cheesey Sausage Muffins 60
  Chris's Breakfast 70
  Crazy Crust Pizza.....................63
  Italian Meats Lasagna 122
  Sausage Balls 18
Seafood
  Butterflied Shrimp, Fried 151
  Crab Cakes.............................. 148
  Crab Salad............................... 210
  Double Dip Fried Fish 19
  Fish Francese...........................150
  Fish Tacos................................150
  Fried Shrimp 151
  Jambalaya................................234
  Mustard Fried Fish.................. 149
  Open Faced Tuna Loaf 220
  Salmon Patties 149
  Salmon Pie 149
  Salmon Steaks.........................150
  Salmon Steaks, Glazed 150
  Shrimp & Grits 151
  Shrimp Bisque 233
  Sizzling Rice Soup 234
  Tartar Sauce............................226
  Tuna Salad................................214
Seasonings
  Chris's Rib Rub 223
  Chris's Special Seasonings 223
Smoked Sausage
  Simple Fried Cabbage 184
  Smoked Sausage Hash.............187
  Smoked Sausage Simmer 185
  Southern Fried Cabbage 184
Soups & Stews
  Beef Stew, Dutch Oven 228
  Benefield Chicken 228
  Brunswick Stew 230
  Butterbean Soup.....................229
  Chicken & Dumplings.............230
  Chicken Bone Broth 229

Chicken Noodle Soup 231
Chili 231
Chili for Two...........................231
Corn Chowder 232
Double Meat Chili 232
Hardy Tomato Beef Stew 229
Irish Beef Stew........................230
Jambalaya.............................234
Potato Soup 233
Shrimp Bisque 233
Sizzling Rice Soup 234
Split Pea Soup 234
Steak & Dumplings 235
Tammy's Crazy Soup 233
Tomato Soup 235
Vegetable Beef Soup 236
Vegetable Garden Soup...........236
Vegetable Soup for Two 236
White Chicken Chili.................232
Southern Sides 237
Air Fryer Vegetables...............257
Apricot Glazed Carrots 248
Asparagus, Sauteed................252
Bacon Brussels 252
Baked Potatoes 248
Beans & Peas.........................238
Boiled Okra 253
Broccoli Cheese Casserole 117
Broccoli, Steamed 252
Brussels, Sauteed 252, 253
Brussels, Steamed 253
Buffalo Mac N Cheese............. 116
Butternut Squash 253, 255
Candied Sweet Potatoes..........251
Cheesy Potato Hash 251
Chicken and Dressing 48
Collard Greens.......................246
Corn on the Cob 244
Corn on the Cob Herb Butter ..244
Corn Pudding.........................245
Cornbread Dressing, Granny... 50
Cream & Fried Corn 245
Creamed Potatoes...................248
Easy Green Bean Casserole 120
Fried Okra 254
Fried Okra Deluxe 254
Fried Okra Patties 255
Fried Squash 255
Garlic Mashed Potatoes 251
Glazed Rutabagas...................251
Granny Green Beans 239
Green Bean Casserole 121
Hashbrown Casserole 121
Hashbrown Potatoes............. 250
Hashbrowns...........................75
Hoppin John 243

How to Make the Best Rice 247
Hushpuppies...........................52
Mexican Street Corn 244
Old Timer Squash Casserole....125
Parboiled White Rice..............247
Pinto Beans...........................241
Potato Cakes.........................248
Purple Hull Peas.................... 240
Purple Saute Cabbage.............246
Red Beans & Rice 242
Red Kidney Beans...................242
Red Potatoes 250
Refried Beans.........................242
Ribboned Squash 256
Roasted Vegetables 257
Scalloped Potatoes 250
Shortcut Dressing 50
Skillet Fried Potatoes..............249
Spaghetti Squash 255
Speckled Butter Beans 243
Stewed Cabbage....................246
Stewed Potatoes....................249
Stewed Squash 256
Stewed Tomatoes 257
Succotash 257
Summer Squash Casserole......125
Tater Tot Casserole 126
Tomato Pie 256
Turnip Greens 246
White Rice.............................247
Squash
Butternut Squash 253, 255
Fried Squash 255
Old Timer Squash Casserole....125
Ribboned Squash 256
Spaghetti Squash 255
Stewed Squash 256
Summer Squash Casserole......125
Sweet Potato
Cheesecake, Sweet Potato.......101
Sweet Pot Cheesecake Pie 175
Sweet Pot Fried Pies................178
Sweet Pot Pecan Pie...............176
Sweet Potato..........................177
Sweet Potato Pie.....................177
Sweet Potato Pound Cake.........98
Sweet Potato Souffle 125
Sweetened Condensed Milk
Fruit Dip 16
Key Lime Pie 169
Lemon Cream Pie 169
Lemon Icebox Pie 170
Martha Washington Balls 141
Millionaire Pie 172
T

Tenderized Beef
Fried Cubed Steak 25
Fried Round Steak 33
Nana's Steak Fries 25
Swiss Steak 35
Tomatoes
Fried Green Tomatoes 15
Stewed Tomatoes 257
Tomato Gravy 226
Tomato Mozzarella Salad 214
Topping
Cinnamon Sugar 161
Coconut Topping 84
Crumble Topping..................... 156
Frozen Fruit Topping 95
Meatloaf Topping....................224
Peach Topping 158
Sour Cream Pie Topping.......... 164
Strawberry Topping 158
Streusel Topping......................71
Streusel Topping, Muffins........ 60
Tammy's Meringue.................. 166
Tuna
Creole Tuna Casserole 126
Tuna Loaf 220
Tuna Salad.............................214
Turkey
Roasted Turkey Breast 202
Thanksgiving Turkey.............. 204
Turkey Crockpot Dinner 203
Turkey Parmesan 220
Turkey Stroganoff 36
Turnip Greens
Turnip Greens 246
U
Upside Down Cakes
Apple Skillet Cake 80
Peach Skillet Cake 95
Pecan Upside Down Cake 112
Pineapple Skillet Cake 97
V
Vegetables
Baked Potato........................... 3
Blooming Onion........................ 2
Brussels, Roasted 2
Corn on Cob............................ 5
Dill Pickles...............................11
Fried Green Tomatoes 15
Home Fries.............................. 6
Potato Chips 7
Potato Skins............................ 7
Sweet Potato Souffle 125
Vegetable Beef Soup 236
Vegetable Garden Soup...........236

Safe Minimum Internal Temperature Chart

Safe steps in food handling, cooking and storage are essential in preventing foodborne illness. You can't see, smell or taste harmful bacteria that may cause illness. In every step of food preparation, follow the four guidelines to keep food safe:

- **Clean** — Wash hands and surfaces often.
- **Separate** — Separate raw meat from other foods.
- **Cook** — Cook to the right temperature.
- **Chill** — Refrigerate food promptly.

Cook all food to these minimum internal temperatures, as measured with a food thermometer, before removing food from the heat source. For reasons of personal preference, consumers may choose to cook food to higher temperatures.

Product	Minimum Internal Temperature and Rest Time
Beef, Pork, Veal and Lamb Steaks, Chops and Roasts	145 degrees F (62.8 degrees C) and allow to rest for at least 3 minutes
Ground Meats	160 degrees F (71.1 degrees C)
Ground Poultry	165 degrees F
Ham, Fresh or Smoked (Uncooked)	145 degrees F (62.8 degrees C) and allow to rest for at least 3 minutes
Fully Cooked Ham (to Reheat)	Reheat cooked hams packaged in USDA-inspected plants to 140 degrees F (60 degrees C) and all others to 165 degrees F (73.9 degrees C).
All Poultry (Breasts, Whole Bird, Legs, Thighs, Wings, Ground Poultry, Giblets and Stuffing)	165 degrees F (73.9 degrees C)
Eggs	160 degrees F (71.1 degrees C)
Fish & Shellfish	145 degrees F (62.8 degrees C)
Leftovers	165 degrees F (73.9 degrees C)
Casseroles	165 degrees F (73.9 degrees C)

United States Department of Agriculture. (n.d.). *Safe Minimum Internal Temperature Chart*. Retrieved from:

https://www.foodsafety.gov/food-safety-charts/safe-minimum-internal-temperatures

KITCHEN
Conversion & Cooking Chart

DRY MEASUREMENTS

½ oz	1 tbsp	¹⁄₁₆ C	15 g	-
1 oz	2 tbsp	⅛ C	28 g	-
2 oz	4 tbsp	¼ C	57 g	-
3 oz	6 tbsp	⅓ C	85 g	-
4 oz	8 tbsp	½ C	115 g	¼ lb
8 oz	16 tbsp	1 C	227 g	½ lb
12 oz	24 tbsp	1½ C	340 g	¾ lb
16 oz	32 tbsp	2 C	455 g	1 lb

LIQUID MEASUREMENTS

1 oz	6 tsp	2 tbsp	30 mL	⅛ C	-	-
2 oz	12 tsp	4 tbsp	60 mL	¼ C	-	-
2⅔ oz	16 tsp	5 tbsp	80 mL	⅓ C	-	-
4 oz	24 tsp	8 tbsp	120 mL	½ C	-	-
5⅓ oz	32 tsp	11 tbsp	160 mL	⅔ C	-	-
6 oz	36 tsp	12 tbsp	177 mL	¾ C	-	-
8 oz	48 tsp	16 tbsp	240 mL	1 C	½ pt	¼ qt
16 oz	96 tsp	32 tbsp	470 mL	2 C	1 pt	½ qt
32 oz	192 tsp	64 tbsp	950 mL	4 C	2 pt	1 qt

Spoons
1 tbsp
3 tsp
½ oz
15 mL

Butter
1 stick
½ cup
¼ lb

Egg Timer
Soft - 5 min
Medium - 7 min
Hard - 9 min

Dash / Pinch
¹⁄₁₆ tsp   ⅛ tsp

1 gallon
4 quarts
8 pints
16 cups
128 fl oz
3.8 liters

1 quart
2 pints
4 cups
32 fl oz
946 liters

1 pint
2 cups
16 fl oz
470 liters

1/4 cup
4 tbsp
12 tsp
2 fl oz
60 ml

1 cup
16 tbsp
8 fl oz
240 ml

Herbs
1 tsp dried =
1 tbsp fresh

OVEN TEMPERATURES

°F	225	250	275	300	325	350	375	400	425	450	475	500
°C	110	120	140	150	170	180	190	200	220	230	240	260

Melissa's SOUTHERN STYLE KITCHEN
melissassouthernstylekitchen.com

Kitchen Conversions Retrieved from: https://www.melissassouthernstylekitchen.com/free-printable-kitchen-conversion-chart/